Contemporary Encounters with Ancient Metaphysics

We would like to dedicate this volume to our partners:
qui nolet fieri desidiosus, amet.

Contemporary Encounters with Ancient Metaphysics

Edited by Abraham Jacob Greenstine and
Ryan J. Johnson

EDINBURGH
University Press

Edinburgh University Press is one of the leading university presses in the UK. We publish academic books and journals in our selected subject areas across the humanities and social sciences, combining cutting-edge scholarship with high editorial and production values to produce academic works of lasting importance. For more information visit our website: edinburghuniversitypress.com

Edinburgh University Press Ltd
The Tun – Holyrood Road, 12(2f) Jackson's Entry, Edinburgh EH8 8PJ

First published in hardback by Edinburgh University Press 2017

Typeset in 10/12 Adobe Sabon by
IDSUK (DataConnection) Ltd, and
printed and bound in Great Britain by
CPI Group (UK) Ltd, Croydon CR0 4YY

A CIP record for this book is available from the British Library

ISBN 978 1 4744 1209 4 (hardback)
ISBN 978 1 4744 3742 4 (paperback)
ISBN 978 1 4744 1210 0 (webready PDF)
ISBN 978 1 4744 1211 7 (epub)

Contents

Part III Epicureans, Stoics, Skeptics, and Neo-Platonists

Part IV Postscript

Acknowledgements

We would like to thank Carol MacDonald at Edinburgh University Press for all her patience and help, along with Ersev Ersoy. We thank Bibliopolis for the opportunity to translate and include this provocative essay by Barbara Cassin, and Presses universitaires de France for the permission to translate and include the pieces by Aubenque and Deleuze. We are both extremely grateful to the faculty at Duquesne, especially Dan Selcer, Ron Polansky, Jennifer Bates, who have been model thinkers, teachers, and professionals. The help, both great and small, from our colleagues and friends, including Tom Sparrow, Michael Weinman, Graham Harman, Tom Eyers, George Yancy, Claire Griffin, Gottfried Heinemann, Charlie Salem, Dave Mesing, Dan Smith, Clifford Robinson, Martin Krahn, Bethany Somma, Tristana Rubio, Greg Recco, Jim Bahoh, Brooke Holmes, Matt Lovett, and John Protevi has been invaluable for the process of putting this volume together. We want to express our love and thanks to our partners – Andreea Greenstine and Erin Rutherford – for their support and conversation. We are grateful to all of our translators, Clayton Shoppa, Jared Bly, and Sam Galson; Jared provided editorial support on all three translations, and Sam was gracious enough to humor translation questions at all hours of the day. Most of all, we would like to thank all of our contributors for their amazing contributions, which we are fortunate to be able to present here.

Note on the Text

In the essays that follow we have typically kept Greek words in a Greek script, rather than transliterating them, especially so as to distinguish them from Latin terms and also later appropriations of the Greek terms (for example, Deleuze's *Chronos* and *Aion*). Greek terms in quotations are presented as they are in the source material. The major exceptions are the three translations (the essays of Cassin, Aubenque, and Deleuze). In these Greek terms are rendered the same way as in the original essays. For Deleuze, this is barely an issue (he mentions *physis* once); Aubenque mostly keeps the Greek terms in Greek, although he speaks of the aporetic and autarchic; Cassin keeps the Greek script for any quotation over a certain length, but her essay is filled with shorter Greek passages that she transliterates.

Each essay is followed by its own bibliography. Again, the exceptions are the translations, in which citations are limited to the notes and mostly follow the original texts.

Notes on Contributors

Pierre Aubenque is Professor Emeritus at the University of Paris-Sorbonne and Secretary General for L'Institut international de Philosophie. He produced a great number of now classic texts in the scholarship of the history of ancient philosophy, including *Le problème de l'être chez Aristote*, *La prudence chez Aristote*, *Sénèque*, *Problèmes aristotéliciens*.

A. J. Bartlett is a Fellow at Monash University. Bartlett's recent publications include *Badiou and Plato: An Education by Truths*, and *Badiou, Deleuze, Lacan* (with Justin Clemens and Jon Roffe). He is also co-editor of *The Praxis of Alain Badiou* and *Alain Badiou: Key Concepts*, translator of Badiou's *Mathematics of the Transcendental*, and is the series editor (with Jon Roffe and Justin Clemens) for Rowman & Littlefield of *Insolubilia: New Work in European Philosophy*.

Emanuela Bianchi is Assistant Professor of Comparative Literature, and affiliated with the Department of Classics and the Program in Gender and Sexuality at New York University. She recently published *The Feminine Symptom: Aleatory Matter in the Aristotelian Cosmos* and the edited the volume *Is Feminist Philosophy Philosophy?*

Jared C. Bly is a graduate student in philosophy at Villanova University where he is in the preliminary stages of preparing a dissertation on critical theory and aesthetics, engaging such figures as Walter Benjamin and Gilles Deleuze. He is also preparing a book-length translation of Patrick Vauday's *The Invention of the Visible*.

John Bova is a Research Affiliate at the University of New Mexico. He recently earned his PhD from the Department of Philosophy at Villanova University with a dissertation entitled, "A Metalogical Approach to the Problem of Reflexivity in Platonic Dialectic." His forthcoming projects include works on Plato, Sartre, and Badiou, and a philosophical interpretation of the phenomenon of "non-first-order-izability" in mathematics.

Barbara Cassin is Director of the Centre Leon-Robin at the Sorbonne. She edited the seminal *Dictionary of Untranslatables: A Philosophical Lexicon*, and is also the editor of several book series, notably *L'Ordre philosophique*. Her most recent book in English is called *Sophistical Practice: Towards a Consistent Relativism* (2013). In 2012, the Académie Française honored her work with the *Grand prix de philosophie*.

Gilles Deleuze taught at University of Paris VIII at Vincennes for two decades. He published widely on the history of philosophy, politics, literature, film, and art, and is author of several books and publications, including *Difference and Repetition*, *Anti-Oedipus*, and *A Thousand Plateaus*.

Sam Galson holds a PhD from Princeton University and is currently seeking a postdoctoral appointment. His main interests are Latin literature and its reception, especially Ovid and Seneca, the classical tradition in the history of science, and Renaissance philosophy.

Abraham Jacob Greenstine is a Fellow and Doctoral Candidate in Philosophy at Duquesne University and the Universität Kassel. His dissertation is on not-being in Aristotle's philosophy. He served as editorial assistant to the journal *Ancient Philosophy*. He is one of the founders and organizers of the Pennsylvania Circle for Ancient Philosophy and the Pittsburgh Summer Symposium in Contemporary Philosophy.

David Hoinski teaches philosophy at West Virginia University and is the President and CEO of Studium Consulting. He earned an MPhil in modern philosophy at KU Leuven and a PhD in philosophy from Duquesne University. He is currently working on a book about philosophical autobiography.

Ryan J. Johnson is Assistant Professor of Philosophy at Elon University. He was a contributing editor (with Daniel Price) and author of *The Movement of Nothingness*, and author of the forthcoming book *The Deleuze-Lucretius Encounter*.

Kurt Lampe is Senior Lecturer at the University of Bristol. He runs the AHRC-funded international network on Stoicism and Continental philosophy (stoicisms.wordpress.com). He is author of *The Birth of Hedonism: The Cyrenaic Philosophers and Pleasure as a Way of Life* and has published articles and book chapters on Socrates, the Cyrenaics, psychoanalysis, and existentialism.

Paul M. Livingston is Professor of Philosophy at the University of New Mexico. His books include *Philosophical History and the Problem of Consciousness*, *Philosophy and the Vision of Language*, and *The Politics of Logic: Badiou, Wittgenstein, and the Consequences of Formalism*. His newest book, *The Logic of Being: Realism, Truth, and Time*, focuses on Frege, Plato, and Heidegger, and will be published in 2017 by Northwestern University Press.

Catherine Malabou is Professor of Modern European Philosophy at Kingston University London and the European Graduate School. She is author of *The*

Future of Hegel, *The Heidegger Change*, *What Should We Do with Our Brains?*, *The New Wounded*, *Ontology of the Accident: An Essay on Destructive Plasticity*, *Changing Difference*, and others. She is co-author of *Counterpath* (with Jacques Derrida), and *You Be My Body for Me* (with Judith Butler).

Ronald Polansky is Chair and Professor of Philosophy at Duquesne University and editor-in-chief and founder of the journal *Ancient Philosophy*. He is author of a commentary on Aristotle's *De Anima* and a commentary on Plato's *Theaetetus*, and is the editor of the *Cambridge Companion to the Nicomachean Ethics*.

Daniel Price is Honors Faculty at the University of Houston, and specializes in Contemporary French and German philosophy. He is the author of *Touching Difficulty: Sacred Form from Plato to Derrida*, and a contributing editor (with Ryan J. Johnson) of the recently published collection of essays entitled *The Movement of Nothingness*.

Eric Salem is Tutor at St John's College, Annapolis. He has translated Plato's *Sophist*, *Phaedo*, and *Statesman* (all with Peter Kalkavage and Eva Brann), and is the author of *In Pursuit of the Good: Intellect and Action is Aristotle's Ethics*.

Clayton Shoppa is Assistant Professor of Philosophy at Saint Francis College. He writes about the contemporary relevance of Aristotle's logic and metaphysics. He is the co-author of *What Is an Environment?*

Adriel M. Trott is Associate Professor of Philosophy at Wabash College. She is the author of *Aristotle on the Nature of Community* as well as articles on Irigaray, Badiou, and Rancière.

Gert-Jan van der Heiden is Professor of Metaphysics at the Department of Philosophy of the Radboud University Nijmegen and a member of its Center for Contemporary European Philosophy. His books include *Ontology after Ontotheology: Plurality, Event and Contingency in Contemporary Philosophy* and *De stem van de doden. Hermeneutiek als spreken namens de ander* (*The Voice of the Dead. Hermeneutics as Speaking for the Other*).

David Webb is Professor of Philosophy at Staffordshire University. Recently he authored *Foucault's Archeology: Science and Transformation*. He is currently working on an English version of selected works by Jean Cavaillès, a book called *Understanding Nihilism*, and is the co-general editor of the seven-volume *Edinburgh Critical History of Philosophy*.

Gina Zavota is Associate Professor at Kent State University. She has published widely on Neoplatonism and on twentieth-century-century French and German philosophy and is co-editor of *Husserl: Critical Assessments of Leading Philosophers* (with Donn Welton and Rudolf Bernet). She is currently working on a book on Merleau-Ponty and materialist ontologies.

CHAPTER I

A Thousand Antiquities

Abraham Jacob Greenstine and Ryan J. Johnson

"Let all our accounts begin with a dedication to Thales."[1]

FOUR ANCIENT TALES

We begin with four tales of ancient philosophers.

First, the time *When Thales Fell in the Well*. Thales was from a prominent Milesian family, and had dedicated himself to the contemplation of nature. Of particular interest was the nature of the heavens: he learned to determine when the sun would be eclipsed and the dates of the solstices. One night, as he was intently examining the stars, he lost track of his feet and fell. Some say he fell into a well, where his maidservant heckled him; some say he toppled off a precipice and died.[2] We should all be so lucky to experience such staggering thought, contemplating the heavens and being knocked off our feet.

Second, the time *When Heraclitus Covered Himself in Shit*. Heraclitus, who had learned all things through his study of himself, had always been a contentious fellow. Having left his home of Ephesus to inhabit the mountains, he ate whatever he could forage. Soon, however, he became swollen and sick, and so returned to the city to seek medical help. He interrogated the doctors, asking whether they could they desiccate a torrent; they could not understand his meaning. Taking matters into his own hands, he covered himself in cow manure, perhaps expecting himself to thereby be purged. He died: either from the manure, from the dropsy, or perhaps from being mauled by a pack of dogs that could not recognize him as human.[3] Again, the power of the elements proved too much for an ordinary life.

Third, the time *When Pyrrho Walked into Traffic*. Pyrrho had been an unsuccessful painter, until he joined the philosopher Anaxarchus on his travels with the campaigns of Alexander. (By the way, Anaxarchus, "the Happy," later bit off his own tongue and spat it at his tormentors, but that is a story for another time.) Pyrrho returned from this journey transformed. Perhaps it was his studies with the Persian Magi and Indian Gymnosophists, perhaps it was the teaching of Anaxarchus, or perhaps it was something else in the war campaign. Whatever caused it, Pyrrho now denied that anything is really one way or another. Soon, he became reckless, going wheresoever he felt, no matter what dangers seemed to be before him: he would walk into traffic, nearly fall off cliffs, and approach feral dogs. He survived only through the efforts of his friends, who had to follow him closely to prevent disaster.[4] The violence of penetrating thought can cause us to do the strangest things.

Fourth, the time *When Lucretius Went Mad from a Love Potion*. Titus Lucretius, a member of one of the oldest Roman patrician families, was "driven mad by a love philtre and, having composed between bouts of insanity several books (which Cicero afterwards corrected), committed suicide at the age of forty-four."[5] This is basically all we know about the life of Lucretius. Let us suggest, at the reader's behest, that perhaps this love potion was not a magical elixir at all, but might have instead been Epicurus' now lost work *On Nature*. Perhaps it was the force of the theory of atoms that drove Lucretius not only to write *De Rerum Natura*, but also to madness and suicide.

PENSÉE BRUTE

Scholars typically read these stories as parodies, caricatures supposedly circulated by rival philosophical schools. The first three are recorded in the invaluable *Lives of Ancient Philosophers* by Diogenes Laertius, who is criticized for being too concerned with the superficial details of philosophers' lives while lacking the intellectual acumen necessary for adequately discussing their doctrines. The story of Lucretius is told by Jerome, who perhaps sought to defame this pagan Epicurean so as to persuade Christian readers to not take the beautiful verses of *De Rerum Natura* seriously. More recently, philosophers and classicists have interpreted these anecdotes as winsome allegories covering up the more sober philosophical doctrines contained within. However charitable this hermeneutic may be, we offer a more blatant and explicit tactic for engaging these tales. With our readers' indulgence, let us risk historical accuracy for philosophic force. Let us ask: What if these stories are actually true? What if we take them seriously? What would such a serious hermeneutic say about the status of metaphysics in antiquity?

On our reading, these stories express the impact of the violent submission of life to theory. These are not fanciful tales or playful caricatures, but are accounts of how the concepts erupt in thought and disrupt the mundane. These stories go beyond ethics and into madness: these are not models to follow or habits to cultivate. Some of the actions are done deliberately, but none should be imitated. Only one of the thinkers – Pyrrho – survives his tale. These philosophers fail to care for themselves, even when they try. Instead, they care for an idea: Thales for the movement of the stars, Heraclitus for the mixtures of the body, Pyrrho for the impossibility of assent, Lucretius for the truth and repose of atomism. It is this care for theories and concepts, an abnormal, unusual care, beyond the care of the self or of one's own life, that we call metaphysics, *pensée brute*, raw thought.

Who has not been taken, if not knocked down, by a thought that sends a tremor through our everyday lives? Who has not been left stuttering and muttering when trying to explain a poignant insight into the cosmos? Metaphysics simultaneously moves us as it compels us; its incorporeal events have real, lasting impacts on our lives, as these four curious stories sharply convey. They are not mere anecdotes; rather they present philosophical encounters that exceed our ordinary concepts, that decenter us, that put us into danger even as we stroll down the road.

In addition to these four ancient tales, we offer the reader a new selection of tales of fundamental encounters. The essays that follow express the emergence of a reshaped relationship between ancient and contemporary philosophies. Each of the nineteen contributors to this volume encounters something from antiquity that provokes thought: an argument, a *corpus*, an object, a life, a myth, a system. Although these stories cross, in an instant, over two thousand years of philosophy, they are as provocative and eventful as the earlier ancient ones. The encounters they present are the same in kind as the vision of the heavens that knocked Thales off his feet and the imbibing of the potion that drove Lucretius mad. While these contemporary philosophers might not appear to act as bizarrely or dangerously as Heraclitus or Pyrrho, the force of ancient metaphysics still erupts in their ideas and systems.

PURE METAPHYSICS

The site of these encounters is pure metaphysics as raw, brute thought.[6] The tonic note of this conception of thought is Gilles Deleuze's bold claim: *Je me sens pur métaphysicien*, "I feel like a pure metaphysician."[7] There are, of course, many precedents for this thought, some of which are under consideration in the essays that follow. However, while many of the other philosophical movements of the past hundred years turned away from metaphysics, Deleuze's proclamation sounds a clarion call for the need to raise again the classic questions of first philosophy. The call for this new metaphysics, pure without necessarily being abstract, has been taken up in this century by various continental realists, materialists, and ontologists, who all share with the ancients a drive to think the nature of things. Thus this pure metaphysics departs from the dominant trends of contemporary thought. It deviates from the deconstructive condemnation of metaphysics as the highest form of a hegemonic project that is destined to fail. It diverges from the analytic turn to linguistic and grammatical analyses in place of the supposedly gratuitous complexities of ontological systems. It distances itself from Heidegger's fixation with the origins. It refuses to constrain philosophy to the limits of experience, consciousness, history, society, or politics. Instead, pure metaphysics puts forward a thought which endeavors to overcome these limits, which seeks their conditions and their truth in being as such, in the nature of things. It forces us to respond, sometimes strangely, to those ancient concepts: the one and the many, truth and falsity, potentiality and actuality, materiality, genesis, the intellect, the cosmos, and the divine itself.

Not all of today's metaphysical thinkers, perhaps not even every contributor to this volume, would be pleased with us characterizing their projects as "metaphysics." Yet despite (or perhaps because of) the divergent approaches of metaphysics, there is a point of convergence that differentiates this set of contemporary thinkers from the so-called post-metaphysical projects of phenomenology, deconstruction, historicism, hermeneutics, and the philosophy of the analysis of language. The latter traditions have had inordinate influence on the focus and shape of mainstream ancient philosophy scholarship; nevertheless, recent continental metaphysics has quietly developed new styles of approaching ancient thought. While these original encounters are today more vibrant than ever, until this volume they have been mostly overlooked in contemporary scholarship. In this book we not only address these varied, volatile, and novel confrontations, but we also seek to provoke a way of thinking about the philosophical canon that might lead to further transformative engagements with the problems of ancient metaphysics. Hence, at our most ambitious, we intend to generate new forms of contemporary metaphysics. We heed Deleuze's proclamation and offer you now a small collection of contemporary encounters.

"A JOKE MEANT TO MAKE PEOPLE WHO LIKE US LAUGH"

This was Deleuze's response to Michel Foucault's quip about the twentieth-century eventually becoming known as the "Deleuzian century." Yet despite the dominance of Deleuze's voice in the introduction thus far, this book is not bound by his thought. Pure metaphysics need not be Deleuzian: indeed many of his critics and detractors have been driven to this task. Rather than indicating a single system of thought, we instead point to an attitude shared across diverse projects. From new materialists to political ontologists, from naturalists to feminists, from dialectical materialists to speculative realists, something new has been bubbling in contemporary philosophy, and it is time to tell these tales. While the two of us were provoked to develop this book by the writings of Deleuze (one of us more directly than the other), what follows is certainly not merely Deleuzian. It is much more than that. If anything, we hope to showcase a thousand antiquities, a multiplicity of contemporary engagements with ancient metaphysics. To say that this still sounds very Deleuzian is, perhaps, not to get the joke.

The ancient texts under consideration originated in the greater Mediterranean, and in particular the Greek and Roman worlds, from the sixth century BCE to the end of antiquity, around the fourth century CE. More specifically, our volume is organized by three sites of engagement with the ancient world: (1) Plato and the Academy; (2) Aristotle and the Lyceum; and (3) the Hellenistic schools of the Epicureans, Stoics, and Skeptics. Beyond these major sites, there is also a foray into the post-Hellenistic world of Plotinus, and some minor excursions to the huts and paths of the Presocratics and Sophists. On the other side of the engagement, the tradition of contemporary continental metaphysics stretches from Bergson and the wartime rationalism of Albert Lautman, through Deleuze's self-nomination as a *pur métaphysicien*, passing by the renewed attention to ontology in thinkers such as Agamben and Badiou, up to the various materialisms and Speculative Realisms that populate the twenty-first-century continental landscape. We have no pretention of being either definitive or complete. Plenty of essential ancient and contemporary thinkers are missing: Anaxagoras, Theophrastus, Academic Skeptics, Epictetus, post-Plotinian Neoplatonists, Foucault, Castoriadis, Jane Bennett, Žižek, Brassier, Iain Hamilton Grant, and so on. Perhaps, then, more encounters are called for, encounters with ancient ethics and politics, with ancient psychology and theology, with ancient logic and physics. Yet here our focus is metaphysics.

This volume is thus a timely incursion into the field of metaphysically focused history of philosophy. The essays do not merely rehearse overlooked contemporary interpretations of the ancients, but, more importantly, they reconsider what it means to think, with the ancients, about the nature of things. In essence, these encounters attempt to "do metaphysics," using ancient philosophers as collaborators to contribute to contemporary problems and concepts. The problems of metaphysics persist through changing tastes in politics, economics, and religion, and they remain because they constantly demand our response. We take up this demand now and respond with a new collection of classically informed yet progressive-minded philosophical movements.

THE ENCOUNTERS

Barbara Cassin's "The Muses and Philosophy: Elements for a History of the 'Pseudos'" (1991; translated by Samuel Galson), investigates Plato's attempt in the *Sophist* to distinguish the philosopher from the sophist. Cassin pinpoints the slippery operation of the *pseudos* through the texts of Parmenides and Hesiod. Yet Parmenides' rejection of not-being allows the sophist to claim infallibility. Plato's Eleatic Stranger shows that Parmenides' rejection of not-being is self-refuting (thus the Stranger's famous parricide is just as much Parmenides' suicide). Further, although the Stranger ultimately fails to find a criterion for truth or falsity, he nevertheless establishes a place for the *pseudos* in the distinction between *logos tinos* (speech of something) and *logos peri tinos* (speech about something). Ultimately, Cassin argues that reality of *pseudos* is a condition for the possibility of language, and indeed involves the very materiality and breath of language.

Catherine Malabou's "Odysseus' Changed Soul: A Contemporary Reading of the Myth of Er" examines the political and ontological meaning of Odysseus' choice of a private life in the Myth of Er of Book X of Plato's *Republic*. In this Myth, when it is Odysseus' turn to choose the paradigm of his next life, he picks the life of a private person who minds his own business. This unexpected choice, echoing the philosopher's return to the Cave in Book VII, gives a model for deconstructing sovereignty without assuming total impotency. Departing from Agamben's discussions of the *homo sacer*, Malabou links together the departures and returns of Odysseus, Socrates, and Er. Malabou casts Socrates as the anti-Bartleby, who by means of φρόνησις simultaneously rejects tyranny and complacent impotency.

Daniel Price's "Plato's Protagoras: The Authority of Beginning an Education" follows Derrida's re-reading of Hegel's framing of philosophical history through to Plato's *Protagoras*. Price, seeking an alternative to the Hegelian frame, inquires into the place of the virtuous subject in Plato. In the *Protagoras* Price finds that the unity and goodness of virtue claims our subjectivity, not vice versa. This claim on our subjectivity orients us to the task of providing a ground for the unity of virtue. This does not concern the authority of a teacher, who demands that we reject any thought that is not owned, that does not pass through the lens of self-conscious self-appropriation. Instead it signifies the emergence of subjectivity through the claims that are made upon us by language.

John Bova and Paul M. Livingston's "Univocity, Duality, and Ideal Genesis: Deleuze and Plato" elaborates an unorthodox yet powerful dualism in the writings of Plato. This dualism accounts for the structural origin of both supersensible ideas and the sensible particulars which participate in them. Further, this duality extends to the reflexive level of theory itself, recognizable in the incompatible metalogical demands for consistency and completeness. Bova and Livingston connect this formal dualism to Deleuze's discussions of ideal genesis and the paradoxes of becoming. They show a presence of a proper "Platonism" of the Idea in Deleuze, and establish thereby the potential for a recuperation of Platonic dualism in the context of the Deleuzian univocity of being.

Adam J. Bartlett's "'Adjust Your Dread': Badiou's Metaphysical Disposition" is the final encounter with Plato. Bartlett considers how Badiou extends the Platonic gesture through his famously provocative ontological principle: mathematics is the science of being qua being. Beginning with a reflection on Parmenidean and Heraclitean metaphysical tendencies, Bartlett follows the trail of Badiou's "Platonism of the multiple," a "metaphysics without metaphysics," which eschews post-Kantian philosophies of finitude. Against the anti-metaphysical dread of the failure to think being, Badiou returns philosophy to itself by showing that ontology is a condition of philosophy, rather than its own project. Since ontology per se is mathematics, philosophy regains the freedom to think again the complex of being, truth, event, and subject.

Pierre Aubenque's "Science Regained" (1962; translated by Clayton Shoppa) was originally published as the concluding chapter of *Le Problème de l'Être chez Aristote*, one of the most important and original books on Aristotle's *Metaphysics*. In this essay, Aubenque contends that the impasses which beset the project of first philosophy paradoxically become its greatest accomplishments. Although science stabilizes motion and thereby introduces necessity into human cognition, human thought always occurs amidst an inescapable movement of change and contingency. Aristotle's ontology, as a discourse that strives to achieve being in its unity, succeeds by means of the failure of the structure of its own approach: the search of philosophy – dialectic – becomes the philosophy of the search. Aubenque traces this same structure of scission, mediation, and recovery across Aristotelian discussions of theology, motion, time, imitation, and human activity.

Emanuela Bianchi's "Aristotle's Organism, and Ours" offers an account of Aristotelian thought in which the aspirations to organismic unity and healthy functioning as a sign of superiority are continually vitiated by unassimilable material factors. These factors can be understood through the paradigmatic figure of the female offspring. Bianchi names this the "feminine symptom" of Aristotelian philosophy, that which is both necessary for and disruptive of the normal operation of teleology. While contemporary philosophical and scientific critiques have undermined the theoretical priority and holism of the organism, Bianchi, by returning Aristotle's discussion of the ontogenesis of the gendered organism, analyzes the normative and topological dimensions of our thinking about the organism, and thereby reimagines its contemporary status.

Adriel M. Trott's "Does It Matter? Material Nature and Vital Heat in Aristotle's Biology" questions whether the difference between form and material in Aristotle is itself a formal or material distinction. Trott, framing her investigation with a discussion of the feminist critiques of the form/matter binary, argues that form and material, rather than being mutually exclusive, are distributed on a gradient, as contraries. Aristotle's account of vital heat shows how the two-sex model slides into a one-sex model whose difference is located on a continuum: if woman is defined in terms of distance from man, a fluidity exists between these positions, whereby the difference between them is not a difference of form or kind, but a difference in heat, one of degree. Through this reading, Trott criticizes the myth of a link between femininity of matter (without devaluing the status of either), and shows that matter is rendered always-already meaningful for Aristotle.

David Hoinski and Ronald Polansky's "The Modern Aristotle: Michael Polanyi's Search for Truth against Nihilism" shows how the general tendencies of contemporary philosophy of science disclose a return to the Aristotelian emphasis on both the formation of dispositions to know and the role of the mind in theoretical science. Focusing on a comparison of Michael Polanyi and Aristotle, Hoinski and Polansky investigate to what degree Aristotelian thought retains its purchase on reality in the face of the changes wrought by modern science. Polanyi's approach relies on several Aristotelian assumptions, including the naturalness of the human desire to know, the institutional and personal basis for the accumulation of knowledge, and the endorsement of realism against objectivism. Hoinski and Polansky emphasize the promise of Polanyi's neo-Aristotelian framework, which argues that science is won through reflection on reality.

Abraham Jacob Greenstine's "Diverging Ways: On the Trajectories of Ontology in Parmenides, Aristotle, and Deleuze" asks what is ontology – how do we speak being? Starting from Deleuze's claim that there is only one ontology, Greenstine successively interrogates the projects of Parmenides, Aristotle, and Deleuze. These three, in dialogue with one another, agree that there is some discourse on being, but disagree about its scope, method, and content. For Parmenides, ontology is a path to the truth, a narrative that leads us to attributes of being itself. For Aristotle, ontology is a knowledge of the first principles, an account that clarifies the many senses of being in order to recognize the divine cause of being itself. For Deleuze, ontology expresses only a single proposition, and being has but a single attribute: being is univocal. By contrasting these projects, Greenstine seeks to outline ontology as such.

Eric Salem's "Object and Οὐσία: Harman and Aristotle on the Being of Things" is the last encounter with Aristotelian philosophy. Salem shows that Graham Harman aims to revive realism by putting objects back at the center of metaphysical inquiry. Harman traces his own thinking back to Aristotle, whom he considers to be the first object-oriented philosopher. Yet Harman, by rejecting the ontological importance of nature, universalizing intentionality to all kinds of object-object relations, and defending the reality of objects that Aristotle would not consider to be genuine οὐσίαι, claims to provide a weirder version of Aristotle's theory of substance. Salem finds that the ideas of each can temper the excesses of the other: the cosmos of Aristotle corrects Harman's overly expansive ontology, while the carnival of Harman supplements Aristotle's insufficient account of autonomy and unity. Further, both provoke us to again ask – what is a thing?

Gilles Deleuze's "Lucretius and Naturalism" (1961; translated by Jared Bly) is the first version of an essay that would later appear in an altered form in the appendix to Deleuze's 1969 Logique du Sens, "Lucrèce et le Naturalisme." Here Deleuze shows how Lucretius, in the first truly noble deed of philosophical pluralism, articulates his atomism as a means to determine the speculative and practical object of philosophy as "naturalism." To distinguish, in humanity, what belongs to myth and what belongs to nature; to distinguish, in nature, what is really infinite and what is not: such is the practical and speculative object of naturalism. One of the most profound constants of naturalism is to denounce everything that is the cause of sadness, everything that requires sadness in order to exercise its power. From Lucretius to Nietzsche, the same goal is pursued and attained: to transform thought and sensibility into affirmations.

David Webb's "On Causality and Law in Lucretius and Contemporary Cosmology" argues that the laws of physics, rather than being immutable, must instead be subordinate to and coordinated by local regularities of causality. Webb develops this idea through a reading of the contemporary cosmology of Unger and Smolin, who seek to address problems of contemporary physics by undermining the presuppositions of scientific absolutism. Webb finds these ideas in Lucretius, who postulates that the motion of atoms is fundamentally a matter of chance. Law-like regularity indeed emerges, but only through the chance coming into being of systems that exhibit stability and a degree of recursion. This stability is never universally binding, but itself may fall apart at some time. Webb concludes by considering Michel Serres' reconceiving of physical laws as neither universal nor immutable.

Ryan J. Johnson's "On the Surface: The Deleuze-Stoicism Encounter" investigates Deleuze's reworking of Stoic ontology and the theory of incorporeals. Contrary to the traditional interpretation, Johnson argues that there are three, not four, primary incorporeals: space, λεκτόν, and time. Deploying Deleuze's thinking of the intensive-extensive ontological distinction, Johnson shows that each of the three incorporeals are paradoxically structured by the slight Stoic surface-without-thickness separating and connecting their respective extensive and intensive dimensions (place/void, verb/noun, Aion/Chronos). It is through this strange ontology of the incorporeals that the Stoics become the initiators of a new image of philosophy that generates a lineage of thought leading, eventually, to Deleuze himself.

Gert-Jan van der Heiden's "Contingency and Skepticism in Agamben's Thought" articulates an encounter between Sextus Empiricus and Giorgio Agamben. Contrary to the usual epistemological reading of ancient skepticism, van der Heiden points out the ontological import of skeptical problems. Van der Heiden focuses especially on how skeptical and quasi-skeptical terms (such as ἐποχή and οὐ μᾶλλον, the Platonic εὐπορία, and the Pauline καταργεῖν) underlie Agamben's ontology of contingency and potentiality. Thus van der Heiden uncovers a peculiar potentiality of the skeptic. The skeptic has the power to withhold assent, to refuse to affirm or to deny any particular belief; this is the habit of skeptical thinking itself, a power that is not subordinated to any sort of actuality.

Gina Zavota's "Plotinus' 'Reverse' Platonism: A Deleuzian Response to the Problem of Emanation Imagery" attempts a radical rethinking of the Plotinian question of emanation through the lens of Deleuze's account of ontological individuation and actualization. Zavota notes that, despite its widespread acceptance as a Plotinian concept, Plotinus himself acknowledges the inadequacy of the language of emanation. Rather, just as Deleuze's virtual Idea does not impose order upon the plane of consistency but instead simply indicates divergent lines of generation, Plotinus' One does not predetermine the organization of things from above. Instead, the variety of generated objects, from the Intellect down to the barest material particulars, self-organize through the inherently generative operation of contemplation or turning towards the One. Thus contemplation is an act of differentiation, and Plotinus' philosophy can be read as a counter-Platonism or divergent-Platonism.

Kurt Lampe's "From Metaphysics to Ethics (with Bernard Stiegler, Heraclitus, and Aristotle)" serves as the postscript to the volume, the final encounter of this collection. Lampe considers Stiegler's appropriations of Greco-Roman philosophemes to think together the metaphysics-ethics doublet, linking first philosophy with the cultivation of the self. In particular, Lampe focuses on the classic fragment of Heraclitus, φύσις κρύπτεσθαι φιλεῖ ("nature loves to hide," or, with Stiegler, "*physis* loves to withdraw"), and on Aristotle's determination of the divine as the thinking of thinking. Through these, Lampe showcases Stiegler's philosophy of technics, which otherwise seeks to overturn the transcendent and originary regimes of being and truth known as "metaphysics."

NOTES

1. Purportedly from a letter from Anaximenes to Pythagoras. As recorded in Diogenes Laertius, *Lives of Eminent Philosophers* (London: Heinemann, 1925), II.4.
2. Ibid. I.22–3, II.4; Plato, *Theaetetus* (in *Opera: Volume I*, Oxford: Oxford University Press, 1995), 174a.
3. *Lives of Eminent Philosophers*, IX.1–6.
4. Ibid. IX.58–62.
5. St. Jerome, *Chronological Tables*, translation with additions to Eusebius' *Chronicles*, (http://www.attalus.org/translate/jerome2.html, June 1 2016), 171st Olympiad.
6. Of course, we grant that our use of the term "metaphysics" is somewhat anachronistic to ancient philosophy; nevertheless, we should not accept the myth that the word originates from a late bibliographical organization of Aristotle's work (see Myles Burnyeat, *Map of Metaphysics Zeta* (Pittsburgh: Mathesis Publications, 2001), p. 7 fn. 4; Stephen Menn, "On Myles Burnyeat's *Map of Metaphysics Zeta*," *Ancient Philosophy*, 31 (2011), pp. 161–202, at p. 200 fn. 49).
7. Arnaud Villani, *La Guêpe et l'Orchidée: Essai sur Gilles Deleuze* (Paris: Belin, 2000), p. 130.

PART I

PLATO

CHAPTER 2

The Muses and Philosophy: Elements for a History of the *Pseudos* [1991]

Barbara Cassin

Translated by Samuel Galson

(The liar) takes advantage of the undeniable affinity of our capacity for action, for changing reality, with this mysterious faculty we possess that enables us *to say* "The sun is shining" when it is raining cats and dogs.[1]

The philosopher, guard-dog of the truth and of the desire for truth, is committed to *alētheia*. The sophist, this wolf for as long as there have been philosophers, is committed to the *pseudos*. *Pseudos* names, from its origin, and indissolubly, the "false" and the "lie" – the "falsehood," therefore, of one who deceives and/or deceives himself. It is the ethico-logical concept par excellence. The *Sophist* of Plato explicitly marks this double bind, which joins the sophistic and *pseudos* in the eyes of philosophy: the sophist is an imitation, a feral counterfeit of the philosopher,[2] because the sophist chooses the domain of the false, the semblance, the phenomenon, opinion – in a word, all that is not. Philosophy of appearances and appearance of philosophy: sophist simulator-dissimulator.

I would like to attempt to pinpoint the *pseudos*, primarily through Parmenides and Hesiod, in order to determine the manner in which the sophistic lodges itself there, so as to understand, through Plato, how philosophy at its beginnings domesticates the very idea of *pseudos*, and organizes the place of the sophistic. Place the *alter ego* in the structure: on the one hand, the *pseudos*, the possibility of choosing the *pseudos*, is a condition of the possibility of the very existence of language; in other words, not everyone is a sophist, but in order to speak, there must be sophists. On the other hand, the interpretation of the *pseudos* in terms of *mimēsis* blocks every assignment of the criterion and confuses the imputation: "Sage or sophist?," the Stranger wonders to the end.

One further word about the *pseudos* before the great ancestors mount the stage. Not on what it signifies, but on how it signifies it. *Pseudos* (like *phēmi*, *fari*, which mean the act of pronouncing) has the root **bha*, "breathe." With *pseudos* it is a matter of the breath in language, of the irreducibility of breath – I could have used the title: "On the breath in language" – the **bha* in the *logos* – in every sense of the word, because, as everyone knows, the sophist does not lack an air.

I. PARMENIDES OR HESIOD: WHAT PLACE FOR THE *PSEUDOS*?

I.1. Parmenides. "Is not": the impossibility of the "*pseudos*" and the habit of words

The possibility of the *pseudos* is linked to the existence of not-being. For if what is not, in the simplest sense, is not, if it is not in any way, then obviously there could only be being, and the saying of being. The term *logos* says this plenitude of saying and being as they reveal each other, this "thought-speech" proper to Greek, which Martin Heidegger, contemplating one of the most Parmenidean fragments of Heraclitus, renders as "the Laying that gathers."[3]

Such is the very situation that the *Poem* of Parmenides inaugurates at the origin of western thought. The term *pseudos* does not appear in the preserved fragments. I would like to say that it cannot, that it should not appear there. For *pseudos* names the mode of being of what is not, while the *Poem* is there to assert that what is not, absolutely is not. In its place emerges the term *doxa*, or rather its plural, *doxai*.[4] "Two-headed" mortals do not know to which "opinion" to dedicate themselves; while the truth, and it alone, "untrembling heart" which characterizes the path of being, is always "persuasive," just as "persuasion," and it alone, is always "true."[5]

Some textual waypoints to authenticate the monody. In fragment 2, the goddess speaks,[6] articulating the "only two ways of inquiry that one can think":

ἡ μὲν ὅπως ἔστιν τε καὶ ὡς οὐκ ἔστι μὴ εἶναι,
πειθοῦς ἐστι κέλευθος, ἀληθείῃ γὰρ ὀπηδεῖ,
ἡ δ' ὡς οὐκ ἔστιν τε καὶ ὡς χρεών ἐστι μὴ εἶναι,
τὴν δή τοι φράζω παναπευθέα ἔμμεν ἀταρπόν·
οὔτε γὰρ ἂν γνοίης τό γε μὴ ἐὸν, οὐ γὰρ ἀνυστόν,
οὔτε φράσαις.

This one: that is and that (it) is not (capable of) not being,
Is the way of persuasion, for (persuasion) accompanies truth.
That one: that is not and that is necessarily not being,
I tell you is an impracticable path,
Because you could not know that which exactly is not
    (indeed, it is inaccessible)
Nor say it.[7]

On one side then, taken in an original mutual belonging, of which Martin Heidegger henceforth will have made every historian of philosophy aware, are being, thinking,[8] saying,[9] truth, but also, as is seldom not forgotten, persuasion. On the other: "is not" and that is all. One cannot deploy – think, say – the identity of the "is not": that is why the path is impracticable.

To attempt to add something to the "is not," to pronounce, for example, an untameable statement like "not-beings are,"[10] amounts to embarking on a "phantom path."[11] If, however, we are seeking habit, custom, it is here that it speaks, or rather, makes some sound: this phantom path is that of "*ethos*, with its multiple experiences," it is the very thing that forges *ethos*, character, about which ethics treats. Opposed to this, by refuting its composite statements, is *logos*, which keeps "is" as the word of the sole way. It is as if the opposition of being and not-being, or more exactly of being and the being/not-being mixture, furnished the first co-ordinates of the opposition between logic and ethics. Here is fragment 7 and the beginning of fragment 8:

οὐ γὰρ μήποτε τοῦτο δαμῇ εἶναι μὴ ἐόντα·
ἀλλὰ σὺ τῆσδ' ἀφ' ὁδοῦ διζήσιος εἶργε νόημα
μηδέ σ' ἔθος πολύπειρον ὁδὸν κατὰ τήνδε βιάσθω,
νωμᾶν ἄσκοπον ὄμμα καὶ ἠχήεσσαν ἀκουήν
καὶ γλῶσσαν, κρῖναι δὲ λόγωι πολύδηριν ἔλεγχον
ἐξ ἐμέθεν ῥηθέντα. μόνος δ' ἔτι μῦθος ὁδοῖο
λείπεται ὡς ἔστιν·

This statement shall never in fact be tamed: not-beings are. But you, turn your thought away from this way of inquiry. Let not a habit with its multiple experiences draw you down this path: to direct an eye without aim, and an ear and tongue ringing with echoes; but by means of the *logos* make yourself a judge of the refutation, with its multiple disputes, that I have just uttered. There remains only the word of the way: is.[12]

The situation, more complex than it first appeared, is therefore as follows. On the one hand, we must say that the *pseudos* is impossible because not-being is not, because being and not-being do not mix, because the *logos* says always and says only being. Such is the case when one lets oneself be guided by the goddess, when one is a sage, or perhaps merely a philosopher. But we must also admit that the opinions of mortals, that which appears to them, *doxai, ta dokounta*[13] closely resemble the *pseudos*, because they are "words," "names,"[14] which are believed to say "true" things, that is, things that are, while in fact the words and things have everything except being:

τῷ πάντ' ὄνομ' ἔσται,
ὅσσα βροτοὶ κατέθεντο πεποιθότες εἶναι ἀληθῆ,
γίγνεσθαί τε καὶ ὄλλυσθαι, εἶναί τε καὶ οὐχί ...

> They will be a name, therefore: all the things
> that mortals, convinced that they are true, have supposed
> come to be and disappear, are and are not.[15]

The impossibility of the *pseudos*: there is only being, the *logos*, ontology. The habit of words: there is also, beside the *logos* and making itself pass for it, the *flatus vocis*, a conventional effect of breath.

I.2. Hesiod. The pair *"pseudos-alēthes,"* and the mimetic

The joint between *alētheia* and *doxai*, between *on* and *dokounta* is doubtless one of the most delicate and controversial points in the interpretation of Parmenides. We can measure the difficulty better by confronting it with another source of Greek thought, one which we customarily think of as non-philosophical, although its kinship is recognizable:[16] Homer, and, accordingly, Hesiod.

The term *pseudos* is this time liberally pronounced. One of the most significant sequences is found both in book τ of the *Odyssey*,[17] and in the prologue to the *Theogony*.[18] Odysseus, unrecognizable, tells Penelope, as if he were not himself, but Aithon the Cretan, how he received Odysseus and his companions at his home for twelve days: ἴσκε ψεύδεα πολλὰ λέγων ἐτύμοισιν ὁμοῖα, "He feigned many falsities while speaking, similar to authentic realities."[19] And this is for Penelope, for the games of Penelope, to dissolve.

Essential here, in my opinion, is the appearance, paired with *pseudos*, of a term other than *alēthes*: *etumos*. The doublet of *etumos*, *etētumos*, already for Parmenides qualifies the path *"which is and which is real* (τὴν δ' ὥστε πέλειν καὶ ἐτήτυμον εἶναι),"[20] as opposed to the path "unthinkable and anonymous, which is not true/is not a true path (οὐ γὰρ ἀληθής ἐστιν ὁδός)." However, the two words do not mean the same thing. We know well, perhaps too well, the extent to which *alētheia* faithfully names the recollection, the unveiling of being within, through, in, as *logos*. *Etumos* – coming from the same family as *etazō* ("put to the test," "examine") and doubtless *etoimos* ("ready," "available," and so "imminent" and "effective," as well as "zealous," "courageous") – means rather, as we observe, "reality," *Wirklichkeit*. In "etymology," for example, it designates the heart of the word, its most profound eponymy; it marks in a terminological fashion, for Democritus in particular, the register of the real in its most inescapable authenticity – atoms and void – as opposed to the conventional – sensible qualities and probably too the words which designate them, sweet, or hot.[21] Linked, certainly, in any case no less essential, is the explicitly mimetic relationship which in this sequence seems to be constitutive of the false.

In the *Theogony*, it is the Muses, "the daughters of great Zeus, of the well-fitted words," "who know well how to make use of words,"[22] who address themselves to Hesiod, making use of the same words as Odysseus:

ποιμένες ἄγραυλοι, κάκ' ἐλέγχεα, γαστέρες οἶον,
ἴδμεν ψεύδεα πολλὰ λέγειν ἐτύμοισιν ὁμοῖα·
ἴδμεν δ', εὖτ' ἐθέλωμεν, ἀληθέα γηρύσασθαι

Shepherds of the fields, wretched things of shame,[23] like bellies,
We know how to say many false things similar to authentic realities,
But we know how, when we wish, to intone truths.[24]

This time, it is quite clear: *pseudos* and *alēthes* are two possible modalities of the *etumos*, two ways of enunciating what is actually real. Two ways which, in addition, are available to the same speaker, who has the ability, therefore, to exercise something like a choice. It is this pairing, with a *pseudos* built mimetically upon the real (*pseudea/homoia*) rather than on the true, through a difference with the immediate and conspicuous vocalization of truths, that the philosophical tradition will retain and accommodate, in the place and position of the exclusive monody of "is."[25] But as for the sophistic, it plays, between Parmenides and Hesiod, in both scenes at once.

II. SOPHISTIC INFALLIBILITY

II.1. Parmenides, guarantor of sophistic infallibility

If philosophy in one way or another will believe that it ought to renounce Parmenides, that is because sophistry, with an unanswerable consequence, draws from the Parmenidean interdiction the guarantee of its own infallibility. It seems to me that its argumentation is twofold and sets off not only (with Gorgias, for example) from the path of being, but also (with Protagoras) from the pseudo-path of opinions.

II.1.1

The first type of argument: if not-being is not, the *pseudos* is impossible, and one who speaks always speaks the truth. Two major texts, often cited, bear witness to this deduction:

• The fragment of Antisthenes, cited by Proclus,[26] which draws the conclusion from what could be called the exclusivity of being: πᾶς γάρ, φησί, λόγος ἀληθεύει· ὁ γὰρ λέγων τι λέγει· ὁ δέ τι λέγων τὸ ὂν λέγει· ὁ δὲ τὸ ὂν λέγων ἀληθεύει, "All speech is veridical; for the one who speaks says something, but one who says something says what is; and one who says what is, is veridical." Aristotle, at the moment in which he refutes this argument by showing the necessity of complicating it, indicates its essence: "the false *logos* is properly speaking *logos* of nothing (ὁ δὲ ψευδὴς λόγος οὐθενός ἐστιν ἁπλῶς λόγος)."[27] Every *logos* is *logos* of something; the false *logos*, not being the *logos* of anything, is not *logos*, and so is not.

- The *Treatise on Not-being* by Gorgias, which, in its second part ("if it is, it is unknowable"), draws the conclusion from the identity of being and thinking: δεῖν γὰρ τὰ φρονούμενα εἶναι, καὶ τὸ μὴ ὄν, εἴπερ μή ἐστι, μηδὲ φρονεῖσθαι, "It is necessary that what is represented is, and that what is not, if it indeed is not, is also not represented."[28] On this basis, whatever statement one pronounces must in fact be: if, paraphrasing the *Prometheus* of Aeschylus, I say that "chariots run upon the ocean," then chariots run upon the ocean.[29]

II.1.2

I would construct the second type of argument in the following manner. There can be no difference between *alētheia* and *doxa*: if there are only two ways, and if that of not-being is impracticable, we can deduce that the way which we practice is indeed that of being. A consistent Parmenides necessarily entails the coincidence of "being" and "phenomenon," as of "truth" and "opinion." Here we recognize the thesis of Protagoras, such as it is presented as much by Plato as by Aristotle. From this perspective, the clearest statement of the *logos* of Protagoras is found in *Metaphysics* Γ 5: τὰ δοκοῦντα πάντα ἐστὶν ἀληθῆ καὶ τὰ φαινόμενα, "everything which is the object of opinion is true, as well as everything which appears";[30] Aristotle, then, knows well how to show that for Protagoras as for Heraclitus, and indeed for Parmenides as well, the identity of being and thinking necessitates this collapse.[31]

We have seen that the sophistic procedure, whose seriousness consists of taking Parmenides at his word, whether it departs from being or from *doxa*, from "logic" or "ethics," renders sophistry and philosophy indiscernible, and blocks every refutation in advance.

II.2. Sophistic poetry

Correspondingly, the "materiality" of language, the "minuscule and unapparent" corporeity that is breath and its modulation, is constitutive and essential to all *logos*; it could not be isolated from its relation to being, as if being could have on the one hand breath, and on the other *logos*: on the contrary, it is breath which makes of *logos* "the great master capable of accomplishing the most divine acts."[32] A sophist does not lie, does not trick, does not make noise, but, always and completely, speaks: καὶ λέγει ὁ λέγων.[33]

If we are attempting to understand what sense a sophist can still give to the term *pseudos* while it is ontologically barred, we can seek assistance anew from the *Encomium of Helen*. Gorgias there begins with a series of magnificent affirmations: "Good order for a city is to be well supplied with men, for a body it is beauty, for a soul wisdom, for an act excellence, for a speech truth."[34] Truth is simultaneously the essence and excellence, the *kosmos*, of *logos*. Yet, by making this encomium, Gorgias aims to "demonstrate that those who denigrate Helen are in the wrong (*pseudomenos*), and to show the truth."[35] The *pseudos* is the "acosmicity" of the speech:[36] we should not understand by this its chaos, as much as a way of pushing it to the limit, driving it outwards, accomplishing it as the "master," as the "tyrant" that it is. From such a perspective *pseudos* is nothing but the most extreme manifestation, the point of omnipotence, of the *logos* committed to being by Parmenides, the perverse but sovereign effect of ontology.

I have studied elsewhere[37] how the sophists thought the *logos* positively, not in terms of ontological adequacy, but of logological efficacy: in terms of fabrication, of fiction. It is thus that one indeed persuades, by "forging false speech" (*pseudē logon plasantes*)"[38] (to the extent that *logos* is not only capable of the eternal present – of Parmenidean being – but is also capable of time in its becoming), everything to which it is the function of the muses, the sirens, and the soothsayers to be related. That is why we must say that sophistry is Parmenidean (not-being does not exist, there is no *pseudos*) and Hesiodic (the false is never anything but a turn of the truth, right inside this "veritable reality" produced by language). But from both points of view, the result is the same: it is impossible to make a division between *logos* and sound, simply because there is no sound.

The task of Parmenidean philosophy, in this regard at least, consists in trying again and always to operate the *krisis*, if not between being and not-being, at least, in any case, between sound and *logos*, opinion and truth, true and false.

III. THE *SOPHIST* OF PLATO: PARRICIDE AND SYNTAX

The refuge of the sophist is impregnable:

– We are really (*ontōs*), my dear friend, engaged in an investigation of the utmost difficulty. For appearing and seeming (*to phainestai kai to dokein*, "to be an appearance and to be an opinion") without being, saying things without saying the truth, all that has always been full of perplexity, before just as now. For how must one speak, in order to say or to believe that falsehoods really are (*ontōs einai*), without remaining caught in a contradiction in saying so – this is of an utmost difficulty, Theaetetus.
– Why is that?
– The audacity of such a discourse is to suppose that not-being is. Unless that were so, falsehood would not come into being. Yet the great Parmenides, my child, when we were children, did not cease from beginning to end to attest to this, saying every time in prose as in verse: 'This statement will never in fact be tamed: not-beings are. But you, turn your thought away from this way of inquiry.'[39]

Plato marks, without the least ambiguity, the consequence that leads from Parmenides to sophistry: without fail, if not-being is not, then there is no *pseudos* – or: if Parmenides, then Gorgias.

On the basis of the end of this dialogue, a text as familiar as it is difficult, I would like to make some clarifications concerning the Platonic localization of the *pseudos*, that is to say its definition and its conditions of possibility.

III.1. The parricide: no *"logos"* for Parmenides

The possibility of the *pseudos* goes, as is known, through "parricide."[40] The parricide does not consist of braving the interdiction by taking the way, effectively impracticable, of not-being. It consists, rather, of engaging, in the full knowledge of the facts, with the pseudo-way that mortals follow out of habit: to defend oneself against the sophists, one must put the to the question the *logos* of Parmenides' rack,[41] and "force not-being to be, in a certain regard, and, in its turn, force being, inversely, to not be, in a certain way (βιάζεσθαι τό τε μὴ ὂν ὡς ἔστι κατά τι καὶ τὸ ὂν αὖ πάλιν ὡς οὐκ ἔστι πῃ)."[42] To put it yet another way, it is necessary to tame the mixed statements, to successfully make of them something other than sound.[43]

It will first be noted that in this partitioning of sound and *logos*, the initial operation consists of making the *logos* of Parmenides confess that it is itself only sound. What then do Parmenides' two verses "confess"? First, that one cannot find "on what to lay," "or to apply" this "word,"[44] "not-being," one cannot "bring it onto the scene" (*poi . . . epipherein*):[45] that is why "it is necessary to affirm that one who would attempt to pronounce 'not-being' does not even speak (οὐδὲ λέγειν φατέον, ὅς γ' ἂν ἐπιχειρῇ μὴ ὂν φθέγγεσθαι)."[46] Parmenides, in contrast to Wittgenstein, will have said too much of it: anything except stating the second way, or putting into words the pseudo-path of mortals, is already too much for the *logos*. Further, by saying, as here, *mē eonta*, Parmenides visibly "attributes" (*prospherein*)[47] number, which is to say being, to not-being, something he already does just with the singular (properly understood: "not-being" involves unity).

I want to stress these two critiques – through *epipherein* (to speak is to go to lay the word on the thing) and through *prospherein* (to speak is also to attribute qualities, predicates, to a subject) – for the two registers that they determine will be reprised, we shall see, at the moment of the definition of the *pseudos*. They corroborate, in fact, the fundamental distinction invented by Plato as a war machine against the Parmenido-sophistic "discourse": the distinction between *logos tinos*, "speech of something" (a simple substantivation of the sophistic *legein ti*, "to say something"), and *logos peri tinos*, "speech which is about," "which concerns something." There are thus two ways in which the supposed *logos* undertakes to "harmonize," "to adapt being to not-being (ὂν ἐπιχειρεῖν μὴ ὄντι προσαρμόττειν)":[48] two ways that Parmenides thus lays his own trap, and that the Poem of the goddess becomes confused with the noisy habit of mortals.[49] We shall say, in conclusion to this point, that to commit this parricide is first of all to understand how Parmenides committed suicide.

III.2. The "come-back" of Parmenides, or being dialecticized[50]

The parry against the sophist consists, therefore, of rendering "logical" the mixture of being and not-being: indeed "hope" emerges as soon as the Stranger manages to make manifest that "being and not-being involve equal amounts of perplexity,"[51] as soon as a symmetry, a commensurability, between being and not-being can be envisaged. The solution proceeds through the examination of the greatest genera and of their mixture or community. It concludes with the famous reciprocal determination of being and not-being: "each time we say (*legomen*) not-being, we do not say an opposite of being, but only something different."[52] Thus, when we pronounce a word and its negation, for example "beautiful" and "not beautiful," we put "one being face to face with another being (*ontos pros on antithesis*)."[53]

The Stranger thus returns as conqueror over the Parmenidean quotation: after the impotence and the audacity that provided the context for its first occurrence,[54] the second is characterized by self-satisfaction.[55] Not only has he succeeded in demonstrating that "not-beings are," but he has also "fully illuminated the *eidos* that is found to be the one of not-being," to the point of daring to conclude with a phrase that, although untranslatable, in his mouth earns the right not to be a play on words, τοῦτό ἐστιν ὄντως τὸ μὴ ὄν ("this is beingly not-being").[56] In doing so, he well and truly sends the *alogon* packing – what at the same time both escapes and blocks discursivity – this supposed opposite of being.[57]

Yet one must carefully assess the situation that this triumph establishes. It seems that in fact a backlash is produced: not only does parricide come back to an inquiry on suicide, but moreover it is a suicide very poorly committed. For after all, insofar as not-being is not thinkable except as an other (namely, and very precisely, another being), the privilege of being remains excessive.[58] One could even legitimately speak of exclusivity, could say that there is only being, and that it can happen quite simply that being relates to itself under the figure of the other: Parmenides not dead, but at most (and by the way, this is the very term that Plato introduces)[59] dialecticized.

III.3. Syntax as parry against the efficacy of "*logos*" ("*peri . . . hōs*")

In any case, if non-beauty is not less than beauty, we still do not have hold of the *pseudos*. The Stranger, in his vocabulary of the community of forms, takes from the sophist the objection according to which, even if not-being participates in being, all the same, nothing proves that speech and opinion themselves participate in not-being (the condition required for the existence of falsehood and simulacrum).[60] From the perspective that we have just outlined, the objection is very grave, because in all rigor with not-being one would say, again and always, something that is. Of two things, the one summarizes everything: either not-being is not, and there is no *pseudos*, or not-being is, and there is no *pseudos*. Here we find again the double torsion of the sophistic argument, through Parmenides and through Hesiod.

The solution, in which the Platonic innovation consists, is a new inquiry which bears upon "words."[61] I shall recount, in the relation to Parmenides, two significant features.

III.3.1. The word and the interlace

First of all, Plato thematizes, even canonizes, a shift of terminology which definitively invalidates the Parmenidean distinction between *logos* and *onoma*. We know that, from the *Sophist* on, "*onomata*" now generically designates "words," which can be specified as *onomata* or "names" (designating agents), and *rhēmata* or "verbs" (designating actions).[62] As for *logos*, it designates the "combination," the "syntax" (*sumplokē*)[63] of at least one name and one verb: we thus no longer pass from sound to speech, but from the imposition of a word, from the nomothetic, to determination, to discursivity (οὐκ ὀνομάζει μόνον ἀλλά τι περαίνει).[64] For example, *logos* is the "word," in the present case, "the name that we utter for this interlace (τῷ πλέγματι τούτῳ τὸ ὄνομα ἐφθεγξάμεθα λόγον."[65]

One can hence deduce that "is," the word of the way, is not a *logos* any more than "short" or "horse." Parmenides reproached mortals for creating with their words an incompatible mixture of being and not-being. The Stranger reproaches Parmenides for remaining at the level of words and not knowing how to mix compatible words in order to pass to *logos*. Once again, the *Poem* of Parmenides read by Plato, as sound, then word, is a not-yet of language.

III.3.2. "Speaking of" and "speaking about" ("logos tinos" and "logos peri tinos")

A second remark, or, as the Stranger says, "another little thing."[66] This mutual incompatibility of certain words outlines at most an infra-logic, a misuse of words which spoils language. Apparently nothing allows us to advance in the determination of the false and in its difference from the truth. Unless we are to locate, interlaced amidst the *logos* itself, a function which is similar to nomination, and another which is similar to the interlace: it is from the interlace as interlace that the "quality" of *logos* will emerge.

Such is, I think, the sense of the distinction, very often obliterated or badly understood, between *logos tinos* and *logos peri tinos*, that the Stranger then introduces.[67] The complement (in the genitive, without a preposition) is equivalent, as we see, to the possessive. "Theaetetus is seated" is a *logos* which belongs to Theaetetus, which depends on him, not (of course) in the sense in which Theaetetus would be its speaker, but in the sense in which it comes to lay itself upon Theaetetus, to speak of Theaetetus. This first function is the literal reprisal of the Parmenido-sophistic function: it always concerns the necessity (ontological *sensu stricto*) of saying something when one speaks, and hence the obligation to be that is proper to what we would today call (at the risk of obliterating the very possibility of the problem) "reference." To be assured of this fact, it is sufficient to consider the tranquil force of the affirmation which opens and closes our passage: "discourse is necessarily, each time that it is, discourse of something; that it be not discourse of something is impossible."[68] Compare this with the very principle of the Parmenidean confession: "he who does not say something says absolutely nothing"[69] which rendered impossible, unworkable, every refutation of the Parmenido-sophistic position. Nothing has changed: Parmenides, Gorgias, or Plato share the same evidence that Aristotle alone would manage to transform into a prejudice.

However, and herein lies the innovation directly conditioned by the syntactical interlace, this function of efficacious nomination finds itself doubled by a function of "surrounding," a – if I may put it like this – "peristic" function.[70] This latter function, in contrast to the other, permits the introduction of, and even unites itself with, the "quality" of the discourse.[71] In fact, the determination of the quality of the discourse, that which makes the difference between "Theaetetus is seated" and "Theaetetus flies," and which unfolds itself in terms of "true" and "false," requires the space of the *peri* in order to be deployed: it concerns that which "revolves around" the very thing of which the discourse is discourse, that which one "attaches" to this thing. Even if the genitive alone (the "reference") and the complement of *peri* (the "subject") make only one – Theaetetus – the *peri* alone introduces the possibility of a *hōs*, of a syntactical articulation with "that," "like," or "as," which does not reduce itself to the interlace of word and verb.

We can convince ourselves that this *hōs* is indeed the prize of the analysis by comparing the new definition of true and false with the provisional definition proposed in order to lead into this part of the demonstration. The latter fitted, in fact, into the sophistic mold in its use of direct objects: "To have as an opinion or to say not-beings, such is in a certain manner the falsehood which is produced in thought and in discourses."[72] The new definition, on the contrary, at once refers to a *peri* and involves a *hōs*.

Before giving the text, a precaution: this conjunction is unfortunately not easy to understand and translate. It is without a doubt one of the most truly equivocal little words in the Greek language, probably deriving from the fusion of five different words.[73] One must know, in particular, that, like *hoti*, *hōs* can simply introduce a substantival clause, just as in the Parmenidean statement of the ways (a usage present at this very place in the *Sophist*);[74] followed by a participle, it can also signify "as," that is to say, "in a quality of," "in the way in which" (and in this case it approximates the Aristotelian *hēi*, "insofar as"); but it can also very commonly denote the unreality of an "as if." I would be tempted, provisionally, perhaps, to perceive in its three successive occurrences a slippage from one sense to the other, leading finally to the mimetic.

The first occurrence: "Of the two discourses," says the Stranger (speaking of "T. is seated" and "T. flies"), "the true says of the beings which revolve around you that they are (τὰ ὄντα ὡς ἔστι περὶ σοῦ)"[75] – which clearly implies another sense of *hōs* and another analysis of *peri* than "the true says the beings as they belong to you." "Of course!," Theaetetus would answer. The Stranger continues: "The false says it of others (*hetera tōn ontōn*)."[76] – "Yes" – "It says not-beings as they are (*ta mē onta hōs onta*)"[77] – "Agreed." The Stranger goes on to clarify the formula: "It says beings which, although they are really beings, are other when they concern you" (*ontōs*[78] *de ge onta, hetera peri sou*)."[79] "In fact, many beings and many not-beings revolve around every subject,"[80] which are such only in relation to it. Considered in isolation, they are both beings. But some are nevertheless not-beings since they are "others": it seems to me that one must understand here at once "other than the subject" (flying does not belong to this Theaetetus to whom I am speaking, and who is currently seated opposite me), and, consequently, "other than themselves." For each at the same time "is" considered in itself, but, when related to the subject, when measured in terms of this subject of the *logos* which gives (if I may put it this way) the tone of the is, each, nonetheless "is not."

It is this last interpretation of alterity, the auto-alterity of predicate/predicate by consequence of the hetero-alterity of predicate/subject, that the final, recapitulative, definition gets behind, and which at the same time clearly makes the sense of *hōs* advance towards an "as if."

> Thus, when one says about you things that are other as if they were the same, that is, not-beings as if they were beings (*peri de sou . . . thatera hōs ta auta kai mē onta hōs onta*), such an assemblage of verbs and names seems in every respect to constitute, in all being and in all truth (*ontōs te kai alēthōs*), false discourse.[81]

The measure of being and sameness is always provided, as in the Parmenidosophistic discourse, by the subject. But the perception, produced by the theorization of syntax as such, of the subject as a center of gravity of predicates, allows us to distinguish (in relation to the subject) two classes of predicates. To situate a predicate badly, that is the false.

III.3.3. The failure of discrimination

So be it. Yet, for all that, it will be immediately noted that no criterion of choice is given. What permits me each time to decide if Theaetetus is flying or if he is seated? The Stranger does not breathe a word of it, making at most an implicit appeal to the evidence of perceived reality: "Theaetetus, with whom I am currently conversing, flies."[82] We all know, and he as well, the extent to which other examples would be less favorable: from "not-being is," to "the current king of France" (the modern version of the goat-stag) "is bald," while passing through "this contribution is of limpid clarity."

What Plato offers us, instead of a rule of discrimination, is the place of the mimetic, in this way outlined by the *hōs* as an illusion about predicates: one can say that the mimetic exists, but not when it exists, no more than where to locate the model and where the image. The Stranger, militant on behalf of mixture, has proved the existence of the *pseudos* in discourse, but he has not in fact provided himself the means to make the *krisis* of the cases.

III.4. The trap of resemblance

Dialogue pleasant and deceiving, or pleasantly sophistic, because transfixed by the mimetic.

The Stranger, of whom one asks from the beginning whether he is man or god, philosopher – and perhaps therefore insane – or sophist, is not Socrates. He merely resembles him, directing the dialogue with Theaetetus in his place, "as" him. But Socrates himself more and more resembles this sophist that is hunted, definition after definition, to the point that his cathartic midwifery no longer manages to distinguish itself from the *genei gennaia sophistikē*,[83] "well born by birth" ("authentic and truly noble," as it is translated), the wolf-dog of a resemblance so "slippery" that it cannot be escaped.

It is here that we return, after the true and the false, at the very end of the dialogue, to the dichotomies of the mimetic.[84] The Stranger makes them fly past at a gallop: the human production of images that are simulacra produced without instruments . . . in order to choose, in the end, against the naifs who think they know what they do not know, the "ironic imitator" – Socrates again. But arborescence that follows, the final one, is still more revelatory: opposed to the popular orator, not one but two personages emerge together, as ever: "sage or sophist (*sophon ē sophistikon*)."[85] A doubt that is only alleviated by a "thesis," which is once more enunciated by Theaetetus: "sage is impossible, because we have posited that this one knows nothing."[86] "Imitator of the sage": such is, then, "in all truth and in all being (*alēthōs . . . ton pantapasin ontōs*),"[87] like the *pseudos* earlier, the sophist. But what? "Philosopher" and "sophist" both make contact with "sage," the same paronym? Who can pretend that they will be distinguished?

"To separate," this *khōris* exactly for which Aristotle will reproach Plato, "to separate, . . . belongs to he who absolutely deprives himself of the Muses and of philosophy (*amousou tinos kai aphilosophou*)."[88] To show that "discourse is one of the classes of being," that it participates in being, that it is: this is the mixture that, with and against Parmenides, makes philosophy triumph.[89] The Muse remains. She is, I believe, what one then wins, when one shows that discourse also participates, with and against Hesiod, in not-being. For this sharing is the condition of the *pseudos* and of *mimēsis*.[90]

Pseudos, mimēsis. One does not distinguish the false from the true any more than the evil intention from the good, the wolf from the dog, the sophist from the philosopher. It is not within the *logos*, within "logic," that we can find the criterion that permits standardization; it is not on account of logic that there will be ethics. Until Plato, in any case, the only *krisis* that logic succeeds in establishing is reducible to that of Parmenides, that of all or nothing: either one is not even speaking, one is making sound (of the **bha*) with the mouth, or one is in the *logos*. At most we could add, in the place of the Parmenidean "I, the truth, am speaking," a more Hesiodic: "I, the Muse, am speaking," "I *alethe* as I *pseude*."

The following stage, which is already the one of modernity, opens doubtless with Aristotle, under the effect of two slight modifications, both anchored
in the attention to the principle of non-contradiction: the passage from *legein
ti* or *logos tinos* to *sēmainein ti*, "to signify something which has a sense for
itself and for another," which undoes the entanglement in which Plato remains
trapped between *legein* and *einei*. And the substitution of *kata* for *peri*: only
the semantics of the categories permits the stabilization of the syntax of subject
and predicates, and the reformulation of the difference between true and false.
The *hōs* no longer designates an illusion about the predicates, but the senses
of the verb to be and the possible modalities of the appearance of a subject. It
remains to be seen whether the definition of truth in terms of adequacy that
necessarily follows ever really manages to escape the mimetic trap enclosed
within phenomenology. "The proposition 'snow is white' is true if and only if
the snow is white."[91] But "those who ask . . . if the snow is white or not need
only look at it."[92]

NOTES

[This essay was originally published as "Les Muses et la philosophie. Eléments
pour une histoire du '*pseudos*,'" in Pierre Aubenque (ed.), *Études sur le "Sophiste"
de Platon* (Naples: Bibliopolis, 1991), pp. 291–316. – eds.]

1. Hannah Arendt, "Truth and Politics," in *Between Past and Future*.
2. Plato, *Sophist* 231a.
3. Martin Heidegger, *Logos (Héraclite, fragment 50)*, in M. Heidegger, *Essais
   et Conférences*, trans. André Préau (Paris, 1958), pp. 249–78.
4. Hermann Diels and Walther Kranz [D.-K.], *Die Fragmente der Vorsokratiker*, 28 B 1.30; 8.51.
5. *Pistis alēthēs*, fr. 1.30.
6. *Ereō, muthon*, fr. 2.1.
7. Fr. 2.3–8.
8. Fr. 3.
9. Fr. 6.1.
10. *Einai mē eonta*, fr. 7.1.
11. The expression is from Denis O'Brien, *Le Poème de Parménide* (text,
    trans., and critical essay), in *Études sur Parménide*, ed. Pierre Aubenque
    (Paris, 1987), I, p. 224.
12. Fr. 7, 8.1–2; trans. O'Brien, modified; the construction of 7.1 is a particu-
    lar subject of dispute.
13. Fr. 1.31.
14. *Glōssa, onoma, onomazein* are thus understood in opposition to *logos*. Cf.
    Ernst Hoffman, *Die Sprache und die Archaische Logik* (Tübingen, 1925),
    and the recent commentary of P. Aubenque, "Syntaxe et sémantique de
    l'être," in *Études sur Parménide*, II, pp. 118–21.

15. Fr. 8.38–40; trans. O'Brien, I, p. 42. But there is another possible construction: "everything that mortals could very well assign to it will be a name (. . .) being born as well as perishing" (trans. Beaufret). This is equivalent from the point of view that concerns us: there are words about which mortals believe that they are true, and which nevertheless are nothing but words.

16. Cf. Alexander P. D. Mourelatos, *The Route of Parmenides* (New Haven, CT and London, 1970), and, for example, my own article, "Le chant des Sirènes dans le Poème de Parménide," in *Études sur Parménide*, II, pp. 163–9.

17. *Odyssey*, 19.203.

18. *Theogeny*, 19ff.

19. "How well he knew how to give the appearance of truth to so many lies!," trans. Bérard; "all of these lies, he gave them the aspect of truths," trans. Jaccottet.

20. Parmenides, fr. 8.18.

21. For *eteēi* in Democritus, cf. D.-K. 68 B 6, 7, 8, 10, and especially the group B 9, 117, 125, where the opposition passes between sensible qualities, which are *nomōi*, and the atoms and void, which are *eteēi*. Sextus (= D.-K. 68 B 9) translates this pair in terms of "truth" and "opinion." It is true that the relationship between *eteēi* and *alētheia* is established at fr. 117: "we know nothing *eteēi*, because truth is in the abyss." Finally, we must note that the sequence ἐοικότα τοῖς ἐτύμοισιν is found in Xenophanes (D.-K. 21 B 35), in a fragment too brief to be easily interpreted; but Xenophanes also says, at fr. 8, that he would have needed twenty-five years in order to "know how to really speak on this (*legein etumōs*)."

22. *Artiepēiai*, *Theogeny*, v. 29

23. It is not without interest to note that *to elenchos*, "reproach," "disgrace," "shame," and *ho elenchos*, "refutation," are two substantival formations of the same verb, *elenchō*.

24. *Theogony*, 26–8.

25. For an interpretation of *doxa* as if it had to do with such a *pseudos*, cf. Rémi Brague, "La vraissemblance du faux (Parménide, fr. I, 31–32)," in *Études sur Parménide*, II, pp. 44–68.

26. Proclus, *in Crat.* 385D, ch. 37 Pasquali.

27. Aristotle, *Meta.* Δ.29, 1024b31ff.

28. Aristotle, *MXG*, 980a10–11.

29. Ibid. 980a13ff. Cf. Barbara Cassin, *Si Parménide* (Lille, 1980), pp. 518–21 and 528–39.

30. *Metaphysics* 1009a8.

31. Cf. Barbara Cassin and Michel Narcy, "Parménide sophiste," in *Études sur Parménide*, II, pp. 277–93.

32. Cf. Gorgias, D.-K. 82 B 11 (II, p. 190 = Hel. 8): λόγος δυνάστης μέγας ἐστίν, ὃς σμικροτάτῳ σώματι καὶ ἀφανεστάτῳ θειότατα ἔργα ἀποτελεῖ.

33. *MXG*, 980b4.

34. D.-K. 82 B 11.1.
35. Ibid. 2.
36. Ibid. 1.
37. On the new type of relation to being, no longer said in but produced by the *logos*, and the shift from *pseudos* to *plasma* which already occurs in Gorgias, I will permit myself to refer to "Du faux ou du mensonge à la fiction," in *Le Plaisir de Parler*, B. Cassin (ed.) (Paris, 1986), pp. 2–29.
38. Gorgias, B 11.11.
39. Plato, *Sophist*, 236d–237a.
40. Ibid. 241d3.
41. *Basanizein*, ibid. 241d6 = 237b2.
42. Ibid. 241d6–7.
43. I agree, ultimately, with the analysis that Monique Dixsaut, "Platon et le *logos* de Parménide," in *Études sur Parménide*, II, pp. 242–6 proposes of this passage.
44. *Tounoma*, *Sophist*, 237c2.
45. Ibid. 237c2; cf. 237c7ff., 10ff. See also the reprisal at 250d7–8, and its modification at 251a9.
46. Ibid. 237e5ff.
47. Ibid. 283b3.
48. Ibid. 238C5ff.
49. On the series of verbs which make understood that there could be no orthology of not-being because there is no -logy of it at all, but only sounds, *Sophist*, 238c10–12 can be compared to *Cratylus*, 429e1–430a5 on the subject of false names.
50. ["Come-back" is in English here and below in the original essay. – eds.]
51. *Sophist*, 250e6ff.
52. Ibid. 257b3–4.
53. Ibid. 257e6.
54. Ibid. 237a.
55. Ibid. 258d.
56. Ibid. 258e3.
57. Ibid. 258e8.
58. Michel Narcy, in B. Cassin and M. Narcy, *La Décision du Sens* (Paris 1989), insists on this point.
59. *Sophist*, 253d2ff.
60. Ibid. 260d5–e3.
61. Ibid. 261d2.
62. Ibid. 261d2; 262a1–7.
63. Ibid. 262c6, d4; cf. *sumplokē tōn eidōn*, 259e5ff.
64. Ibid. 262d3ff.
65. Ibid. 262d6.
66. Ibid. 262e3.
67. Ibid. 263a: περὶ οὗ τ᾽ ἐστὶ καὶ ὅτου, a4; περὶ ἐμοῦ τε καὶ ἐμός, a5.

68. Ibid. 262e5ff., reprised at 263c10–11, "it is counted among the impossibilities that there be a discourse which is a discourse of nothing."

69. Ibid. 237e1ff.

70. On the importance of *peri*, cf. Michel Narcy, "A qui la parole? Platon et Aristote face à Protagoras," in *Positions de la Sophistique*, ed. B. Cassin (Paris, 1986), pp. 83ff.

71. Plato, *Sophist*, 262e8, *kai poion tina*; cf. 263a11, b2.

72. Ibid. 260c2–4.

73. Cf. L. S. J., s.v. ὡς, end.

74. For example at *Sophist*, 261a9, b1.

75. Ibid. 263b4ff., cf. d.1

76. Ibid. 263b7; "others, which are still counted among beings," conforming to the very definition of not-being and to the Parmenidean *come-back*.

77. Ibid. 263b9.

78. *Ontōs* is the text of the manuscripts, cf. Narcy in *La Décision du Sens*, op. cit., pp. 91ff.; for a different interpretation of *hōs*, cf. ibid. pp. 90ff.

79. *Sophist*, 263b11.

80. Almost the same phrase (and the Stranger refers us to it) describes the manner in which being and not-being revolve around each *eidos* and the manner in which, in the plural this time, beings and not-beings revolve around each subject (ibid. 263b11ff., 256e5ff.).

81. Ibid. 263d1–4.

82. Ibid. 263a8.

83. Ibid. 231b7ff.

84. From ibid. 265b.

85. Ibid. 268b10.

86. Ibid. 268b11–12.

87. Ibid. 268c3ff.

88. Ibid. 259e2.

89. Ibid. 260a1–7.

90. Ibid. 260d–e.

91. Alfred Tarski, "La conception sémantique de la vérité," in *Logique, Sémantique, Métamathématique*, trans. under the direction of Gilles Granger, II, p. 271.

92. Aristotle, *Topics* 11, 105a5–7.

CHAPTER 3

Odysseus' Changed Soul: A Contemporary Reading of the Myth of Er

Catherine Malabou

PREAMBLE

In April of 2014, while I was in residence at the Townsend University Center at UC Berkeley, I taught a four-week graduate seminar entitled "Animation/Reanimation: New Starts in Eternal Recurrence," and, in relation to that seminar, I delivered publically the Una's Lecture, entitled "Odysseus's Changed Soul: A Contemporary Reading of Plato's Myth of Er." Two years later, in April of 2015, I revised this lecture in preparation for publication in the present volume, and delivered it as a new talk at UC San Diego. The title of the lecture this time was "Plato Reader of Agamben, From *Homo Sacer* to the Myth of Er." In both versions, I referred to Giorgio's Agamben *Homo Sacer: Sovereign Power and Bare Life*, and this for four main reasons. First, because Er, as Plato describes him, immediately appeared to me as a possible figure of the *homo sacer*. Second, because the myth addresses the issue of the choice (αἵρεσις) of lives by the souls of the dead before their reincarnation, and because "life" here is to be understood as ζωή and βιός at the same time. Third, because the myth proposes in its own terms a reflection on sovereignty, and fosters what seems to be the first critique of it, thus already articulating a distinction between βασίλεια and the pure principle of exception, that is the very specific combination of injustice and violence that Plato calls tyranny. Fourth, and in this case inverting the direction of analysis from that of Agamben's, because Plato's argument may be read as an anticipated response to Agamben's insistence on "impotentiality" as a possible deconstitution of sovereignty. Socrates, as I argue, is the anti-Bartleby par excellence, and incarnates quite another version of such a deconstitution.

I am then reading Plato through Agamben, and Agamben against himself through Plato.

I then sent my paper to Jacob Greenstine, who helpfully informed me of the recent publication in English translation of Agamben's *The Use of Bodies*, the final volume in the *Homo Sacer* project, which contains a short chapter entitled "The Myth of Er."[1] I had not yet bought the book, and at first felt upset with such a coincidence. Would this chapter challenge, or worse obviate, both my approach to Plato and my use of *Homo Sacer I*? Reading the chapter, I was relieved to discover that Agamben's and my interpretations differed on all points, except perhaps when it comes to the insistence on the importance of the choice of lives and the meaning of the soul as a site of both differentiation and imbrication of ζωή and βίος. Apart from this, he and I do not focus on the same parts of the myth, and Agamben does not say anything about what is for me the most important point, that is Odysseus' choice of life, which is in no way comparable to others. My interpretation of the part played by Odysseus allows me to read the interaction between the three characters Er, Odysseus, and Socrates as a fluid process of identity exchange which underlies the reflections on justice developed in the myth, an exchange which is not considered by Agamben.

I then decided, in agreement with Jacob, to publish my text as it was, with just a few added references to *The Use of Bodies* when they appeared necessary.

The Myth of Er forms the conclusion of Plato's *Republic*. Socrates introduces the tale by explaining to Glaucon that the choices we make and the character we develop in this life will have consequences after death. He narrates this myth in order to give an account of the reward and punishment that the just and the unjust person, respectively, receive after death. The story begins as a man named Er, the son of Armenias of Pamphylia, is given a chance to witness what occurs in Hades and is brought back to life to tell what he has seen.

Er is supposed to have died in battle, but when the bodies are collected, ten days afterwards, Er remains undecomposed. Two days later he revives on his funeral pyre. When he wakes up, he tells others of his journey in the afterlife. His destiny is, then, one of a messenger. When Er's soul arrives in Hades, as Socrates tells, the judges there "said that he was to be a messenger to human beings to tell them about the things happening there, and they told him to listen to and look at everything in the place."[2]

WHAT DOES ER SEE IN HADES, AND WHAT CAN HE TELL US ABOUT THE AFTERLIFE?

We can distinguish three main moments of the myth.

First, we are told that the souls of those judged to have lived justly are sent upwards to heaven to enjoy a beautiful sojourn for a thousand years. The souls of those judged to have been unjust, by contrast, go under the earth to be punished. The souls of those who committed serious crimes (tyrants, mostly) receive especially severe punishment and are finally thrown into Tartarus. In a thousand years all the souls, except those eternally damned, join from up above and from down below, and travel to the center of the Universe, which is a meadow reigned over by Necessity.

In a second moment, the souls come before Lachesis, one of the three Fates, and are told to choose the lives that they are going to live for the coming reincarnation. Samples or models of lives (τὰ τῶν βίων παραδείγματα) are displayed, and the souls are each to pick up one from among them in turn. The order in which they choose has been decided by a lottery. After making the choice, each soul elects its own guardian (δαίμων), and is insolubly bound to the chosen life. A "sort of spokesman" declares: "your daimon will not be assigned to you by lot; you will choose him. The one who has the first lot will be the first to choose a life to which he will be bound by necessity."[3]

In a third and last moment, the souls drink from the river Lethe and forget everything. They are then born again to this world. Of course Er is not judged, does not choose any life sample and does not drink from the river – he comes back as the man he used to be to tell the living what he has seen. He opens his eyes to find himself lying on the funeral pyre, early in the morning, and able to recall his journey through the underworld.

I will focus here on a specific moment of the myth, that of the choice of lives. A puzzling problem appears at this point. In most cases, the souls pick up the same kind of life as the one they are used to. Plato writes: "Er said it was a sight worth seeing how the various souls chose their lives, since seeing it caused pity, ridicule, and surprise. For the most part, their choice reflected the character of their former life."[4] There is a major exception to such a repetition, though. The myth exposes a case of someone who does not select the same sample, but chooses, on the contrary, a new kind of life, a life which is not the same as his former one. This case is that of Odysseus, who is the last to choose. Socrates tells that Er reported: "Now it chanced that Odysseus' soul drew the last lot of all, and came to make its choice. Remembering its former sufferings, it rejected love of honor, and went around for a long time looking for the life of a private individual who did his own work, and with difficulty it found one lying off somewhere neglected by the others. When it saw it, it said that it would have done the same even if it had drawn the first-place lot, and chose it gladly."[5]

Odysseus chooses a different soul, a different life. He chooses to "become a private individual who did his own work,"[6] βίον ἀνδρὸς ἰδιώτου ἀπράγμονος, translated by Allan Bloom as "the life of a private man who minds his own business."[7]

This choice is highly perplexing. What could motivate it? Of course, it might be related to what Socrates said a little bit earlier, regarding the best kind of choice. The just, Socrates declared, "will know to choose the middle life in such circumstances, and avoid either of the extremes, both in this life, so far as is possible, and in the whole of the life to come. For this is how a human being becomes happiest."[8]

We can then understand Odysseus' decision as being commanded by such an imperative. At the same time, the extremes which Socrates speaks of are "wealth and other evils," and "tyranny or other similar practice."[9] None of these "irreparable evils" were committed by Odysseus. So what is Odysseus trying to avoid in choosing this middle life? Again, the text claims: "remembering his sufferings." But is such a reason sufficient for him to choose to stop being the hero that he is?

Commentators do not generally pay much attention to this puzzling case. To my knowledge, the only genuinely profound analysis of Odysseus' choice is that of Patrick Deneen, in his beautiful book *The Odyssey of Political Theory: The Politics of Departure and Return*. He writes:

> Many commentators on the Myth of Er do not pause to reflect on the grounds or rationale for admiring the particular life that the soul of Odysseus chooses. Those few that have reflected on the grounds for Odysseus's soul's specific choice agree that it is noteworthy, but disagree on the grounds.[10]

What they generally disagree on is whether Odysseus, when choosing to become a private man who minds his own business, chooses (without saying it) the life of Socrates. Alan Bloom, for example, declares: "The wise voyager Odysseus gains higher status [in the myth]. All he needed was to be cured of love of honor (a form of spiritedness), and he could live the obscure but happy life of Socrates."[11] According to Seth Benardete, on the contrary: "Socrates himself seems never to have been Odysseus. His *daimonion*, he said, was probably unique."[12]

The complexity of Odysseus' gesture seems to add to the general difficulty of interpreting the myth, underscored by many readers. Stephen Halliwell, for example, affirms: "Given the *Republic*'s wavering images of the afterlife, Er's story appears out of nowhere, professing to carry an eschatological authority that the *Republic* not previously envisaged."[13] Or: "In a visionary mode whose complexity tests the limits of understanding, [. . .] the narrative raises more questions than it can answer."[14] Julia Annas, for her part, claims that the myth of Er is "a painful shock," offering a "lame and messy ending" to "a powerful and otherwise impressively unified book."[15] Odysseus' choice seems only to confirm this shocking ending! What about this uninteresting, neutral, and banal model of life, that of a private bourgeois minding his own business? The conclusive part of the *Republic* seems to definitely disappoint.

Let's try to propose another reading of this passage. It must be noticed first that the myth stages a strange interplay between the three characters – Er, Odysseus, and Socrates – which reveals a complex structure of identity and difference. Each of them, in a way, might exchange his part with the two others. First, the myth of Er has striking resemblances with Odysseus's journey in

Hades as related in book XI of *Odyssey*. Second, Er's voice is, in fact, that of Socrates, to the extent that Socrates is the one who speaks and tells us what Er has seen. Third, Socrates himself shares common characteristics with both Odysseus and Er. It seems that Er, Odysseus, and Socrates exchange names in a loose or fluid identification process. Nevertheless, Odysseus's new life – the life of "a private man who minds his own business," or "does his own work" – does not match any of these three characters. As Deneen notices:

> Odysseus seems to choose exactly the life that most opposes his past history and seemingly his own disposition. In the pages of the *Odyssey*, neither is Odysseus a private man (*idiotēs*) – after all he is king of Ithaca, even when he is absent from his island – nor does he "mind his own business." Indeed, minding one's own business requires one to avoid "being a busybody" (*polupragmonein*) or literally avoid "doing many things" (cf. 433d). Odysseus – he of "many ways" (*polutropos*) – is the supreme example of the human who does many things. [. . .] The man who is neither private nor avoids "doing many things" is said to choose the seemingly opposite life when his soul is given the choice of all possible lives after death.[16]

Socrates is a private man in the sense that he does not seek public office, but he nevertheless does many things and certainly does not mind his own business. His life is neither obscure, nor happy. As for Er, he is a soldier, an occupation which by definition is not a private one, and as a witness, he precisely does not mind his own business. So the exchangeability of these three characters contrasts with the unappealing style or mode of Odysseus' chosen second life. Again, we do not see exactly what motivates this choice, and why it appears to be the best one.

Unless – unless we imagine a reincarnation of the myth of Er itself, a return of the myth in the twenty-first century, a new life, a rebirth of the narrative in a new framework or new "life paradigm." Would this help us to interpret Odysseus's choice differently?

I imagine the myth of Er coming back today to help us propose a solution to one of the major political and philosophical issues of our time: that of thinking beyond, or after, sovereignty. More precisely, I imagine Plato coming back on the scene today to discuss Giorgio Agamben's statement in *Homo Sacer* according to which it has become necessary to think "beyond the principle of sovereignty," beyond the "sovereign ban," and to "have moved out of the paradox of sovereignty."[17]

Is not this myth a very profound example of what deconstructing sovereignty may mean? In choosing to become a private man who minds his own business, in renouncing being the king of Ithaca, Odysseus would dismiss or relinquish his sovereignty.

According to Agamben, the paradox of sovereignty consists in the fact that everything which sovereignty includes as an essential part of its definition is at the same time excluded by this definition itself. In reverse, what sovereignty excludes from its concept is at the same time essentially included in it. This strange situation, which constitutes the very foundation of sovereignty, its fundamental logic, follows from the fact, as Agamben subtly shows, that the concept of sovereignty coincides with the concept of exception: exception is the rule. Sovereignty, Agamben argues, implies "the state of exception as a permanent structure."[18] If supreme power is founded on exception, then there is no way in which we can rigorously distinguish between the exceptional and the regular. Agamben again: "The paradox of sovereignty consists in the fact the sovereign is, at the same time, outside and inside."[19] Outside and inside the juridical order, outside and inside nature, outside and inside violence, outside and inside the law. The book establishes no less than fifteen "zones of indistinction" between the outside and the inside.

What allows the paradoxical structure of a zone of indistinction to exist is a certain type of relation: the relation of the self with itself. Sovereignty is by definition and precisely the very form of this being-in-relation with itself. This erases the difference between normality and excess, the allowed and the forbidden, between the inside and the outside. The sovereign is everything – the same and the other – all at once. Agamben: "It has often been observed that the juridico-political order has the structure of an inclusion of what is simultaneously pushed outside. [. . .] Confronted with an excess, the system interiorizes what exceeds it through an interdiction and in this way 'designates itself as exterior to itself.' [. . .] We shall give the name *relation of exception* to the extreme form of relation by which something is included solely through its exclusion."[20]

Deconstructing sovereignty thus implies the interruption of self-foundation, of self-sufficiency, of, again, the relation of the sovereign's self to itself defined as the origin of all limits or boundaries, as that which decides on the interior and the exterior, the inclusion and the exclusion, the rule and the exception.

It is possible to see Earth and Hades as Greek versions of the inside/outside dichotomy. This is what Heidegger, in *Parmenides*, demonstrates when commenting on the myth of Er.[21] He shows how in ancient Greece the relationship between interiority and exteriority, the inside and the outside, are thought in terms of relationships between the earth, or the above, and the underground. We know that from the beginning of the *Republic*, Plato's reflections on power, sovereignty (βασιλεία), and justice, are constantly sustained by a determination of the relationship between this world and the other world underneath. The myth of Er teaches us that if nothing changes in Hades, in the world underground, if the unjust chooses the same model of life again, then tyranny and abuse of sovereignty in general will never end and justice will never reign. Which is another way of saying that if sovereignty cannot renounce being both the interior and the exterior, the legal and the illegal, life and death, the sub- and the superterrestrial, then the Republic cannot actualize itself as the achievement and accomplishment of the philosophical ideal of justice. Again, something has to change, to be interrupted. It is at this point that Odysseus' choice appears and situates itself.

In order to sustain such an interpretation, I have to go further in the reading of the interplay between Er, Socrates, and Odysseus. Er exactly coincides with the definition of the *homo sacer*, even if the first identifiable figure of the *homo sacer* is, according to Agamben, Roman and not Greek. For him the first concrete emergence of *homo sacer* as a political category is the *devotus*, a man who is devoted by the consul, the dictator, or the praetor "in order to save the city from a grave danger."[22] The *devotus* is the symbol of the sovereign, to the extent that the *devotus* is exposed to death in his place. Armed on horseback and plunged into the thick of his enemies, the *devotus* wears a special cloak and appears openly before both armies. "What is the status of the living body that seems no longer to belong to the world of the living?"[23] The *devotus*, Agamben continues, either dies – and the ritual of devotion is thus accomplished – or he survives. What "happens to the surviving devotee? [. . .] The surviving devotee is a paradoxical being, who, while seeming to lead a normal life, in facts exists on a threshold that belongs neither to the world of the living nor to the world of the dead: he is a living dead man."[24] Er is precisely a surviving *devotus*, a living dead.

Following Agamben's characterization, we might see Er as the very symbol of the most extreme effect of sovereign power. Er is "the living pledge to his subjection to a power of death,"[25] he has "entered into an intimate symbiosis with death without, nevertheless, belonging to the world of the deceased."[26] Moreover:

> The surviving devotee, *homo sacer*, [. . .] [is] a bare life that has been separated from its context and that, so to speak surviving its death, is for this very reason incompatible with the human world. In every case, sacred life cannot dwell in the city of men. [. . .] we are confronted with a residual and irreducible bare life which, must be excluded and exposed to a death that no rite and no sacrifice can redeem. [. . .] [A] life that may be killed but not sacrificed.[27]

We remember the distinction made earlier in the book by Agamben between the two Greek words for life, ζωή and βίος (transliterated in Agamben's work to *zōē* and *bios*). As we know, ζωή means bare life, that is, natural life. It expresses "the simple fact of living common to all living beings (animals, men, or gods)."[28] βίος means qualified life, the way of life, the choice of a life in general; it indicates "the form or way of living proper to an individual or a group."[29] The life of the *homo sacer* is bare, stripped from its quality. A life that can only be killed.

Moving away from sovereignty, interrupting the sovereign's relationship to itself, implies for Agamben that bare life itself becomes a form of life rather than being a murderous ontological result. We have to invent creative and affirmative ways of erasing the borders between bare and qualified life, so that the very notions of inside and outside, inclusion and exclusion, themselves disappear. Emancipation from sovereignty necessitates "a constitution and installation of a form of life that is wholly exhausted in bare life and a *bios* that is only its own *zōē*,"[30] that is, a unity between symbolic and biological life. Such a constitution would prevent any violent dissociation between them. The problem is how to conceive such a unity, the indifference or non-difference between βιός and ζωή. Odysseus helps us to address this specific problem.

FROM ER TO ODYSSEUS

We just saw that Er was, as a living dead, a life "separated from its context."[31] In both his κατάβασις, his descent, his journey through Hades, and his ἀνάβασις, his ascent and awakening on the pyre, Er does not have a form of life, a βιός, what Plato names a model of life – βίου παράδειγμα – any longer. While travelling through the underground, he is no longer a soldier but instead a nobody, a witness with no qualities. He does not choose a new life like the other souls. He is not simply a soul itself: he is still embodied. He survives as a living being in the realm of death.[32] We do not know anything about the life he will lead when he returns as a surviving *devotus* among the living. How will Er return to life? How will he give a βιός to his ζωή? Odysseus shows him the way.

We should remember that the sight of the souls choosing their lives "caused pity, ridicule, and surprise."[33] One reason for the grotesquerie of this scene is the fact that all the models of lives mix bare life and qualified life, each is a βιός and a ζωή at the same time. Some human souls choose to be reborn as animal souls, for example that of a swan, a lion, an ape, or an eagle. Even great and famous human beings are taken in those exchanges. Er saw

> the soul that once belong to Orpheus, he said, choosing a swan's life: he hated the female sex because of his death at their hands, and so was unwilling to be conceived in a woman and born. He saw the soul of Thamyris choosing a nightingale's life, a swan changing to the choice of a human life, and other music animals doing the same. The twentieth soul chose the life of a lion. [. . .] Similarly, souls went from the other animals into human beings, or into one another.[34]

There are no strict frontiers, in these models, between natural and social life, human and animal existences. Even if the soul's choices are motivated by past experiences, most of the time their results are very similar to the previous ones, as noted above. It is clear that Plato is looking for a way to save this absence of a boundary from either chaos or sheer repetition. Socrates reports that there is a sort of "exchange of evils and goods for most of the souls."[35] Those who were formerly rewarded chose poorly while those recently punished are patient with their choices: but this remains a single transaction, not a transvaluation proper. Whatever the mythological dignity of the personages (Orpheus, Ajax, Agamemnon, Atlanta, etc.), whatever the kinds involved (human, animal, man or woman, gentle or fierce beast, athlete or craftswoman, etc.), whatever the transformation (exchanging a qualified life for a ζωή or a ζωή for a qualified life, or a qualified life for a qualified life, or a ζωή for another ζωή), this metempsychosis does not open a new future, it does not resolve the problem of justice, and it does not deconstruct the threat of tyranny immanent to sovereignty. The task is to discern the right measure of the fusion and communication between the two dimensions of life.

Odysseus' choice – a case which certainly is not a simple exchange – allows us to consider a new way of joining or bringing together ζωή and βίος, a way that does not suggest any abuse of power or tyrannical sovereignty. The model of life he chooses implies a neutralization of the distinction between βίος and ζωή. Odysseus chooses the life of a man whose qualification is that of having none. The myth does not specify what kind of occupation he has. In what sense is such a choice genuinely different from the others? What is the political meaning of Odysseus' gesture? Socrates shows us the way.

FROM ODYSSEUS TO SOCRATES

According to Deneen, Odysseus' choice is not only exemplary for Er, it also represents a philosophical answer to one of the main concerns in the *Republic*. Odysseus' choice is a veiled answer to a problem with the famous image of the cave: how does one who has exited the cave return? "In the *Republic*," Deneen writes, "Odysseus's choice of souls in Book 10 has significant implications for the philosopher's choice whether to redescend to the cave in Book 7."[36] We will see that this second orientation is not separated from the first one: the question of the philosopher's redescent involves also the status of philosophical life as an indiscernible state between βίος and ζωή.

As we know, with the allegory of the cave Socrates depicts our condition as chained within a cave such that we cannot recognize the truth, describes the ascent of the philosopher out of this condition, and then posits the possibility of his redescending. "The Cave allegory describes the macabre deathlike existence in the cave, the true life afforded by ascent, and the unwilling return to the underworld."[37] This situation is strikingly similar to the one described in the myth of Er, except in the myth the return is a return to this life. Yet the question is the same in both cases: how are we to return?

There is, apparently, no doubt that Socrates urges the philosopher to descend into the cave again. "If the philosopher refuses to descend," Deneen writes, "the solution of the philosopher-king to the problem of justice proves impossible."[38] Socrates is adamant about this point: it is not permitted "to stay there [above ground] and refuse to go down again to the prisoners in the cave and share their labors and honors, whether the inferior ones or the more excellent ones."[39]

Of course, as Socrates admits in the course of his analysis, reentering the cave involves the risk for the philosopher of being put to death by the hands of the crowd. Thus Glaucon raises the crucial question: "You mean that we are to treat them unjustly, making them live a worse life when they could live a better one?"[40]

The question of whether the philosopher, having reached the bright land of truth above the cave, would choose to redescend to the subterranean region and try to rule has been a source of much controversy for readers of the allegory of the cave. "Would the philosopher seek to rule the inhabitants of the Cave at the risk of his own life?"[41]

Deneen reminds us that "the thesis that the philosopher would refuse to redescend was primarily established by Leo Strauss [in *The City and Man*] and popularized by Allan Bloom in his 'Interpretive Essay' appended to his translation [of the *Republic*]."[42] Elsewhere Bloom declares:

> It is true . . . that the potential philosophers must be compelled to leave the cave as well as return to it. But once out, they recognize how good it is to be out. They never see a reason to go back, and compelling them to go back is said to be good for the city, not the philosophers. If they thought it good to go back, they would not be good rulers. It is only by going out that they became aware that the kallipolis is a cave, nay Hades, and to be in it is as to be a shade.[43]

Again, Socrates admits that there is significant danger in the philosopher's redescent. He asks about the returned philosopher:

> Now, if he had to compete once again with perpetual prisoners in recognizing the shadows, while his sight was still dim and before his eyes had recovered, and if the time required for readjustment was not short, wouldn't he provoke ridicule? Wouldn't it be said of him that he had returned from his upward journey with his eyes ruined, and that it is not worthwhile even to travel upward? And as for anyone who tried to free the prisoners and lead them upward, if they could somehow get their hands on him, wouldn't they kill him?[44]

Odysseus's choice offers an answer to precisely this dilemma: if the wise individuals are to return, they must not reveal themselves as who they really are. They have to return in disguise. We may thus understand that the model of life chosen by Odysseus is a mask. Nevertheless, the kind of disguise that Plato here proposes is other than the one Odysseus chose in *Odyssey*, namely his disguise as a beggar, which he wears after he returns to Ithaca from his long journey away. Odysseus dressed this way so that he can accustom himself to the new political situation of Ithaca before he appears as what he really is: the king. In the myth of Er, Odysseus' new life does not coincide with this earlier impoverished transvestment. Dressed as a poor man, Odysseus prepares the moment of his violent revenge. Eventually he reveals himself, starts fighting the suitors, and seeks revenge on the new political order of Ithaca which has been established in his absence. What results from this violence is the threat of permanent wars of revenge, and Odysseus cannot to resolve this threat by himself. He has to implore the help of Athena to put an end to the chaos he himself instigated.

Hiding oneself might be necessary. But most of the time, wearing a mask is not an interruption of tyranny, just its new ruse. In the myth of Er, Plato raises the question of how to disguise oneself not as a temporary ruse, a prelude to violence, but on the contrary as a means to neutralize tyranny. Such a mask is designed to produce a permanent ontological disruption of absolute power. For example, it might be the mask of a private mind minding his own business.

Socrates again indirectly intervenes at this point, helping us to determine what wearing a mask may mean in the case of politics. A striking fact in the myth is that among the various models of lives, τὰ τῶν βίων παραδείγματα, available to choose, the life of a philosopher was nowhere to be found. Strangely, the philosophical does not constitute a sample life. We thus have to guess, by reflecting on Odysseus' choice of disguise, what a Socratic life paradigm might be.

If the philosopher is to become a king without being a sovereign, does this mean that he must renounce all power? Let us turn again to Agamben. He contends that in order to move away from the sovereign exception we have to figure out the existence of a power which is at the same time a non-power. Something that would correspond to the Greek word ἀδυναμία, "impotential-ity," "incapacity." This power would be a specific mode of δύναμις: a potenti-ality that never actualizes itself, that never comes to any form of ἐνέργεια, but instead remains a pure virtuality. The model of life corresponding to this kind of power is not just another mask of violence. It is not about being a beggar out-side and a king inside. Instead it is about being nobody; it is about being a life whose only quality is barrenness. This is the life paradigm of a non-person. For Agamben the model of life of such an impotent, ἀδύνατος soul is certainly not that of Odysseus (who of course appears most of the time as the accomplished energetic figure, the ἐνέργεια par excellence), but that of Melville's Bartleby. Bartleby is the perfect example of a life which is indiscernibly a ζωή and a βίος:

> In modern thought, there are rare but significant attempts to conceive of being beyond the principle of sovereignty. [. . .] But the strongest objection against the principle of sovereignty is contained in Melville's Bartleby, the scrivener who, with his "I would prefer not to," resists every possibility of deciding between potentiality and the potentiality not to.[45]

In challenging Odysseus' sovereignty, does Plato anticipate Melville and sug-gest that Odysseus has to renounce his ἐνέργεια and become a proto-Bartleby?

Is Bartleby the correct philosophical equivalent of a private man who minds his own business? Is Bartleby truly the modern reincarnation of Odysseus, and consequently also that of Socrates? Is impotentiality – or the potentiality of the "not to" – the response to the deconstruction of sovereign power? Is it in this way that the philosopher must descend in the cave again, saying: "I am going, but I would prefer not to"? Deprived of any determined identity? Anonymous? Must the privation of sovereignty entail impotency?

This is, of course, not Plato's answer. We know that Socrates' demon intervenes to discourage him from doing certain things. Yet Socrates would never have uttered a phrase like "I would prefer not to." His paradigm is not that of impotentiality or non-potentiality, but, on the contrary, that of a free and affirmed living being. If there cannot be a model of life for the philosopher, it is because such a thing would be in contradiction with itself, it would stabilize, solidify, the being of a soul whose character is to be essentially in motion. Plato has a name for this specific philosophical mobility and dynamism. It is φρόνησις, often translated as "practical virtue." In reality, φρόνησις is not a virtue, but the virtue of all virtues, what allows each virtue to be what it is. An essential point here is that φρόνησις situates itself right at the crossing between the biological and the spiritual or noetic components of the soul. It occupies the exact middle, between ζωή and βίος. It is strange that Agamben, in *The Use of Bodies*, does not mention φρόνησις when he affirms that "the soul is not (only) *zōē*, natural life, or (only) *bios*, politically qualified life: it is, *in them and between them*, that which, while not coinciding with them, keeps them united and inseparable and, at the same time, prevents them from coinciding with each other."[46]

I do not think that the soul, ψυχή, can be defined as being "in between" ζωή and βίος, as if it, in a certain sense, transcends them. Because Agamben does not address the issue of what a philosophical model of life might be, he transfers onto soul in general what pertains to the activity of philosophy. It is philosophy, in the form of φρόνησις, that works to both hold together and separate these two kinds of lives, and thus constitutes a self-discipline of the soul, because ψυχή is nothing outside the interplay of these two lives. Φρόνησις is the crossing point between the soul understood as the principle of life, animation, sensibility, and sensuousness, and the soul as the principle of contemplation, concentration, and thinking. Φρόνησις is what transforms a purely biological life into a psychic life, a source of animation into an autonomous center of movement and action. Φρόνησις is thus what both displays and suppresses the difference between βίος and ζωή. As Plato says, the philosopher is, in a certain sense, always already dead; but this strange state constitutes the proper strength of the soul. It is a task, an ἔργον, not an impotentiality. It is a force which never results in violence; it is the very ἐνεργεία of justice. As we know, after Plato Aristotle gives a profound analysis of φρόνησις understood as prudence, such that φρόνησις is a way to expose and protect oneself at the same time. If the philosophers have to descend into the cave again, they will have to be cautious, prudent by being able to play with the plasticity of their life, sometimes appearing as pure ζωή, bare life without qualities, sometimes, on the contrary, as philosopher-kings-and-queens, thinkers, wise rulers. Philosophers must let their lives appear in their disappearance, wearing a mask in between. The paradigm of the philosopher appears at the very crossing point between humanity and animality, the beauty and splendor of Odysseus and the banality of a private individual. Socrates is very often compared to an animal, a ray, or a gadfly, for his specific mobility is in between the species. Socrates does not pass from the human to the animal, or from the animal to the human, as ordinary souls do. The plasticity of his soul is the very site of φρόνησις. Therefore, he can be said to be, as Heidegger notices, uncanny: "The uncanny [. . .] has nothing to do with the monstrous or the alarming. The uncanny is the simple, the insignificant, ungraspable by the fangs of the will."[47] The uncanny is always masked. Yet these masks are not artifacts or ruses. Instead they are the necessary detours or differences in the eternal recurrence of the identical.

Return is the central problem of the myth of Er. This problem, in its turn, must be understood through a host of questions: how is it possible to make a non-violent use of one's force and power when lost in the crowd, when alone in tyranny, when possibly exposed to murder? How is it possible to remain sovereign while going beyond sovereignty? Can return be anything other than a lost cause? What model or sample of life should be chosen for such a return? Odysseus' return to Ithaca? The philosopher's return to the depths of the cave? Er's return to earth and life? Plato does not tell us what use Er makes of all that he learnt in Hades. Does he return masked, as a beggar, as a private man, or as a φρόνιμος? Does he become an ungraspable, uncanny character? And are all of these possible returns and becomings different types of *homini sacri*, or do they present an alternative to the very meaning of the *homo sacer*?

To transform Plato into a contemporary theorist of some of the most urgent political issues (such as those of biopolitics, life, and the difference between sacrifice and killing) is not a new gesture. Yet the enigmatic myth of Er has been often overlooked and underestimated. It now appears that this concluding part of the *Republic* is not a disappointment or weak ending at all. On the contrary, through a series of enlightening dissimulations it addresses the capacity to distinguish between force and violence, between kingship and sovereignty, without defending impotency and exalting the absence of decision.

There are three myths of judgement after death in Plato: in the *Gorgias*, *Phaedo*, and the *Republic*. As Julia Annas rightly analyzes, the myth of the Gorgias is relatively simple:

> there is a judgement after death; the good are rewarded and the bad
> punished. [. . .] The *Gorgias* myth, then, expresses a kind of optimism:
> we should not be depressed by the fact that around us we plainly see
> the good suffering and the wicked flourishing, for this is not the end of
> the matter; ultimately there will be a judgement where everyone gets
> what they deserve.[48]

Metempyschosis, or reincarnation, appears in the myth of the *Phaedo*. In the first place, "the *Phaedo* myth appears to be giving basically the same judgement story as the *Gorgias*," but in fact there are "several shifts of emphasis which together downgrade the role of the judging."[49] As it happens, "reincarnation [. . .] appears as a punishment for a bad life, and the highest kind of virtue is said to belong to the philosopher, who by refusing to identify with the body's concerns renders his soul at death 'pure,' unattracted by the body and presumably not liable to reincarnation."[50] According to Annas, though, "reincarnation and the final judgement myth have not been successfully combined,"[51] and the myth ends up confused, and confusing as a whole.

The myth of Er for its part "is more complex than the *Gorgias* myth, without being confused and eccentric like the *Phaedo* myth."[52] Why then has it been considered as disappointing, or at times even repellent? Because "there is no longer any suggestions that [the judgement] is a *final* judgement."[53] The cycles of reincarnation are endless, which means that

> there is no way in which justice gets to predominate [. . .] The afterlife judgement, then, can no longer serve as a moral rectification to individuals, a guarantee that in the end just people do get their due reward. In the Myth of Er the cosmos is horrifyingly indifferent to individuals' moral achievements, and presents no guarantee at all that those achievements will "in the end" get their due reward and not have been thrown away.[54]

As Agamben notices in *The Use of Bodies*, this cosmic indifference pertains to the intermingling of necessity (ἀνάγκη), that sets the condition of choices, and contingency (τύχη), with its lottery and arbitrariness.[55] Of course, "the myth seems to explain the irreparable union of each soul with a certain form of life in terms that are moral and, in some way, even juridical: there has been a 'choice,' and there is therefore a responsibility and a fault (*aitia*)."[56] At the same time, however, all justice is "impossible," because both necessity and the choice are "blind."[57]

A strange conclusion for a dialogue devoted to justice: that justice might not, in the end, triumph! That there is perhaps no reward at all for a life of virtue. To "mind one's own business" then means that we should not expect anything from the gods. The mythical "spokesman" of beyond is clear when he tells the souls: "Virtue has no masters: as he honors or dishonors it, so shall each of you have more or less of it. Responsibility lies with the chooser; the god is blameless."[58] The life of virtue is worth possessing, because it is precisely detached from all hope for gratification or benefit. It does not depend on anyone, and does not wait for any reward. Such is, perhaps, the ultimate significance of kingship: indifference to gratifications. Desire of justice for itself. From Er to Odysseus to Socrates, the voices of the living dead still resonate to tell us that such a desire, in its utmost fragility, is what will, eternally, recur and survive.

NOTES

1. Giorgio Agamben, *The Use of Bodies: Homo Sacer IV, 2* [*Use of Bodies*], trans. Adam Kotsko; "The Myth of Er" is the title of chapter III.9, pp. 249–62.
2. Plato, *Republic* [*Rep.*], trans. C. D. C. Reeve, 614d.
3. Ibid. 617d–e.
4. Ibid. 619e–620a.
5. Ibid. 620c–d.
6. Ibid.
7. Allan Bloom, *The Republic of Plato* [Bloom], p. 303.
8. *Rep.* 619a–b.
9. Ibid.
10. Patrick J. Deneen, *The Odyssey of Political Theory* [Deneen], p. 106.
11. This and the next quotation are quoted by Deenen at pp. 106–7. See also Bloom, p. 436.
12. See also Seth Benardete, *Socrates' Second Sailing*, p. 229.
13. Stephen Halliwell, "The Life-and-Death Journey of the Soul: Interpreting the Myth of Er," p. 460.
14. Ibid. p. 445.
15. Julia Annas, *An Introduction to Plato's Republic*, pp. 349, 353.
16. Deenen p. 107.
17. Giorgio Agamben, *Homo Sacer: Sovereign Power and Bare Life* [*Homo Sacer*], pp. 47–8, 59.
18. Ibid. p. 38.
19. Ibid. p. 15.
20. Ibid. p. 18.
21. Martin Heidegger, *Parmenides* [Heidegger].
22. *Home Sacer* pp. 96–7.
23. Ibid. p. 97.
24. Ibid. pp. 98–9.
25. Ibid. p. 99.
26. Ibid. p. 100.
27. Ibid. p. 100.
28. Ibid. p. 1.
29. Ibid.
30. Ibid. p. 188.
31. Ibid. p. 100.
32. On this point, see the powerful study by Claudia Baracchi, *Of Myth, Life, and War in Plato's Republic*.
33. *Rep.* 620a.
34. Ibid. 620a–d.
35. Ibid. 619d.
36. Deneen p. 112.

37. Ibid. p. 113.
38. Ibid.
39. *Rep.* 519d.
40. Ibid.
41. Deneen p. 116, which attributes this question to Dale Hall, "The *Republic* and the 'Limits of Politics.'"
42. Deneen p. 126.
43. Allan Bloom, "Response to Hall," quoted by Deneen p. 113.
44. *Rep.* 516e–517a.
45. *Homo Sacer* p. 48.
46. *Use of Bodies* p. 261.
47. Heidegger p. 101.
48. Julia Annas, "Plato's Myths of Judgement," pp. 122–3.
49. Ibid. p. 125.
50. Ibid. pp. 126–7.
51. Ibid. p. 127.
52. Ibid. p. 129.
53. Ibid. p. 131.
54. Ibid. p. 135.
55. See *Use of Bodies* p. 251.
56. Ibid.
57. Ibid. p. 256.
58. *Rep.* 617e.

BIBLIOGRAPHY

Agamben, G., *Homo Sacer: Sovereign Power and Bare Life*, trans. D. Heller-Roazen (Stanford: Stanford University Press, 1998).

Agamben, G., *The Use of Bodies: Homo Sacer IV, 2*, trans. A. Kotsko (Stanford: Stanford University Press, 2015).

Annas, J., *An Introduction to Plato's Republic* (Oxford: Clarendon Press, 1981).

Annas, J., "Plato's Myths of Judgement," *Phronesis*, 27.2 (1982), pp. 119–43.

Baracchi, C., *Of Myth, Life, and War in Plato's Republic* (Bloomington: Indiana University Press, 2001).

Benardete, S., *Socrates' Second Sailing: On Plato's Republic* (Chicago: University of Chicago Press, 1989).

Bloom, A., "Response to Hall," *Political Theory*, 5.3 (1977), pp. 315–30.

Bloom, A., *The Republic of Plato*, 2nd edn (New York: Basic Books, 1991).

Deneen, P. J., *The Odyssey of Political Theory: The Politics of Departure and Return* (Lanham, MD: Rowman & Littlefield, 2003).

Hall, D., "The *Republic* and the 'Limits of Politics,'" *Political Theory*, 5.3 (1977), pp. 293–313.

Halliwell, S., "The Life-and-Death Journey of the Soul. Interpreting the Myth of Er," in G. R. F. Ferrari (ed.), *The Cambridge Companion to Plato's Republic* (Cambridge: Cambridge University Press, 2007), pp. 445–73.

Heidegger, M., *Parmenides*, trans. A. Schuwer and R. Rojcewicz (Bloomington: Indiana University Press, 1992).

Plato, *Platonis Opera*, ed. J. Burnet, vol. 4 (Oxford: Clarendon Press, [1902] 1968).

Plato, *Complete Works*, ed. J. M. Cooper (Indianapolis: Hackett, 1997).

Plato, *Republic*, trans. C. D. C. Reeve (Indianapolis: Hackett, 2004).

CHAPTER 4

Plato's Protagoras: The Authority of Beginning an Education

Daniel Price

I was going to have said that Hegel was blunt, but his reputation precedes him, no doubt, and such an obvious lie would have cast suspicion on the rest of my contribution. Let me say, instead, that he has the virtue of being certain of his interpretation of the history of philosophy, certain of how each part fits into the framework he provides, and certain that providing a framework is the task of philosophy as such. And if even Hegel can be forgiven for any particular misreading, the more troubling betrayal lies in the certainty that philosophy is defined and framed through the articulation of claims – through situating the agency of language in the action of contestation oriented by the progress of science. This framing is the most difficult for academics to avoid, for the technologies of argument (whether consciously Hegelian or not) dominate teaching and publishing throughout the modern academy. That this technology is at stake, and that merely arguing for a more humanistic technology or more open stance toward unconventional claims will not solve the problem,[1] is the difficulty and contribution I seek to draw out of Plato's *Protagoras*.

At the broadest level, the Hegelian frame is the embodied structure of subjective grasping or comprehension, and Socrates, Plato, and Aristotle are seen as the great precursors to Hegel's insight. Hegel is not accusing the Athenian philosophers of believing that humans possess rationality, or use some sort of rationality as a tool; in fact, his continuing attraction for continental philosophers rests in the idea that participation in the activity of the world constitutes a developing language, unbound by a priori rules of reason or reified ideas of subjectivity.[2] The Athenian trio, Hegel tells us, were the first to turn to the authority of a moral claim in a subject's apprehensions (Socrates' emphasis on the task of philosophy), of the conceptions themselves (Plato's ideas), and then finally of the process of perfecting those conceptions in a self-conscious appropriation of the reality of one's situation (Aristotle's ἐνέργεια as ontological foundation grasped in ἐντελεχεία).[3] The authority of one's own certainty, as guaranteed by the process of staking claims and counterclaims in terms of powerful and explanatory grounds, is the crux of the turn to the subject in modernity – and to pretend to argue against it from the grounds of a different framing would be to miss the point. To simply refuse the beginning of thought, and the task of thinking with others, by ceding the ground to those who are certain that, at the very least, the task of philosophy is to make well-formed and intelligible claims, is to betray the claim of authority, beyond the self.

Hegel's clearly demarcated march from Socrates through Aristotle around the authority of subjectivity, as engaged in knowing the world as the true place of one's own activity, has been replaced in our times with a rather muddy sense that people produce meaning, and my purpose is to make the productivity of the frame explicit as well as to demonstrate why this general frame of actively produced meanings is inappropriate to at least part of Plato's project. The final section, in fact, suggests that "framing" is the wrong metaphor for philosophical work in Plato's own terms. By way of foreshadowing, one can say that Hegel's Aristotle returns to λόγος at the end of the process of a grasping act, as the truth of the meaningfulness of the situated self, in an apprehension of what is completed, and thus communicable, for thought. The authority of λόγος rests in achieving a delimited form that expresses the truth of a subjectively grasped situation. For Hegel's Socrates, the λόγος is already there in the beginning (ἀρχή), but the knowing subject is stripped of its situation, and thus philosophy relies on the authority of λόγος as ἀρχή, without understanding the true place of communication in causation (specifically, the active giving of form). In Socrates, the λόγος is internalized, then separated from itself; in this separation, meaning becomes transcendent, becomes universal or common (κοινός) to all, but loses its contact with its own true ground in actuality.

This separation from embodied consciousness that Hegel here identifies as a weakness in Socrates, in order to then overcome it in the progress toward the Aristotelian framing of philosophy, we will see as the authority of beginning, and as the refusal of a framing through determinate judgement. More simply, the authority of beginning, in a λόγος that evokes reasons that it cannot possess, will allow us to break with the frame where truth must only have a determined or achieved form.[4] Hegel is more comfortable than I am with separating Socrates from Plato, and we should note that, in some of the texts under consideration, he is offering an account of Socrates as he leads into Plato. My interest, again, lies in the frame that the account of Socrates provides for the general opposition between Plato and Aristotle, which in turn becomes the basic framing movement of all philosophy as such as understood by Hegel and those of us who follow – or drown – in his wake. Whether Hegel's claims about Plato and Socrates create a coherent and convincing set of true statements about the content of Plato's writings is not particularly material for this task, even if it is otherwise interesting.

In a volume on recent appropriations of Greco-Roman philosophy, it is worth mentioning that Hegel's arguments about the Greeks resonate with contemporary concerns, and also worth mentioning that the difference between resonance and framing is itself already at stake in reading Plato against Hegel. As with the seemingly endless deferrals Plato inserts at the beginning of his dialogues, as one friend recounts to another what someone else said about a conversation, the beginning does not establish the frame within which the answer will be redeemed, but it does begin the question that sets the stage and marks what will have been resonant or empty – signal or noise.

I read Hegel reading Plato because Derrida wanted to resurrect a certain subjective productivity, an inescapable violence, as a tool against the Heideggerian attacks on technology and humanism.[5] These polemics are wrapped both within and against the politics of a waning Marxism and Foucault's anti-humanist histories, and at our distance we can now see Derrida as a last great defender of the careful study of the humanities while the academic establishment bunkers into an increasing irrelevance and complains of being under attack from both modern technology and deconstruction. But to contextualize the interpretation of a historical moment this way is to imitate the pedantic footnotes to the *Symposium* explaining what a youthful Alcibiades might mean to Plato's readers, while it is instead necessary to understand the resonance of the questions, and how a philosophical tone can span generations. In other words, what is in question is the meaning of the claim that context determines the production of meaning; inserting that question into the trajectory of a particularly resonant historical reading of Plato is the task at hand.

We pretend to remember – as a retelling of the story, so not beyond contestation, but not as part of the argument – that Derrida had used a certain return to Plotinus, and the idea of the trace, to resuscitate Plato against Heidegger, and to establish the force of intelligible presence in the world, as text, and not in the individual, as conscious.[6] The echoes of this deployment are felt throughout contemporary thought as the demand to read attentively to differences at the margins, or to celebrate the explosive potential of careful exegesis. Frames are imposed, but since they "never arrive" at a completed framing that exhausts the material at hand, they also provide the movement forward – such is the justice of deconstruction. Except for those directly in Derrida's wake, however, the call to recapture the study of the humanities through a rehabilitation of critique feels increasingly stale – it smells of humanism, in one form or another, and there is a great anxiety to avoid any sort of subject-oriented philosophy.[7]

Instead of responding from within the (admittedly shared) anxiety, though, let us ask why we feel that compulsion of the subject – and whether, as Hegel had claimed, we live within the claim of the subject, and the authority to speak of one's own situation, or whether we are ruled by a different beginning. With the philosophical ἀρχή, with the authority of beginning, we ask a question of how time enters into our philosophical account of the world[8] – or whether it does such as a constant frame, like the supposed fact that everything happens "in" time, framed by the past, or conditioning our present. If the event of time, as the embodiment of novelty in the apprehension of a shared world, is a constant aspect of every framing, then the hope for redemption is contained in every moment, as the promise of transcendence. The idea that hope, as a hope for a messianic future, is hope for the fulfillment of a promise already given, and that the embodiment of this hope is the activity of language, is the core of Hegel's enduring legacy, from Bloch and Benjamin to Derrida – that is, the self's presence to the world is supposedly filled with contour, with the feeling of its force, and Hegel teaches us that these contours constitute the truth that the words must strive to capture. The alternative we pull from Plato's *Protagoras* is that the ἀρχή does not demand truth, nor a passage through the embodied feeling of a soul framed by its conditioning context; rather, it demands that we begin, and remain true to the orientation toward beginning. It is not the fact of an overdetermined present, with too many people saying too many things, that makes it possible to speak; it is the call to speak well that makes it imperative to engage with the confusion and to begin.

In the short account of Socrates from the *Lectures on the History of Philosophy* I wish to consider, Hegel begins by offering a translation of an early paragraph of Aristotle's *Magna Moralia*, and then explains its meaning in his own terms. First, and with attention to Hegel's German rendering, Aristotle:

> Socrates has spoken better about virtue than Pythagoras, although also not completely right, since he made the virtues into a kind of knowing [*Wissen*] (ἐπιστήμας). This is clearly impossible. For all knowing is tied to a ground (λόγος); the ground, however, is only in thinking; with this, all the virtues are set within insight [*Einsicht*] (knowledge [*Erkenntnis*]). In this, he works against himself since he effaces [*aufhebt*] the illogical – receptive – side of the soul [*Seele*], namely passion [*Leidenschaft*] (πάθος) and ethical life [*Sitte*] (ἦθος), which indeed also belong to the virtues.[9]

In the *Magna Moralia* Aristotle goes on to say that Plato makes progress by separating the logical and illogical parts of the soul, but fails to separate virtue from being and truth. Hegel ignores this side of Aristotle's criticism of Plato for now. For his sights are set on the implicit and unified ontological truth that would ground Socrates' turn to the ethical subject, and he does not want to follow Aristotle in a categorization of different modes of subjective being. Now Hegel:

> This is a good criticism. We now see that what Aristotle saw lacking in the determination [*Bestimmung*] of virtue in Socrates was the aspect of subjective actuality – what we nowadays call heart. 'The good is essentially only an inward seeing [*Eingesehenes*].' Knowledge [*Erkenntnis*] is thus the singular moment for virtue. Virtue is determining [*bestimmen*] yourself according to universal goals, not according to particular goals. However, virtue is not only this insight

[*Einsicht*] or this consciousness, that virtue would be, [since] it is still lacking the man, the heart, the soul [*Gemüt*] that would be identical with it – the moment, we can either say the being or the realizing in general; and this aspect of being is that which Aristotle names the illogical. If the good has this reality, as universal reality, then it is, as universal being, ethical life; or the reality as individual consciousness, that is passion; for passion is also a determination [*Bestimmtheit*] of the individual subjective will. Insight lacks, so to speak, substantiality or material. However, it is in the vocation [*Bestimmung*] of virtue to allow for this [materiality], which, as we saw, had actually vanished – this is the real spirit of a people, where consciousness returns into itself. Even so, this [Socratic conception of virtue] is merely the subjective determination of insight, without the reality of ethical life and, for the individual, [without the reality of] pathos.[10]

Allow me, schematically, to point to two claims that are problems for Hegel's account, both as exegeses of Plato's texts and as possible philosophical positions in their own right: (1) the good is seen inwardly in an act of apprehension, (2) virtue is embodied in placing the interests of society over those of the individual, since society provides the true determinations of individuality. Hegel's claim is that Socrates has already seen that one must turn to the subject as frame for correct predication (or delimitation) of the truth, but that an unclear grasp of the meaning of objectivity makes it impossible to see that orientation as anything but the subjugation of the individual to the abstract and foreign authority of λόγος. Because λόγος is internal and has no communicated or exterior truth – or rather, because the authority of what is communal and illogical but still actual and capable of causing effects is not recognized – the moral subject remains oriented within a merely abstract frame. One might be tempted to translate Hegel's complaint here into ontological terms by saying that Socrates forgets that no virtue exists without the individual who instantiates the quality in a concrete situation or determining social context. Beyond the fact that this would be a poor reading of Plato, this formulation of the problem risks misunderstanding the very specific frame that the act of completing a judgement provides in Hegel's account. Only after Socrates' supposed insight into the nature of seeing the good (as an inward apprehension controlled by knowledge), does the return to the situation serve as a genuinely philosophical frame.

For Hegel, the determinations of experience frame thought, which in turn, once it achieves a recognized form within the community, acts as determination and frame for the next experience. This insight into the subject as enacting a frame when grasping reality is hence the measure he uses to interpret all of philosophy, and the lens that lets him see philosophical history as truthfully culminating in the subject who becomes conscious of her or his historical being. In this Hegelian light, Socrates' success is to have seen the active or productive role of the subject's conceptions; his fault was to have presumed to know them in their empty universality as orientation toward the truth, as if beyond the embodied context of a specific time. Our question is whether we can give some space to a thought that is not determined by the paradigms of production and thus understand what type of ground Socrates' turn to λόγος might otherwise provide.

Although Socrates and Plato perhaps do share with Hegel a sense that the subject constitutes the proper place of philosophical inquiry, the meaning of that turn, I will argue, is not embodied in some nascent – but incomplete – understanding of the subject's apprehension of a distinct and intelligible determination of thought. The subject does not occupy the place of λόγος in order to frame experience as meaningful or to give light to bare intuition. To deny this τέλος to the structure of the inquiry, on my part, allows me both to avoid the reification of a knowing subject who occupies the place of a completed separation from the world and to see the sense of the philosophical project as such in terms of an orientation – a gesture or a bodily attitude – that grounds the place that the knowing and rational subject will later come to occupy. The subject is controlled by the demands of knowledge, or of λόγος more generally, and does not have knowledge at his or her disposal for any particular purpose in order to do anything – not even in order to express the truth of the situation we already find ourselves within. Beginning with the orientation toward, with the search for a truth beyond one's particularity, need not imply the abandonment of the place of that beginning, however. The education to virtue is not completed in the political individual, capable of action, but rather education is always begun in the determination to turn toward the good that lays claim to us. The moral claims of the beginning (ἀρχή) are not, in themselves, claims for authority based on having caused or empowered the actual. A claim that holds us but does not rest on the power of creating effects thus provides the clue that lets us break with the metaphysics of subjective framing that Hegel makes explicit for us.

Perhaps because I am a masochist, my plan is to reread one of the dialogues that would seem most clearly to embody the deliberate transition toward identifying virtue with determined contents of thought already implicitly possessed by a pre-existing rational subject.[11] That dialogue – Plato's *Protagoras* – is not one of the most frequently read works, and I will begin with a bit of a summary of its argument before moving toward my brief account of how knowledge and virtue are connected in its unfolding conclusions.

THE MOVEMENT OF PLATO'S *PROTAGORAS*

The revival of rhetoric and relativism has occasioned a growing interest in the doctrines of Protagoras[12] – who continues to be best known for the claim that "man is the measure of all things," attacked by Socrates in Plato's *Theaetetus* and *Cratylus*. In the *Theaetetus*, Protagoras' saying is supposed to be synonymous with the idea that perception (αἴσθησις) is knowledge (ἐπιστήμη). Plato then has Socrates equate perception with seeming (φαινόμενον) and shows that it is impossible to have true statements derive from seeming, since all men equally possess seeming and there would be no way to distinguish a true from a false λόγος on the basis of seeming alone. In the *Cratylus*, the aphorism means, quite directly, that things are what they seem to each of us, without reference to sensation. The refutation is similar, although this time we speak of whether a man may be wise, not of the truth of individual propositions. Plato has the interlocutor accept the claim that things must have a distinct reality or substance (οὐσία) of their own, independent of us, since otherwise one could not distinguish the wise from the ignorant.[13] Both dialogues use Protagoras as a foil for separating claims of truth from human affective presence, and both would seem to support the idea that Socrates and Plato do not understand what it would mean for affective presence to fulfill an intuition, or for the intuition to become common when it takes on communicable limits. In the secondary literature in general, it is still taken for granted that the search for a proper discourse determines meaning and that truth is attained when subjects learn to control their language. At stake is the commonplace that knowledge is advanced through claims that can be affirmed or refuted, and that are guaranteed by following the form of inquiry Socrates embodies (as opposed to the sophists). Unfortunately, this commonplace conclusion inverts the sense of truth's relation to the subject, as a power to speak the truth displaces the claim of the truth upon a speaker. To see the difference, I should aver, is not to capture a more subtle claim within the discourse, but to pay attention to the time in which the claim arises – so that time's emergence as claim can make sense as a post-subjective understanding of truth and the call to speak in its name.

The dialogue entitled *Protagoras*, for its part, does not contain the claim that man is the measure of all things. It may, in fact, contain representations of Protagoras' own views, especially in two long monologues – one a μῦθος and one a λόγος – purporting to explain the nature and origin of mankind and his virtues. These monologues are, perhaps, more or less accurate representations of Protagoras' own writing, given that they contain numerous elements that exceed the dramatic frame Plato provides. The dialogue as a whole is usually taken to be aporetic, and is also usually taken to represent one of the "early" or "Socratic" dialogues.[14] It is usually said to be a moral dialogue, since it is concerned with the virtues of men in society, although like many dialogues it does occasionally play on an idea of ἀρετή that would be foreign to our current sense of virtue. If I am correct in my interpretation, there is a strong sense in which all of Plato's dialogues are moral, since each concerns the proper stance of the subject who possesses, and is possessed by, λόγος.

In its broadest strokes, Plato's *Protagoras* concerns itself with the question of whether virtue can be taught. It is initially framed within an encounter between Socrates and an unnamed friend intent on getting some sexual gossip concerning Socrates and Alcibiades. Socrates, instead, tells of his encounter with a wisdom that far exceeds physical beauty and begins to recount his meeting with Protagoras. The story Socrates tells begins before dawn, when a youthful friend who wishes to engage Protagoras as a teacher asks Socrates to act as an intermediary; however, instead of closing the deal for the youth, he enters into an examination of what is taught by a sophist. Socrates asks him what a sophist is, and what they claim to teach. He seems intent on showing that unless the sophist is an expert in some sort of craft (τέχνη), and the student is proposing to change into that sort of craftsman, then there is nothing that a sophist really teaches. Since sophists teach how to give good grounds – "clever speaking" is surely a poor translation of δεινὸν λέγειν[15] since it conveys nothing of the sense of power involved – and these grounds do not pertain to a particular craft, they must be giving us general guidelines for producing effects without truly knowing what they teach. Here Socrates refers to sophists as confectioners, pretending to sell nourishment for the soul but only providing sweets. He uses a similar example in the *Gorgias*,[16] but there denies sophistry even the status of τέχνη, saying it is only a kind of empirical guesswork. In the *Protagoras*, the lack of knowledge means that the sophist himself may not know whether the doctrines he peddles as nourishment will help or damage the soul.[17]

The conclusion drawn, too quickly, in the secondary literature is that this metaphor embraces the idea that only single ideas, clearly possessed and disseminated as distinct pieces of information, can serve as true knowledge. The metaphor, however, is introduced in the *Protagoras* at a point where Socrates still maintains that virtue, as the orientation toward doing what one should do, is not teachable. It may be that Socrates wishes to warn us against uninformed teachers, without claiming that informed teachers actually succeed in teaching virtue. The role of the information one must have in order to teach, in fact, is considerably complicated by the demand that virtue be unified in a way that τέχνη, of itself, is not; even the τέχνη καὶ ἐπιστήμη of measurement that grounds the specific judgements from which courage is determined at the end of the dialogue[18] would be oriented toward the unity of the virtues, not the actual possession of virtue in a knowing (and thereby unified) subject.

In spite of his doubts, Socrates nevertheless takes his friend to speak with Protagoras. He asks the sophist the same questions he had asked the friend, but does not get the same answers. Instead, Protagoras says that in fact all practical intelligence is sophistry, although most sophists have been afraid to go by the name.[19] He thus accepts explicitly the definition in terms of τέχνη that Socrates' youthful friend had rejected.[20] Socrates then presses Protagoras, at two decisive points separated by a long digression, on what it means for virtue to be unified.[21] For his part, Protagoras suggests that we should look for the origin of virtue, and indeed of λόγος itself, within the human need to organize into societies for survival.[22] Our true being, Protagoras suggests, is embodied in having powers or capacities that we use to manipulate the world to achieve our own ends. In the myth, the gods allowed humanity τέχνη so that they may survive as a species, and through this τέχνη we were able to invent λόγος, although Zeus had to intervene later and give everyone a share of justice and shame so that we could live together in cities.[23] Those that understand the power of manipulation that λόγος provides are able to give shape to the city, the virtuous being those who act in accord with what is best for that city and not solely for the self. The many, however, are manipulated, not liberated, by the rhetorical power of the few.[24] There are long apparent digressions on the proper form for a discussion as such, against having flute girls at parties, and on the interpretation of a poem by Simonides, discussing the difference between being good and becoming good (although this is often seen to be merely a sarcastic parody of the sophists, there are perhaps pertinent arguments here, as well).

At the beginning of the dialogue, Socrates argues that virtue cannot be taught, since no one recognizes any expert above themselves in matters of virtue (as they would if it were a τέχνη), and since the best people in Athens seem incapable or unwilling to teach virtue to their children.[25] He goes so far as to say that at first he believed that no human intervention could account for good people becoming good.[26] By the end, Socrates argues that virtue itself is a type of knowledge (ἐπιστήμη), and would thus be accessible to teaching.[27] He does not say that virtue is dependent on knowing, nor that you need knowledge in order to enact your virtue properly, however. He says that knowledge is virtue.[28] The example that demonstrates the equivalence, used in similar fashion in a number of other Platonic dialogues, is courage; however, here the example of courage has a very specific weight because the question arises within the discussion of whether virtue is unified.[29] One must have knowledge in order to be courageous and not merely foolhardy; however, the knowledge that grounds courage is unified and arises from the goodness of this unity, not from the control exercised over individually articulated (and therefore "unified") bits of knowledge. The decisive sense lies in the virtue of the soul being knowledge, and not just being dependent on knowledge for its proper utilization.

The dialogue ends without any definitive conclusions, although there are several lessons one can draw fairly confidently, at a very general level, that are important to us. (1) The λόγος of humanity enables correct civic action to take form regardless of popular opinion and not as the manipulation of popular opinion for personal advantage. (2) Λόγος is shared (κοινός) and allows us to distinguish between just and unjust activity. (3) The unity of virtue and knowledge answers the question of what is shared, and of what constitutes political τέχνη. I have been careful to word these conclusions in such a way as to avoid the sense that a subject who precedes a situation frames propositions about that situation either falsely or truly. Nor can a subject be framed by these situations, given Plato's insistence on knowledge as providing the grounds for every decision we actually take. With an eye toward Hegel, the question, again, is whether one can find in Plato a type of knowing that provides grounds without framing individual instances within determining judgements or in historically determined conceptual schemes.[30]

My purpose for the rest of this paper is direct: I wish to find the sense of placement that Plato may assign to the subjects who know, or are virtuous, such that they are neither mute in their sensuous presence to the world nor fulfilled through achieving an understanding of that affective presence. In other words, through understanding the place the subject occupies as oriented by learning virtue, we move against the frame that Hegel proposes (who was perhaps merely following Aristotle after all). I hope to indicate, if not prove, only one thing: the unity and goodness of virtue claims our subjectivity – our subjectivity does not possess that goodness, either as permanent characteristic or in the fleeting feeling of presence to the world, and then express meaning in accord with that possession. In order to be true to Plato's own sense, we have to see how he transcends the body and the immediacy of its evidence. In order to avoid the Hegelian frame, a more difficult task, we must reconstruct the call to which Plato responds, and how he there avoids the frame of knowledge understood as a type of determination made by a subject within the world (either as the cause of that world or as a part of the unfolding causal relations that constitute the world as such).

AGAINST THE APPREHENSION OF THE GOOD IN INSIGHT

I had suggested earlier that Protagoras' own words may be replicated in the long monologues he delivers when he first encounters Socrates.[31] At the very least, they do afford a consistent account of man as the measure of all things. He begins with a myth about the acquisition of τέχνη by humanity, and then explains how the various virtues contribute to the survival of the species. When first asked whether the virtues are unified, Protagoras says that the virtues must be unified "like the parts of a face,"[32] since he wants to defend their unity of function as all belonging to individual humans as tools for achieving something.[33] From Hegel's point of view, the refutation of Protagoras' myth about the origin of humanity rests on the insistence that virtue must be known in its truth, and cannot be merely lived toward as a practical orientation. But Plato himself does not emphasize the completed side of knowledge, nor its being grasped as a delimited concept within interior insight.

In general, and extending back at least to the dismissive treatment of the idea that man is the measure of all things in the *Theaetetus* and *Cratylus*, the fact that an individual perspective cannot count as the truth for a multiplicity of subjects, that there must be some substance beyond what we individually cause to exist in creating mental images, has counted as enough of a rebuttal against Protagoras.[34] In this dialogue, however, the sense in which the object must be beyond the self is less clear, given that the education of virtue is supposed to touch on situated individuals as directed toward their own development when beginning an education.[35] The individual subjective nature of the call to pursue virtue is, after all, what Hegel himself identifies as Socrates' contribution to philosophy. Our problem, most directly, may be the attempt to interpret the refutation in terms of true and false predication. The point about true and false λόγος may not indicate that a subject faces a decision about how to actualize a belief through predication, but rather that a truth claims us, constitutes our subjectivity as unified in that claim, and then is betrayed by ignorance (which, in turn, may lead to false statements). Perhaps it is the possibility of betrayal, not the free choice between different modes of predication, which separates the Socratic subject from the Euthydemian subject, who is in constant possession of the truth (or of appearances), and from the Protagorean subject, who possesses λόγος as a tool for controlling the world. It is not that the wise man knows how best to survive, how best to utilize the power of λόγος; rather, wisdom consists in knowing that we are claimed by the unity of virtue and that this claim, because of the authority it bears on our orientation as the beginning (ἀρχή) of thought and action, is the same thing as virtue.

With this transformation of the meaning of subjectivity in mind we can make sense of Socrates' refutation of Protagoras: he does not deny that λόγος, justice, and political τέχνη all help humanity, but rather he denies that their *unity* rests in providing that help. There is a tendency in the literature to say that their unity is found in a subject who possesses or controls knowledge, through the proper application of the craft of λόγος, but only because we have accepted the broad outlines of the subjective frame. To know that unity is required of you, for example (and in contrast with that framing), may not constitute a positive piece of information, but may still serve as the common "ground" (here no longer in the sense of λόγος, as Hegel suggests, but of ἀρχή) from which the sense of our place in the world gains its orientation. Socrates may have meant nothing more when he insisted that his wisdom was found in knowing that he did not know.[36]

In the *Protagoras*, Plato allows Socrates to frame the dialogue negatively. After the return to the question of the unity of virtue, Socrates leads Protagoras to see that courage – like all other human virtue – relies on knowledge. The further step, which collapses virtue into knowledge, depends on the claim of beginning (ἄρχειν) that knowledge puts on us to respond. He asks Protagoras how he understands the relation between knowledge and human will, but clearly expects assent.

> . . . the uninformed (ἀτεχνῶς) think that mankind possesses knowledge, not that knowledge rules (ἄρχειν) mankind, but rather something else, like desire, or pleasure, or eros, or often fear. They imagine knowledge to be like a captive slave, pushed around by absolutely anything else. Now, is this your view, or do you think that knowledge is noble, and such as to rule (ἄρχειν) over man, and that he who knows the good and the bad will never do anything contrary to knowledge's command, and that intelligence (τὴν φρόνησιν) is sufficient aid for humanity?[37]

It is only by an anachronism – like Hegel's insistence that knowledge is only real when possessed by an individual in a moment of apprehension – that one could say that Socrates proposes that the individual's knowledge or rationality exercises control over the individual's passions. Rather, the nobility of knowledge claims our obedience because it holds to the primary, to what begins; knowledge does not impose itself, like an efficient cause, but commands us by orienting us towards what commands our obedience within knowledge.

AGAINST DETERMINATIONS – INDIVIDUAL OR SOCIETAL

Plato's *Protagoras* does not have the long examinations of place one finds in the *Republic* or the exhortation to take up the place assigned to you by the gods in the *Apology*. Recalling Hegel, we might say that it should have them, since we are situated by cultural and affective forces that determine the true meaning of virtue. Very briefly, Hegel's dominant metaphor here is spatial and captures a sense of participation as owing one's being to that which causes the determinations to take on a specific shape; this is what he understands by ἀρχή. Hegel thought that this framing metaphor was beyond question, and that Socrates had discovered its importance when he turned to λόγος as the "ground" of virtue. The German *Grund* can have the sense of reason, but only in the way we speak of having a reason for our actions. We do not say, as far as I've ever heard, that I have a ground for my virtue except when one has grounds for doubting the integrity of an act. In Plato's dialogue virtue is supposed to be equivalent to the ground (as claim and ἀρχή) itself, and not in need of a reason for coming into existence. Rather, the virtuous subject assumes a position with regard to the unity of virtue, taking that orientation as the beginning of education. Only if we accept the claim that there is no unity outside of human apprehension, and its companion claim that unity of sense is produced through an act of subjectivity, would we say that λόγος is an insufficient ground for virtue, in need of both individual πάθος and ethical life.

Protagoras, in his monologue concerning the teaching of virtue, says that we all cause the learning of virtue when we correct our children, using "threats and blows" as if the children were twisted pieces of wood in need of straightening.[38] He is claiming that Socrates has mistakenly drawn the conclusion that no one taught virtue[39] because he failed to see that everyone was constantly teaching it. Socrates does not directly respond to Protagoras' claim, but asks, instead, about the unity of virtue. Following a common reading, we would perhaps explain that the unity begins with the subject's knowledge and not with the beliefs inherited from society. A true education would then be possible, and Socrates could begin teaching virtue on his own once they cleared the imposters out of the competition. But this assumes that knowledge aids virtue, or in Protagoras' terms, that humans use knowledge, and all other virtues, as tools to further their own ends – yet we have seen that Socrates specifically excludes this sense of virtue.

Between the two direct examinations of the unity of virtue, Protagoras takes over the dialogue and purports to identify a contradiction in Simonides.[40] Socrates' response is tortured, but he saves Simonides by claiming that there is a difference between becoming good and being good. Simonides had said that it is hard to become good, and yet criticized a saying of Pittacus that claimed it was hard to be good.[41] At first, Socrates claims that there is no contradiction since Simonides might mean that the good is a hard path to follow, but easily maintained once achieved.[42] Protagoras does not allow this to stand, and Socrates takes a more extreme – and more interesting – tack. It is, as a matter of fact, impossible to be good, not just hard to be good, since such an honor is reserved for god alone.[43] Socrates turns to the example of a doctor. A doctor becomes a good doctor through study, and the good doctor may become a bad doctor through bad implementation of his knowledge. But a bad doctor cannot implement his knowledge in a good way, since what makes him bad is the lack of knowledge, and his action itself does not change his state of ignorance.[44] This claim should have struck Protagoras as false. Surely a doctor may chance upon a cure, or grope toward a better and better practice of medicine, he might respond. If Socrates is convincing here, it is because knowledge precedes or begins the activity, and in fact gives orientation to the individual who knows. The sense of precedence, however, is not equivalent to the idea that a piece of information, separate from human existence, causes a human apprehension to take its particular form. There is no correct framing through the power of determination that causes the form to be unified and powerful. Rather, it is the claim on human knowing – the claim to find what rules, or begins, in order to become good – that breaks with this model of causality. The good, if it were possible, would exist outside of chance and circumstance, but no more mysteriously than the doctor who knows what to do before having to do it. The bad is always the result of ignorance, and thus of circumstances overwhelming our capacity to act in accord with knowledge.[45]

One might be tempted to see this as a problem of predication: the doctor may only be called good or bad insofar as she acts in accord with knowledge or not. In that case, however, the entire digression on Simonides is frivolous, if not merely absurd, since there is no reason one would privilege possessing knowledge over acting well in the determination of what constitutes acting well (acting as a good doctor acts). More fundamentally, it would also fail to shed any light on the question of whether an education oriented by virtue changes one's being as subject, and not just the predicates that would apply to that subject.[46] Protagoras, although for slightly different reasons than Hegel, had assumed that education changes you, and Socrates counters that change only comes through ignorance of the eternal, which is why ignorance is evil. In the case of education, however, the orientation toward that atemporal unity beyond the subject's capacity constitutes the demand – the beginning – of virtue itself. For one sees that the self is changed by acquiring knowledge, but since that knowledge is eternal, and the virtuous self begins its education in being oriented by knowledge, the student can remain faithful to the task of knowledge and still be under way toward learning.

Of greatest interest to a reading of Socrates against Hegel, here, is the fact that the subject is not grounded within a network of cultural and material causes. Nor is the subject merely turned toward the abstract universal, as if the ground of the unity of knowledge existed without human apprehension, or Socrates were merely ignorant of that place where the ground takes shape. The subject neither frames appearances nor is framed by an encompassing and explanatory ground such as we find in Hegel's sense of λόγος. Instead, by orienting oneself toward the task of providing a ground (as leading and ruling) for the unity of virtue, one sees the authority of beginning in terms of the orientation and not in its ability to produce effects, such as a true representation of the forces that cause or ground a particular. As the *Protagoras* teaches us, one does not ask knowledge to cause something else to happen; one responds to knowledge's virtue when we begin our activity, as an orientation toward what could sustain the truth before we act, unified as a good action only insofar as we embrace the task and do not betray the intelligence of beginning.

Meandering with Plato's *Protagoras*, we have not come to a new place for beginning – much less do we have new reasons to read Plato's works. Rather, we see a gesture of beginning and of staying true to that gesture. The authority of this task begins in the never present unity of sharing a future, and not in the unified past of having all been present to the same culture, the same words, or the same context. I do not travel through determination to get there; we live only in the words we have not yet said; we are compelled to reach out toward words because of that future beyond our desires, otherwise than our embodiment, and only named in its absence; we do not posit a realm beyond ourselves where happiness awaits; we walk with our friends and explore the arguments, driven not to betray the reasons that we began.

NOTES

1. See Bernard Stiegler, *La Technique et le Temps, 1: La Faute d'Epiméthée* and *La Technique et le Temps, 2: Désorientation*.
2. See Catherine Malabou, *L'Avenir de Hegel*.
3. Hegel's reading of these three foundational thinkers is found in the first two volumes of his *Vorlesungen über die Geschichte der Philosophie* (G. W. F. Hegel, *Werke*, vols 18 and 19 [*Werke*]). The treatment of Aristotle's reliance on ἐντελέχεια draws from Aristotle's *Metaphysics* Λ, as in 1071a–1072a.
4. There is a variety of attempts to escape the frame of determinate judgements in the continental tradition, and a smaller number in Anglo-American circles. Hans Georg Gadamer, *Gesammelte Werke*, vol. 7 (*Die Idee des Guten zwischen Plato und Aristoteles* [*Die Idee des Guten*]) defends the idea that questioning precedes the moment of Hegelian determination. Drew Hyland's reading of Plato's *Charmides*, *The Virtue of Philosophy*, does a nice job of interpreting Plato himself along these lines. John Sallis' *Being and Logos* concentrates on the possibility of distinguishing sophists from philosophers. Mitchell Miller's *Plato's Parmenides: The Conversion of the Soul* represents something of this current in the Anglo-American tradition. One finds a persistent eulogizing of the value of being open-minded in both traditions.

Richard Robinson's *Plato's Earlier Dialectic* influentially emphasizes the idea that the ἔλεγχος does not serve to produce new correct opinions, but "to wake men out of their dogmatic slumbers into genuine intellectual curiosity" (p. 17). However, he continues to argue that the basis of knowledge is knowing what something is, and that knowing an essence as a predicate counts as the basis for the proper use of a word within a given context. He sees the ἔλεγχος as a method, or as a rhetorical tool, for achieving determinate knowledge, even if it does not begin there. One may also mention Charles L. Griswold, Jr, "Relying on Your Own Voice: An Unsettled Rivalry of Moral Ideals in Plato's *Protagoras*." Griswold claims that one gains one's own voice in assuming responsibility for the self as soul, and thus in becoming the "true speaker" or "true author" of one's views. The emphasis is not on predication, nor on the Hegelian sense of determination, but rather is on the practice of assuming moral responsibility for one's voice. Throughout, my question is simply whether one sidesteps Hegel by avoiding the moment of determination, or whether instead one remains within Hegel's interpretation to the extent that one keeps the subject in the place of framing (and thus staging, or encompassing) what is present. If it is true that one cannot so easily escape Hegel, it may be true that our sense of "being open" to the world, or to new interpretations, already closes us off from the moral claim that truth holds on us.

5. At least, this is the development of the early Derrida's trajectory that I defend at length in Daniel Price, *Touching Difficulty.*

6. Ibid. part I.

7. It is impossible to provide an objective barometer of the mood in philosophy, but the allure of Speculative Realism and/or Object-Oriented Philosophy lies in its refusal to embrace the primacy of knowing as subjective activity. See Graham Harman, *Towards Speculative Realism*, and Quentin Meillassoux, *After Finitude.*

8. That this is Heidegger's question, in, for example, "The Question Concerning Technology," and the tortured and untranslatable plays on the earliest beginning as what is trusted in the search for truth. We will not be following Heidegger, but do note that much of the contemporary rethinking of technology is an echo of this question. See, for in-depth overviews, Thomas Brockelman, *Žižek and Heidegger: The Question Concerning Techno-Capitalism*, and Timothy Campbell, *Improper Life: Technology and Biopolitics from Heidegger to Agamben.*

9. *Werke*, vol. 18, p. 474. The translation is my own; square brackets are my insertions of the German word or the grammatical referent; rounded parentheses are Hegel's own. The Aristotle passage comes from *Magna Moralia* I.1 1182a15–23.

10. *Werke*, vol. 18, pp. 474–5; my translation.

11. I think of this as the traditional reading, although it is to some extent post-Kantian. Paul Natorp, *Platos Ideenlehre*, is very explicit about this reading, and is so specifically in relation to the *Protagoras* as Plato's first great

dialogue (because it establishes the opposition between idea and experience, and thus allows for the function of the Kantian determinate negation to be performed, even though the determination of the meaning of the sensible world through the categories of the ideas is not an explicit claim in the dialogues (pp. 10–18, 214)). One might also see Gregory Vlastos, "The Unity of the Virtues," for an elaborate defense of the unity of virtue being located in the knowing subject who controls the process of predication itself.

12. Joseph Margolis ties his larger project directly to Protagoras in "Metaphysique radicale." On the side of rhetoric, one has Edward Schiappa, *Protagoras and Logos*, and Antonio Capizzi sees Protagoras as the great precursor to humanism in an interesting commentary in *Protagora*.

13. Gerold Prauss, *Platon und der Logische Eleatismus*, turns his reading of Plato around the problem of the possibility of false statements.

14. Charles Kahn, "A New Interpretation of Plato's Socratic Dialogues," labels it one of the proleptic dialogues; it is supposed to prepare the students for future teachings.

15. Plato, *Protagoras [Pro.]*, ed. Burnet, vol. 3, 312d7–9.

16. Plato, *Gorgias*, vol. 3, 463b–466a.

17. *Pro.* 313d–314b.

18. Ibid. 356c–d, 357a–b.

19. Ibid. 316d–e.

20. Ibid. 312b.

21. Ibid. 329d, 349b. Actually, Protagoras claims to teach the τέχνη of political life at 319a, but allows that this constitutes virtue as such by allowing Socrates to make the substitution at 320a–b.

22. Ibid. 320d–328d.

23. Ibid. 322a–d.

24. Ibid. 317a.

25. Ibid. 319b–320c.

26. Ibid. 328e.

27. Ibid. 361a–b.

28. Terry Penner, "The Unity of Virtue," argues for the importance of a strong interpretation of the equivalence, although for different reasons than I employ. Vlastos, "The Unity of the Virtues," tries to save the unity of the knowing subject through a theory of predication.

29. *Pro.* 349d.

30. See *Die Idee des Guten*, chapter 2, where Gadamer suggests that a movement between τέχνη and virtue itself is implied in the *Protagoras*, and argues that virtue is not a τέχνη.

31. *Pro.* 320d–328d.

32. Ibid. 329e.

33. Ibid. 330b.

34. It may be important to note that one can go the other way, with Plato, and say that the creation of images is itself the process of moving toward (or within) the good, but to say so would be to accept the Hegelian frame

and insist that Plato was not guilty as charged. My hope is to avoid that frame altogether. Jean-François Mattéi's *L'Etranger et la Simulacre* is the most sustained reading of that productivity, but one sees it, as well, in John Sallis, "Mimesis and the End of Art," where Plato is presented as a precursor to Hegel's understanding of productivity.

35. *Pro.* 313d–314c.
36. Plato, *Apology*, vol. 1, 21d, 23b.
37. *Pro.* 352b5–c7.
38. Ibid. 325d.
39. Ibid. 319b–320c.
40. Ibid. 339b–d.
41. Ibid.
42. Ibid. 340c–d.
43. Ibid. 344b–c.
44. Ibid. 345a.
45. Ibid. 344e–345c.
46. Ibid. 313a–b.

BIBLIOGRAPHY

Aristotle, *Aristotelis: Metaphysica*, ed. W. Jaeger (Oxford: Clarendon Press, 1957).

Aristotle, *Magna Moralia*, in F. Susemihl *Aristotle*, vol. 18 (Cambridge, MA: Harvard University Press, 1969), pp. 446–684.

Brockelman, T. P., *Žižek and Heidegger: The Question Concerning Techno-Capitalism* (London: Continuum, 2008).

Campbell, T. C., *Improper Life: Technology and Biopolitics from Heidegger to Agamben* (Minneapolis: University of Minnesota Press, 2011).

Capizzi, A., *Protagora: Le Testimonianze ei Frammenti* (Florence: G. C. Sansoni, 1955).

Gadamer, H. G., *Gesammelte Werke*, vol. 7 (Tübingen: Mohr, 1985).

Griswold, C. L., "Relying on Your Own Voice: An Unsettled Rivalry of Moral Ideals in Plato's *Protagoras*," *Review of Metaphysics*, 53.4 (1999), pp. 283–307.

Harman, G., *Towards Speculative Realism* (Winchester: Zero Books, 2010).

Hegel, G. W. F., *Werke*, Vol. 18-19 (Frankfurt: Suhrkamp, 1999).

Heidegger, M., "The Question Concerning Technology," in M. Heidegger, *Basic Writings* (New York: Harper Perennial, 2008), pp. 307–42.

Hyland, D., *The Virtue of Philosophy* (Athens: Ohio University Press, 1981).

Kahn, C., "A New Interpretation of Plato's Socratic Dialogues," *Harvard Review of Philosophy*, 5.1 (1995), pp. 26–35.

Malabou, C., *L'Avenir de Hegel: Plasticité, Temporalité, Dialectique* (Paris: Vrin, 1997).

Margolis, J., "Metaphysique radicale," *Archives de Philosophie* (1991), pp. 379–406.

Mattéi, J.-F., *L'Etranger et la Simulacre: Essai sur la Fondation de l'Ontologie Platonicienne* (Paris: Presses Universitaires de France, 1983).

Meillassoux, Q., *After Finitude* (London: Continuum, 2008).

Miller, M., *Plato's Parmenides: The Conversion of the Soul* (Princeton: Princeton University Press, 1986).

Natorp, P., *Platos Ideenlehre* (Leipzig: Meiner Verlag, 1903).

Penner, T., "The Unity of Virtue," *Philosophical Review*, 82.1 (1973), pp. 35–68.

Plato, *Platonis Opera*, ed. J Burnet, 5 vols (Oxford: Clarendon Press, 1915–16).

Prauss, G., *Platon und der Logische Eleatismus* (Berlin: Walter de Gruyter, 1966).

Price, D., *Touching Difficulty* (Aurora, CO: Davies, 2011).

Robinson, R., *Plato's Earlier Dialectic*, 2nd edn (Oxford: Clarendon Press, 1953).

Sallis, J., "Mimesis and the End of Art," in J. Sallis, *Double Truth* (Albany, NY: State University of New York Press, 1995), pp. 171–90.

Sallis, J., *Being and Logos*, 3rd edn (Bloomington: Indiana University Press, 1996).

Schiappa, E., *Protagoras and Logos: A Study in Greek Philosophy and Rhetoric*, 2nd edn (Columbia: University of South Carolina Press, 2003).

Stiegler, B., *La Technique et le Temps, 1: La Faute d'Epiméthée* (Paris: Galilée, 1994).

Stiegler, B., *La Technique et le Temps, 2: Désorientation* (Paris: Galilée, 1996).

Vlastos, G. "The Unity of the Virtues," in G. Vlastos, *Platonic Studies* (Princeton: Princeton University Press, [1973] 1981), pp. 221–65.

CHAPTER 5

Univocity, Duality, and Ideal Genesis: Deleuze and Plato

John Bova and Paul M. Livingston

In *Difference and Repetition*, Gilles Deleuze outlines a theory of ideas as problems, existent on the level of a virtuality distinct from, but irreducibly related to, that of their incarnation in a variety of specifically constituted theoretical domains:

> Following Lautman and Vuillemin's work on mathematics, 'structuralism' seems to us the only means by which a genetic method can achieve its ambitions. It is sufficient to understand that the genesis takes place not between one actual term, however small, and another actual term in time, but between the virtual and its actualisation – in other words, it goes from the structure to its incarnation, from the conditions of a problem to the cases of solution, from the differential elements and their ideal connections to actual terms and diverse real relations which constitute at each moment the actuality of time. This is a genesis without dynamism, evolving necessarily in the element of a supra-historicity, a *static genesis* which may be understood as the correlate of the notion of *passive synthesis*, and which in turn illuminates that notion.[1]

Deleuze's identification of ideas with problems is adopted, in part, from the novel synthesis proposed by the mathematical philosopher Albert Lautman in a series of essays of the 1930s and 1940s, of an unorthodox but textually grounded Platonism and the mathematics of his time.[2] Deleuze takes Lautman's work to provide at least partial means for a reconciliation of structure and genesis, so that an account of the virtual structure of an idea-problem can at the same time, and without irreducible tension, function as an account of its real genesis in a specific, concrete domain. This yields Deleuze's understanding of ideal genesis, which involves at once an account of the origin of "actual terms and diverse real relations" and an account of the origin of those "differential elements and ideal connections" that precede and determine them. The principle underlying both origins is that of a paradoxical structural becoming which realizes the concrete relations characteristic of a particular field on the basis of a prior "dialectic" of formal/structural relationships, in particular those of limit, unlimitedness, multiplicity, and unity.

In this essay, we consider the formal and ontological implications of one specific and intensely contested dialectical context from which Deleuze's thinking about structural ideal genesis visibly arises. This is the formal/ontological dualism between the principles, ἀρχαί, of the One (ἕν) and the Indefinite/Unlimited Dyad (ἀόριστος δυάς), which is arguably the culminating achievement of the later Plato's development of a mathematical dialectic.[3] Following commentators including Lautman, Oskar Becker, and Kenneth M. Sayre, we argue that the duality of the One and the Indefinite Dyad provides, in the later Plato, a unitary theoretical formalism accounting, by means of an iterated mixing without synthesis, for the structural origin and genesis of both supersensible Ideas and the sensible particulars which participate in them. As these commentators also argue, this duality furthermore provides a maximally general answer to the problem of temporal becoming that runs through Plato's *corpus*: that of the relationship of the flux of sensory experiences to the fixity and order of what is thinkable in itself. Additionally, it provides a basis for understanding some of the famously puzzling claims about forms, numbers, and the principled genesis of both attributed to Plato by Aristotle in the *Metaphysics,* and plausibly underlies the late Plato's deep considerations of the structural paradoxes of temporal change and becoming in the *Parmenides,* the *Sophist,* and the *Philebus.*

After extracting this structure of duality and developing some of its formal, ontological, and metalogical features, we consider some of its specific implications for a thinking of time and ideality that follows Deleuze in a formally unitary genetic understanding of structural difference. These implications of Plato's duality include not only those of the constitution of specific theoretical domains and problematics, but also implicate the reflexive problematic of the ideal determinants of the form of a unitary theory as such. We argue that the consequences of the underlying duality on the level of content are ultimately such as to raise, on the level of form, the broader reflexive problem of the basis for its own formal or meta-theoretical employment. We conclude by arguing for the decisive and substantive presence of a proper "Platonism" of the Idea in Deleuze, and weighing the potential for a substantive recuperation of Plato's duality in the context of a dialectical affirmation of what Deleuze recognizes as the "only" ontological proposition that has ever been uttered. This is the proposition of the univocity of Being, whereby "being is said in the same sense, everywhere and always," but is said (both problematically and decisively) of difference itself.

BECOMING AND THE DYAD: DELEUZE'S PLATO

In the opening pages of *The Logic of Sense*, Deleuze considers the structure of a pure and paradoxical "becoming whose characteristic is to elude the present."[4] This becoming is exemplified, according to Deleuze, by the "pure events" of Alice's transformations in *Alice's Adventures in Wonderland* and *Through the Looking-Glass*. An event involves an "essence of becoming" through which it moves unlimitedly in both of two opposed directions at once, Alice becoming (for example) in the same moment both larger than she was and smaller than she becomes. According to Deleuze, this paradoxical and bidirectional structure provides the formal basis for a theory of the conditioning of phenomena that, including their change and becoming at a fundamental level, does not relegate this conditioning to the static resemblance between a model and its copy. As yielding such a theory of conditioning, the structure of paradoxical and unlimited becoming also helps to define an original structure of genesis, at the formal basis of the virtual which is the "characteristic state of Ideas."[5] Indeed, as Deleuze goes on to suggest, the structure of unlimited becoming is opposed, already in Plato, to the dimension of fixity, measure, and rest. The two produce a profound and deep dualism at the root of Plato's understanding of temporal genesis, one that is to be sharply distinguished from the more familiar "dualism" of the sensible and the supersensible:

> Plato invites us to distinguish two dimensions: (1) that of limited and measured things, of fixed qualities, permanent or temporary which always presuppose pauses and rests, the fixing of presents, and the assignation of subjects [. . .] and (2) a pure becoming without measure, a veritable becoming-mad, which never rests. It moves in both directions at once. It always eludes the present, causing future and past, more and less, too much and not enough to coincide in the simultaneity of a rebellious matter.[6]

Deleuze briefly quotes two passages in which this problematic becoming is evidenced in Plato's dialogues, in connection with the problem of the relationship of temporal flux, change, and becoming, limitless in itself, to whatever fixes quantities and gives order. The first of these is Socrates' example in the *Philebus* of the hotter and the colder, which cannot (as Socrates argues) "take on a definite quality" since, as they are always "going a point further," cannot stop and become fixed without becoming something other than themselves.[7] This requires, according to Socrates, that both the hotter and its opposite be characterized under the heading of the "unlimited" (ἄπειρον), as against that which is characterized, by contrast, by "limit" (πέρας). Hence a distinction is drawn, among everything that is, between these two types, along with their mixture and its cause, the principle of which is established earlier in the dialogue as one suggested or given by the gods. The other example comes in the

Parmenides, in the course of the development of the implications of the second hypothesis about the One, and in particular the consequences of its partaking in time. According to this hypothesis, Parmenides suggests, the One will be characterized by "coming-to-be both older and younger, and neither older nor younger, than the others and they than it."[8] By virtue of this becoming, according to Parmenides, both younger and older go "toward their opposites [. . .] the younger coming to be older than the older, and the older younger than the younger," though neither, again, can actually attain a fixed relationship to the other, since then they would cease becoming and no longer come to be anything at all.

In thus evoking the duality between a dyadic principle of unlimited becoming, on the one hand, and the fixity of limit, on the other, Plato thus points, according to Deleuze, to a "more profound and secret dualism hidden in sensible and material bodies themselves," one that does not characterize the distinction between the "intelligible and the sensible," between "Idea and matter" or between "Ideas and bodies."[9] Rather, it is a dualism between "that which receives the action of the Idea and that which eludes this action," according to which, while "limited things lie beneath the Ideas," there is nevertheless still "even beneath things . . . [a] mad element which subsists and occurs on the other side of the order that Ideas impose and things receive."[10] This Platonic dualism between (on the one hand) what Plato characterizes as the One or Unity and (on the other) an irreducibly dyadic principle of the unlimited, further characterized as that of the "Great and the Small" thus offers, on Deleuze's reading, a general structural framework for accounting not only for the relationship of "participation" between sensible things and Ideas, but even for the very constitution of both on the basis of the deeper structural and dialectical relationships it formulates.

It is the same Platonic dualism which, as modern scholarship has demonstrated, plausibly underlies some of the puzzling views about forms and numbers attributed elliptically to Plato by Aristotle in the course of his doxography of earlier principles in the *Metaphysics*:

> Since the Forms are the causes of all other things, [Plato] thought
> their elements were the elements of all things. As matter, the great and
> the small were principles; as substance, the One; for from the great
> and the small, by participation in the One, come the Forms, *i.e.* the
> numbers.
>
> But he agreed with the Pythagoreans in saying that the One is
> substance and not a predicate of something else; and in saying that
> the numbers are the causes of the substance of other things, he also
> agreed with them; but positing a dyad and constructing the infinite out
> of great and small, instead of treating the infinite as one, is peculiar
> to him; and so is his view that the numbers exist apart from sensible
> things, while they say that the things themselves are numbers, and
> do not place the objects of mathematics between Forms and sensible

things. His divergence from the Pythagoreans in making the One and the numbers separate from things, and his introduction of the Forms, were due to his inquiries in the region of definatory formulae (for the earlier thinkers had no tincture of dialectic), and his making the other entity besides the One a dyad was due to the belief that the numbers, except those which were prime, could be neatly produced out of the dyad as out of a plastic material.[11]

In this passage and others, Aristotle attributes several deeply puzzling claims to Plato. These include the claims that Forms have elements which are also the elements "of all things," that numbers can be "produced out" of the dyad of the Great and Small, which acts as a kind of "material" in combination with the One, and that forms actually are themselves to be identified with numbers as thus produced. Aristotle appears also to claim that Plato held that sensible objects are constituted of forms and the Great and the Small, and that forms are themselves composed of the Great and the Small together with Unity.[12] Aristotle says directly in several places that Plato identified forms with numbers.[13] He also makes the suggestions that Plato identifies Unity with the Good (and perhaps that he identifies the Great and the Small, by contrast, with evil), and that Plato treats the "Great and Small" as matter with respect to which the One is form.[14]

Beyond Aristotle's testimony, there is evidence that the development of the problem of number may be closely connected with the content of what have been called Plato's "unwritten" teachings.[15] The sixth-century Neoplatonist Simplicius notoriously reports descriptions of a lecture given by Plato on the Good and attended by Aristotle and others: Aristotle is said to have reported Plato's teaching that the principles of all things, including the Ideas, are the "Indefinite Dyad, which is called Great and Small" and Unity.[16] There is a suggestion in Simplicius' quotations of Porphyry and Alexander that Plato held that Unity and the Indefinite Dyad are also the elements of numbers and that each of the numbers participates in these two principles.[17] The lecture on the Good is said by Aristotle's student Aristoxenus to have confounded Plato's listeners, who expected a lecture on ethics but were instead treated to a discussion of numbers and geometry, leading up to the claim that the Good is to be identified with Unity or "the One."[16] In Platonic scholarship, the attempt to explicate the exact nature and systematic role of the teachings of Plato that can be summarized under the heading of the duality of the ἀρχαί of the One/Good and the indefinite dyad, or the greater-and-less have led to a wide variety of exegetical and substantive accounts.[19] Many of these accounts have attempted, further, to explain why these apparently crucial teachings do not appear in a direct form in any of Plato's dialogues, characterizing them, for instance, as Plato's "oral" or "inner-Academic" teachings, or emphasizing what is seen as their intrinsic connection to a dialogical form of life, which for various reasons cannot be directly represented or replicated in writing. Here, without taking a position on this question of the "unwrittenness" of the theory of duality, we will simply attempt to reconstruct its probable logical form, following in particular modern commentators who discover evidence for it in the dialogues themselves.

In particular, it will be useful to consider the interpretations of the doctrine of duality which arise in the twentieth century from two rather disparate lines of scholarship. One of these lines, arising from Julius Stenzel and passing through Oskar Becker, culminates in Lautman's reconstruction of the ideal genesis of numbers and ideas on the basis of a "superior" dialectic of virtual relations. It is this line which, as we have already seen, most directly influences Deleuze in his conception of ideal genesis on the level of the virtual. But another strand, largely or wholly distinct from the first but just as useful for understanding the probable logical form of Plato's doctrine, is inaugurated in recent "analytic" scholarship by Kenneth M. Sayre's interpretation of the so-called "unwritten teachings" as, in fact, literally *written* in several of the late dialogues, and explicable on the direct basis of the mathematical theories and leading problems already known to Plato.

THE PRINCIPLES IN THE TWENTIETH CENTURY: STENZEL, BECKER, LAUTMAN, AND SAYRE

In his 1927 work *Mathematical Existence*, Oskar Becker, following Julius Stenzel, theorizes the role of the ἄπειρον, as it figures specifically in the "unlimited Dyad" (ἀόριστος δυάς), as that of a kind of generative potency, at the root of both the existence of "number" and its "generation" in accordance with a temporal or quasi-temporal anteriority to produce an ordering of before and after. Becker suggests that this ordering is subsequently crucial for Aristotle's conception of the infinite, and in particular for its close relationship to his account of time in the *Physics*, according to which time is a counting or numbering of motion, with respect to just this distinction of "before and after." Here, Becker suggests, the thought of time as the continuity of the ἄπειρον, prior to and before the possibility of measurement, has a deeper provenance in the linked conception of time and number that already appears in the somewhat obscure Platonic conception of the dyad.[20] In a later article, "The Diairetic Generation of Platonic Ideal Numbers," Becker, developing suggestions made initially by Stenzel, argues that the generation of numbers can be considered, in close connection with the method of διαίρεσις or division recommended by Plato in a number of late dialogues, identical to that of the diairetic definition of a concept by division. Stenzel had suggested, in particular, that the positive whole numbers may be seen as generated by means of a process of successive binary "division," whereby each number n, beginning with 1, generates $2n$ and $2n + 1$. According to Becker, although this solution tends in the right direction, it does not explain how "ideal" (as opposed to familiar mathematical) numbers can actually be ideas, and it also does not explain how ideas can thereby be thought as dynamically generated rather than simply recovered subsequently by analysis. As an alternative, he suggests that the ideal numbers are generated by a repeated process whereby one divides into two, but in the division the original one is "sublated" or overcome in the division. In this way, the powers of 2 (2, 4, 8, 16, etc.) can be thought of as generated by the symmetrical iteration of binary division itself, while all other numbers are seen as arising from an asymmetrical development of a diairetic tree structure (e.g. 3 is generated by the division of an initial unit, a, into two, (b and c) and the subsequent division of c into d and e, while b remains unaffected; the remaining (unsublated) elements are then three (b, d, and e).) In this way, the actual seriality of number can be seen as generated in a way that is "formally identical" to the structure of the διαίρεσις of concepts that Plato suggests in the *Sophist* and the *Statesman*. Becker also notes the possibility of connecting this to the structure of the division of a continuous quantity by iterated fractional decomposition to produce an exact (rational) point. In this way, the process of διαίρεσις which results in the identification of the constituents of an idea as "monads" or "ones" may be thought to produce examples of the sort that Plato appeals to in the *Philebus*, e.g. the identification of the fixed letters or discrete musical notes from the fluid continuum of possible sounds.

Albert Lautman's 1939 work, "New Research on the Dialectical Structure of Mathematics," draws on the thesis of his 1938 dissertation, according to which concrete mathematical theories develop a series of "ideal relations" of a "dialectic abstract and superior to mathematics."[21] In particular, Lautman understands abstract "dialectical" ideas as the development of the possibility of relations between what he calls (by contrast) pairs of notions: these are pairs such as those of "whole and part, situational properties and intrinsic properties, basic domains and the entities defined on these domains, formal systems and their realization, etc."[22] The dialectical ideas that pose these relations do not presuppose the existence of specific mathematical domains or objects. Rather, they operate, in the course of mathematical research, essentially as "problems" or "posed questions" that provide the occasion for inquiry into specific mathematical existents. In reference to differing specific mathematical theories such as, for instance, the theory of sets or (in a different way) real analysis, the dialectical relationship of whole and part may be seen as posing a general problem which is to be resolved differently in each domain, on the basis of concrete mathematical research, and thereby partially determines the kind and structure of entities existing in that particular domain. Thus general problems such as the problem of the relationship of formal theories of proof to actual mathematical results, the relationship of whole to part, and (especially) the relationship of continuity and discontinuity pose conditions under which they are resolved concretely, in different ways, in specific mathematical theories. At the same time, the development of the specific theories in terms of the particular kinds of structures and entities said to exist therein points back to the general problem and articulates its own more general structure.

The problem, here, thus has a priority over its particular solutions, and cannot be reduced to them. According to Lautman, this priority is not that of an ideality existent in itself prior to its incarnation in a specific domain, but rather that of the kind of problematic "advent of notions relative to the concrete within an analysis of the Idea."[23] In particular, it is only in developing the actual structure and configuration of particular concrete domains that the actual meaning of the governing Ideas is worked out. Here the concrete development of particular domains does not, moreover, exhaust the general problem but rather, typically, suggests new questions and problems in other concrete domains which are also to be related to the same general dialectical structure. Dialectical Ideas, in this sense, "govern" the "intrinsic reality" of mathematical objects and it can even be said, using the Platonic terminology, that the reality of the mathematical objects, as concretely demonstrated in mathematical research, thus resides in their "participation" in the dialectical ideas.[24] But as Lautman emphasizes, this sense of "participation" is quite at odds with the way Plato's conception of participation is typically understood. In particular, whereas participation is often understood as that of an ideal model to objects which in some respect copy them, here the Ideas are understood "in the true Platonic sense of the term" as the "structural schemas according to which the effective theories are organized."[25] What is at issue here is not a "cosmological sense" of the relationship between ideas and their concrete realization such as is developed, for instance, in the *Timeaus*. According to such a sense, which is fundamentally understood by reference to the concept of creation as forming or shaping, the realization of the ideas in concrete reality depends on their capacity to impose law and structure on an otherwise undifferentiated matter, itself knowable only (as Plato in fact suggests) by a kind of "bastard reasoning" or "natural revelation."[26] By contrast with this "cosmological sense" of the relationship between ideas and particulars, it is essential in the case of mathematical objectivity to understand the relationship between the dialectical ideas and the particular mathematical objects as a "cut [which] cannot in fact be envisaged." This is, Lautman says, a kind of "mode of emanation" from dialectics to mathematics that does not in any way presuppose the "contingent imposition of a Matter heterogeneous to the Ideas."[27]

For Lautman, many of the problems that define the "superior" dialectic that ultimately determines specific mathematical domains and their essential problems are evident in the historical concerns of philosophers, for instance with the relationships between the "same and the other, the whole and the part, the continuous and the discontinuous, essence and existence."[28] But the mathematician's activity has an equally significant role, according to Lautman, in giving rise to new problems that have not yet been abstractly formulated. In this twofold enterprise, the task is thus not to demonstrate the applicability of classical logical or metaphysical problems within mathematical theories, but rather to grasp the structure of such theories "globally in order to identify the logical problem that happens to be both defined and resolved" by its existence.[29] This is a peculiar experience of thought, according to Lautman, equally characteristic of the capacity of the intelligence to create as of its capacity to understand. In it:

Beyond the temporal conditions of mathematical activity, but within the very bosom of this activity, appear the contours of an ideal reality that is governing with respect to a mathematical matter which it animates, and which however, without that matter, could not reveal all the richness of its formative power.[30]

Finally, Lautman suggests that this particular experience of exigency, by means of which general philosophical problems communicate with the particular constraints of specific mathematical domains to illuminate the "contours" of such a superior reality, can be witnessed in the late Plato's understanding of the genesis of Ideas and numbers:

All modern Plato commentators [. . .] insist on the fact that the Ideas are not immobile and irreducible essences of an intelligible world, but that they are related to each other according to the schemas of a superior dialectic that presides over their arrival. The work of Robin, Stenzel and Becker has in this regard brought considerable clarity to the governing role of Ideas-numbers which concerns as much the becoming of numbers as that of Ideas. The One and the Dyad generate Ideas-numbers by a successively repeated process of division of the Unit into two new units. The Ideas-numbers are thus presented as geometric schemas of the combinations of units, amenable to constituting arithmetic numbers as well as Ideas in the ordinary sense.[31]

Following Stenzel and Becker, Lautman suggests that the diairetic "schemas of division" of Ideas in the *Sophist* can themselves be traced, in their logical structure, to the schemas of the "combination of units" that are also responsible for the generation of the ideas-numbers. Both are then genetically dependent upon a kind of "metamathematics" which unfolds a time of generation that, though it is not "in the time of the created world," is nevertheless, just as much, ordered according to anteriority and posteriority.[32] This ordering according to anteriority and posteriority is equally determinative, and even in the same sense, with respect to essences quite generally as with respect to numbers themselves. Indeed, following a suggestion by Stenzel, Lautman suggests that this is the significance of Aristotle's claim in the *Nicomachean Ethics* that the Platonists did not admit the ideas of numbers.[33] Since the ideal-numbers are already the principle of the determination of essences as anterior and posterior (i.e. as before and after), there is not (nor can there be) a *further* principle of the division of essences that is prior to or superior to this numerical division itself. In this impossibility of equipping the metamathematics of the ideal-numerical principles of anteriority and posteriority with *another* determination (a "metametamathematics," so to speak), we witness once again, according to Lautman, the necessity of pursuing the dialectic in which the mathematical problems and the ideal relations communicate with and articulate one another.[34] In particular, in such a dialectic, and only in it, are to be found the problematic conditions and the possibility of mutual illumination in which the more original structures constitutive of anteriority and posteriority as such – and hence of time and genesis, in an original sense – can be brought to light.

In a remarkable analysis, Kenneth M. Sayre has argued that the content of the so-called "unwritten teachings" that link the problems of number with those of the structure of forms and the Good can be largely recovered from Plato's middle and late dialogues themselves. According to Sayre, it is thus not necessary to speculate about the esoteric content of the Platonic teachings alluded to by Aristotle, since they are actually present in dialogues such as the *Philebus*, *Parmenides*, and *Sophist* (among others). Sayre reconstructs Aristotle's statements as clearly attributing five distinct claims about forms, sensible objects, numbers, and the Great and the Small. Among these are the claims that sensible objects are constituted of both forms and the Great and the Small, and that forms are themselves composed of the Great and the Small and Unity.[35] As Sayre notes, while the claim that the forms are the principles or causes of sensible things is familiar from many of Plato's dialogues and is present as early as the *Phaedo*, the suggestion of a composition of the forms themselves by more basic principles would be, if it can be attributed to him, a significantly novel element of the late Plato's thinking about them. Sayre sees this late conception as developed both thematically and methodologically in Plato's descriptions of the method of dialectic in the *Sophist*, the *Statesman*, and especially the *Philebus*, where at 16c–e, Socrates describes a "god-given" method for pursuing problems of the one and the many generally, including (it appears) with respect to the distinctive unity exhibited by forms. On Sayre's reading, the passage is meant to formulate a methodological response to the question of how the kind of unity (μονάς) that a form is can characterize indefinitely many changing particulars, without thereby becoming dispersed among them and losing its unity. The problem is a specification of the more general question of how the properties and characteristics of individuals are thinkable at all, given that they are subject to ceaseless change in time.

Thus specified, the problem does not simply involve the unity of forms as such, over against sensible beings thought as completely undifferentiated or irreducibly multiple. Rather, since it is also the question of how sensible things are themselves thinkable as enduring unities despite the unlimitedness of their possible change, its solution involves a unified accounting for the unity of both. Since sensory objects would, if (somehow) deprived of the relationship to Forms that allow them to be thought as distinct individuals having definite characteristics, also have no definite character and in this sense be indistinguishable from the ἄπειρον, the problem is that of characterizing how determinate forms are themselves defined and gain application to the changing particulars.[36] The elements of a solution to this are to be found, Sayre suggests, in the *Philebus*' development of cases in which a number of specific characteristics are distinguished out of a continuum of possible variation, such as the identification of particular letters from the continuum of vocables, or the identification of discrete musical notes from the continuum of sound.³⁷ In this way, a particular discrete number of intermediate forms are introduced between the general and continuous form (for instance sound itself) and the specific instances, for which the intermediate forms then serve as measures.³⁸

As Sayre suggests, the methodology may be considered a further development of the method of the collection or division (or σύνθεσις and διαίρεσις) proposed in the *Statesman* and the *Sophist*. As is suggested there, the key methodological idea is that the definition of a thing begins by collecting a number of instances of the kind to be defined with a view to discerning the general form they have in common. The form, once found, is further articulated or qualified by a repeated διαίρεσις or division of its several components, until a unique set of specific characteristics is identified that distinguishes the particular kind of thing in question from others similar to it. As Sayre notes, however, the major and glaring difference between the description of the "god-given" method in the *Philebus* and the descriptions of the dialectician's art in the *Sophist* and the *Statesman* is that the latter two involve no mention either of the ἄπειρον, or of the need to distinguish among indefinitely many single things to articulate what is in itself a continuum having the character of the "unlimited" in the sense of indefiniteness. Sayre sees the account given in the *Philebus* as responding to a problem about unity and the ἄπειρον – both in the sense of the "indefinitely many" and that of the indefinitely continuous – that is already posed in the *Parmenides*.³⁹ The idea of a unified collection of individual members, or a whole composed of parts, implies both that there is a sense of unity characteristic of the collection as a whole and that there is a sense of unity characteristic of each member as a unique individual. Unity in both senses must be imposed on what is in itself non-unified in order to produce the determinate structure of whole and part.⁴⁰ The possibility of identifying an individual as part of such a collection must thus result from the combination of a principle of Unity, in both senses, with a contrasting principle of the indefinitely many or multitudinous. This is what Plato calls in the *Parmenides* the ἄπειρον πλῆθος and which, Sayre suggests, can also be identified with the (later) mentions of the "indefinite dyad" or, indeed, "the Great and the Small" of which Aristotle speaks.

On this basis, Sayre argues that the final *Philebus* account of forms and participation involves a twofold application of the imposition of Unity on the Great and Small: first, in order to produce the determinate forms themselves, and second, in the imposition of the forms thus produced, now functioning as "measures," on the Great and Small again to produce the characteristics of particular sensible objects.⁴¹ If this is right, both the Forms and sensible things are composed from the two principles, although according to different modes of combination. This suggestion of a unitary genesis ultimately underlying both the forms and their sensory participants allows Sayre to contest both of two conflicting interpretations of the role of the πέρας and the ἄπειρον in the *Philebus*. On the first of these, the relationship between limit and the unlimited is analogous to or anticipatory of Aristotle's account of form and matter; here, the unlimited is accordingly said to be a kind of undetermined potentiality of objects to acquire certain properties.[42] On the second existing view, the "unlimited" is not attributed directly to objects at all, but is rather a set of concepts which admit of variation as less or more.[43] Sayre argues that both views have potentially fatal internal problems. The first, in particular, has difficulty explaining why the imposition of Unity should produce particular objects that are in some sense valued as ordered as opposed to bad or disordered elements corresponding to other points on the same continuum. But the second has difficulty explaining how the mixing of Unity and the Indefinite could produce determinate individuals and not simply determinate types. Both existing alternatives, Sayre argues, are furthermore difficult to square with the text. A better alternative is to construe the combination of Unity with the ἄπειρον as having the twofold application, both to the generation of forms and, once again, to the specification of particular objects, that Aristotle also suggests in his own gloss on Plato's theory of forms and numbers. In each case, the combination allows for determinate measure to be imposed upon what would otherwise be the ἄπειρον character of what would become or change indefinitely and without limit.

THE STRUCTURE OF PLATO'S DUALITY

As we have seen, the dualism of the One and the Unlimited Dyad, if indeed it can be attributed to Plato and has roughly the structure that Stenzel, Becker, Lautman, and Sayre suggest, plausibly underlies a uniform Platonic account of ideal structural genesis. According to this account, both ideas and their participants, and even the underlying structure of their becoming in the "now," have their genesis in the interaction of the two "principles" (ἀρχαί) of the dualism. This raises the pressing question of the relationship of this "two" to the "one" of being which Deleuze affirms as the univocity of being, and relates to his ontology of difference. To address this question on the level of a formal and meta-formal analysis, we will first briefly underline several structural features that constrain the interpretation of Platonic dualism as we have reconstructed it here, following the contemporary commentators.

Plato's dualism, which is literally a dualism of the One and the Two, is a dualism of a radical and unfamiliar kind, as can be shown by contrasting its structure with that of some more familiar ontological proposals. First, it is not a dualism of substances or types of entities. Neither is it the "two-worlds" dualism of vulgar Platonism (and vulgar anti-Platonism), which stop with the first distinction between a form and its sensible participant without pushing on, as Plato's dualism does, to the question of the ground of the identity and difference of the two terms that are thereby related. Again, given its structure, Plato's duality cannot be understood as the duality of two mutually complementary parts within a larger given whole, or of an opposition of forces which could, even in principle, be reconciled or reinscribed into a larger unity. (It may be that it can, however, be understood as the affirmation of the impossibility a priori of such a final synthesis, a point to which we will return.)

Both familiar dualisms, and also familiar cases of duality, consist in pointing out two things: two types of things in the case of dualism, two complementary parts of something in the case of intratheoretical dualities. Plato complicates this in perhaps the most decisive way possible in a single move. The "two" that he asks about are the two consisting (first) of the one and (second) of the two. This "second," moreover, is itself irreducibly dual: paradoxically split, in a way that affirms unlimited becoming in both of two opposed directions, and can thus in itself find no stopping point, on pain of not being what it is. This is sufficient to ensure that, even if the two "principles" of the one and the dyad are thought together, the thought will itself be irreducibly dual and dualizing. Rather than inscribe them within a single static field, or subsume them to the principle or possibility of a higher reconciliation, their work, if they really are ἀρχαί, will include a rebound upon the discourse and even the thought that, naming them, claims to get a synoptic view of them. Whether this application of the Two to its own thought ruins the possibility that any articulable dualism can be true or any true dualism articulable is a question to which we will return (in a twofold way) in the final section.

At the same time, and for the same reason, the inscription of the One as one element of the dyad in the Platonic dualism does not in any way indicate an incipient or approximate monism of the One. If the Platonic dualism indeed affirms the possibility of a uniform accounting for both being and becoming, it is not because it reduces the two to any given one. It is rather essential to its structure that it affirm an irreducible basis for both in the two principles it introduces, without any possible reduction of their difference, and it is in this way that it plausibly witnesses Plato's final overcoming of Eleaticism, while also subverting in advance any Neoplatonic reduction to the One. Indeed, because of (what we might call) the irreducibly "dyadic" character of the dyad, there is no possible deduction or derivation of it from the contrasting principle of the One. And although, as is witnessed in the complex dialectics of the *Parmenides*, the idea of an irreducible alterity may yield a profound sense of the difference, the duality that is at stake here is not simply the opposition of the One and the Other(s). In treating the dyad as a principle opposed to the One, Plato articulates a more structurally complex configuration of relationality in which any relativity of the other(s) to the One, if it is not to lead to a false correlation of the two, must be redoubled with an incommensurable counter-correlativity from the side of the Dyad.[44]

Thus by contrast with, for instance, the Aristotelian relativity of matter to form, or the Schellingian/Hegelian "identity of identity and difference," here, through the very dyadic character of the dyad, the dualism of the One and what is other to it is in no way overcome, suppressed, reduced, or sublated by the assumption of an existing One-All. Rather than being overcome in such a way, dualism is rather apportioned, continually rediscovered, and deployed more aggressively, not only on the "ontological" level of entities but also on the level of the very logic of the account which systematically inscribes dualism in the structure of what is, without tacitly reinscribing it within a single total and consistent system. Here, what Hegel identifies as the flaw of indeterminate negation is seen to be rather the form in which truth of duality is final: the relation by which an opposed A and B can be fixed and projected into a synthetic AB turns out to be merely an AB in the sense of A or an AB in the sense of B.[45]

Because of the formal level on which the dualism operates, that is not only intratheoretically, but also metatheoretically, it is such as to split not only the ontological field to which it is applied, but also the theoretical position from which it finds any possible application. In this respect it reflexively takes itself up within its own scope, inscribing an irreducible two not only on the level of the principles grounding being and becoming, but also (as a "metalogical" or "metaformal" duality between completeness and consistency) on the level of any possible application of principles to being and the norms that govern it.[46]

In particular, if "two" here is not just the quantity of the principles, as in Aristotle's doxography, but the very essence of a split ἀρχή, then any argument for limiting the possibilities of knowledge's access to principles that does not make essential use of the duality risks missing the intrinsic logic of the topic. Thus, one can emphasize completeness, underscoring that the two together generate all things. This produces a total system, which happens to rest on two principles. But this would simply be another theory of everything, as though instead of a one-all, we had here simply a two-all. This is the line of many who refer to ideal genesis, including, for instance, many of those who follow the "systematic" reconstructions of the Tübingen school. And it is also, of course, a tendency of Plato's thought.[47] But the difference from monism is then only momentary and superficial, and nothing is easier than for improvers of the system, beginning with Neoplatonism, to repair lapsed monism by representing multiplicity and its disasters, the very stuff of existence according to the dualist account, as merely privative. Or one can emphasize consistency, pointing to how the "two" of the dualism together provide, in any concrete case, a coherent account of the determinate being of a thing. But this is to ignore or deny the inconsistency inherent to its becoming, its tendency to overleap boundaries and subvert identities through the continuity of its potentially limitless change in both directions, and thus to communicate directly, in the most banal of its changes, with infinite multiplicities that exceed the resources of a given consistent theory. Beyond either of these strategies, what is necessary to grasp the reflexive bearing of the Platonic duality on the very structure of ἀρχή as such is, rather, to emphasize its tangled and iterative structure, whereby the one is doubled by its other only in order for any unity of the two to be split once more, and in unlimited fashion. A radically dualist ontology of the Platonic sort, then, can only be maintained with a shift in the ontological function of knowledge. The task of ontology no longer takes the form of a progressive completion of a One-All, or a filling in of the gaps of a total account of all the beings that is in itself capable of both completeness and consistency. Rather, the one and the all are simultaneously present to us, not as starting points for a deductive or genetic chain whose existence would tacitly neutralize their ontological potential, but as norms of theoretical construction. It is then only the reflective acknowledgement of a failure, at once mathematical and philo-sophical, to realize them simultaneously that leads us to posit the irreducibility of the dyad as what there must have been, such that the projected synthesis of consistency and completeness absolutely is not.

This makes possible a kind of dialectical analysis which has a wholly dif-ferent tendency from Aristotelian essentialism, insofar as it inscribes in place of any harmonious unity between thought and being in adequate knowledge rather an irreducible conflict of the norms of completeness and consistency. This is a conflict which indeed plays itself out immanently in knowledge, allowing it thereby to participate essentially in the duality of the principles itself. The metalogical or metaformal theory that results, as much as it remains a theory of the ἀρχή, shares as many characteristics with an an-archy. If the One, in its duality, is here still identified with the Good, then Platonic dualism structurally demands a conversion which would here separate the Good from the ideal of the Perfect, blocking any possible ontotheology.

UNIVOCITY AND DUALISM: ONTOLOGICAL QUESTIONS

How, then, does Plato's irreducible "two" stand with respect to what Deleuze affirms, early in *Difference and Repetition*, as the only possible ontological proposition and finds at the basis of any possible formal/ontological articula-tion of the irreducibility of difference the proposition that Being is said in a single sense? On this point, we conclude by offering two distinct suggestions, whose compatibility is itself a difficult question, and which arise from the overlapping but different perspectives of the two present authors.

First suggestion: Deleuzian side

If the univocity of being – the single sense of its saying – were indeed thought here as an ontic first principle or an undivided ἀρχή, it would indeed deny or restrict the duality of the Platonic "two." It would re-inscribe them within a logic of simultaneous completeness and consistency, and vitiate the iterated difference in which the duality maintains itself, as we have argued, in being applied to itself along with whatever is and becomes. But in order to reconcile the univocity of being with the original duality at the ontological and meta-logical basis of ideal genesis, and thereby distinguish it completely from any principle of ontological monism, it may be sufficient to recall the specification which Deleuze immediately gives it. This is the specification that, though being is said in one and the same sense, that of which it is said is nothing other than difference itself.

More specifically, Deleuze writes: "In effect, the essential in univocity is not that Being is said in a single and same sense, but that it is said, in a single and same sense, *of* all its individuating differences or intrinsic modalities."[48] The several "formally distinct senses" which articulate these differences or modalities of difference are, at the same time, univocally affirmed and said in the same way, in terms of a being "equal" for all. In briefly tracing the history of the univocity of being, Deleuze finds that Scotus affirms it as being's neutrality with respect to the distinction of its finite and infinite modalities, while Spinoza does so by affirming unitary substance as distinct from the modes, and Nietzsche by affirming the repetition in which only difference returns.[49] Each one thereby avoids an onto-theological unification of beings into the totality of a One-All, but only by affirming instead an irreducible duality or multiplicity of the ἀρχή itself, on the level of principles or of the differentiating modes of that of which univocal being is said. But if the ontological proposition of the univocity of being thus does not contravene, in each of these cases, the equal affirmation of an irreducibly split doctrine of determining modes, then maybe all that is needed to affirm a parallel separation, and thus to recover a Plato beyond or before the ontotheological closure, is to remove the priority marked in Plato's own thought by his identification of Unity with the good and flatten the hierarchy it implies. To do this would be, instead of Plato's own preference for the One over the dyad, to hold the "two" of the Platonic duality rigorously equal and their priority undecidable, thereby affirming the equal right and power of the two with respect to the ideal and real genesis they effect.

Second suggestion: Platonic side

The reflexive problem of the split application of the duality to itself must be given its due if it is to be answered satisfactorily. What can it mean to give one theory that holds it to be true and articulable that there are two ultimate principles, two ἀρχαί? There is a strong prima facie case that any such theory refutes itself, and this has led to a widespread prejudice against dualism in contemporary thought. For Plato's logic of the "one-over-many" does not seem to stop at the terms of any known duality. In order to say that there are two of something, we seem to need to make essential use of a unity which precedes and surpasses the duality. This poses no problem when speaking of, say, two cows. But when, in order to say that there are two ἀρχαί, it appears that we must appeal to a single univocal concept of ἀρχή, we seem to approach a destructive interference of form and content. For, if we are in possession of such a concept, we can take it, in correspondence with the entirety of its extension, to be the higher genus which is the proper object of our philosophical attention. Thus the conditions for the articulation of a duality of ἀρχαί seem to be incompatible with its truth, and it appears that a dualist theory must be either meaningless or self-refuting.

This relentless reassertion of totality in and by means of theory may indeed characterize any conceivable strictly intratheoretical dualities, and the way in which such dualities, however stark, tend to reinforce the one-all of the theory in which they appear. For this reason, it is important to emphasize the metalogical character of the duality of ἀρχαί. This theory, if true, shares the essential characteristic of formal theories with the expressive power of arithmetic: the one-all that seems demanded to make their questions sensible is subverted by the answers those questions receive. The objection to dualism can then be reversed and taken as a criterion of adequacy. If we take a dualism of ἀρχαί seriously, ontologically and logically, then at some point that thesis, which seems to rest on our possession of a prior concept of ἀρχή, has to step out of order and retroactively split that concept itself. The duality of the ἀρχαί must retroact upon the concept of ἀρχή in a logical experience which, if it is to output the dyad, can only be negative, that is the experience of the impossibility, a priori, of their synthesis.

The unity of the ἀρχή that we need in order to ask the ontological question is then only the unity of the problem – specifically, a problem about synthesizing the norms which appear ontologically as the one and the dyad, and metatheoretically as consistency and completeness. Metalogical difference or metalogical duality thus depends essentially on metalogical negation and vice versa. This negation is ontologically affirmative, not in the manner of the extension of a concept, but in that of the truth of a theorem.

Lautman and Deleuze have taken some of the first steps toward such an ontological recognition of what metamathematics shows us, and have done so, crucially, in terms of an experience of the difference between problem and solution. However, the price of selecting this point of interface is that it may be necessary to curtail Deleuze's tendency, in suggesting that the One is only the univocity of difference, to project univocity beyond the threshold of the question or problem, celebrating rather the affirmation of difference as such and in itself. Along similar lines, it would apparently also be necessary to reconsider whether Deleuze, in dealing theory the power thus to decide between affirmation and negation, tends to leave without a place an ontological affirmation that takes the form, exactly, of a metalogical negation.

NOTES

1. Gilles Deleuze, *Difference and Repetition* [DR], p. 183, translation slightly modified.
2. Anglophone study of this neglected philosopher was jumpstarted by Simon Duffy's 2011 translation of his collected works: Albert Lautman, *Mathematics, Ideas, and the Physical Real*. Recent studies of Lautman in relation to Deleuze include Simon Duffy's "The Role of Mathematics in Deleuze's Critical Engagement with Hegel," and "Lautman's Concept of the Mathematical Real," as well as Eleanor Kaufman, *Deleuze, the Dark Precursor: Dialectic, Structure, Being*.
3. Note that one should not be misled by parallel structure when naming the principles. The One is probably not best identified with "limit" (πέρας) but with the formal cause of the limit, which is at the same time the limit of limit's power to distinguish itself from the unlimited, if indeed the Good is what causes the mix, as Lautman would say, of limit and unlimited in the *Philebus*. For the One to appear as limit already requires the presence

of the Dyad as that in which limits can come to be; thus it is already to be working on the plane of participation-instances. Similarly, it is the implicit identification of the indefinite negation "unlimited" with the positive content, "Dyad" or "great-and-small" which is dialectically provocative in Plato's naming of that principle.

4. Gilles Deleuze, *The Logic of Sense* [*LS*], p. 1.
5. *DR* p. 111.
6. *LS* pp. 1–2.
7. Plato, *Philebus* [*Phil.*], 24b–d. For editions of Plato, we use the Loeb series (see bibliography).
8. Plato, *Parmenides*, 154a.
9. *LS* p. 2.
10. Ibid. p. 2.
11. Aristotle, *Metaphysics* [*Meta.*], A.6 987b14–987b35. This passage is slightly modified from W. D. Ross's translation found in *The Complete Works of Aristotle*, ed. Jonathan Barnes. Ross here notes that this reading of the end of the first paragraph, "come the forms, *i.e.* the numbers," and not merely "come the numbers," is the one in accordance with the Greek of the manuscripts.
12. These claims are suggested by the continuation of the passage quoted above: *Meta.* 988a10–17. For further discussion, see Kenneth Sayre, *Plato's Late Ontology: A Riddle Resolved* [Sayre], pp. 90–4.
13. For example, Aristotle, *Meta.* 991b9, *De Anima* 404b24.
14. Aristotle, *Meta.* 988a7–17, 1091b13–14, *Physics* 187a17.
15. Aristotle refers to Plato's "so-called unwritten teachings" at *Physics* 209b14–105.
16. For references and discussion, see Sayre pp. 76–7.
17. Ibid. p. 77.
18. Ibid. p. 77.
19. There is more than one way in which a list of theses can be compiled from these prose accounts. For some examples see Sayre pp. 94–5, and also Mitch Miller, "'Unwritten Teachings' in the *Parmenides*," and Dmitri Nikulin, "Plato: *Testimonia et Fragmenta*." The last also contains an overview of the secondary evidence for the existence of Plato's thought on the principles, for a fuller archive of which see Konrad Gaiser's *Testimonia Platonicum*, in Greek and German at the end of his *Platons Ungeschriebene Lehre*, and John Findlay's selections, in English, appended to his work *Plato: The Written and Unwritten Dialogues*. Sayre's argument depends upon establishing the strength of a chain of synonyms for the Dyad. He maintains a list of their incidence in the commentators at http://www3. nd.edu/~philinst/plato.html.
20. Oskar Becker, *Mathematische Existenz*, 6.b.i.C.
21. Lautman, *New Research on the Dialectical Structure of Mathematics* [*New Research*], p. 199. He refers here to Lautman, *Essay on the Notions of Structure and Existence in Mathematics* [*Essay*].

22. *New Research* p. 204.
23. Ibid. p. 200.
24. Ibid. p. 199.
25. Ibid. p. 199.
26. Ibid. p. 199.
27. Ibid. pp. 199–200.
28. *Essay* p. 189.
29. Ibid. p. 189.
30. Ibid. p. 190.
31. *New Research* p. 190.
32. Ibid. p. 190.
33. Aristotle, *Nicomachean Ethics*, I.4.
34. *New Research* p. 191.
35. Sayre p. 161.
36. Ibid. p. 124.
37. Ibid. p. 126. See *Phil.* 17a–e.
38. Sayre pp. 125–6.
39. Plato, *Parmenides*, 157b–158b.
40. Sayre p. 64.
41. Ibid. p. 180.
42. Ibid. p. 137.
43. Ibid. p. 139.
44. It may be possible to read the split names of Being in the *Sophist* in precisely this way, so that neither naming the One as Rest correlative to Motion nor naming the Dyad as the Different correlative to Identity succeeds in articulating a relation between the identity of the One and the motion of the Dyad. At the same time, the reappearance of two different, unrelated, relations in the place where one tries to get one to work for all would then succeed in showing something of the split "ontological difference" which cannot there (despite the new possibilities opened up by a "parricide" which yet remains Eleatic) be explicitly affirmed.
45. Given the complicated structure this implies, relating (as we shall see) constitutive ideas of consistency, completeness, and negation, what kind of logic should be used to treat this structure formally? Since it is plausible that closely formally-related problems arise in the context of set theory, for example in connection with Russell's paradox, it may be that set theory or second-order logic can provide the requisite expressive power. See Paul Livingston, *The Politics of Logic*, chapters 1 and 8, for instance, for one development of the connection of issues treated here as arising through Plato's dualism with Russell's paradox and related structures. At any rate, it seems likely that, whatever logic is adopted, an essential reference to crucial limitative and paradoxical results of metalogic or metamathematics will be needed to make formal sense of the structure.
46. The idea of making essential interpretive and ontological use of a metalogical duality between completeness and consistency was introduced by one of

the authors (Bova) in conversation with the other author (Livingston) around 2008, and is central to the argument of John Bova, *A Metalogical Approach to the Problem of Reflexivity in Platonic Dialectic* (where an extended version of some of the remarks of the present section can also be found), for an ultimately ethical recuperation of the Platonic dialectic on metalogical/metamathematical grounds. For another development, see Livingston, *The Politics of Logic*, especially chapter 1.

47. There is nothing remarkable about the fact that systematic and ontotheological tendencies can be found in Plato. What is remarkable is that there are also points of resistance to those tendencies internal to the Platonic text, and not incidentally but at its heart.

48. *DR* p. 36.

49. *DR* pp. 39–42.

BIBLIOGRAPHY

Aristotle, *The Complete Works of Aristotle: The Revised Oxford Translation*, ed. J. Barnes, 2 vols (Princeton: Princeton University Press, 1984).

Becker, O., *Mathematische Existenz: Untersuchungen zur Logik und Ontologie Mathematischer Phänomene*, 2nd edn (Tübingen: M. Niemeyer, [1927] 1973).

Becker, O., "The Diairetic Generation of Platonic Ideal Numbers," *New Yearbook for Phenomenology and Phenomenological Philosophy*, 7 ([1931] 2007), pp. 261–95.

Bova, J., *A Metalogical Approach to the Problem of Reflexivity in Platonic Dialectic* (Villanova: http://search.proquest.com.ezp1.villanova.edu/dissertations, 2016).

Deleuze, G., *Difference and Repetition*, trans. P. Patton (New York: Columbia University Press, [1968] 1994).

Deleuze, G., *The Logic of Sense*, trans. M. Lester and C. Stivale, ed. C. V. Boundas (New York: Columbia University Press, [1969] 1990).

Duffy, S., "The Role of Mathematics in Deleuze's Critical Engagement with Hegel," *International Journal of Philosophical Studies*, 17.4 (2009), pp. 563–82.

Duffy, S., "Lautman's Concept of the Mathematical Real," in S. Duffy, *Deleuze and the History of Mathematics: In Defense of the "New"* (New York: Bloomsbury, 2013), pp. 117–36.

Findlay, J. M., *Plato: The Written and Unwritten Dialogues* (New York: Humanities Press, 1974).

Gaiser, K., *Platons Ungeschriebene Lehre: Studien zur Systematischen und Geschichtlichen Begründung der Wissenschaften in der Platonischen Schule* (Stuttgart: Klett, 1963).

Kaufman, E., *Deleuze, the Dark Precursor: Dialectic, Structure, Being* (Baltimore: Johns Hopkins University Press, 2012).

Lautman, A., *Lés Mathématiques, les Idées et le Réel Physique* (Paris: Vrin, 2006).

Lautman, A., *Essay on the Notions of Structure and Existence in Mathematics*, in A. Lautman, *Mathematics, Ideas, and the Physical Real*, trans. S. Duffy (London: Continuum, [1938] 2011), pp. 87–193.

Lautman, A., *New Research on the Dialectical Structure of Mathematics*, in A. Lautman, *Mathematics, Ideas, and the Physical Real*, trans. S. Duffy (London: Continuum, [1939] 2011), pp. 197–219.

Livingston, P. M., *The Politics of Logic: Badiou, Wittgenstein, and the Consequences of Formalism* (New York: Routledge, 2012).

Miller, M., "'Unwritten Teachings' in the *Parmenides*," *Review of Metaphysics*, 48.3 (1995), pp. 591–633.

Nikulin, D. V., "Plato: *Testimonia et Fragmenta*," in D. Nikulin (ed.), *The Other Plato: The Tübingen Interpretation of Plato's Inner-Academic Teachings* (Albany, NY: State University of New York Press, 2012), pp. 1–38.

Plato, *Cratylus, Parmenides, Greater Hippias, Lesser Hippias*, trans. H. N. Fowler (Cambridge, MA: Harvard University Press, 1977).

Plato, *The Statesman, Philebus, Ion*, trans. H. N. Fowler and W. R. M. Lamb (Cambridge, MA: Harvard University Press 1975).

Plato, *Theaetetus, Sophist*, trans. H. N. Fowler (Cambridge, MA: Harvard University Press 1977).

Sayre, K. M., *Plato's Late Ontology: A Riddle Resolved*, 2nd edn (Las Vegas: Parmenides, 2005).

CHAPTER 6

"Adjust Your Dread": Badiou's Metaphysical Disposition

A. J. Bartlett

WHAT IS THE FORM OF THE DISCOURSE?

What is the problem of which metaphysics is the inquiry? Passing by Heidegger's imagistic allusions to soil, extrapolated from Descartes's letter to Picot outlining the arborescence of philosophy (a metaphor Deleuze turned on its side),[1] perhaps it was the great rival to Heraclitus, Parmenides,[2] who, eschewing organic metaphor altogether, truly expressed it best: the same is to think as to be.[3] The gap, indistinction, or indiscernibility between "thought" or thinking and "what is," by no means necessarily a "separation" to be resolved, is what metaphysics names, and it goes without saying that working out the places and operations implies and entails a lot of toing and froing, of back and forth, of *fort/da*.[4]

Parmenides' injunction, or perhaps declaration – it is important to remark the type of his utterance – is then in no way an answer, definitive, or even propositional, for nothing is to be tested or verified as such. Rather it is the task for philosophy to take up, the consequences philosophy draws each and every time it exists. Every time it is made, this declaration marks the recommencement of philosophy, and it provokes, every time, the question: "What is the form of the discourse by which being lets itself be said?" The answer, evident in the developed orientations to it – analytical, phenomenological, existential, formal, etc. – in turn positions being and thought with regard to each other. It decides: what of being can be thought, and thus what (is) not. In other words, it establishes being for thought – whether as potential, limit, chaos, imaginary, whole, indeterminate, inconsistency, and so on. Immediately, we can see that

Parmenides' declaration – maybe even a declaration of war or πόλεμος contra Heraclitus, the type of declaration the latter would have to respect – separates the thought of being from the imperative of nature, insofar as insisting on the indifference of being and thought is to unify them only in terms of the void – the nothing that is. What makes them indifferent cannot be something or other, some third thing relative to them. There is literally nothing to tell them apart.[5] In other words, it is by no means necessary to the thought of being that being and nature be conflated as φύσις, or in any other fashion, hidden or vital, driven or willed. As such, it becomes possible to say that if being can be thought outside the varieties of adequation, then nature does not exist.[6] Being can be thought not only as not nature per se, but by a form of thought that is absolutely un-natural and absolutely rational – right up to the point of demonstrating as consistent the inconsistency at its own heart. Thus, by existing, this discourse – being the thought of being qua being – refutes natural being by being what it is not. To jump ahead, this means that the thought of being as such can be the thought also of real change: thinking what is in exception to it. Metaphysics is not constrained to be either the impossibility of change, as in Parmenides, or the all of change, as in Heraclitus. Metaphysics is the site of a war on two fronts.

What form of discourse can think being, such that the void of being's relation to thought is at its core, yet can think the what is-not-being-qua-being as rational for it? For Alain Badiou, following and extending Plato, mathematics alone is capable of such a thinking: it is, he says, the science of being qua being.[7] Mathematics (qua discourse) is ontology. The entirety of *Being and Event* is the demonstration of the veracity of the consequences of this philosophical decision. Invoking all necessary qualifications and precautions against the over-excitable (both analytic and continental), this has been the most misunderstood decision of Badiou's philosophy: mathematics thinks or is the discourse of or the science of being qua being.

In the first instance, then, philosophy is divorced from ontology.[8] Extrapolating on his own interrogation of this decision via set theory – which couples to it a theory of the event, the generic form of a truth, and thus its "subject" – Badiou will argue that mathematics has always been ontology.[9] Not that mathematicians are decidedly ontologists, but, given that what they work on is literally nothing, not-being as object, as substance, or as an "empirical given," it is being itself which they inscribe in the numbers and letters which make up their discourse. Out of the void, then, which, as Badiou establishes, is the "name of being"[10] – the name of what is un-presented in presentation as such, pure multiplicity and not One – ontology constructs an entirely consistent and infinitely extensive system of thought. Thus mathematics thinks of being what of being can be thought. Philosophy, then, as Descartes alluded to, is under conditions; yet it thinks in its own terms, relative to the concepts and categories it renders thinkable, the thought of being as such. This makes of mathematics itself a thought, something philosophy after Plato has always been less than willing to grant. Even when it has shown mathematics all due respect, philosophy has almost always assumed that it can go one better when it comes to thinking what it is to be. Philosophy has considered its operators conceptually superior to the technical (or aesthetic) specificities of mathematics, even when it is plainly number which is at stake – the one and the many, parts and wholes, the finite and infinite.

If mathematics is integral to philosophy as a condition, just as art, politics, and love are also conditions for Badiou, at the level of what can be thought of being as such, it is also crucial in that it demonstrates that the thought of being is both possible and consistent, thus rational and not indeterminate, senseless, or theological. Mathematics is a discourse which is not reducible to or subsumable within the framework of language: neither the well-made language of logical positivism and its heirs in the analytic tradition, nor the poetic, fragmentary form it takes in post-Heideggerian postmodernisms, nor, finally – though this constitutes an entirely distinct relation in Badiou's thought – the place assigned to language in psychoanalysis.[11] But let us stop here, as the introduction of mathematics is to get ahead of the game, as it were, given that in the paper whose analysis forms the bulk of this essay,[12] Badiou posits this interruption of metaphysics hitherto only at the end and under the signification of what he calls a Platonic gesture.

THE *KNOWLEDGE* OF METAPHYSICS

The declaration of Parmenides, under all its possible interpretations, remains the recognizable core of all metaphysics. It is audible for instance in the famous "know thyself," which for Plato can only be a task: not because being is ineffable, but because it already contains a division, which is to say it insists on a thought of the void as what must be traversed. The knowing of the self is the knowing of the division at the core of thought as the impetus to thought. The problem evoked here is of the in-discerning of inside/outside, finite/infinite, mediation/immediacy, and so on, all relays of the initial decision on being being thought. A distinct strategy since Nietzsche, broadly agreed to by a coterie of seemingly diverse and opposed thinkers in the twentieth century, has been to deny the problem as such. For if, as a problem of metaphysics it is "metaphysical," and if metaphysics is what must end for the thought of being to truly be, then the question, in Wittgenstein's terms, is outside the sayable as such. The upshot of this strategy is to say that "the same is to think as to be" is itself propositionally unsayable, and so should not be said if one wants to make sense. Even if Heidegger does reopen the question of being qua being as an anti-Platonic gesture, and so in terms of being as being said, he did so under the injunction of language or of the poem. This reopening is, in a certain sense, to comply with Wittgenstein's injunctions about the coincidence of the limit of thought and world as only thinkable to language. What is without language is nonsense for Wittgenstein, while for Heidegger the poem speaks being since it is free of what annuls it as such: Plato's idea, the inaugural and mathematically conditioned gesture of metaphysics.

Hegel already pointed out that those who claim to abandon metaphysics can often be seen to do so on metaphysical grounds. It is always, for them, Hegel says, the question of identity – or of a unity in some way. Today's version of this identity is surely the market as imagined in the Hayekian sense as at once beyond our reason yet amenable to it in some way – in fact, as that to which human being naturally tends. It is reasonable, the refrain goes, that we do not know what the market knows – such knowledge being virtually absolute and so beyond our capacities. What the market knows and we never can attain, is precisely, the ends of our reason nevertheless. It is our limit and our destiny. Its potential is what we act out, thus making known to us our true nature. This non-knowledge at the heart of our knowledge which is thus the very knowledge of our being, the very thing we cannot know, is a sophistic convenience, which is to say it is an ideology at the level of practice. Ideology should not be understood as a negative term here; it just marks a function. What is negative about ideology is its use as a negative by those who practice it necessarily and deny it actually – in fact, denial and occlusion are the positivist essence of ideology.

For Hayek et al., and as we know there are many in this et al. (known to it and unknown to themselves both) the market is not an ideology and not, thus, a metaphysics. It is supposedly a fact of our existence, and the fact or pragmatics of our existence is to naturally fall short of knowing by nature: thus we cannot know; better we submit to this nature than attempt to scale the mountain of what we are capable. If we reconcile ourselves to this finite framework, empirically attested or, as the self-styled anti-metaphysicians like to say, "evidence-based" (so long as we agree the parameters), what we are capable of will be revealed in good order as in accord with such a nature. But clearly this is the assumption that consists in metaphysics: the assumption of the true nature of our nature or what we might call subject as subjection. It is one option but, as always, relies on a priori conditions off limits to creatures like us. So these conclude with what they contend, and thought (in the sense of an intervention on this construction itself) becomes an annoyance best disavowed, just as Plato's Socrates was disavowed by the panoply of "patrons of the flux" and thinkers of the state contemporary to him. Thus thought, in the sense that aims at that of which we are capable, must be precisely exceptional to facts of existence, not being some creature of the limit, thus, not being the subject of this constraint regulated by the rule of language, world, sense, nature, or horizon. In other words, thought requires a subject-figure that does not by the necessity of its nature return to the rule.

What, then, does it means to hold that nature does not exist? If such can be thought, thought that interrupts the adequation between nature and language, Being and beings, then a whole swathe of metaphysical and anti-metaphysical traps might be sprung – given that, on either side, some sort of natural ineffability serves to unify their opposition. Badiou's ontological intervention is to show that the rule as such, which is always some assumption of what it is to be – φύσις, market, fact, etc. – posits itself as incomplete, thus leaving open the space precisely for: first, some form of thought that can think incompleteness as such, in other words actual infinity; and second, some subject which is not at all reducible to some rule. Thus something else can be thought. Certainly the theme of the impasse is explored constantly in Plato, and in Plato the geometric paradigm, as the "Platonist" Gregory Vlastos labels it, serves as that which forces the impasse to which all the Athenian language games concede, with great shows of satisfaction. If, on the contrary, this impasse can be thought, we avoid precisely the circularity inherent to classical metaphysics and to its supposed contraries: in this sense both metaphysics and anti-metaphysics succumb to the same circle.[13] It would then be this same/difference, rather than metaphysics as such, that needs to be terminated altogether.

PLATONISM IS AN ANTI-PLATONISM

In his first *Manifesto for Philosophy*, Alain Badiou announces his project under a double Platonic disposition: as a "Platonic gesture" correlated to a "Platonism of the multiple."[14] The latter phrase marks the renewed necessity of an ontological project in the wake of and contra Heidegger; the former the formal arrangement for the thinking of truth or truths. Since a truth is what is truly new, this makes truth (once again) "a new word in Europe (and elsewhere)."[15] This double dispensation is necessary, Badiou declares in the *Manifesto*, if philosophy – a term he happily interchanges with metaphysics – is to "return to itself" and not submit to the incessant calls for its end: that its ends be circumscribed, that it end, or that it has come to its end. Against this tendency toward ends, philosophy, Badiou argues, is possible: "The crux of the matter is to know what the following means: taking *one more step*. A step within the modern configuration, the one that since Descartes has bound the three nodal concepts of being, truth and the subject to the conditions of philosophy."[16] In several works Badiou gives shape and form to what such a renewed philosophy must traverse and pass through; it is to this adversary that he gives the catch-all term "anti-Platonism."

I have explored this self-situation more fully elsewhere,[17] but for a general picture we can adduce: the vitalist (Nietzsche, Bergson, Deleuze), the analytic (Russell, Wittgenstein, Carnap), the Marxist, the existentialist (Kierkegaard, Sartre), the Heideggerian, and that of the "political philosophers" (Arendt and Popper).[18] In Badiou's words, "ultimately the 20th century reveals a constellation of multiple and heteroclite anti-Platonisms." Taken together, "their anti-Platonism is incoherent" but what unites them is that each ostensibly accuses Plato of being ignorant of something essential to philosophy and "this something is identified with the real itself" (e.g. change for the vitalists, language for the analytics, concrete social relations for the Marxists, negation for the existentialists, thought in as much as it is other than understanding for Heidegger, democracy for the political philosophers).[19]

Badiou identifies this anti-Platonism, such is its ubiquity and extension, as what passes today for Platonism as such – that is it forms the hard-core of what is the received wisdom on Plato. This "Platonism" is then

> that common figure, montage of opinion, or configuration that circulates from Heidegger to Deleuze, from Nietzsche to Bergson, but also from Marxists to positivists, and which is still used by the counterrevolutionary New Philosophers (Plato as the first of the totalitarian 'master thinkers'), as well as by neo-Kantian moralists. "Platonism" is the great fallacious construction of modernity and post-modernity alike. It serves as a type of general negative prop: it only exists to legitimate the "new" under the heading of anti-Platonism.[20]

Badiou elaborates three predominant "philosophical" tendencies derived from this anti-Platonist collective: (1) the hermeneutic tendency, whose central concept is interpretation; (2) the analytic, whose concept is the rule; and (3) the postmodern, concerned with the deconstruction of totalities in favor of the diverse and the multiple. What they have common is a commitment to language, its capacities, rules, and diversity such that language is the "great historical transcendental of our times."[21] The obvious consequence of this fundamental accord, for Badiou, is a commitment to the end of metaphysics and thus philosophy since Plato. Plato thus marks the point of an inception that must be reversed. Contemporary "philosophy" or anti-Platonism, he says, effectively "puts the category of truth on trial."[22]

Nonetheless, Badiou agrees with two allegedly anti-Platonic claims that arise from the contemporary critiques: Being is indeed essentially multiple;[23] and Plato does indeed mark a singular and decisive point in the history of thought. Here Heidegger as much as Deleuze is a central figure of reference.[24] However, in regard to the first point of agreement, to say that being is multiple today is to say, as noted, that it falls under the regime of mathematics qua ontology and not "language." Badiou's position is thus to invert this accusation and argue that it is precisely Plato's conception of what there is that matters, and what there is are truths whose ontological status is at once undecidable and generic and whose presentation is eventual, thus exceptional, and subjective.[25] In regard to the second point, Plato is to be understood as the incitement to thought, through whom thought is given "the means to refer to itself as philosophical" and thus "independently of any total contemplation of the Universe or any intuition of the virtual."[26] Plato is decidedly not the moment at which thought turns to despair.[27] For Badiou, the rejection of the linguistic (re)turn is predicated on the existence of "a regime of the thinkable that is inaccessible to this total jurisdiction of language."[28] What is required therefore is a "Platonic gesture" whose condition is a "Platonism of the multiple."

"METAPHYSICS WITHOUT METAPHYSICS"

In the essay under consideration here, entitled "Metaphysics and the Critique of Metaphysics,"[29] Badiou names this Platonic project, noting the paradoxical form of the utterance, as a "metaphysics without metaphysics":[30] a metaphysics that in its first indication cleaves itself, as dialectical, from a pre-Kantian "classical metaphysics" and from the post-Kantian (but not simply Kantian) modern negative variant, "archi-metaphysics."[31] However, this Hegelian dialectical metaphysics must itself give way to the second Platonic gesture, to a mathematical and thus ontological reconsideration of "the links between finitude, infinity, and existence."[32] This second gesture ensures that being and truth remain thinkable in their division and, moreover, that this division not be characterized or overdetermined by any extrinsic knowledge as to their coupling: not by a theory of correspondence, adequation, transcendence, or language.[33]

As so often in Badiou's work a negation provides the impetus of interrogation. So he moves from the rejection of anti-Platonism to an analysis of the impossibility of the void as what marks the history of ontology from Aristotle to Heidegger (passing by Spinoza, Leibniz and Hegel, as seen in *Being and Event*), to disprove the positive assertion of "democratic materialism" that no exception exists to its double remit of bodies and languages.[34] Conversely, we also often see the affirmation of an impossibility, contrary to what particular philosophies conceive to be their rational kernel: in reading Hegel, we find Badiou's counter-affirmation of the inexistence of the whole; in Deleuze, the counter-affirmation of the impossibility of the *eventum tantum* (or even the thesis that multiplicity drives the Deleuzian metaphysics); in Aristotle or Spinoza, the counter-affirmation that the void insists for thought.[35]

These interrogations have in common the axiomatic that organizes Badiou's philosophy: that the One is not, and, if the One is not, then the nothing is. This axiomatic, which contemporary post-Cantorian mathematics provides, is the basis both of a reinterrogation of philosophy *tout court*, and a point of orientation for the present of philosophy. The critique of prior metaphysics, then, begins in this same way: claims to "the end of metaphysics" organize the entire contemporary system of reference, from Kant to the present. For such post-Kantians, metaphysics is either obsolete or in crisis. That it is dying, or it should die; that it is in crisis, or that it be radically overhauled such that the means of its confinement attest to the rightful antipathy of contemporary "rationality" – much as Guantánamo Bay, in the global sense, or Nauru or Manus Island, in the Australian context, serves the hubris of an empty reason.[36]

The productions of this "opera of the end,"[37] as Badiou calls it, vary. He delineates four "librettos":[38]

1. *Critique.* Kant's critical limitation of the reaches of dogmatic metaphysics (as we shall see, this is the metaphysics which accounts for or even counts the indeterminacy of God in its systematics) as too ambitious

or categorically promiscuous; the intellectual, political and historical exhaustion of what metaphysics was supposed to provide as the virtue of knowledge or its guarantee.

2. *Positivism*. A rational positivism, as "mathematized experimentation" based in the empirical sciences (or in a knowledge of them) substitutes its virtues for the exhausted guarantees of an indeterminable God. Comte, Wittgenstein, and Carnap serve to name the arbiters of this paradigm for Badiou here.

3. *Dialectics*. The dialectical refusal of any metaphysics of the one in the sense of eternal, stable entities supported by "fixed categories through which metaphysics," as the "mutilation of a complete form of thought," "allows something like a submission to death to prosper." Hegel, Marx, Nietzsche, Freud, and Lacan name this deposition of the "principle of identities" in the name of the real of contradictions and "concrete becomings."

4. *Hermenuetics*. Suggesting Heidegger without naming him, positing the epochal nature of the return of the dead Gods: "that which discerns under the name of metaphysics the nihilistic disposition of the entire history of the West." This disposition is what must be reversed and thus metaphysics itself must, via a patient hermeneutics, come to nothing. Its origin, as it were, must be unfounded such that the history of the present be revoked. Natural being, φύσις, "holds sway" against the Idea.[39]

These four operas, Badiou avers with all seriousness, do violence to philosophy as cry, insult, and mockery. Eschewing a more extended account of Badiou's somewhat ironical review of the charges – including Kantian hubris, Comtean physical and political pathology, and Heideggerean global terrorism[40] – what we need to note is that their general consensus turns on the impossibility of metaphysics to think the new. For Kant, nothing new is achieved in all the "chatter and bustle" of metaphysics, which has effectively remained unchanged since Aristotle; for Comte, metaphysics is not only a sickness ("but is it so different for Kant? And will it be so different for Wittgenstein, or Heidegger?"),[41] but also the ideological apparatus of a certain formation of power. In both cases, it blocks "a strategic passage: the passage between philosophy and social order" or "the 'social installation' of anti-metaphysical philosophy."[42] As for Heidegger, the reign of metaphysics as Idea suppressing the nature of being as coming forth culminates in the *enframing* of the entire earth qua technology. Thus, while referring to Nietzsche as the last metaphysician via his "will to power," Heidegger finds the "the truth of Being . . . replaced by machination's erection of 'goals' (values)."[43] As with the Platonism of the anti-Platonists, the metaphysics of the anti-metaphysicians is what it is because it leaves something out: "the true nature of what is."[44] And thus "what is to be feared in [metaphysics] is precisely the apparent weakness of its content."[45]

Ultimately, then, what is left out is thought itself, given it must name what addresses itself to this "what is" under the mode of a formal clarity – whether that be of the critical, positivist, hermeneutical, or clearing type. But we might venture, it is thought as a peculiar form of salvation – not just for Heidegger, clearing space for the Gods, but for Kant too, so as to save humanity itself as author of subjective reason; and for Comte, as access to the world as such devoid of "vagueness" and "equivocity."[46]

What remains over in each of these thinkers, we can say, pre-empting Badiou's exposition, is the supposition that metaphysics stripped bare reveals the extant truth of being as such. One is reminded here of Nietzsche's comment regarding truth being a woman and philosophers being "clumsy" and "unskilled."[47] Badiou says: "What makes metaphysics fearsome is that it ignores the discipline of the true questions in favour of an indeterminacy that any signifier of mastery whatsoever can come to inhabit."[48] Metaphysics thus is fiction: the search for (the) truth (of being) in name only – hiding in fact a true indifference to it. Thus the anti-metaphysician (so, physicians of the cure) are the true champions of truth. After Heidegger, putting into play the adage that the cure is often worse than the disease, Badiou avers that much of contemporary philosophy, in a strange parody of this claim against the indifference of metaphysics, simply excises truth from all consideration – other than, perhaps, as virtual adjunct to an affective knowledge: the logical rule in analytic philosophies, or the transcendental ground for the equality of opinions or perspectives in postmodernisms.

So this is the horn of the dilemma for the varia of anti-metaphysicians – the proper approach to being is occluded as metaphysics, which posits an indeterminacy at the heart of its rationality. Anti-metaphysics counts indeterminacy qua indeterminate in what can be thought. It not only holds off from interrogation of the indeterminate as indeterminate, but occludes the necessity for the indeterminate in the very form of its rationality. Hence anti-metaphysics is a dogmatic metaphysics, asserting as reasoned the full place of the indeterminate – God as we know it, but as Badiou says, any "master signifier" whatever – and thus feeding off of its "own inability to attain knowledge."[49] Badiou notes that Kant had already spotted what Heidegger makes palpable as the necessity of its end: "that of the indifference of non-knowledge" qua the question of Being.[50] Because Badiou's interrogation of the anti-metaphysicians as the proponents of an "archi-metaphysics" allegedly subversive of and directed towards power "dogmatics" shows how they maintain being in the place of being undecided, this master signifier must be dealt with. The surprise is how they go about it.

Badiou is able to weave together under this designation of an archi-metaphysics[51] – a designation none of its proponents aspire to – its critical, positivist, and hermeneutic strands. He shows how the delimitations of each, real in their operational form, nonetheless conform in the orientation and structure of their address: annunciation (indifference), determination (of the indeterminate), and desire (end). Badiou is thus able to show how certain utterances and determinations of Heidegger resonate back into Kant (for example, the analysis of the power of metaphysics as occlusion), and that Comte pre-empts Heidegger's claims for the ontotheological destination of metaphysics, the famous "forgetting of forgetting." Badiou cites Comte: "'Metaphysics' – he writes – 'is in fact nothing but a form of theology gradually enervated by dissolving simplifications.'"[52]

These decidedly un-casual remarks highlight what each archi-metaphysician in their own defense would no doubt seek to occlude. So Badiou demonstrates the negative nature of their conceptual alliance. "Indifference, simplification, abstraction, separation, dissolution: such are the operations through which, under the accepted name of metaphysics, the power of a neutral thought, or of the object-less argument, establishes itself. The power of the undecided and the undetermined as such."[53] I cite this to pre-empt: for everything archi-metaphysics opposes of dogmatic metaphysics, Badiou, in slightly different terms and by subtractive rather than strictly negative operations, will affirm. But in affirming that thought must affirm the existence of the indeterminate as thinkable, Badiou, via the contemporary mathematics of set theory, breaks also with the dogmatist schematic, such that the infinite or indeterminate is not potential, and so off limits to thought as such, but actual. And so, contra archi-metaphysics – and the latter distinction draws many more contemporary thinkers into the archi-metaphysics remit[54] – what is, the infinite, is actually thinkable as such: it is not the known or determined un-thought of all thought. The infinite is neither ineffable nor determined. After Cantor, the infinite is not off-limits to thought. The saving grace of archi-metaphysics, that it knows the infinite qua indeterminate, whereas the dogmatists treated it as resource for knowledge, saves only the indeterminate whose thought it was to have deposed. The indeterminate – on the basis of the say-so of dialectics but not as a dialectics – must therefore be thought again. Hence the indeterminate becomes actual, not virtual: thinkable, but outside the constrictions of language (critical, positivist, hermeneutic).

Just as Plato was wont to do with Homer, Hesiod, Heraclitus, and Protagoras, Badiou will ally these hermeneuts and critical reasoners with the contemporary positivists or "partisans of linguistic empiricism"[55] for whom metaphysics, by its utterances, makes no sense – the holy grail of logical positivism. Citing Wittgenstein and Carnap, but following the former through the chicanes of the final propositions of the *Tractatus*,[56] in which Wittgenstein imposes, by turns subtly and in sledgehammer style, the limits of our world as being the limits of our knowledge (language): beyond this being-said is what is mystical.[57] Hemmed in by this tautology of sense making, reminiscent of the great Protagoras,[58] we are condemned to say, as subjects of metaphysics, only what can be said. Such a trajectory is of course proper to philosophy, Wittgenstein says. To take the

> propositions of natural science – i.e. something that has nothing to
> do with philosophy – and then, whenever someone else wanted to say
> something metaphysical, to demonstrate to him that he had failed to

give a meaning to certain signs in his propositions. Although it would
not be satisfying to the other person – he would not have the feeling
that we were teaching him philosophy – *this* method would be the
only strictly correct one.[59]

It is curious that the motif of a certain stealth must appear in this archi-metaphysics, that thought itself is too much for us to bear. So we must outsource
what is right to a logic of sense that remains apart from and exceeds that of
which we are capable. Yet this stealth and this mysticism claims to be rationally deduced. Once again we see the unconscious at work: "For Wittgenstein,
metaphysics denotes the void in signification, just like for Heidegger it denotes
the void in the problematic or the question, and for Comte the void in scientific denotation."[60]

Something is missing, the fact of the question – whether as statement or
law or as the presence in thought of being itself. Yet, as Badiou mischievously
points out,[61] when it came to love for Comte, an unsayable remains in play.
As for Wittgenstein, the mystical, as noted, is given its place relative to sense:
"just the facts, ma'am," do not after all exhaust our experience. And, completing the trilogy, Heidegger's ever-returning saving God marks this same "void"
place. Thus archi-metaphysics sets itself a task in contradiction to its original
target of critique: to "over-determine the undetermined,"[62] which is to say,
for archi-metaphysics "the last recourse to the metaphysically undetermined,
poses itself with a certain intensity.[63]

So the problem for archi-metaphysics in its contrary delimitation of
dogmatic or classical metaphysics is what to do with the indeterminate that
dogmatics simply assumes to be there for it. The power of dogmatics lay in its
use of this indeterminacy; the correction of archi-metaphysics is to determine
this unknowable unknown, to, as Badiou puts it,

replace it with what we shall call an archi-metaphysics, that is, with
the suspension of sense to an undetermined that is purely and simply
left to the historial indeterminacy of its coming. Archi-metaphysics is
the replacement of a necessary undetermined with a contingent one,
or: the established power of an unknown master is opposed by the
poetics or prophetics of the to-come.[64]

This is exemplified in Kant – to whom Wittgenstein and Heidegger and
Comte pay their own particular homage[65] – by the shifting of God to regulative idea, from knowledge to "matter of faith." We thus recover religion
within the limits of reason alone, while leaving God as indeterminate to his
own devices. Once again, the limits of reason are coordinated with those of
experience, enabling a closed world without any place for what is in exception to it. What Kant regulates is the place of the indeterminate as such,
such that it be at any time God, man, rule, or law: whatever must name
that space as off limits to thought as saving reason. This, for Badiou, is the

great terror of critical, positivist, or hermeneutical archi-metaphysics – the ruin of the concept. The sophistry of it – which in a certain sense is also a conceit – can be put in this way: to know what cannot be known; to have the knowledge of what cannot be known to knowledge. Thus, as ever, in thrall to this indeterminacy at the limit of a conceit, all thought is reduced to a form of expression or a making sense or a language game which requires that it never overstep the mark marked out for knowledge beforehand, so that it never strays into "metaphysics." To reverse a favorite citation of Badiou from Mao: for archi-metaphysics, "we will *not* come to know all that we do not know." Or: we must not because we cannot.

It is no coincidence that what is common to the three creatures of archi-metaphysics is a reductive approach to mathematics. Badiou, taking Kant as exemplar, compares them unfavorably to Leibniz, Spinoza, and Descartes in terms of the proof of God (or whatever master signifier you like). For Badiou, the rationalism of these latter three, derived in good measure from their specific, extensive and knowledgeable interrogations of what mathematics thinks, trumps the former insofar as this rationalist metaphysics "blunt[s] indeterminacy and expose[s] transcendence to a rational control more rigorous than could ever be exerted by positivism's Humanity, Kant's moral subject, or the poet of hermeneutics."[66]

Certainly Hegel, Badiou argues, recognizes this rationalist advance in dogmatic metaphysics over archi-metaphysics. Hegel in fact recognizes and takes as fundamental for thought itself that axiomatic alignment of thought and being, conceived by Parmenides. In other words, the subject/object dichotomy – the subject of thought and the object of its thought qua unknowable being – essentially concedes in advance and militates against what it supposes as the mark of the human and subject as such – its very subjectivity. Or, at least, one side of subjectivity, that which is not so much subject as subjective; which is to say, that which would be subject not to the limits of language and world but to what is in exception to it and thus become a maker of its world as such. As Hegel puts it: "that thinking in its immanent determinations and the true nature of things form one and the same content."[67]

If Hegel points the way, he still is not the answer for Badiou. What this means is that Hegel recognizes an essential aspect of dogmatic metaphysics that archi-metaphysics cannot see, and that is the exceptional nature of the indeterminate. Exceptional, then, in some form of thinkable relation to thought itself, not excluded from, but immanent to it. As Badiou writes: "A being, philosophically accessible as a name, can be said to be essentially undetermined if amongst the predicates that permit its definition is the claim that this being exceeds, in its very essence, any predicative determination available to an understanding such as ours."[68] And: "The name of 'metaphysics' will then be given to that discursive disposition which claims that an undetermined being, as we have just defined it, that is, a being whose determination exceeds our cognitive power, is required in order to complete the edifice of rational knowledge."[69]

Let us here note: Hegel does not endorse classical metaphysics, but recognizes in it the power of the concept – to make a "predicate of the impredicable."[70] But only insofar as this determines the question or marks the site from which the question of being thought must take its orientation. We can call this site negation, though that is only indicative of an operation at this site. This site is what is nothing for the efforts of predication and can thus have no bearing on reason; but for Hegel – and Badiou in another way again – this being which exceeds determination in its essence (not its substance) is what must not be excluded from thought as such or else an integral aspect of the thought of being, namely that which is in exception to it, cannot be thought.

In other words, rational knowledge, classical metaphysics, would be that which takes on its own ἀπορία as itself, that admits a thinking exists capable of working through what exceeds it without either reducing its essence to knowledge or knowing its essence to be unthinkable as such. Rather it constructs a discursive framework capable of supporting and articulating as real what is nothing to knowledge. Thus, as Badiou says, "that it be able to place, within a discursive framework available to all – an argumentative and not a revealed framework, in other words a *rational* framework – a point of indeterminacy that may, from that moment on, harbour any signifier of mastery whatsoever."[71] In Badiou's determination of a set-theory ontology, this role is taken by the void: Ø. The nothing as name of being, that is!

But before we return to this metaphysics without metaphysics we must continue to see what dogmatic metaphysics admits which archi-metaphysics – the metaphysics of contemporary philosophy – refuses to know as knowledge. Badiou recognizes in this classical schema the sense given to what is pursued by Aristotle – metaphysics as the science of being qua being. Let us note first that this makes metaphysics the same as ontology for Badiou. Ontology, he says elsewhere and everywhere in his work, quoting Aristotle, is "the science of being qua being." We must also note that ontology, for Badiou, thinks also the exception, and thus the place or site of the coming to be of that which is not being qua being. What is not being qua being for Badiou is what the event names within a situation of being, and as such marks the place of the possible coming forth of a new truth of that situation as in-exception to it – an immanent exception. All truth such that it must come to be is subjective, the subject being the finite support of an infinite truth (infinite in its being). For Badiou, the subject is the meta-physical category par excellence, being what is between what is not being qua being and its being a body in a determinate world: as such, having "no place to be."[72] It requires a meta-physics because "of the subject, there can only be a theory. 'Subject' is the nominal index of a concept that must be constructed in a singular field of thought, in this case philosophy."[73] Thus: to think and to be.

But again this is to get ahead of ourselves in the sense that what forms the framework of the rationality of a classical metaphysics – that one may prove an existence without thereby determining what exists – is correlated to the notion of the indeterminate as One, while for Badiou, adhering to this same determination as to the power of a metaphysics qua the concept, rationality – mathematics (as for post-Aristotelian rational metaphysics) – dictates that being is not One. For the classical world, the One – in Plato, the Good which is not an Idea – serves as the determination of the indeterminate such that a thought can think it. That is to say its existence is thinkable while its essence remains indeterminate. Or:

> That one may prove an existence without thereby determining what exists is the core of metaphysics as power.
>
> Metaphysics is classical, or dogmatic, when it grants the undetermined point of its apparatus the rationality of its existence.
>
> This point is crucial. What classical metaphysics after Plato borrows from mathematics is the demonstration of existence purely on the basis of the concept. Metaphysics is at base the recognition of a pure existence. Meaning that this existence, which cannot be empirically attested, and the being of whose content is beyond the measure of our cognition, can nonetheless be rationally demonstrated.[74]

For Badiou, then, this is what is essential to classical metaphysics or what a classical metaphysics under the condition of the rational force of mathematics shows us to be crucial for thought as such: that existence is rationally shared between the undetermined and the determined, the infinite and the finite. In other words, that the transition from the finite to the infinite is "by way of existence,"[75] the decision that existence is not reducible to known knowledge, or that "there exists" is the recommencement and not the end of thought. A "thought" that is, in Badiou's words from *Being and Event*, "nothing other than the desire to finish with the exorbitant excess of the state."[76] That is, with a predication in excess of itself as what Plato called a false conceit of knowledge – knowing what must not be known.

> In the end nothing, is more corrosive for philosophy than to separate itself from this [rational] regime, which creates, beyond that which can be empirically attested, the real of a simple possibility, and destines thought to the only thing that matters, its absolute identity with the being that it thinks.[77]

For Badiou this "subsumption of the existential" by the mathematical – which Hegel has pointed to – is both shared in common by Plato, Leibniz, Spinoza, and Descartes, and missed by Kant, and by extension the positivists and hermeneuts.[78] However, Hegel thinks that this rationality is lacking in terms of the absolute, that this rational apparatus lacks, if you like, the form of its rationality – which has to be given by speculative dialectics. As Badiou notes and laments, here as elsewhere,[79] Hegel was himself not shy in deprecating mathematics. But it is with respect to the infinite that Hegel does not fall into line with the anti-metaphysics of archi-metaphysics which, for Badiou, prides itself precisely on reducing knowledge to the dimensions of the finite alone; of what, in other language, can be demonstrated to be constructible relative to any posited existence.

This also links Hegel to dogmatic metaphysics, which, as we have seen, gives us a "rational treatment of the existence of the infinite,"[80] thus holding at bay the finitist demands of constructivist-empiricism, which render death as the horizon of the knowing subject. Dogmatic metaphysics is a discourse of the effective proof of the infinite – proof as what assures the "mathematicitiy of existence."[81] Its proof is in its discourse, that infinite being is sayable beyond knowledge as what we will (have) come to know. Thus the anti-metaphysics of archi-metaphysics must separate out the infinite from what can be thought, from the subjective capacity for thought. Denying the discursive capacity of mathematics is one step in this deposition, returning us, Badiou says, to an empirical finitude that "Plato would not have failed to consider as anterior to any philosophy whatsoever."[82] Thus in these terms archi-metaphysics is a sophistry: at least insofar as it is hostile to what mathematics effects as real with regard to the infinite (and so what is not real with regard to the finite).[83]

Badiou notes here that Kant recognizes another feature of metaphysics that treats it less in terms of it being an operation of thought than of it being something integral and indeed natural for thought itself. This biological metaphor, Badiou notes, is fundamental.[84] Hence Kant can recognize metaphysics as an existence of nature such that it underpins cognition – the always there – and he can at the same time displace it from the subjective framework of this same cognition. Hence it is always there, in the nature of thought, as that which must be overcome or maintained in its proper place as excessive to reason, relative to the faculties available to the transcendental subject. "Kant is very close in the end to collapsing his critique of dogmatic metaphysics into an equally dogmatic metaphysics of the nature of thought and of the ultimate ends of the contradiction between the transcendental organisation of the understanding and reason's urge-to-transcendence."[85] In concentrating his attention on the faculties of cognition and the determination toward transcendence wherein the nature of this thought is annulled as, again, without knowledge, in the literal not relative sense, Kant exacerbates or even, as Badiou suggests here, dogmatizes the separation of thought and being all over again. Thus in recognizing existence qua metaphysical – the natural thought of "what is" so to speak – and separating it off from what is the subject's cognitive capacity qua subject, Kant "augments rather than decreases the part played by the undetermined, and consequently the recurrent possibility of a veritable metaphysical obscurantism."[86] "Augments," because Kant determines its existence, and "obscurantism," because there must be an existing part of thought unable to be thought by thought as such. Previously the indeterminate had no existence and thought was limited by it: now an indeterminate is posited to exist such that thought itself must render it inexistent.

The dialectical challenge to this, which points the way out, is to propose a real determination of the undetermined that endows metaphysics with its power – the power to "infinitise the finite."[87] So dialectics seeks this answer as the means to have done with the transcendental indeterminacy that organizes and orients classical or dogmatic metaphysics; that is the form of its existence so to speak, while not lapsing back into what it considers worse. Thus, to be "neither Kantian, nor empirico-positivist, nor phenomenologico-hermeneutic."[88] Badiou names in this neither-nor vein – besides and in debt to Hegel – Lenin, contra the double injunction empirico-criticism, and both Freud and Lacan with regard to the "cunning power" of negation and its realization in terms of the subject of the unconscious. The power of the theory of negativity in each, thus that which marks out what inexists as real for any possible knowledge of being as such, maintains discursively this to-and-fro between the finitude of a being and the infinity to which it owes its determination.

However, Hegel's praise of classical metaphysics, in the sense of its rational relation to existence, opens onto what is for him the problem of how the conceptual apparatuses it uses to grasp or name the existence of the indeterminate are themselves constructed. Thus its forms of (pure) thought, *pace* Kant here, are themselves uncritically deployed; that is to say, what metaphysics brings to bear as thinking itself is pure determination. Metaphysics is indeterminate *in actu*, we could say, and not just its object. Indeed, the (life of the) object is precisely what must be thought for Hegel, such that being and thought are the same. Being must be thought, in other words, such that we can come to know what thought is – the rational determination of its concepts and categories.[89]

This entails for Hegel, Badiou argues, that:

Each and every category, whether it be being, nothingness, becoming, quality, quantity, causality, and so on, ultimately consists of a definite time of determination, if only one has the patience to follow the true movement of transformation whereby each category takes place as the exteriorization and dialectical truth of the preceding ones.[90]

This is, then, logic, the logic of determination replacing dialectics, a move Hegel says he owes to Kant. The point being that dialectics is destined for higher things while the destitution of metaphysics is carried out by logic. As Badiou describes it, "'Logic' means: a regulated process of determination, whereby the undetermined absolute (for example being, being as such) lets integral singularity take place as the ultimate immanent specification of itself. Logic is here the logic of determination, which leaves no indeterminacy behind, and which, in this sense, abolishes metaphysics."[91] But in this form it clearly has its roots in Aristotle. One of the ironies of Kant's claim against the science of metaphysics not changing since Aristotle is that the logic Kant has recourse to is itself unchanged since Aristotle. So Kant is in the manner of repetition: despite himself, nothing new.

Determination here means to count what shows itself as tending toward its proper end, there being only one. As there is nothing indeterminate for knowledge, knowledge being the extent of determination, metaphysics has no proper end and so by extension there is no knowledge of it: or what it speaks of cannot be known and so is not. Metaphysics is an empty discourse, outside logic, nothing. But in a sense this is an auto-abolition, at least if we ascribe to Kant the nomination archi-metaphysician because the indeterminacy he invokes as nothing is the one that sustains his philosophy as object – being as such or the thing-in-itself. This is the case, Badiou argues (following Hegel), because Kant's critique of classical metaphysics (ostensibly that it begins with "special objects" – soul, god, the world, etc. – and "forgets" the categories that allow for the capture of these objects as objects) pushes so far against the object that the categories obtain "an essentially subjective signification."[92] The object becomes then almost absolutely indeterminate – thus an "infinite obstacle," as Hegel put it.

"It is this operation," Badiou asserts – thinking of what he elsewhere calls Kant's "obscurantist attachment to pious moralism"[93] – "that creates the radically unknowable. It allows the placing of all signifiers of conformism and of moralising oppression in the beyond of the supra-sensible."[94] Hence what Kant calls knowledge is reconciled to a faith that what cannot be thought – qua radical indeterminacy – must be, for this very reason, the site of the Good to whose wisdoms we logically submit. It is a perverted Platonism insofar as, for Plato, under the sign of the Idea, thought names the commensurability of the known and unknown.[95] What enables an-other thinking of the indeterminate possible is mathematics, which, moreover, allows that a situation be rethought beyond what logically constrains it. Referring to Plato "in passing," Badiou notes that this is the courage of thought, one which:

> Attempts to put an end at the same time to both the objectivity
> of the undetermined in classical metaphysics and the subjective
> finitude which, in critical archi-metaphysics, stands alone before the
> undetermined absolute. Essentially, dialectical argument poses that a
> category of thought is only such on condition that it exhausts without
> remainder that which is thought in thought through this category. Or,
> to quote Hegel, if the category remains a form of absolute thought,
> there cannot also be the surplus of "a *thing-in-itself*, something alien
> and external to thought."[96]

Badiou reduces the principles of Hegel's argument – indeed that argument is at stake – to two points, which we can summarize. First, that it is by the movement of thought itself that any undetermined will come to be determined or that the "gap" between finite and infinite is the locus of thought itself, the kernel of its procedure as such. In Badiou's own ontological formalization this locus is centered on the first infinite set – that of all ordinals – and thus the concept of a limit, which can be marked as such and traversed, is critical to it. Referring to Hegel, Badiou remarks that this is what the real is rational means and moreover this implies that to the extent that thought is thinkable, it is thinkable absolutely. So thought as absolute and not the absolutely indeterminate. This thought, Badiou remarks, takes time, being the labour of the concept – what Plato referred to, speaking of hard things being worth doing, as "the long detour." Second, and now contra archi-metaphysics (and still classical qua objects) dialectics claims that the categories of thought are not simply, singularly, subjective: rather dialectics is a form of thought adequate to its objects as such. In other words, its categorical determinations are those adequate to that which it thinks, which is to say it can only think categorically with regard to what it thinks. Categories are not first a priori and then addressed to an object thus making of the object, which cannot be thought, a knowledge. In this way dialectics is that form of thought which is conceptual and, as Badiou avers, absolute: no indeterminacy remains over on either side. There is then a category for every determinate content and "the becoming of concepts exhausts the real."[97] Thus: "not only, and contrary to what Hamlet declares, is there nothing in the world which exceeds our philosophical capacity, but there is nothing in our philosophical capacity which could not come to be in the reality of the world."[98]

This is what philosophy is constrained to think, the thought of the absolute, which is not, as we can see here, the thought of the One or the whole as such, but of the Two. As Badiou notes, the change in the form of the transcendental under positivist and hermeneutic direction, from subjectivity to language, changes nothing in terms of this schema. Rather, as we have seen already, "we are dealing here with a reinforcement, by means of a synthesis between criticism and positivism, and soon, via cognitivism, with a hermeneutics of intentionality, of all that which for the past two centuries has taken place in the way of archi-metaphysics."[99]

Now as we have said, dialectics points the way – it opens up these determinations of the (being of the) One to the Two which founds them in order to rethink entirely what is thought as being or, as Badiou says, referring again to Plato beyond Hegel – which is of course where he wants to get to recommence philosophy for today – "between the absoluteness of the concept and the creative freedom of negation."[100] The problem is that while dialectics opens this question to thought, dialectics itself is behind the game in regard to what is thinkable of this relation between the finite and the infinite. "Hegel himself underestimates [. . .] the link between finitude, infinity, and existence within a mathematical paradigm,"[101] Badiou argues. If we were thus tasked to reexamine the "axioms of classical metaphysics," to re-intervene on the question posed there of the rationality of the indeterminate, "we would learn that, as Descartes once glimpsed, it is possible, in light of contemporary mathematics, and namely of the Cantorian treatment of the infinite, to begin purely and simply with the infinite."[102]

Thus the form of the relation that has hitherto underpinned "speculative ontology," and so also classical and archi-metaphysics, which comes in the two dialectical couples of the-one-and-the-many and the-whole-and-part, is no longer thinkable. Set-theoretic ontology, contemporary mathematics, has substituted for them a wholly other double relation, one based in the actuality of the infinite, and which, woven from the void, thinks no objects whatsoever: belonging, "which indicates that a multiple is counted as element in the presentation of another multiple" and inclusion, "which indicates that a multiple is a sub-multiple of another multiple."[103]

> Set theory sheds light on the fecund frontier between the whole/parts relation and the one/multiple relation; because, at base, it suppresses both of them. The multiple-whose concept it thinks without defining its signification-for a post-Cantorian is neither supported by the existence of the one nor unfolded as an organic totality. The multiple consists from being without-one, or multiple of multiples, and the categories of Aristotle (or Kant), Unity and Totality, cannot help us grasp it.[104]

Badiou's notion of a "metaphysics without metaphysics" is thus subject to this contemporary mathematical condition. That the infinite can be thought undermines the necessary object of an archi-metaphysics and posits by this thought the absoluteness of the concept. Thus it has no need to posit the indeterminate at all, given that mathematics renders such a notion superfluous to the thought of being – indeed "metaphysical." But of course this mathematical materialism of the infinite, to wax rhetorical, also breaks with dialectics. The axiom schema of set theory, while historical in terms of its invention, has no recourse to what Badiou refers to here as "the theme of a historial auto-determination of the undetermined."[105] That is to say, set theoretical ontology has no recourse to a notion of immanent becoming to account for being, being thought. As the discourse of presentation as such, set theory thinks infinity directly and is the means of its coming to be. Hence we have our Platonic gesture or affirmation: "in a style bereft of any hyperbolic transcendence of the Good (and therefore outside of metaphysics) that for everything which is exposed to the thinkable there is an idea, and that to link this idea to thought it suffices to decide upon the appropriate axioms."[106]

As we have said this "demand to the world that it adjust its dread to rich and numbered postulates,"[107] apropos and contra Heidegger (the "last universally recognizable philosopher"),[108] is the task Badiou has taken up, as for him any philosophy must, confronted with the inventions and interventions of the forms of thought that are its conditions. Badiou's anti-metaphysical metaphysics is thus what he calls the return of philosophy to itself – which means also that philosophy is integrally divorced from ontology per se. Mathematics, we might say, bequeaths philosophy the freedom of thought it had erroneously supposed as its alone – which is to think again the complex of being, truth, and subject.

NOTES

1. See M. Heidegger, "Introduction to 'What Is Metaphysics?'" It is not without interest that, like the pre-Socratics, Parmenides and Heraclitus, who sold the all of truth, Heidegger considers metaphysics to be concerned with the whole (essence/existence, Being/beings) and not the arcana of the pieces (to use Heraclitus' allusion).

   For Descartes see "To the French Translator of the Principles of Philosophy serving as a preface," in *The Principles of Philosophy*. For Deleuze (and Guattari) see *A Thousand Plateaus*, "Introduction: Rhizome": "We're tired of trees. We should stop believing in trees, roots, and radicles. They've made us suffer too much. All of arborescent culture is founded on them, from biology to linguistics. Nothing is beautiful or loving or political aside from underground stems and aerial roots, adventitious growths and rhizomes" (p. 15). To be fair, Descartes is not mentioned in this passage, and is named only a few times in the entire text (Chomsky and psychoanalysis are the primary referents, but the discussion points back to a classical even biblical approach). What is clear is that what is at stake is a certain form of the subject.

2. See Plato, *Theaetetus*, 152e (translations of Plato are from *Complete Works*, ed. John Cooper):

   > Let us take it as a fact that all the wise men of the past, with
   > the exception of Parmenides, stand together. Let us take it that
   > we find on this side Protagoras and Heraclitus and Empedocles;
   > and also the masters of the two kinds of poetry, Epicharmus in
   > comedy and Homer in tragedy.

   Elsewhere he calls them "patrons of the flux." See also 180d–181a (emphasis added):

   > But I was almost forgetting, Theodorus, that there are other
   > thinkers who have announced the opposite view; who tell us that
   > "Unmoved is the Universe," and other similar statements which
   > we hear from a Melissus or a Parmenides *as against the whole
   > party of Heracliteans*. These philosophers insist that all things are
   > One, and that this One stands still, itself within itself, having no
   > place in which to move.
   > [. . .] we have got ourselves in between the two parties; and
   > if we don't in some way manage to put up a fight and make our
   > escape, we shall pay for it, like the people who play that game on
   > the line in the wrestling schools, and get caught by both parties
   > and pulled in opposite directions.

3. A literal translation from the Greek is rendered "to think and to be is the same thing." Published translations vary.

4. See Sigmund Freud, *Beyond the Pleasure Principle*, pp. 8–11. Note: "Finally, a reminder may be added that the artistic play and artistic imitation carried out by adults, which, unlike children's, are aimed at an audience, do not spare the spectators (for instance, in tragedy) the most painful experiences and can yet be felt by them as highly enjoyable."

5. See Ray Brassier, "Presentation as anti-phenomenon in Alain Badiou's *Being and Event*." Brassier understands Badiou's invoking of Parmenides' maxim as meaning "thinking and being are both nothing" (p. 63). Thus there is no identity between them and this lack of predication is the point of the same. For Brassier, critical of Badiou's position here, this results in an impossibility of distinguishing "between discourse and world, thought and reality, logical consequences and material causes" (ibid.).

6. See Alain Badiou, *Being and Event* [BE], p. 140:

> If it is clear that a natural being is that which possesses, as its ontological schema of presentation, an ordinal, what then is *Nature*, that Nature which Galileo declared to be written in "mathematical language"? Grasped in its pure multiple-being, nature should be natural-being-in-totality; that is, the multiple which is composed of *all* the ordinals, thus of all the pure multiples which are proposed as foundations of possible being for every presented or presentable natural multiplicity. The set of all the ordinals – of all the name-numbers – defines, in the framework of the Ideas of the multiple, the ontological substructure of Nature.
>
> However, a new theorem of ontology declares that such a set is not compatible with the axioms of the multiple, and could not be admitted as existent within the frame of onto-logy. Nature has no sayable being. There are only *some* natural beings.

Hence Nature does not Exist.

7. *BE* pp. xiii, 3–4.

8. François Laruelle calls this an act of "cultural 'matricide'" which is the core, he says, of Badiou's inherently conservative, Maoist, "re-education of philosophy." "Rather than an invention, re-education is a particular type of repetition; one that seeks to modify everything while conserving for it the destination and the ends of philosophy." "Re-education," Laruelle continues, "makes use of mathematics, and then logic, only as pedagogical disciplines safeguarding the correct image of thought – a project that some would not hesitate to call a bootcamp." The explicit implication is that Badiou is a reformer rather than a revolutionary (to use the well-worn charge) – a clever accusation vis-à-vis what underpins Badiou's thought: real change. Whether Laruelle successfully makes his case for Badiou's authoritarian conservatism is another matter: his concentration on

mathematics reduces Badiou's other conditions to oppressed adjuncts of this science, and that his interrogation draws on a particular political – itself well-worn – orientation to Maoism and Platonism gives pause. But Laruelle is at least militantly honest in his address. He is a philosopher, not a commentator – the two being deliberately conflated in our mediatic age to the exaltation of the latter, the debilitation of the former. François Laruelle, *Anti-Badiou: On the Introduction of Maoism into Philosophy*, pp. vii–xii.

9. *BE* p. 435. In Alain Badiou, *Logics of Worlds: Being and Event II* [LW], the mathematical logic of Category Theory provides the onto-logic of appearing – or what is being-appearing as such. See also Alain Badiou, "Mathematics and Philosophy," pp. 15–16, apropos the distinction between mathematics and logic – mathematics being the science of being qua being:

> In my work [. . .] logic pertains to the coherence of appearance.
> And if the study of appearance also mobilizes certain areas
> of mathematics, this is simply because, following an insight
> formalized by Hegel but which actually goes back to Plato, it
> is of the essence of being to appear. This is what maintains the
> form of all appearing within a mathematizable transcendental
> order. But here, once again, transcendental logic, which is a part
> of mathematics tied to contemporary sheaf theory, holds sway
> over formal or linguistic logic, which is ultimately no more than
> a superficial translation of the former.

For a summary appraisal of Badiou's move from set theory to category theory see A. J. Bartlett and A. Ling, "Translators' Introduction: The Categorial Imperative."

10. *BE* pp. 52–9.

11. On Badiou's relation to psychoanalysis, specifically Lacan, for whom anyway "mathematization alone reaches a real" (Jacques Lacan, *The Seminar of Jacques Lacan, Book XX*, p. 131.), see A. J. Bartlett and Justin Clemens, "'The Greatest of Our Dead': Badiou's Lacan," *Badiou and Philosophy*, ed. Simon Duffy and Sean Bowden, and "Not Solvable by Radicals: Lacan, Topology, Politics."

12. See the final section on "Metaphysics Without Metaphysics."

13. Just as in our parliamentary systems, democracy presumes the role of reason for the insurgency of natural capitalisms.

14. Alain Badiou, *Manifesto for Philosophy* [MP], pp. 97–101, 103.

15. *BE* p. 3; Badiou takes this from Saint-Just, who said "happiness is a new word in Europe."

16. *MP* p. 32.

17. See A. J. Bartlett, *Badiou and Plato: An Education by Truths* [BP], and A. J. Bartlett, "Plato."

18. "Pour aujourd'hui: Platon!" These seminars are part of an ongoing series given at the Collège de France over three years 2007–8, 2008–9, and 2009–10. The 2007–8 seminars and Badiou's seminar on the *Republic* given in 1989–90 (just after the publication of *Manifeste pour la philosophie*) are reproduced in full on François Nicolas' website. The notes which reproduce the seminars are by Daniel Fischer: http://www.entretemps.asso.fr/Badiou/seminaire.htm. All translations of these seminars are my own.

19. Ibid., from 24 October 2007: http://www.entretemps.asso.fr/Badiou/07-08. htm.

20. Alain Badiou, *Deleuze: The Clamor of Being* [DCB], pp. 101–2. After praising Deleuze as "the most generous" anti-Platonist, "the most open to contemporary creations," Badiou concludes: "all that Deleuze lacked was to finish with anti-Platonism itself" (ibid.).

21. Alain Badiou, *Infinite Thought* [IT], p. 46. Badiou invokes this tripartite schema in a variety of texts and with a series of nuances, the latter dependent on the topic at hand. In the essay "The (Re)turn of Philosophy *Itself*," Badiou contends that this discourse concerns itself with "language games, deconstruction, [. . .] heterogeneity without end, *différend* and differences, the ruin of Reason, [and] the promotion of the fragment [. . .]" (p. 20).

22. *IT* p. 6. In seminars from 2007, Badiou also notes another form of contemporary Platonism, "la Platonism mystique," which he links to the events of May 1968 and, he says, is manifest in the work of Guy Lardreau and Christian Jambet (see "Pour aujourd'hui: Platon!" of 5 December 2007). See also *LW* p. 522: "What may be called 'Platonism' is the belief that in order to come close to this ideal, it is necessary to mathematize, by hook or by crook. This is opposed by all the doctrinaires of sense or meaning, be they sophists or hermeneuticists – all of them, at bottom, Aristotelians."

23. *MP* p. 85.

24. On Deleuze's compatibility with the "linguistic turn" and the "great lineage of contemporary sophistry" and, therefore, with the discourse of the contemporary state see *LW* p. 386.

25. For a discussion of these features of truths, see *BP*.

26. *DCB* p. 102.

27. In speaking of the function of ἀπορία within the Platonic dialogues and within the history of philosophy more generally, Samuel Scolnicov, in *Plato's Metaphysics of Education*, at p. 50 observes that it registers in two ways. For the sophist it registers as despair, as the beginning of the end, while for the philosopher it is an incitement: the site, if you like, of a recommencement. We return to this in the next section.

28. Quoted in Peter Hallward, *Badiou: A Subject to Truth*, p. 16; from Alain Badiou, "L'Entretien de Bruxelles," p. 21.

29. Alain Badiou, "Metaphysics and the Critique of Metaphysics" ["MCM"], trans. Alberto Toscano.

30. Ibid. p. 190.

31. See Alain Badiou, *Theory of the Subject* [*TS*], "On the Side of the True," pp. 116–24.
32. "MCM" p. 190.
33. See further *TS* p. 122:

> The inventory gives us four philosophical names for truth: coherence, repetition, totality, torsion. There are no others. The "adequation" of Aristotle and Saint Thomas has never been anything but a nicety out of a dictionary. To say that there is truth when the spirit agrees with the thing does not dispense anyone from looking for the effective law of the agreement in question. Aristotle and Saint Thomas offer their solutions to this problem, which, like all others, are distributed in the system: coherence, totality, repetition, torsion.

34. *LW* p. 1. Equivalently, for democratic materialism "there are only individuals and communities" (ibid. p. 8). Badiou counters this with a metaphysics of the subject which is never a body as such. See ibid. p. 37:

> That is the content of Book I, which is a metaphysics in the strict sense: it proceeds as though physics already existed. The advantage of this approach is that we can immediately see the (subjective) forms of 'life' that the materialist dialectic lays claim to, which are the forms of a subject-of-truth (or of its denial, or of its occultation). This study obviously remains formal as long as the problem of bodies, of the worldly materiality of subjects-of-truth, has not been treated. Given that a subjectivizable body is a new body, this problem requires that one know what the "appearance" of a body means, and therefore, more generally, that one elucidate what appearing, and therefore objectivity, may be.

35. See *DCB*, or *LW* pp. 281–7. For a contrary view on this last impossibility see Jon Roffe, *Badiou's Deleuze*, pp. 119–20.
36. In order to serve a (re)newed will to classification, determination, and circumscription of peoples, and thus a metaphysics all too human and thus without truth, Australia runs an offshore "archipelago" of detention for would be seekers of asylum, specifically those who arrive by boat and from countries Australia is actively involved in rendering uninhabitable one way or another: military and surveillance support of the Sri Lankan state against the Tamils, wars in Afghanistan and Iraq etc., and the usual "run of the mill" exploitation and corruption of resources and peoples a functioning democracy requires. The status and treatment of these people is subject to periodic, formulaic, and ineffective criticism from external and international agencies, including the UN. This has no effect because the logic of classification, determination, and circumscription is impeccably contemporary and global,

and would-be critiques only serve to repeat it after their own fashion. Hence the critical (liberalist) posture, including empirical "data" and hermeneutic nuance, is its own repetition, lacking the capacity or the knowledge to break with its own form. The irony of Australia's terror of arrivals by sea should be lost on no one familiar with its short history; that this irony affects a symptom in Lacan's clinical sense, would bear analysis. This is also to say that philosophy is worth nothing, considered as an academic game.

37. "MCM" p. 174.

38. Unless otherwise noted, the following four paragraphs quote from "MCM" pp. 174–5.

39. *BE* p. 123.

40. Speaking of Comte/Heidegger, Badiou says at "MCM" p. 178: "on the one hand, a civil servant failing to attain his professorship, on the other, the planetary reign of technology, with a little of what I'd like to call ontological ecology. It is, as it were, a Franco-German difference."

41. Ibid. p. 176.

42. Ibid. p. 177.

43. Quoted at ibid. 177. Badiou quotes from Martin Heidegger *Nietzsche, Volume III* [*Nietzsche*], p. 175.

44. "MCM" p. 178.

45. Ibid.

46. Ibid. p. 179.

47. Friederich Nietzsche, *Beyond Good and Evil*, "Preface."

48. "MCM" p. 178.

49. Ibid. p. 179.

50. Quoted at ibid., again from Heidegger, *Nietzsche*.

51. "MCM" p. 181.

52. Quoted at ibid. 179, from Auguste Comte, *Discours sur l'Esprit Positif*, p. 20.

53. "MCM" p. 179.

54. Deleuze most emphatically and contentiously, even if it is undeniable he affirms the indeterminate as without the form of its thought. Indeed it is un-contentious to speak of Deleuze as a metaphysician – he is not one for the end of philosophy – thus it is the shape of his metaphysics that matters, and as a good Aristotelian it is still Kantian at the level of being as being thought, as One virtual or indeterminate as such (consider *DCB*). For other archi-metaphysicians, see *MP* pp. 47–52.

55. "MCM" p. 180.

56. Ludwig Wittgenstein, *Tractatus Logico-Philosophicus* [*TLP*], from 6.4 forward.

57. Ibid. 6.522.

58. "Of all things the measure is Man, of the things that are, that they are, and of the thing that are not, that they are not." For this translation: Jacqueline de Romilly, *The Great Sophists of Periclean Athens*, p. 97–8. Protagoras' assertion concerning the gods is exemplary also as precursor to Wittgenstein's

fondness for the limit: "I am unable to know whether they exist or do not exist or what they are like in form; for there are many hindrances to knowledge, the obscurity of the subject and the brevity of human life," quoted in Diogenes Laertius, *Lives of Eminent Philosophers*, 9.41.

59. *TLP* 6.53.
60. "MCM" p. 180.
61. Ibid.
62. Ibid.
63. Ibid. p. 181.
64. Ibid.
65. Ibid.
66. Ibid. pp. 181–2.
67. G. W. F Hegel, *Science of Logic* [*SL*], p. 45. Quoted by Badiou at "MCM" p. 182.
68. "MCM" p. 182.
69. Ibid.
70. Ibid. p. 183.
71. Ibid. p. 182.
72. Book I of *Logics of Worlds* is entitled "Formal Theory of the Subject (Meta-physics)."
73. *LW* p. 47.
74. "MWM" p. 183.
75. Ibid. p. 184.
76. *BE* p. 282. Badiou continues:

> Nothing will ever allow one to resign oneself to the innumerable parts. Thought occurs for there to be a cessation – even if it only lasts long enough to indicate that it has not actually been obtained – of the quantitative unmooring of being. It is always a question of a measure being taken of how much the state exceeds the immediate. Thought, strictly speaking, is what un-measure, ontologically proven, cannot satisfy.

77. "MCM" p. 184.
78. Ibid. Hence in their rationality, Badiou remarks, "these thinkers were and remain of a calibre which Kant could never lay claim to" (ibid.). See also *LW* p. 353:

> Kant is the inventor of the disastrous theme of our 'finitude' [. . .]
>   Nevertheless, once he broaches some particular question, you are unfailingly obliged, if this question preoccupies you, to pass through him. His relentlessness – that of a spider of the categories – is so great, his delimitation of notions so consistent, his conviction, albeit mediocre, so violent, that, whether you like it or not, you will have to run his gauntlet.

79. See, for example, Alain Badiou, "Philosophy and Mathematics: Infinity and the End of Romanticism." For a different view of Hegel on mathematics (of the infinite) see Simon Skempton, "Badiou, Priest, and the Hegelian Infinite."
80. "MCM" p. 184.
81. Ibid.
82. Ibid. p. 185.
83. Badiou's definition of sophistry can perhaps be summed up as hostility to the place of mathematics, which is not reducible to language, relative to philosophy.
84. "MCM" p. 185.
85. Ibid.
86. Ibid.
87. Ibid. p. 186.
88. Ibid.
89. For Badiou, as noted above, mathematics does not treat with objects and moreover the very conception of the subject is determined by Badiou to be "objectless." See, for example, Alain Badiou, "On a Finally Objectless Subject," trans. Bruce Fink, in Eduardo Cadava, Peter Connor and Jean-Luc Nancy (eds.), *Who Comes After the Subject* (New York: Routledge, 1991), pp. 24–32. In *Logics of Worlds*, Badiou develops a new theory of objects, which in turn has no recourse to a subject. An object appears for a world.
90. "MCM" p. 187.
91. Ibid.
92. Ibid. p. 188.
93. *LW* p. 240.
94. "MCM" p. 188.
95. Platonism, as Badiou conceives it and takes up, is both the "knowledge of ideality" and "the knowledge that access to ideality is only through that which participates in ideality" (Alain Badiou, *The Concept of Model*, p. 92). Or: "The Idea is the occurrence in beings of the thinkable" (*BE* p. 36). In this sense, of maintaining the "co-belonging" or "ontological commensurability" of "the knowing mind and the known" (Alain Badiou, "Platonism and Mathematical Ontology," p. 49), Plato is Parmenides' heir or his patricide: and we could venture, given the pronounced "fidelities," and more clearly the intervention that is *Being and Event*, Badiou is Heidegger's – the last anti-(archi)metaphysician.
96. "MCM" p. 188; the Hegel quotation is from *SL* p. 45.
97. "MCM" p. 189.
98. Ibid.
99. Ibid. p. 189.
100. Ibid. p. 190.
101. Ibid.
102. Ibid.

103. *BE* p. 81.
104. Ibid.
105. "MCM" p. 190.
106. Ibid.
107. Ibid.
108. *BE* pp. 1, 481. Badiou's intervention in "Metaphysics and the Criticism of Metaphysics" on the question of metaphysics today, thus essentially on Heidegger, is a double irony: (1) that he uses the words of the poet (Mallarmé) to conclude this intervention on the famously and resolutely "poetic ontology" of Heidegger; (2) that he invoke dread, where the concept of dread or anxiety, distinguished from fear, is one Heidegger uses in "What Is Metaphysics" to insist on being as thought under the orientation of the nothing. But for Badiou the nothing can be thought – this is the adjustment that anxiety (after Lacan) opens up as possible for us at the point of a decision – being can be thought, and as such we can go on.

BIBLIOGRAPHY

Badiou, A., *Theory of the Subject*, trans. B. Bosteels (London: Continuum, [1982] 2009).

Badiou, A., "On a Finally Objectless Subject," trans. B. Fink, in E. Cadava, P. Connor, and J.-L. Nancy (eds.), *Who Comes After the Subject* (New York: Routledge, [1988] 1991), pp. 24–32.

Badiou, A., *Being and Event*, trans. O. Feltham (London: Continuum, [1988] 2005).

Badiou, A., *Manifesto for Philosophy*, trans. N. Madarasz (Albany, NY: State University of New York Press, [1989] 1999).

Badiou, A., "L'Entretien de Bruxelles," *Les Temps Modernes*, 526 (1990), pp. 1–26.

Badiou, A., "Mathematics and Philosophy: The Grand Style and the Little Style," in A. Badiou, *Theoretical Writings*, ed. R. Brassier and A. Toscano (London: Continuum, [1992] 2004), pp. 3–20.

Badiou, A., "Philosophy and Mathematics: Infinity and the End of Romanticism," in A. Badiou, *Theoretical Writings*, ed. R. Brassier and A. Toscano (London: Continuum, [1992] 2004), pp. 21–38.

Badiou, A., "The (Re)turn of Philosophy *Itself*," in A. Badiou, *Conditions*, trans. S. Corcoran (London: Continuum, [1992] 2008), pp. 3–22.

Badiou, A., *Deleuze: The Clamor of Being*, trans. L. Burchill (Minneapolis: University of Minnesota Press, [1997] 2000).

Badiou, A., "Platonism and Mathematical Ontology," in A. Badiou, *Theoretical Writings*, ed. R. Brassier and A. Toscano (London: Continuum, [1998] 2004), pp. 49–58.

Badiou, A., "Metaphysics and the Critique of Metaphysics," trans. A. Toscano, *Pli: Warwick Journal of Philosophy*, 10 (2000), pp. 174–90.

Badiou, A., *Infinite Thought: Truth and the Return to Philosophy*, ed. and trans. J. Clemens and O. Feltham (London: Continuum, 2003).

Badiou, A., *Logics of Worlds: Being and Event II*, trans. A. Toscano (London: Continuum, [2006] 2009).

Badiou, A., *The Concept of Model*, trans. Z. L. Fraser and T. Tho (Melbourne: re.press, 2007).

Badiou, A., "Pour aujourd'hui: Platon!," notes of D. Fischer (http://www.entretemps.asso.fr/Badiou/07-08.htm, 2007–8).

Bartlett, A. J., "Plato," in A. J. Bartlett and Justin Clemens (eds.), *Alain Badiou: Key Concepts* (Durham: Acumen, 2010), pp. 107–17.

Bartlett, A. J., *Badiou and Plato: An Education by Truths* (Edinburgh: Edinburgh University Press, 2011).

Bartlett, A. J. and Clemens, J., "'The Greatest of Our Dead': Badiou's Lacan," in S. Duffy and S. Bowden (eds.), *Badiou and Philosophy* (Edinburgh: Edinburgh University Press, 2012), pp. 177–202.

Bartlett, A. J. and Clemens, J., "Not Solvable by Radicals: Lacan, Topology, Politics," in M. Constantinou (ed.), *Badiou and the Political Condition* (Edinburgh: Edinburgh University Press, 2014), pp. 232–51.

Bartlett, A. J. and Ling, A., "Translators' Introduction: The Categorial Imperative," in A. Badiou, *Mathematics of the Transcendental*, trans. A. J. Bartlett and A. Ling (London: Bloomsbury Academic 2014), pp. 1–10.

Brassier, R., "Presentation as anti-phenomenon in Alain Badiou's *Being and Event*," *Continental Philosophy Review*, 39.1 (2006), pp. 59–77.

Comte, A., *Discours sur l'Esprit Positif* in *Traite Philosophique d'Astronomie Populaire* (Paris: Fayard, 1985).

de Romilly, J., *The Great Sophists of Periclean Athens*, trans. J. Lloyd (Oxford: Clarendon Press, [1988] 1992).

Deleuze, G. and Guattari, F., *A Thousand Plateaus: Capitalism and Schizophrenia*, trans. B. Massumi (Minneapolis: University of Minnesota Press, 1987).

Descartes, R., *Selections from the Principles of Philosophy*, trans. J. Veitch (Project Gutenberg, [1881] 2003).

Diogenes Laertius, *Lives of Eminent Philosophers*, trans. R. D. Hicks (London: Heinemann, 1925).

Freud, S., *Beyond the Pleasure Principle*, trans. J. Strachey (New York: W. W. Norton, [1920] 1961).

Hallward, P., *Badiou: A Subject to Truth* (Minneapolis: University of Minnesota Press, 2003).

Hegel, G. W. F., *Science of Logic*, trans. A. V. Miller (New York: Humanity Books, 1999).

Heidegger, M., "What Is Metaphysics?," trans. D. F. Krell, in M. Heidegger, *Pathmarks*, ed. W. McNeil (Cambridge: Cambridge University Press, [1929] 1998), pp. 82–96.

Heidegger, M., "Introduction to 'What Is Metaphysics?,'" trans. W. Kaufman, in M. Heidegger, *Pathmarks*, ed. W. McNeil (Cambridge: Cambridge University Press, [1949] 1998), pp. 277–90.

Heidegger, M., *Nietzsche, Volume III: The Will to Power as Knowledge and as Metaphysics*, trans. D. F. Krell (San Francisco: Harper & Row, [1961] 1987).

Lacan, J., *The Seminar of Jacques Lacan, Book XX: On Feminine Sexuality, the Limits of Love and Knowledge, 1972–3*, trans. B Fink, ed. J.-A. Miller (New York: W. W. Norton, 1998).

Laruelle, F., *Anti-Badiou: On the Introduction of Maoism into Philosophy*, trans. R. Mackay, (London: Bloomsbury Academic, [2011] 2013).

Nietzsche, F., *Beyond Good and Evil*, trans. R. J. Hollingdale (London: Penguin, 1973).

Plato, *Complete Works*, ed. J. M. Cooper (Indianapolis: Hackett, 1997).

Roffe, J., *Badiou's Deleuze* (New York: Acumen, 2012).

Scolnicov, S., *Plato's Metaphysics of Education* (London: Routledge, 1988).

Skempton, S., "Badiou, Priest, and the Hegelian Infinite," *International Journal of Philosophical Studies*, 22.3 (2014), pp. 385–401.

Wittgenstein, L., *Tractatus Logico-Philosophicus*, trans. D. Pears and B. McGuiness (London: Routledge, [1921] 2001).

PART II

ARISTOTLE

CHAPTER 7

Science Regained [1962]

Pierre Aubenque

Translated by Clayton Shoppa

Εἶναι καὶ ἐνταῦθα θεούς.[1]

The previous chapters'[2] conclusions may seem negative: the science without name, to which editors and commentators will give the ambiguous title *Metaphysics*, seems to oscillate without end between an inaccessible theology and an ontology incapable of tearing itself away from dispersion. On the one hand, an object too distant; on the other, a reality too close. On the one hand, a God ineffable since, immutable and one, he escapes from the grasp of a thought that divides that of which it speaks; on the other, a being that, insofar as it is in motion, escapes, through its contingency, from a thought that speaks only in order to compose that which is divided. The two projects of Aristotle – the one a unitary discourse about being, the other a first and thereby foundational discourse – each seem to result in failure.

But if we analyze the causes of this failure, of which all that has survived under the name *Metaphysics* is only the meticulous description, we realize that the case of theology and the case of the one discourse about being (what we have called ontology) are, in reality, neither identical nor even parallel. The human incapacity [*L'impossibilité humaine*] for theology is not Aristotle's own discovery; Plato himself had suspected it in the first part of the *Parmenides*, by recovering [*retrouvant*] the profound sense of the old Greek wisdom of limits: one must not try to search, human that one is, to know that which is beyond the human. But, in Aristotle, the impossibility of a theology is not only encountered and recorded; it is progressively justified, and this justification of the impossibility of theology paradoxically becomes the substitute for theology itself. The impossibility of thinking God outside of movement leads to the theory of the unmoved First Mover. The impossibility of applying to God the human experience of thinking, that is to say the thought of another object, leads to the definition of God as Thought that thinks itself. More often, however, this impossibility is not counterbalanced, or rather is not concealed, under the form of apparently positive affirmations. It presents itself overtly through negations: God does not live in society,[3] he has no need of friends,[4] he is neither just nor courageous,[5] and, more generally, is not virtuous, since he is better than virtue.[6] Finally, by putting these negative litanies about divinity one after the next, we notice that by demonstrating both the inadequacy of human discourse – and, more generally, of human experience – for the perfections of God, and the impossibility for humanity to coincide with a principle from which it is separated by movement, we have filled an entire branch of knowledge, which can only be called theology. This, which we encounter for the first time in Aristotle, and from which a certain tradition will benefit, is only a theology paradoxically realizing itself by demonstrating its own impossibility, a first philosophy constituting itself by establishing the impossibility of climbing back up to the principle; the negation of theology becomes negative theology. And yet, this consequence, which the Neoplatonic tradition will only have to discover in the texts of Aristotle, is not expressly assumed by Aristotle himself. The negativity of theology is simply encountered in the mode of failure; Aristotle does not accept it as a realization of his project, which was incontestably to make a positive theology. In other words, this negativity conveys the limits of philosophy, not an unexpected overthrow of these limits. Aristotle does not yet take part in the negations in which his successors will delight. The negative discourse about God translates the powerlessness of human discourse and not the infinity of its object.

The same cannot be said for ontology. The failure of ontology manifests itself, not on one level, but two: on the one hand, there is no one λόγος about τὸ ὄν; on the other, since being as being is not a genus, it is not even the case that τὸ ὄν is one. If we can repeat about ontology what we said already of theology – namely, it exhausts itself, but at the same time realizes itself, in the demonstration of its own impossibility, and therefore the negation of ontology is confused with the establishment of a negative ontology – we can add here that this ontology is doubly negative: negative, first in its expression, yet also in its object. The negativity of ontology not only expresses the powerlessness of human discourse but also the negativity of its object. Here the consequence is that these two negatives, far from adding themselves together only to make ontology the shadow of a shadow, end up, on the contrary, counterbalancing themselves: the difficulty of human discourse about being becomes the most faithful discourse of the contingency of being. Being is no longer the inaccessible object that would be beyond our discourse; but it reveals itself in the very fumbling of our approaching it: being, at least this being of which we speak, is none other than the correlate of our difficulty. The failure of ontology becomes the ontology of contingency, that is to say of finitude and of failure. It is this reversal that may be recognized in the fact that the aporia is itself an approach: the infinite trampling of the question – "What is being?" – becomes the image most similar to a being that is never quite what it is and never ends up coinciding with itself. The absence of a path (πόρος) becomes a plurality of ways: the inability of human discourse to bring out the unique sense of the word "being" does not lead us to deny being all sense, but rather to let the irreducible plurality of categories arise where it unveils itself. One could say about the philosopher what Sophocles says about the human, that it is παντοπόρος ἄπορος,[7] a being so rich in resources that it is impoverished. But it would be necessary to add that the detours by which the philosopher approaches being are not as much attacks on its simplicity, as the exact expression of a great detour through which the simple is realized in its instability, that is by its moving away from itself.

But one could object that our commentary is here as alien to lived Aristotelianism as Neoplatonism is to what is effectively negative in Aristotelian theology. Does Aristotle, in the case of ontology, assume this transmutation of the failure in the adequate expression of being? It appears that the dual role played in Aristotelian philosophy by motion provides the beginning of an answer to this question. If motion is, for Aristotle at least as much for Plato, that which, by separating being from itself, introduces negativity into it, motion is also that through which being endeavors to regain [retrouver] its lost unity. The foundation of the scission is at the same time its corrective. Admittedly, it is better for a being not to have to move. But, if it is movable by nature, it is better that it moves than rests: the mobility of the animal is worth more than the lethargy of the plant, and the continuous movement of the celestial spheres is worth more than the movement, interrupted by stops, of the beings of the sublunary world. Motion is both what pulls beings furthest away from God and the only route that remains to draw nearer to God, so that, although God is defined above all by motionlessness, the beings incapable of rest are strangely those closest to God: "It is good to persuade oneself that the ancient traditions, and especially those of our fathers, are true, when they teach us that there is something immortal and divine in the things that are in motion."[8] The fact that Aristotle successively valorizes motion and immobility certainly betrays the convergence of two opposed traditions in his works. But Aristotle's original contribution is to establish a complex relation – whether one might call it from means to end, or again from imitation to model – between these two contradictories, motion and motionlessness. Certainly, the idea was not new, as Plato had already said, "time is the moving image of eternity."[9] With this he tried to express that the movements of the celestial spheres, of which time is the measure, imitate, through their regularity, the eternity of what is properly unchanging. But this relation remained accidental for Plato: it is because of its regularity that this movement imitates immobility, not because of its movement. More profoundly, Aristotle will show how from even within the humblest motion will be born the substitute for a motionlessness that is, at the same time, denied and replaced by its contradictory (since the end of motion is nothing other than its suppression). In the same way that one only works in order to stop working,[10] that one makes war in order to stop fighting,[11] in this way, too, one only moves in order to stop moving. But imagine a being that lives in a world where work, war, and more generally movement are natural, that is ineradicable [insupprimables]; thus the laborious effort we make to escape work, the bellicose effort to escape war, and the mobile effort to free us from movement will become the substitute for leisure, for peace, for impossible immobility. It will hence be by its infinity, and not only by its regularity, that movement will imitate motionlessness, that is will strive to raise itself to this level without ever reaching it; motion will tend toward it, if we are allowed this anachronistic metaphor, the way in which the convergent line indefinitely closes in on the asymptote.[12] All the movement of the world is merely an impotent effort, and yet it is always reborn through its striving to correct its mobility and to approach the divine.

If such a scheme is never expressly thematized by Aristotle, as it is by the Neoplatonists, it appears in too many passages for their convergence to be the result of chance. The same oscillation between depreciation and rehabilitation is found [se retrouve] in connection with time and contingency, each of which are linked to movement – the first because it is the measure, the second because it is the consequence. One often cites the text of the *Physics*, where time appears as the source of rupture, of scission.[13] But it needs to be compared with the passage from *Nicomachean Ethics*, where time is presented as "the benevolent auxiliary" of the mind and of human action.[14] Time is what keeps humans from being immortal, but it is also that through which humanity "immortalizes itself as much as it can."[15] In an equally celebrated passage from *On Generation and Corruption*, Aristotle also shows how not only the cycle of the seasons, but also the linear series of generations corrects the mortality of individuals through the permanence of species.[16] The infinity of time, rendering possible the indefinite return of the same, here makes up for the finitude of beings in time, as if the source of their finitude were at the same time the site of their salvation. The same ambiguity may be found [se retrouverait] in relation to contingency: how does the same philosopher who depreciates contingency as the degradation of necessity, who attributes to it the failures of Nature and the production of monsters, raise arguments, more affective than rigorous, against those who deny the contingency of the future? If there were no contingency, he says, "no longer would it be worthwhile to deliberate nor to make any effort";[17] yet humans deliberate and act, showing that they are a "principle of the future";[18] thus it is contingency and its implications, that is a suspension of the principle of contradiction, that must be accepted as the condition of the possibility of deliberation, of action, and of human labor. The negation of contingency leads to "the lazy argument"; conversely, it is the moral rejection of laziness (yet, of all human states, this one might most resemble the motionlessness of the divine) that provides Aristotle with the principle for a paradoxical rehabilitation of contingency,[19] which, rendering human activity possible, gives itself its own corrective.

Motion supplements, through its infinity, the finitude of moving beings: how does this remark, which seems to pertain to physics, to biology, even to anthropology, concern ontology, that is the discourse about being? Is not discourse foreign to the movement of which it speaks? Moreover, does it not immobilize motion by speaking it? Does it not redouble the finitude of its object with the impossibility of coinciding with it where it is? But here a remark intervenes that (apparently incidental in Aristotle's text) bears a decisive inflection, a remark with which Aristotelianism perhaps most opposes the philosophy of Plato, a remark which will permit the restoration of the possibility of a coherent discourse about being in motion: discourse itself is movement. To those who deny the existence of motion, such as the Eleatics, Aristotle retorts that to deny motion is still to attest to it, for even the negation of movement is movement: "Suppose there might be false opinion, or mere opinion, even if there is imagination, even if there is variable appearance, then motion exists; indeed, imagination and opinion seem to be some motions."[20] One might think that this remark aims at only imagination and opinion, which are unstable, while νοῦς, διάνοια, and ἐπιστήμη are always defined as a stop or a rest in motion.[21] But we have seen that, for Aristotle, rest was the contrary, and not the contradictory, of motion, and therefore had sense only within mobility in general. In the *De Anima*, after having affirmed the incompatibility of the soul and movement,[22] Aristotle nevertheless recognizes that the passions of the soul are motions;[23] yet we know that the thoughts, of which words are signs (σημεῖα), are presented in the *De Interpretatione* as so many "passions of the soul" (παθήματα τῆς ψυχῆς).[24] Finally, in *De Memoria*, Aristotle shows that memory is not one faculty among others, but instead permeates all intellectual activity, since the thought of a being who lives in time cannot itself be anything but a temporal thought; the soul cannot think without images:[25] if we recall here that imagination is essentially motion and that intellection is a rest in motion, we will realize that for the human, who is a being in time, self-stabilizing thought exercises itself only through images in motion. Human thought has escaped so barely from this temporal condition that not only is it in time, but it thinks in time; the timeless itself cannot be thought except through the schema of temporality, in the same way that the non-quantitative is thought through the quantitative,[26] and that, in a general way, what is beyond the categories, being immobile, cannot be approached except through the categories themselves (in a necessarily inadequate way).

But what is a source of inadequacy, when it concerns the thinking of the intelligible (that is, the immobile), is transmuted, when it concerns the thinking of being in motion, in a process that makes its very mobility adequate to the mobility of its object. Human thought is a thought in motion of a being in motion, an inaccurate seizure of the inaccurate, a search whose very distress is an image of the negativity of its object. It is because human thought is always separated from itself that it coincides with a being that never manages to coincide with itself. If there is no native familiarity between the soul and the intelligible, as was the case for Plato, this same distortion restores, through a detour, the familiarity of the soul with its effective object (which is not intelligible). The very obscurity of the soul to itself becomes more illuminating than clarity.

Only if all the affections of the soul (and, through them, the discourses that express them) pertain to motion, are there degrees in this dependence. Rest, although it belongs to the class of the movable, is evidently what, inside a being in motion, most repels motion itself. The stabilizing thought, that is science,[27] is obviously less capable, even though it only comprehends within motion, of fitting what is moving in movement itself. Science frees necessity (what cannot be otherwise) on a ground of contingency (what can be otherwise). But if contingency can never be entirely banished from its horizon, science is less attentive to the horizon itself than to the stable cores that it discovers therein. Thus it will be necessary to have recourse, not to this, but to another discipline of the soul in order to think, not this or that domain within the horizon, but the horizon itself. If, in the sublunary world, necessity arises from a ground of contingency, there is a thought more open, a discourse more general, than the thought and discourse of necessity, a thought to which belongs the thinking of the sublunary world as a horizon of the events that are produced therein (that is, as a contingent world). We have already encountered and described at length above this thought that is open to the indeterminate, this discourse that moves beyond all classes: it is what Aristotle names *dialectic*.

Although Aristotle does not ever clearly express himself regarding the relations of dialectic and motion – relations that, already present in Zeno's works,[28] become explicit again in the later history of dialectic – it is perhaps not without significance to note in Aristotle's attitude the same swaying over dialectic as over movement, time, and contingency. Devalued in relation to science, dialectic recovers [*retrouve*] in what seems to disqualify it – its excessive generality, its instability, its uncertainty – the opportunity to affirm an unexpected superiority. We will not dwell here on this duality of aspects, which we have described at length,[29] but it illustrates once again this reversal that, without ever being thought as such by Aristotle, structures his effective speculation at each instant, and in accordance with which finitude finds in itself not only the yearning for a salvation coming from the outside (as with the Platonists), but also the means of its own redemption. Humans are, in a sense, condemned to think dialectically because they lack the intuition of an origin from which they are irremediably separated and of a totality in which they are a fragment; but they find that the dialectical character of their approach here fits what is incomplete in being as being (which is itself only the index of an impossible unity). The dialectical method, Aristotle tells us, never allows us to seize the essence of anything;[30] but could it facilitate an intuition of essences in a world where we only encounter quasi-essences that, separated from themselves by movement, always with the power to be another thing, are never entirely what they are?

A remark in Book Z will let us specify and justify the fundamental role of dialectic in an ontology that is above all an ontology of finitude, that is of scission. Aristotle says that there are two kinds of beings: beings primary and in themselves, that is the immobile and simple beings, which are their own quiddity (since they are nothing other than essence and "essence is, according to us, quiddity");[31] but there is another kind of being, which are not only essences and which maintain, therefore, more complex relations with their quiddities than the first: such beings, says Aristotle, are not *immediately* (εὐθύς) their quiddity.[32] Hence what characterizes the quasi-essences of the sublunary world (as opposed to the simple and immutable essences) is that they are separated from themselves; but what first brings them together and allows them to be named as essences is that they can coincide with themselves, if not immediately, at least by a detour.[33] Thus the necessity of a *mediation* between something and itself that at once contrasts the unchanging essences and the sensible essences and, at the same time, allows these and those to be equal; only, what is an original unity in one case will be a derived unity in the other, what coincides with itself will only be restored, from the ground of the scission, by the implementation of laborious intermediates. We saw what these intermediaries are in the domain of theoretical knowledge: they are demonstration and dialectic. But it should be clarified here that demonstration (of which Aristotle repeatedly emphasizes the mediating function) is only, one might say, a mediation *for us*, which is required by the dispersion of our perspective, not by the dispersion of its object. No movement of demonstration has any other purpose than to show that the external relation between a subject and an apparently accidental predicate (for example, between Socrates and mortality) is in reality the deployment of the inner unity of an essence, the middle term (here, humanity). Contrarily, dialectic intervenes whenever one is unable to call the apparent dispersion to a real unity, therefore whenever the reality of the scission forces the search for unity into an endless movement. Unlike demonstration, dialectic thus does not lead us to the intuition of an essence that would subsequently render the search for mediation superfluous. It is not mediation towards an essence, but rather is the substitute of the essential unity where this unity is not found [*est introuvable*]; it is the mediation that does not stop mediating by its own movement; it is not an intermediary between a beginning and an end, in which it could rest, but rather the intermediary that gives itself to itself for its beginning and its end.[34] This explains how dialectic, although lower in value than demonstration and intuition, is nevertheless invoked in extreme cases – those where the demonstration and the intuition are defective. Such is the case, as we have seen, for the intuition of principles: such is the case, when it is about showing, between sensible being and its quiddity, a unity that is properly onto-logical, that is a unity that depends solely on the discourse we have concerning it, a discourse that would collapse without it. This might seem to contradict the function, which Aristotle assigns to intuition, of being the faculty of extremes, and the function, which he assigns to discourse, of being the faculty of intermediaries (μεταξύ).[35] Yet here, where intuition is lacking, it is necessary that discourse compensates for its silence; and here, where this silence keeps quiet before the beginning and the end, discourse will never stop trying to recover a foundation that escapes it. The more extreme the object of speech is, the greater the detour will be. Thus not just anything, but, because it is the faculty of intermediaries, only dialectic can supplement the silence before the extremes. The failure of intuition is the reality of the dialectic.

Dialectical mediation seems therefore to have no other purpose than itself; the question – *What is being?* – is still raised, and the dialogue of the philosophers over it will have no end. But one might then ask whence comes the impulse that prevents this research and indefinite dialogue from constantly spoiling in its failure. A detour is a detour and not an endless drift [*une derive sans fin*], only if it is the condition for a return. Dialectic has sense only if it aims at its own suppression, that is at intuition, even if this intuition is always in the future [*jamais future*]. Mediation has sense only if it aims at a rediscovered immediacy [*une immédiateté retrouvée*], in the same way that movement is expended toward rest, or rather, since rest remains always restless, toward the Prime Mover. It is a paradoxical relation, according to which the inferior term is both the negation and the realization – on a humbler level – of the superior term, and which Aristotle, as we have seen, designated under the name *imitation*. Sublunary nature imitates the subsistent nature of celestial Bodies in the same way that the circular motion of the First Heavens imitates the motionlessness of the Prime Mover.[36] The cycle of seasons imitates the movement of the celestial spheres. The circular generation of living beings imitates the eternal return of the seasons. Finally, in the highest degrees of the series, "art imitates nature,"[37] and human poetic speech is an "imitation" of their actions.[38] The last two formulas, which often have been superficially interpreted in the sense of a realist aesthetics (according to which art is merely a doubling of reality), take a far deeper sense if returned to the general framework of Aristotelian metaphysics. Then it will become clear that nothing prevents the work of art or the technical object from resembling its model as little as corruptible beings resemble the incorruptible beings that they nevertheless "imitate." Aristotelian imitation is not a descending relation from model to copy, as it is in Platonic imitation, but an ascending relation through which the inferior being strives to achieve, with the available means, a bit of the perfection it sees in the superior term, a perfection that the superior could not make descend to the inferior. Platonic imitation required the Demiurge's power. Contrarily, Aristotelian imitation supposes a certain impotence on the part of the model, since it is this impotence for which it compensates. When Aristotle affirms "art imitates nature," it is wrong to focus on just one of the terms of this phrase, for he also says that art "completes what nature could not carry out."[39] If what we have said is accurate, these two phrases do not oppose, but complement each other. To imitate nature is not to double it superfluously, but rather to supplement its shortcomings,[40] to complete itself – not even to humanize, but simply to naturalize. To imitate nature is to render nature more natural, that is to strive to close the scission that separates it from itself, from its own essence or idea. In clearer terms, it is to use contingency[41] against itself to regulate it, to ensure that the nature of the sublunary world imitates, despite its contingency, the order that reigns in Heaven. When Aristotle wonders what could happen "if shuttles were to weave themselves,"[42] he expresses the unattainable idea[43] of human art: to ensure that the tool or the machine reproduces the spontaneity of living, and more profoundly, the circularity of the celestial movements, themselves an image of the motionlessness of the divine. The ideal technique for Aristotle, an ideal that he knows is unattainable, but which is still to be used as a regulative principle of research and of incomplete actions, is, in the strictest sense of the term, that of *automatism*: not because he sees in it, at first, a means of mitigating mankind's grief,[44] but because the act of self-motion is, by its circularity (which renders superfluous any distinct mover of the movable), the highest imitation of the unmoved motion of God.

The example of human art, which is only a particular case of movement in the sublunary world (one of reflective and voluntary movement), illustrates the paradox of an imitation that only imitates motionlessness through movement, and necessity through contingency.[45] There is imitation, however, because there is – in art and in nature, in the sublunary world and in the celestial world, in the celestial world and for God – an identity of the end, which is the Good. It is the Good to which human work and action aims, like the movements of a nature that does nothing in vain. But this identity of the end does not explain what appears at first sight as a diversity of means. In reality, it is not a matter of the different means that will be used on both sides, as if motionlessness was a means in the same way as movement. The truth is that there is, on one side, a use of means (movement), and, on the other side, the immediacy of the end and the means: even though movement has no other end than its own suppression (thereby betraying its merely instrumental function), motionlessness is itself its own end. What therefore separates the imitator from the imitated is not the diversity of more or less complex means used to attain a certain end, but the need for a mediation on one side and the absence of mediation on the other. Thus the remark according to which we make use of means only to do without them acquires its full sense; for it is precisely what is Good that can do without mediation. In effect, Aristotle borrows from Plato this idea that the Good is defined by its sufficiency, by the fact that it lacks nothing in being what it is, that it is "autarchic."[46] Some will then object that this definition of the Good only makes more problematic its imitation by a world in which evil appears as a consequence of motion:[47] how can contingency, the power-not-to-be, imitate the subsisting perfection of God, who, lacking nothing, is entirely what he can be, and cannot be other than he is? In particular, how can humans – as inhabitants of the sublunary world, that is as not being self-sufficient, as having need of the force of movement – how can they thus imitate the autarchic motionlessness of God? We henceforth know the answer: this imitation is only paradoxical because it goes through a detour: motion, the site of all cosmological and human mediations. The world and humanity indirectly realize [*réalisent médiatement*] what is immediately in God, because humanity and the world have need of means to coincide with their end, a coincidence that is immediately realized in God. But mediation has no other sense and no other reason to be except to restore, through a detour, the immediacy that it is not.[48]

Imitation, as Aristotle intends it, pertains more to πρᾶξις than to ποίησις; it does not lead to works that would be so many "imitations" (μιμήματα) of a model. Rather it exhausts itself in its very movement, as if the failure of its aim became here, too, its own reality. Imitation then appears less like the realization of a copy than like a degraded image of the subsisting act of the model. It is perhaps one of Aristotle's most constant intuitions: to see the movements of the world and the restlessness of humans as so many stopgaps, as so many substitutes, compared to the autarchic unity of the divine. During our analysis we have given many examples of this substitutive function that Aristotle assigns more or less consciously to many experiences in the sublunary world: frequency (ὡς ἐπὶ τὸ πολύ) is the substitute for necessity, circular generation the substitute for eternity, dialectic the substitute for intuition, human art the substitute for a faulty nature, the worried activity of humans the substitute for an act that has no need to be active in order to be what it is. We can now add: mediation is the substitute for unity.

Humanity now appears as the privileged agent of this immense effort of substitution, by which the sublunary world compensates, by imitating, for the failures of a God who could not descend to it, but who at least offers it the spectacle of his own perfection. An agent among others, certainly, for humanity only extends a movement of substitution that animates both the revolution of the celestial spheres as well as the shivering of the humblest of plant and animals. Yet it is the privileged agent, for, with humanity, the substitution becomes conscious: all beings are moved by an aspiration for the divine, whose perfection they imitate; but it is only for humanity that this imitation becomes imitation of a spectacle. Only humanity can access the thought of unity, because we see a highest realization – which itself is still an imitation – in the immutable movement of the celestial spheres. Only humanity knows, even from afar, a bit of what it imitates. It is only through humanity that the obscure motion of the transcendent becomes the ideal of research, of work, and of action. Humanity, living among so many others in the sublunary world, thus becomes the most active substitute of the divine within this world. We have already mentioned this conversion of the divine into the earthly whereby Aristotle – increasingly conscious of what remains distant in the theology of a transcendent God – finally recovers [retrouve], in the humblest movements of beings in the sublunary world, something of the divinity he had, until then, sought in heaven. Εἶναι χαὶ ἐνταῦθα θεούς: there are also gods here below, he observes, taking up the phrase of Heraclitus.[49] A reflection that would go against the most constant dogma of astral theology, that of the separation of the earthly and the divine, if it could not be interpreted thus: what is divine in the sublunary world is perhaps the effort of this world to equate itself to a God (with whom the world is not equal), so that it would not be a received or participated divinity, but rather a vicarious or substitutive one.

Perhaps it is also a conversion of the same order that is hidden in the apparent permanence of statements according to which the human is a mortal god,[50] or contains something of divinity (which is essentially the intellect).[51] In the Protrepticus, where these affirmations are encountered for the first time in Aristotle, they are easily interpreted with reference to astral theology: humans are beings who by their soul (increasingly Aristotle says: by their intellect) participate in the divine since soul or intellect is only a scrap of fire or of sidereal ether.[52] But if the divinity of νοῦς, which implies its extrinsic origin, will be maintained by Aristotle to the end, the allusions to the divinity of humanity seem to become increasingly conventional, as Aristotle turns away from, without repudiating, a too distant theology. At the same time, it is true that the traditional formulation takes on a new sense: what is divine in humanity is no longer what remains in it from its divine origin, but perhaps is, on the contrary, the effort of humanity to recapture its lost origin, to equate itself and to equate the world in which it lives with the immutable splendor of heaven, to introduce to the sublunary world a bit of this unity that God could not or would not put [*faire pénétrer*] into it, but of which he at least gives us the spectacle. The divinity of humanity is no longer the melancholic evocation of an immemorial past during which humans would have lived in the familiarity of the gods,[53] but it is the always open future of humanity, which is to imitate God, that is to substitute for him "as much as possible"[54] by completing itself and by completing the world towards the Idea (εἶδος) of what they are, and what, yet, they never are completely. The divinity of humanity is less the degradation of the divine in the human than the infinite approximation of the divine by humanity. Such an effort of substitution, which takes over, in the sublunary world, for the defective intentions or impotence of God, is ultimately nothing other than the vocation of humanity, who were born "to understand and to act."[55] It is not by rising above themselves but by completing what they are that humans are "immortalized." The divinity of humanity is nothing other than the movement through which always incomplete humans "humanize themselves,"[56] reach or attempt to reach their own quiddity, from which they are (like all beings in the sublunary world) at every instant separated.

Throughout this work in the domain of knowledge we have followed this effort of humanity to overcome the scission, to achieve unity within itself and outside of itself in imitation of the subsistent simplicity of the divine. We tried to show, in turn, how the search for unity was required as the most original need of our language, how the spectacle of unity and thereby the ideal of research were supplied by astral contemplation, how the fundamental obstacle to unity was discovered in motion (the source of every scission), and finally how this motion was its own corrective (since the infinite mediation toward unity became the substitute for unity itself). Applying then the conclusion of this study to its beginning, we discovered that Aristotle's ontology, as a discourse that strives to reach being in its unity, found in the failed structure of its own approach the result that this approach could not supply to it: the search for philosophy, otherwise called *dialectic*, became the philosophy of the search. The search for unity holds the place of unity itself; ontology, which took theology as a model, bit by bit became the sublunary substitute for an impossible theology.

But dialectic, which is the theoretical aspect of mediation, is not the only aspect, for the philosophy of Aristotle is not only a theoretical philosophy. It does not forget that it is also a practical and poetic philosophy, showing thereby that knowledge (or the search for knowledge) does not constitute the only way humanity relates to being. The two other aspects of human existence, which a total philosophy ought also to consider, Aristotle named πρᾶξις (by which he designates the immanent action, principally moral) and ποίησις (that is, productive action, work). A complete investigation into the Aristotelian philosophy of being should therefore include an elucidation and an ontological evaluation of moral action and of work. It would have to show how moral action imitates, through the detour of virtue and of the relation with the other, what, in God, is an immediacy of intention and of act (otherwise called *autarchy*), and how, subsequently, virtuous or friendly mediation realizes, through "the relation to an other," a Good, which in God is a coincidence of self with itself.[57] It would also have to demonstrate how work (which imitates and completes nature) substitutes for the incoherence of the world a bit of the unity whose spectacle it draws from the regularity of Heaven, and how, subsequently, work – by naturalizing nature (that is, by rendering [*rendant*] it almost necessary) and by humanizing humanity (that is, by returning [*rendant*] to it a contemplative vocation) – is for Aristotle also a corrective of the scission, an infinite approximation of leisure, of peace, and of unity. An ontological elucidation of the anthropology of Aristotle would, in a general way, show how the indefiniteness [*l'aoriste*] of human activity imitates the perfection of the divine act, how the accomplishments to be achieved by humans imitates the accomplishment always already achieved by God. While even the most systematized tradition studied separately Aristotle's theoretical, practical, and poetic philosophy, it is necessary here again to make manifest the structural unity of his effective philosophical speculation. Such an elucidation of Aristotelian anthropology, which should be done,[58] would complete the demonstration of how (if not by Aristotle's design, then at least in the reality of his approach) the four aspects of his philosophy (which is only of being and of God because it is of the world and of humanity) are arranged, how an ontology of the scission finds its justification through a physics of motion, and how this ontology, by imitating a theology of transcendence, degrades it but also completes it in an anthropology of mediation. We would then complete the recognition that the metaphysics of Aristotle is only an incomplete metaphysics because it is a metaphysics of incompleteness, and because it is, subsequently, the first metaphysics of humanity, not only insofar as it would not be what it is if the human were a beast or a God,[59] but also because the incompleteness of being uncovers itself through metaphysics as the birth of humanity.

One will ask, it is true, why the tradition has underestimated the aporetic aspects of Aristotle's metaphysics and their human implications. It thus remains to be shown, through a study no less philosophical than historical, how and why the tradition was necessarily bound to be tempted to ignore what was eternally incomplete in Aristotelian metaphysics. The tradition transmits, extends, and thereby, completes; the tradition is what takes over from a beginning and thereby removes what had been begun in it; the tradition is "surprised" no longer; the tradition resolves the aporia even though the aporia is always lived as nascent; the tradition, through commentating, unifies what it believes to be the *membra disjecta* of interrupted work; it orders the fragments without wondering whether these fragments do not tend precisely to show that their object involved no order.[60] In the presence of the failure of the Aristotelian double project of a human theology and a science of being as being, the tradition had the choice between two paths that it followed in turns. The easiest, which was not historically the first, was to deny the failure by attributing it to accidental circumstances, to fill in the lacunae, to unify the dispersion, to compensate for the silences with a commentary all the more abundant when they commented upon a word that was silent. Put simply, such was the way of interpretation of the Arab and Christian commentators of the Middle Ages. It had, it is true, a justification that was not one of ease. Since it had heard another Word [Parole], the silences of Aristotle appeared to it more welcoming to this Word than the competing word of Plato; it was easier to Christianize (or Islamize) an Aristotle who remained below the religious option, than it was to philosophize in terms of a Platonism that was another religion. Sine Thoma mutus esset Aristoteles: the commentary of Saint Thomas will remain for centuries the substitute for the word, at once exemplary and deficient, of Aristotle. This is not to diminish the grandeur and historical importance of Thomism, which, appealing to its Aristotelianism, had an answer to everything, even the effective silences of Aristotle.[61]

The second route was Neoplatonic. It consists in hearing the silence, in collecting the negations, in systematizing not the answers but the difficulties. It consists in recognizing the failure, but to see in it only a ruse, if not of the philosopher himself, then at least of his object. With Neoplatonism the scission went on to become the ironic manifestation of unity, negation the most adequate expression of the ineffable, the impossibility of the intellectual intuition of the condition of a highest apprehension. Everything that for Aristotle fell short of being went on to find itself transmuted in the beyond. As if poverty were the subtlest of riches, the indeterminacy of being as being went on to become the infinite creative power of the One, and the indefinite mediation of humanity towards the One became that by which the One mediates itself for us. Ultimately, such an interpretation was no less systematizing than the preceding one, since it systematized the non-systematic itself. It completed, in its fashion, the incomplete, not by simple extrapolation, but by taking on incompletion itself.

These overly schematic considerations, which should be confirmed by a methodical study of the tradition, have here no other purpose than to suggest why the Aristotle of the tradition is who he is, and why Aristotle as he was is not the Aristotle of the tradition. If it is true, as modern exegesis has increasingly recognized and as we have tried to justify, that the metaphysics of Aristotle is dialectical, that is aporetic, then one will agree that there are two ways to consider the aporia: either in what it calls for or names, that is its solution; or in itself, which is only an aporia insofar as it is not resolved. To resolve the aporia, in the sense of "giving it a solution," is to destroy it; but to resolve the aporia, in the sense of "working towards its solution," is to fulfill it. We believe we have shown that the aporiai of Aristotle's metaphysics had no essential solution, in the sense that they were not resolved anywhere in the

universe of essences; yet, since they do not have a solution, it is always necessary to seek [*cherche*] to resolve them, and this search [*recherche*] for a solution
is, finally, the solution itself. To seek unity is to have already found [*trouvée*]
it. To work to resolve the aporia is to discover it.[62] To never to cease searching
for what it is to be is to have already responded to the question: What is being?
It does not belong to the tradition, whatever that might be, to recapture this
beginning that always begins, this scission that always separates, and this hope
that always returns. To transmit openness is to close it: Aristotle, as the history
of the immediate aftermath of Aristotelianism evidences, was less the founder
of a tradition than the initiator of a question, of which he warned us himself
that it always remained initial, and that the science which poses it was eternally "searching" [*recherchée*]. We cannot extend Aristotle, we can only repeat
him, that is to begin him again. Still, this repetition will never regain [*retrou-
vera*] the irreplaceable naivety of its true beginning. We today know too well
that, since we do not find what we seek, the philosopher finds, in this very
search, what was not sought. Yet this is not a modern thought, but the eternally
archaic sentence of a wisdom that Aristotle already judged to be obscure:[63] Ἐὰν
μὴ ἔλπηται, ἀνέλπιστον οὐκ ἐξευρήσει, ἀνεξερεύνητον ἐὸν καὶ ἄπορον. "If one does
not hope, one will not find [*trouvera*] the unhoped-for, which cannot be found
[*introuvable*] and is aporetic."[64]

NOTES

[This essay was originally published as "La Science Retrouvée," the concluding
chapter of of Pierre Aubenque's *Le Problème de l'Être chez Aristote: Essai sur la
Problématique Aristotélicienne*, 6th edn (Paris: Presses Universitaires de France,
[1962] 2013), pp. 485–507. – eds.]

1. Heraclitus, DK 22 A 9, cited at *Parts of Animals*, I.5 645a21. ["For there
   were gods there too." – trans.]
2. [that is, of *Le Problème de l'Être chez Aristote*. – eds.]
3. *Politics* I.2 1253a27.
4. *Eudemian Ethics* VII.12 1245b14.
5. *Nicomachean Ethics* X.8 1178b9ff.
6. *Nicomachean Ethics* VII.1 1145a26; *Magna Moralia* II.5 1200b14.
7. *Antigone*, v. 360.
8. *De Caelo* II.1 284a2.
9. *Timeaus*, 37d.
10. *Nicomachean Ethics* X.7 1177b4.
11. Ibid. 1177b5, 9ff.
12. Cf. *Politics* I.6 1255b2: Nature tends (βούλεται) toward uniformity, but it
    is powerless (οὐ δύναται) to reach it.
13. Ἡ δὲ κίνησις ἐξίστησι τὸ ὑπάρχον (*Physics* IV.12 221b3). Cf. *De Caelo* II.3
    286a19; *Physics* IV.13 222b13; *De Anima* I.3 406b13.

14. *Nicomachean Ethics* I.7 1098a24.
15. *Nicomachean Ethics* X.7 1177b33. Plato had already said, "mortal nature seeks, to the extent that it is possible, to exist always and to be immortal" (*Symposium* 207d). But what Aristotle adds, and what is decisive, is the demonstration throughout *Nicomachean Ethics* that it is by time and in time, and not by slipping from time, that mortal beings evade the destructive effects of temporality.
16. *On Generation and Corruption* II.10 336b25–34. Cf. *Metaphysics* Λ.6 1072a7–18; *De Anima* II.4 415a25–b7; *Economics* I.3 1343b23; *The Generation of Animals* II.1 731b31. Plato already saw in fertility the substitute for immortality (*Symposium* 206c, 207a–d). The idea will be taken up by Plotinus (*Enneads* III.5.1).
17. *De Interpretatione* 9 18b31.
18. Ἀρχὴ τῶν ἐσομένων (ibid. 19a7).
19. One cannot think that Aristotle could have seen here an argument in favor of the *existence* of contingency. But it had been proven by other means in the analyses of the *Physics* on motion. Note that *De Interpretatione* is generally considered one of Aristotle's last writings.
20. Ἡ γὰρ φαντασία καὶ ἡ δόξα κινήσεις τινὲς εἶναι δοκοῦσιν (*Physics* VIII.3 254a29). Cf. *De Anima* III.3 428b11. One rightly sees in this argument's structure one possible source of the *cogito*. Cf. P.-M. Schuhl, "Is there an Aristotelian source for the '*cogito*'?" *Revue philosophique de la France et de l'Etranger*, 138 (1948), pp. 191–4. This type of argument is not, moreover, isolated in Aristotle's work: probably of a sophistic origin, it forms the ἔλεγχος in the strict sense. Another example of ἔλεγχος is supplied by the argumentation of *Metaphysics* Γ against those who deny the principle of contradiction (to deny the principle of contradiction is still to attest to it). Cf. [*Le Problème de l'Être chez Aristote,*] Part I, Chapter II, §1.
21. *De Anima* I.3 407a32; III.2 434a16; *Physics* VIII.3 247b10, 248a 6–9.
22. Aristotle demonstrates this at length, against the Platonic theory of the self-moving soul, in *De Anima* I.3 (especially 406a2).
23. *De Anima* I.4 408a34ff. *Thought* (διανοεῖσθαι) is named, just as sadness, joy, or anger are, at lines 408b6 and 14. Such movements, says Aristotle, are only said to be of the soul "by accident" (408a30), since the *essence* of the soul is repugnant to movement (406a2): this confirms motion is linked to the corporeal; but since souls *in the sublunary world* are forms *of bodies*, Aristotle is very close to recognizing that motion is (in fact, if not in law) linked to the life of the soul, which, besides, knows to use motion in the attempt to find, through it, rest.
24. *De Interpretatione* 1 16a2ff.
25. *De Memoria* 1 449b31. Cf. *De Anima* III.3 427b14–16, 7 431a16, 8 432a7–14.
26. *De Memoria* 1 449b30–450a9.
27. Cf. [*Le Problème de l'Être chez Aristote,*] Part I, Chapter II, §4.

28. Zeno's arguments that motion cannot exist are, in effect, extraneous to Aristotle's assertion that Zeno would be "the inventor of dialectic" ([Valentine] Rose, [*Aristotelis qui Ferebantur Librorum Fragmenta* (*The Fragments of Aristotle*), 3rd edn,] fragment 65).

29. Cf. [*Le Problème de l'Être chez Aristote*,] Part I, Chapter 3, §3.

30. *Sophistical Refutations* 11 172a15.

31. *Metaphysics* Z.6 1032a5, 1031b39.

32. *Metaphysics* Z.6 1031b31.

33. The expression εὐθεῖα γραμμή designates the straight line as opposed to the circle (*Physics* VII 248a13, 20, b5). Εὐθύς is also used to name straight movement as opposed to circular movement (ibid. VII 248a20, VIII 261b29, 262a12–263a3, etc.).

34. The idea of mediation responds to one of the old torments of Greek conscience: "Men die, said Alcmaeon, because they cannot join the beginning to the end" (Diels, fr. 2: *Problems*, XVII.3 916a33).

35. Καὶ ὁ νοῦς τῶν ἐσχάτων ἐπ ἀμφότερα· καὶ γὰρ τῶν πρώτων ὅρων καὶ τῶν ἐσχάτων νοῦς ἐστι καὶ οὐ λόγος (*Nicomachean Ethics* VI.12 1143a35ff.).

36. The general principle of this imitation is formulated in *Metaphysics* Θ.8 1050b28: "Incorruptible beings are imitated by the beings that are perpetually changing."

37. *Physics* II.2 194a21, 8 199a15. Cf. *Meterology* IV.3 381b6. This thesis is affirmed in the *Protrepticus* (fr. 11 W[alzer, *Aristotelis Dialogorum Fragmenta*]: Iamblichus, IX, 49, 3ff.) against Plato, who had argued in Book X of the *Laws* that nature imitates the finality of art (888e ff., esp. 892b; cf. *Sophist* 265b–266e).

38. *Poetics* 1 1447a16ff., etc.

39. Ὅλως τε ἡ τέχνη τὰ μὲν ἐπιτελεῖ ἃ ἡ φύσις ἀδυνατεῖ ἀπεργάσασθαι, τὰ δὲ μιμεῖται (*Physics* II.8 199a15–17).

40. Cf. *Protrepicus* fr. 11–13 W: the role of art is of ἀναπληροῦν τὰ παραλειπόμενα τῆς φύσεως.

41. Art relates only to the contingent (*Nicomachean Ethics* VI.4).

42. *Politics* I.4 1253b33–1254a1.

43. Too many overlook that the verbs in this sentence are *unreal*.

44. The tools' automatic movement would obviate the master–slave relationship (1254a1). Yet Aristotle speaks of this relationship with the same objectivity he would have for any natural relationship, of which this only a particular case.

45. This paradox was developed brilliantly by Plotinus in the second tract of the first Ennead (*Of Virtues*), where he strives precisely to reconcile the assertion of Plato (*Theaetetus* 176a) that virtue makes humans like God with that of Aristotle (esp. *Nicomachean Ethics* X.8 1178b10ff.), according to which God is not righteous. Plotinus responds that indeed "we become like God through our virtues, although God has no virtues . . . We partake of the order of the intelligible world, the proportion and the harmony, which here below constitute virtue; but intelligible beings

have no need of this harmony, of this order and this proportion, and virtue is not useful for them; nevertheless, it is by the presence of virtue that we are made similar to them" (I.2.1). Plotinus explains there are "two kinds of similarity": one that "requires an identical item in similar beings" and is reciprocal; and one that, uniting the inferior to the superior, the derivative to the original, is only established in difference, and will never achieve reciprocity (I.2.2). In this sense one may say the multiple *imitates* the One, movement motionlessness, disorder order, word silence, friendship loneliness, war peace, discursive thought the Thought that thinks itself, which imitates, in its turn, the Absence of thought, and so on.

46. *Nicomachean Ethics* I.5 1097b8. Cf. *Philebus* 20d, where the Good was said, in the same sense, ἱκανόν.

47. *Metaphysics* Θ.9 1051a17–21 ("Evil is, from its nature, posterior to the potential"; therefore it does not exist independently from sensible things and is foreign to the first and eternal realities).

48. We have endeavored to illustrate this point with an example: that of *friendship*. God, being autarchic, does not need friends. But the worst way for humans to imitate God would be to pretend to do away with friends. Alone with themselves they would spend their time contemplating themselves, which in humans would not be a perfection but a state bordering on animal stupor (ἀναίσθητος, *Magna Moralia* II.15 1213a5). The only way for humans to imitate God, who has no friends, is to have friends, who by their community supplement humanity's finitude: the friendly mediation imitates, by a detour, the divine autarchy. Cf. Pierre Aubenque, "L'amitié chez Aristotle," in *Actes du VIIIᵉ Congrès de Sociétés de philos. de langue française* (Toulouse, 1956), pp. 251–4 (reproduced in *La Prudence chez Aristote*, Paris: Presses Universitaires de France, 1963, pp. 179–83).

49. *Parts of Animals* I.5 645a21.

50. Cf. fr. 61 Rose (Cicero, *De Finibus*, II.13.40: "*Sic hominem. . . , ut ait Aristoteles, . . . quasi mortalem deum*"), and, in a more attenuated and even problematic form, *Parts of Animals* II.10 656a6; *Nicomachean Ethics* VII.1 1145a24, 27, X.7 1177b27, 30. It is here, moreoever, a traditional formulation. Cf. Xenophon *Memorabilia* I 4 (ὥσπερ θεοὶ βιοτεύοντες).

51. Fr. 61 Rose, 1.8, where Aristotle cites either Hermotimus or Anaxagoras: ὁ νοῦς γὰρ ἡμῶν ὁ θεός (cf. *Nicomachean Ethics* X.7 1177b29). Yet "humanity *is* its intellect": about this formula, of Platonic origin (cf. *Laws* XII 959ab), and which often appears in *Nicomachean Ethics*, esp. X.7 1178a2–3, 7, IX.8 1168b31–3, cf. René-Antoine Gauthier, *La Morale d'Aristote* (Paris: Presses Universitaires de France, 1985), pp. 43–5.

52. Cf. [*Le Problème de l'Être chez Aristote,*] Part II, Chapter I, §2. On the link between astral theology and the theme of the soul's divinity, cf. Louis Rougher, *La Religion Astrale des Pythagoriciens* (Paris: Presses Universitaires de France, 1959), Chapter IV.

53. Καὶ οἱ μὲν παλαιοί, κρείττονες ἡμῶν καὶ ἐγγυτέρω θεῶν οἰκοῦντες . . . (*Philebus* 16c).

54. *Nicomachean Ethics* X.7 1177b32. On the meaning of this reservation, see our study, *La Prudence chez Aristotle*, pp. 171ff.

55. Rose, Fr. 61 (Cicero, *De Finibus*, II.13.40: *Hominem ad duas res, ut ait Aristoteles, ad intelligendum et ad agendum esse natum*).

56. If it could coincide with its νοῦς, humanity would not be beyond itself, but would be itself (*Nicomachean Ethics* X.7 1178a2, 7; cf. our commentary on these texts, Introduction, Chapter II, pp. 58ff.). And yet it would be "divine" in this, if it is true that, according to the teaching of astral theology, its essence is divine. It is necessary to reverse the formulation of Ollé-Laprune: "It is precisely the peculiar character of humanity to be completely itself only by rising above itself" (*La Morale d'Aristote*, p. 50). This is because it is usually from below itself [*en deçà de soi-même*] that humanity "becomes divine" by becoming what it is, that is a being of contemplation and leisure. On the use of the verb ἀνθρωπεύεσθαι, cf. *Nicomachean Ethics* X.9 1178b7.

57. The text that seems to us to be essential is *Eudemian Ethics* VII.12 1245b19–19: Ἡμῖν μὲν τὸ εὖ καθ᾽ ἕτερον, ἐχείνῳ δὲ (= τῷ θεῷ) αὐτὸς αὑτοῦ τὸ εὖ ἐστιν. We have commented on this text in our other work, already cited, *L'amité chez Aristote*, p. 253. This is no longer simple coincidence if Aristotle's political ideal is an ideal of *autarchy*. Wary of mediation, for fear that it lives its own life and that the means might become an end, Aristotle wants to limit it as much as possible: hence his condemnation of getting rich [*la chrématistique*], where money, means that it is, becomes "the starting point and the end of exchange," στοιχεῖον καὶ πέρας τῆς ἀλλαγῆς, *Politics* I.9 1257b22. But if the human were perfectly autarchic, there would be no need for cities (*Politics* I 2 1253a28; cf. *Nicomachean Ethics* V.8 1133a27). The relative autarchy of the city is therefore only an imitation, through the detour of a limited and controlled exchange, of the divine autarchy. (Cf. *Politics* I.2 1253a1: ἡ δ᾽ αὐτάρκεια τέλος καὶ βέλτιστον. On the "autarchic" ideal in Greek thinking in general, cf. A. J. Festugière, "Autarcie et communauté dans la Grèce antique," in *Communauté et Bien Commun*, ed. François Perroux [Paris: Librairie de Médicis, 1944] and reprinted in *Liberté et Civilization chez les Grecs*, pp. 109–26.)

58. We tried to propose this particular problem's outlines in our study, *La Prudence chez Aristote*.

59. *Politics* I.2 1253a29; cf. 1253a3–4.

60. Of course it is not here a matter of Aristotle's intention (for this intention was, without any doubt, an intention to order), but the *sense* conveyed of the aporetic *structure* of the Aristotelian *Metaphysics*. Such structure will never be assumed by Aristotle, as it will be later by Pascal (fr. 373, "I would give too much honor to my subject if I treated it with order since I wish to show that it is incapable of this").

61. We are only talking here about the *Aristotelianism* of Saint Thomas and not of his "Thomism." Doubtless the philosophy of Saint Thomas also has its aporetic aspects: the question, *Quid est Deus?*, that already tormented the young oblate of Monte Cassino perhaps does not involve a response more

univocal than the τί τὸ ὄν; of Aristotle. However, this is not our problem. What we aim at here is the use Saint Thomas made of Aristotelianism as a complete system. And, certainly, it was quite necessary that it be so: Saint Thomas sought in Aristotelianism an *instrument*, he could not linger on it without losing it, hence it was necessary for him to close Aristotelianism in order to overtake it. Unfortunately, as regards Aristotle, the tradition has retained more of this closure than this overtaking. Whatever the wisdom of his commentaries, which, in detail, often accede to the difficulties of Aristotelianism (cf., for example, some of the texts cited in [*Le Problème de l'Être chez Aristote,*] n. 4 on p. 242), the fact remains that Saint Thomas has contributed much to substantiate the legend of Aristotle "master of those who know" [cf. Dante's *Divine Comedy*, Inferno IV – trans.], completion of a philosophy which the author of the *Summa Theologica* nevertheless had good reasons to know was fundamentally incomplete. On the fundamental "incompleteness" of the philosophy of Aristotle in regard to Christian thought, cf. the remarks of A. Forest, *La Structure Métaphysique du Concert selon saint Thomas d'Aquin*, p. 315ff.

62. This is the sense which we give to the formulation from *Nicomachean Ethics* VII.4 1146b7: Ἡ γὰρ λύσις τῆς ἀπορίας εὕρεσίς ἐστιν, where λύσις, which is taken on the same level as εὕρεσις, designates the *act* of resolution and not the solution itself.

63. *Rhetoric*, III.5 1407b14.

64. Heraclitus, fr. 18 Diels.

CHAPTER 8

Aristotle's Organism, and Ours

Emanuela Bianchi

How does an entity come to be? The production of artifacts is of course easily explained through the technical human capacity for identifying (and indeed – under capitalism – generating) needs and wants, and designing and manufacturing solutions from cooking vessels to drone weapons. But, despite the advances of systems chemistry, molecular biology, and both ecological and developmental biology, the coming to be or ontogenesis of natural entities remains fundamentally mysterious, both in the sense of the original emergence of living order from its physico-chemical environment, and in the sense of the development of an individual organism from germ cell to adult form. Arguably, it is this latter mystery that is Aristotle's own central problematic (Aristotle's universe is one that maintains itself in perpetuity and therefore questions of cosmic origins and the origin of life do not concern him). This ontogenesis has at least two registers: the metaphysical and the biological – the coming to be of beings qua their being, or the question of how a thing emerges where there was no thing before, on the one hand, and the specific biological mechanisms involved in natural coming to be, on the other. While Aristotle's metaphysics of becoming has perhaps its most programmatic account in the first books of the *Physics*, called by Heidegger the "hidden, and therefore never adequately studied, foundational book of Western philosophy,"[1] the specific mechanisms of natural becoming, at least in the animal kingdom, are covered in *Generation of Animals*.

Technical metaphors of course abound in Aristotle's accounts of coming-to-be: we are all familiar with the bronze sphere or the statue as the paradigmatic hylomorph, the composite of matter and form as essential causes of an entity, the τόδε τι or "this something" that is the central deictic object of Aristotle's ontological investigations.[2] To round out the roster of four essential causes, we might add the moving cause or ἀρχὴ κινήσεως, which is the craftsman himself, and the final cause or "that for the sake of which," the purpose which the object will serve, for which it is made. Nonetheless the primary problem, the wondrous mystery that all this is marshaled to explain, is the natural organism, and it is this that forms the central locus of Aristotle's investigations, and in which the metaphor of technical production plays a pivotal part. The organism – unified, integrated, and complete, an uncreated functional totality of parts and whole – is the very subject and substance of Aristotelian inquiry. As is well known, Aristotle spends the central books of the *Metaphysics* wrestling with how to conceive of such a substance. For, if this substance is a composite of matter and form, the question arises – what is the ground of its unity? How can it be unified or thought of as a unity? Aristotle first examines form, then matter, as possible candidates for the primary substance that would underlie the whole, and finally rejects each in turn, reasserting the irreducibility of the matter-form complex for the τόδε τι. In the text the problem is resolved, in a sense, by a change of frame. By turning, in Book Θ, to the potentiality-actuality schema, Aristotle is finally able to treat the "this," and a fortiori the organism, as a unity that may be understood according to its δύναμις, that is its capacity, potential or possibility – and its ἐνεργεία or ἐντελεχεία, its activity, actuality, and completion.[3] Preparing for this turn, towards the end of Book H, he writes, "the proximate matter [ὕλη] and the form [μορφὴ] are one and the same; the one exists potentially, the other as actuality [<τὸ μὲν> δυνάμει, τὸ δὲ ἐνεργείᾳ]. Therefore to ask the cause of the unity is like asking the cause of unity in general; for each individual thing is one, and the potential and the actual are in a sense one."[4] It is noteworthy that Aristotle is only able to claim any sort of unity for the composite entity once it is considered from the point of view of its development, in process and in motion over time, a motion and process that is, for him, necessarily directed toward an endpoint, a τέλος that has absolute conceptual primacy[5] We will return later to the question of the nature of the unity designated by the potentiality-actuality schema, and in particular that of the "being at completion" indicated by ἐνεργεία and ἐντελεχεία.

This view of the organism as de facto total, unified, and complete-in-itself has had, in turn, a variegated fate in the history of philosophy and in the biological sciences. The organism – especially the animal organism, with its unity, its structure of interrelated parts contributing to the functioning of the whole, its development from relatively simple origins to an extensively differentiated complexity, the way it is distinguished from its surroundings by a boundary (membrane, integument, carapace, or skin), the operations by which it continually connects with and differentiates itself from the external world – the organism maintains and propagates itself through nutrition, growth, healing, reproduction, locomotion, and perception. All of these mark it out as a specific sort of phenomenon in the world that, in virtue of its mysterious unity in complexity, impresses itself upon the philosopher who, like Aristotle, is interested in the "why" of things. In modernity, a nexus of problems grows up around the figure of the organism, exemplified by a vigorous debate that emerges among nineteenth-century biologists. The conflict is between mechanists, who seek to explain all biological processes reductively in terms of purely physical elements obeying a kind of billiard-ball causality, and those who invoke vital forces such as the soul, "entelechies," "archeon," or life itself, a tendency dismissed as an unfortunate and archaic mysticism bearing the name of Aristotelianism.

In philosophy, Kant's Third Critique, *Kritik der Urteilskraft*, argues that the organism cannot be understood by the determinate judgements that observe linear, billiard-ball causality. Instead a different sort of judgement must be brought to bear on this object in order to make sense of its reciprocal arrangement of parts and whole and the apparent purposiveness of its being: reflective judgement. This is not to say that purpose is a part of nature, something Kant strictly denies (since he believes such a notion would require a designer); rather, the idea of a teleology or final cause of nature is necessarily projected upon the organism, by us, as we confront and seek to understand it.[6] This thoroughly modern approach, in which our own perceptual and cognitive apparatuses (indeed our own very organismic being) enters into our knowledge of the organism remains central to twentieth-century phenomenological and psychoanalytic approaches, wherein interest in the organism cannot but reflect, at least in part, our own anthropomorphic and narcissistic obsession with ourselves. Elaine P. Miller has shown how, for example, Nietzsche's dismissal of the ontological significance of the organism in favor of an understanding of nature as multiple, discontinuous, and erratic is rooted in his reading of Kant and Goethe's critiques of teleology.[7] For Nietzsche, the totality represented by the organism is provisional and precarious, an anthropomorphizing abstraction; following both Kant and Goethe, he contends that any sense of teleological purpose is a fiction. This rejection of the unity and totality represented by organicist thinking, and the resulting demise of the organism as a key philosophical entity is, in the twentieth century, paralleled in the biological sciences with the modern synthesis of Darwinian evolutionary theory and Mendelian genetics. The former takes species and populations as more fundamental than individual organisms in driving biological processes, while the latter roots the focus of biology in the microbiological and molecular processes of the gene. This synthesis, as Richard Lewontin puts it, brings biology "at last into conformity with the epistemological metastructure that already characterized physics since Newton and chemistry since Lavoisier."[8] This tendency is felt throughout the biology of the most recent century, with its emphases on materialism in evolution, the molecule, single-celled prokaryotes and archaea, the ecosystem, phylogenetics, and most recently informatics and data-driven approaches. What is absent is the selfsame, midsize, biological organism.[9]

This turn away from the organism and toward processes that unfold over time at both macro and micro levels is found in strains of philosophical thinking stretching from Nietzsche to Henri Bergson, Alfred North Whitehead, Gilbert Simondon, and most explicitly and polemically in the thought of Gilles Deleuze and Félix Guattari. For the latter, the organism represents not simply an anthropomorphic projection, but a truly fascistic imposition of the tendencies of hierarchy, sovereignty, organization, stratification, and Oedipal reproductive sexuality upon an open field of flows, intensities, and indeterminate potentialities designated as the Body without Organs.[10] All of these philosophers, interested in the unfolding of temporal processes, in becoming rather than in static, if not ossified, states of being, have no difficulty invoking ontologies of force: Bergson, for example, in *Creative Evolution*, writes that "life is like a current passing from germ to germ through the medium of a developed organism. It is as if the organism itself were only an excrescence, a bud caused to sprout by the former germ endeavouring to continue itself in a new germ."[11] Bergson certainly does not pass over the organism or living body entirely, for "it is an individual, and of no other object, not even of the crystal, can this be said, for a crystal has neither difference of parts nor diversity of function."[12] And yet, for him this individuation is only a tendency whose limits are made manifest by the phenomena of reproduction taking place over a super-organismic timespan. Of course, since Darwin, the mechanisms by which complexity can arise no longer require an explanation that invokes mystical forces. So, for Bergson, the limitation of mechanistic thinking is not that it cannot account for complex organization, but that it cannot countenance time, and the force that works through time, as real. Indeed, for Bergson mechanism includes not just the classical physical causality of billiard balls, but also a causality that may act by means of releasing (as with the explosive force in dynamite unleashed by a flame) or unwinding (as with the potential energy contained in a spring). Yet mechanism is still insufficient for explaining the push to complexity observable in the phenomenal of life. The force of time, possessing "effective action and reality of its own," is invisible to mechanists, and Bergson sees in this mechanist limitation an unbearable sense of loneliness and dissatisfaction which follows the thought of a process without finality or end.[13] The modern Kantian notion of reflective judgement, in which teleological explanations are invoked insofar as they satisfy us, would seem to be at work here, and yet Bergson is not simply reinscribing the traditional opposition between mechanism and teleology exemplified by the individuation of the organism. For him, the notion of the organism as such, as animated by a vital principle, also runs aground on the shore of the insufficiency of internal finality or "absolutely distinct individuality"[14] as evidenced in the phenomena of reproduction or, indeed, autoimmunity, in which a phagocyte attacks the very organism that sustains it.[15]

Notable in both Bergson's thinking and also in Nietzsche's thought, inflected by Empedocles, is the identification of an anti-teleological, destructive tendency in nature. Bergson affirms that "life does not proceed by the association and addition of elements, but by dissociation and division,"[16] while Nietzsche finds the occasional unifications of life seen at the level of the organism as provisional and desultory, in a world mostly constituted by "erratic and arbitrary forces that encounter each other in unending strife."[17] Nietzsche opposes Aristotle here not simply with his endorsement of Empedocles' proto-evolutionary stance (against which Aristotle repeatedly polemicizes),[18] but also with an echo of Aristotle's student, companion, and critic Theophrastus, for whom "the good is something rare and in few [things], whereas evil is much in number."[19]

The shift away from organismic thinking we are tracing continues in the mid-twentieth-century work of Gilbert Simondon, who incorporates the social collective and sensory environment into the organism's purview in his investigations into individuation. Simondon attends not only to the organism's interactions with its environment or external milieu as inherent to its becoming, but also to its interior milieu, to the pluripotentiality of the developing being – the fact that it could realize any number of developmental pathways. In so doing, he, like Bergson, analyzes the organism's inherent out-of-phaseness with itself, its non-self-sameness, as key to its development. What results is a new conception of "metastability" in which ontogenesis is understood from the point of view of a process of becoming that fundamentally displaces the substantial finality of the adult individual.[20] And in contemporary biology, disciplines such as cellular and molecular biology, genetics, immunology, microbiology, bioinformatics, and approaches such as medical ecology have emphasized the permeability and precariousness of organismic and cell boundaries, as well as foregrounding web-like constitutive interrelationships between and within the organism and its surroundings, both macro and microscopic. The organism has, in Goethean fashion, become multiple rather than unified, and concepts such as the microbiome have come to take its place. In this view, an "organism" is a collectivity of symbiotic beings constantly interacting with their environment, such that, for example, one no longer "catches" a fungal infection such as *Candida albicans* from a hostile exterior environment, but one rather experiences an imbalance that leads to an overgrowth of one element that is already part of one's being qua microbiome.[21] In evolutionary terms, too, the rise of that most unitary of creatures, the eukaryotic single-celled organism, is now widely (if not universally) understood to be the result not simply of accumulated genetic mutations, but of certain chimerical, symbiotic cellular incorporations. Intracellular organelles like mitochondria (the energy-generating centers within cells), chloroplasts (in which photosynthesis takes place), or plasmids are thought to have once been prokaryotic bacteria in their own right, at one time in evolutionary history ingested but not digested by another host bacterium.[22] This leads to a very different view of the organism, and of health and disease, displacing the view that even something as life-threatening as cancer should be thought of as an external enemy to be vanquished. As Dorion Sagan puts it: "[organelles within the cell that were once bacteria] are now generally well behaved, although cancer is noteworthy for the rampant multiplication of the occasionally vampiric mitochondria."[23] In a Foucauldian register, Ed Cohen has shown how the development of discourse on the immune system in the late nineteenth century, so central to the contemporary conception of a healthy and well-defended organism, relies on a political *dispositif* of war and defense against a hostile environment, tracing the roots of the very notion of "immunity" to Roman law rather than to the texture and tissue of biological membranes and processes.[24] According to the new models of the body emerging from these discourses, the notion of the "foreign body," of what is other to the organism, is as much internal as it is external; no amount of fortification can keep this alterity at bay. The phenomena of life, according to these critiques, appear irreducibly plural and relational, the unity of the organism all but disappears, and the "norms" of "normal" and "healthy" versus "pathological" or "diseased" are, as Georges Canguilhem presciently argued from the 1940s onward, no longer easily opposable or extricable.[25]

What, then, can a return to the Aristotelian text offer the contemporary thinking of multiplicity, of networks, of anti-normativity and molecularity? Aristotle's thought is without doubt the site where the organism is instituted as metaphysically hegemonic, where its healthy functioning is offered as a paradigm of being as ἐνεργεία. I seek to show here, in brief, that, against his explicit intentions, there are elements at work in the biological texts that offer a more complex view of the being of the organism.[26] To clarify, I am not arguing that Aristotle was something like a contemporary ecological thinker all along. Rather, I want to offer a picture of his thought in which his valorization of organismic unity and healthy functioning as a sign of what is best are continually vitiated by unassimilable factors – by material forces, compulsions, and vicissitudes that work to undermine any claims to metaphysical and ethical unity. I argue that these difficulties and ἀπορίαι may be best understood through the figure of the female offspring, understood as (what I call) "the feminine symptom." Putting gender at the center of the discourse on the organism will serve, I hope, to clarify some of the stakes of understanding the organism in its normative and topological dimensions, and thus to assist in a reassessment of its contemporary status.

Before developing this notion of the feminine symptom, it is necessary to be as clear as possible about Aristotle's conception of γένεσις, of natural coming to be. In the *Generation of Animals*, as is well known, the male possesses the principle of movement and generation, and the female possesses the material principle. The scene of sexual reproduction thus illuminates in explicit detail the active transfer of a moving, generative, formative masculine principle upon passive feminine matter. The natures of form and matter are not, however, a simple issue for Aristotle. Coming-to-be, as we learn early on in the *Physics*, has three components: a privation of the form to come, the form to which the developing thing is destined, and the matter. The matter is the substrate for the change and abides the process, admitting form's presence from its prior absence. Matter thus "admits of both contraries," as Aristotle puts it in *Metaphysics* Λ, that is the form (A), and its contrary, the privation (not-A).[27] Insofar as the non-material causes (formal, motive, and final) act upon the matter, the matter is transformed into A, while the privation that is form's contrary, not-A, is destroyed.

On the one hand, then, matter is the substrate, the ὑποκείμενον that underlies the form; it is the passive subject of change that persists and endures. On the other hand, it is a site that somehow includes and encompasses privation or lack as a very part of its being, a lack that offers itself up to destruction as form is progressively installed. As the potter forms the jar, the clay (as malleable matter) yields, giving up its formlessness to the destined form. Or, as Aristotle puts it in *Physics* I.9, matter yearns for and stretches out toward (ἐφίεσθαι καὶ ὀρέγεσθαι) the divine and the good. Matter, in this passage, literally desires form, just as, he writes, "the female which desires the male and the ugly which desires the beautiful."[28] Already we notice something odd here. We find matter (which is paradigmatically passive in relation to the masculine form) behaving like an obscure subject of desire, somehow internally motile, vectoral, and inclined or impelled toward form. Likewise, in *De Caelo*, Aristotle explains the movement of the elements toward their proper places – fire and air upward, earth and water downward –with recourse to the notion of an inclination or ῥοπή that manifests in lightness and heaviness – a tendency to move toward proper place which is finally understood according to the potentiality-actuality schema.[29] Here, then, matter is already folded in advance into the potentiality-actuality schema, into a scene of teleological becoming. Its incipient, vectoral orientation toward form is evident not simply because it lies in readiness, waiting to be acted upon and enformed, but rather insofar as it bears in itself an impulsion, an obscure and untheorized, perhaps untheorizable, source of motion. It is obediently and inevitably directed toward form, stretching out and desiring – if not quite actively, then at least in the middle voice: ἐφίεσθαι καὶ ὀρέγεσθαι.

Yet the role of matter in the biological texts, and especially in the biology of sexual reproduction, turns out to be rather more complex than even this duality between pure passivity and obscure impulsivity indicates, especially on account of what is implied by this impulsivity, that is that, in direct contrast to every explicit claim, matter may in fact move itself. In Aristotle's discourse on heredity in *Generation of Animals* and in his account of the role of αὐτόματον in reproduction in the *Metaphysics*, matter is revealed as the source of vicious disruptions that disturb the orderly passing of paternal form from one generation to the next. Let us consider the following highly illustrative quote from *Generation of Animals* IV.3:

> Males take after their father more than their mother, females after their mother. Some take after none of their kindred, although they take after some human being at any rate; others do not take after a human being at all in their appearance, but have gone so far that they resemble a monstrosity, and, for the matter of that, anyone who does not take after his parents is really in a way a monstrosity, since in these cases Nature has in a way strayed [παρεκβέβηκε] from the generic type. The first beginning of this deviation is when a female is formed instead of a male, though (a) this indeed is a necessity required by Nature, since the race of creatures which are separated into male and female has got to be kept in being; and (b) since it is possible for the male sometimes not to gain the mastery [κρατεῖν] either on account of youth or age or some other such cause, female offspring must of necessity be produced by animals.[30]

There is a lot going on here. Nature is capable of straying from its predestined path toward form and the good. In sexual reproduction, things can go wrong and the male fails to gain the mastery (κράτος, a political concept), resulting in a female offspring. The factors and circumstances that may contribute to such an outcome have already been listed by Aristotle, and include factors internal to the organism (the parents may be too young, too old, too fluid or feminine of body) as well as external factors. Indeed, the wind may be in the south, or copulating animals may simply be facing the south, which would contribute to a deficiency of heat, leading to the failure of the masculine principle.[31] If the deficiency is mild, a female is the result, if it is greater, the offspring is a monstrosity. But whence do such deficiencies arise? Clearly, they inhere in the material and environmental conditions of conception, both internal and external, the aleatory, plural, and unpredictable vagaries of the material world, with matter here acting against nature's unfolding rather than for it, acting against the smooth reproduction of masculine form, disrupting its action and its mastery.

At the same time – and here the notion of the feminine symptom comes into view – nature requires such deficiencies in order for the cyclical teleology of sexual generation to occur. What I am calling symptomatic here is that which is both necessary to the teleology and disruptive of teleology, rendering their confluence therefore strictly speaking inexplicable. A formulation from Judith Butler's *Bodies that Matter* may help to clarify this sense of the symptom: "A constitutive or relative outside is, of course, composed of a set of exclusions that are nevertheless *internal* to that system as its own nonthematizable necessity. It emerges within the system as incoherence, disruption, a threat to its own systematicity."[32] If this understanding of symptomaticity – as nonthematizable necessity, as that which both exceeds and founds a system – is deconstructively expedient, the Greek meaning and etymology of symptom, σύμπτωμα, multiplies this serendipity. Σύμπτωμα is literally a falling together (from συμ-, together + πίπτω, to fall), anything that befalls one: coincidence is its Latinate cognate. It may refer to chance, mischance, or calamity.[33] The falling together of the σύμπτωμα suggests both an unexpected, unchosen, forceful downward motion, and an irreducible plurality, the falling of more than one thing together, at the same time. The symptom here describes not only the production of a female offspring as the unexpected conjunction of winds in the south with copulation, but it also involves an unstable valence of matter, such that it is both obedient and destructive, or obedient through its destruction.

If destruction sounds too strong here, a closer examination of the mechanisms involved in sexual reproduction (and, more specifically, in heredity) is in order. First of all, there is the strange transformation of scale from the tiny deviation in temperature to the contrariety or opposition of sexual difference. When the failure of mastery occurs, "the material must change over into its opposite condition. Now the opposite of the male is the female."[34] "Such a small thing may tip the scale and be the cause of heat and cold," says Aristotle;[35] a deficiency of heat causes a transformation into an opposite. Note the shift from a scalar notion of temperature to one of discrete contraries, resulting from an agonistic, politically characterized struggle between spermatic heat and environmental conditions – material conditions that might be either inside or outside the mother's body, indeterminately.

But again, such accidents will necessarily happen. A small deviation from the ideal temperature, then, generates the required female; a larger deviation creates occasional "monstrosities" (τέρατα): calves with two heads, babies with six fingers, and the like. In this way, femininity can be seen to function as a sign of, and a figure for, masculine failure. An error in the concoction of the offspring reveals a susceptibility of the natural, telic unfolding of organismic reproduction to another kind of necessity, a necessity inherent in the forces or compulsions of matter. Aside from noting the deep misogyny in theorizing femaleness as a mild form of monstrosity, and indeed the profound normativity inherent in the Aristotelian cosmos, how are we to understand this ἀπορία, this strange confluence, this necessary coinciding – note the echo of σύμπτωμα here – of two different orders of necessity in the reproduction of the female?

While a consideration of the mechanisms of heredity and of spontaneous generation cannot solve this ἀπορία, it may shed some light on the processes at work and deliver us resources within the Aristotelian text for a rather different conception of the organism than that governed solely by the τέλος of unity and substance. How, for example, may a male offspring resemble his mother, or a female offspring her father? If all goes well, the motion deriving from the male creates a shape after its own pattern, and the male resembles his father. However, if this process fails, such failure may take a number of different paths, depending on which faculty or δύναμις in the male fails to gain mastery. In the case of a son looking like his mother, Aristotle contends that this is a result of a kind of departure from type or destruction – an ἐξίστασθαι of the male power or potentiality (δύναμις), this time not qua male but qua individual. The mother's characteristics then appear, not as a result of the presence or actuality of any formal principle or power on her part, but merely as a result of an absence, an ablation of the sperm's individualizing δύναμις. Aristotle distinguishes two decisive mechanisms: ἐξίστασθαι, a destruction or "departure from type" that permits femaleness or maternal characteristics to appear by default, and λύεσθαι, a lapsing, loosening, or slackening in which case the characteristics of grandparents (of the same sex) and former ancestors comes to the fore. So if the father's δύναμις, qua individual, slackens or loosens, the son resembles the grandfather. Ἐξίστασθαι is thus the result of a pure failure of masculinity, while λύεσθαι signifies that the agent (ποιοῦν), while still there, is acted upon by that on which it acts, presumably by latent δυνάμει residing in the reproductive material (which are never otherwise theorized); thus a heating agent may end up being cooled, or vice versa.[36]

This ἐκ-στάσις of ἐξίστασθαι represents a derangement or departure from where something stands, a putting out of place of the self-standing uprightness of masculinity. The slackening, or loosening, λύεσθαι, is by contrast rather a passive failure; it does not involve the forceful element of violent transformation, but results rather in a μετα-βαίνειν, a walking over, to the next ancestor in line. According to Aristotelian usage, ἐξίστασθαι signifies a departure from being that is an inherent possibility within matter, insofar as matter is the site of the very possibility of being and not being. Matter, then, is the site of a destructive deviation that leads to an overthrow of the masculine power of production and transformation into its feminine opposite.

Aristotle's quite brilliant solution to the problems presented by inherited characteristics thus results in a profound incoherence in terms of his theory of sexual reproduction, because it requires a balance of powers, δυνάμεις, between the sexes that cannot be reduced to the matter–form distinction. There is simply no explanation of how the "information" for the mother's form, the mother's λόγος, can be present in the menstrual blood, even if this has, as he says, the potential to become all the female parts as well as the male parts. If the father's δύναμις qua individual (rather than qua male) fails to master the matter, how can the offspring resemble his or her mother? Aristotle posits no λόγος deriving from the female. Are we then to just assume the presence of the δύναμις or λόγος of the mother's form, qua individual, as well as those of her parents and other ancestors, in the menstrual fluid? This is a substance he has characterized, quite unusually and surprisingly, as πρώτη ὕλη, first or prime matter, supremely passive and ready to be acted upon.[37] Matter, however, is found also to be the site of unexpected disruptions, transformations, and potencies, of the spontaneity designated by αὐτόματον, the chance occurrences of nature.

In chapter Z.9 of the *Metaphysics*, Aristotle indeed pursues the analysis in such a way that leads him to contradict almost everything he says about matter elsewhere. He starts by asserting that in some instances a thing can be generated both by αὐτόματον and by τέχνη, as in the case of health, which may just be present by the chance element in nature, or be brought to presence by the actions of a doctor. He says – using the middle voice – that in such instances the matter is "such that it can be the source of its own motion [οἵα κινεῖσθαι ὑφ' αὐτῆς]."[38] And this is a remarkable statement indeed. However, Aristotle does not emphasize just how singular and complex the notion of "health" is (as a context for these self-initiated motions), even though it appears repeatedly in his discourses as a paradigmatic τέλος. For health may be the end-product and aim of a τέχνη (medicine), but since the "matter" upon which this τέχνη operates is a living body, it is quite unlike a bed or a statue, and thus health also indicates that a body is by nature functioning well, living well, in accordance with its form or actuality, its ἐνεργεία. We might say, then, that insofar as the body for the doctor is analogous to the wood for the carpenter, the body is "matter," but insofar as the body itself is already a hylomorph, a composite of form and matter generated by nature, it is not mere matter at all but a natural "this," an organic unity, that can be theoretically further decomposed into material components (flesh and bone, or menstrual blood, depending on whether it is analyzed it statically or genetically) and form. But Aristotle does not claim this here at all. His statement is, rather, quite explicit: the matter in itself (not just qua the object at hand for the doctor) is self-moving. Nevertheless, Aristotle simply treats health as an example – as if there were many others – of things that are generated both artificially and spontaneously, instead of the remarkable, mysterious, and perhaps unique confluence of material necessity, bodily practices, and medical art, of φύσις, ἔθος, and τέχνη, that it undoubtedly is.

What follows is still more confusing. Things that have the capacity to move themselves can be divided into two kinds: those that can move themselves in a particular way (presumably animals), and those that cannot – he says, "so as to dance [ὀρχήσασθαι]."[39] Such dancing, in the middle voice, is a kind of self-motion without form or end. It is presumably not choreographed or orchestrated, but improvised, mantic, automatic. This matter that moves itself in no particular way (οὐχ ὡδί), dancing in the middle voice, certainly suggests Lucretius's famous dust motes dancing in a sunbeam,[40] but perhaps also the Bacchanalian frenzy: the automatism of women dancing in the mountains, far beyond the confines of the πόλις.

Moving to a discussion of natural becoming and αὐτόματον as spontaneous generation, Aristotle writes:

> But things by nature which are generated spontaneously [ταὐτομάτου] are, as in the previous case, those whose matter can be moved also by itself in the way in which it can be moved by the seed; but things without this capability cannot be generated otherwise than by things like themselves.[41]

Aristotle has just discussed how the seed acts just like things produced by τέχνη, as the source of the seed has the same name (ὁμώνυμον) as the seed's product: a horse reproduces a horse. Likewise, the bed is built from the λόγος or idea of the bed within the carpenter – the idea and the product have the same name. He adds, though, that we must not expect to find this homonymy in every case in nature, since we say that a woman – if not a monster (ἐὰν μὴ πήρωμα ᾖ) – is also produced by a man. Likewise, a mule does not come from a mule.[42] In other words the processes of generation in nature also dance, they are subject to certain aleatory deviations, and in these cases what is produced does not always have the same name as its progenitor – the mating of a horse and a donkey produces something else, called a mule, and a man may likewise produce a woman. Matter's αὐτόματον breaks the homonymy of λόγος.

These deviations, then, the articulating deviations of αὐτόματον, disrupt the νόμος and λόγος of patrilineal and patronymic succession, the paternal logic of the moving cause. Sexual reproduction is thus explicitly given the same aetiology, the same causal explanation, as that of spontaneous generation, in short that "matter has the power to move itself in the same way as the seed."[43] The opaque motion of matter, its automatic spontaneity, is able to intervene in and disrupt the passing down of the patronymic – breaking the homonymy, forcing a shift in the λόγος – between one generation and the next. The αὐτόματον of matter thus articulates both beings and words through time, in a randomly shifting series, in a form of change and temporality characterized by unpredictability, lability, deviation, and opacity. In the phenomenon of αὐτόματον, where the aleatory motions of matter are exposed, we may glimpse a moment of unorthodox Aristotelianism wherein Darwinism is foreshadowed, insofar as automatism is the unthinking, uncaused, undirected, non-teleological engine for transformations of form over generations.

By way of conclusion let me return to the conception of becoming from the *Physics* – that of matter, privation, and form. Here matter is oriented in advance toward its τέλος, and represents a hole or space yearning to be filled, a hole that is only defined by the peg that will come to fill it, as the female desires the male. Nevertheless, it is crucially important to recognize that as soon as matter is understood as thus invaginated, as incorporating a penetrable privation at its heart, such a determination by a τέλος in advance is displaced, and an indeterminate field of becoming is hence necessarily opened. Understanding matter as δύναμις shackles it necessarily to ἐνεργεία as the realization or actualization of a potential for a specific form, but it is precisely as this site of privation that matter enables becoming anything at all, not merely becoming some determinate thing, predetermined by teleology. In its most radical dimension, then, δύναμις as potential or capacity or possibility, as the condition for possibility for becoming in general, must indicate an open field of possibilities. It is a delimited field to be sure, for an elephant does not give birth to a mouse; but within those limits – whatever they may be – the possibilities are theoretically infinite because infinitesimally different.

Aristotle falls just short of acknowledging the plural possibilities inherent in matter, but it is worth recalling his definition of matter as "what is able to both be and not be."[44] Matter thus defined appears as the very site of indeterminacy and the aleatory, the site where A and not-A may both transpire. The potentially infinite field of possibility that matter represents is instead reduced to a simple opposition, the primary contrary of being or not-being. Yet as evidenced by all the ways that nature does not go according to plan, through chance, plural ἀρχαί, and the indeterminacy of matter, the restless rumbling of plural possibilities may be discerned beyond and behind this congealed logical formula of non-contradiction. The female offspring, after all, is not simply a not-A, but rather an opposite or contrary in nature who bears the mark of privation. And this contradiction is negotiated in her very body. Feminine matter may be oriented toward and set along a proper path, but may also, teratologically, go off the rails and in turn (in quite un-Aristotelian fashion) send form itself off the rails, toward other as yet untold shapes and configurations. The vicissitudes of the feminine symptom disclose here a radically non-Aristotelian space or field of contingent pluralities that signifies an always present possibility of other unforeseen kinds of becoming.

Here, then, subterranean and suppressed forces, including environmental factors and unpredictable material conditions, are irreducible, effective factors in the coming to be of the organism. We might thus discern, against all of Aristotle's explicit claims, resources in the Aristotelian text for a vision of the organism not as the bounded, unified totality of the one, but perhaps as developing according to an entirely different topology and logic. In a feminist frame, we might push for a conceptualization according to the Irigarayan topology of the two lips, partly open in intimate proximity to itself and its surroundings, or indeed as irreducibly plural.[45] Or in terms of the leaky, open, penetrable, fungible, and thus "horrifying" bodies of women investigated by feminist theorists such as Margrit Shildrick and Elizabeth Grosz.[46] The ἐξίστασθαι, λύεσθαι, and αὐτόματον, the destructions, slackenings, and compulsions inherent in the materiality of sexual reproduction carry with them the signs of finitude and mortality, of castration, monstrosity, disease and death – those dispersals and divisions evident in Nietzsche's Empedocleanism and in Bergson's *durée*.

The reading of Aristotle offered here, then, demonstrates that at least part of the impetus for a vision of a totalized, cleanly separate, healthily functional, fully hierarchized and stratified organism is an anxious masculinity, eager to inoculate itself from feminine threats of leaky boundaries and bodily dissolution. This would seem to align quite neatly with the philosophical-political critiques of the organism proffered above, stretching from Kant and Goethe to Deleuze and Guattari. But what might we also make of the flight from the organismic paradigm within the biological sciences over the last two centuries? This flight, has, in fact, been quite hotly contested. A slew of early twentieth-century biologists in Germany, the UK, and the US including E. S. Russell, W. E. Ritter, Kurt Goldstein, Agnes Arber, and J. H. Woodger have argued in various registers for the organism's centrality and coherence to the biological sciences, borrowing largely from Kant a thinking of teleology and functionality that does not invoke "metaphysical" principles such as form, design, or final purpose secreted in Nature.[47] Ritter, for instance, invokes the hormone as a chemical secretion that affects the organism as a whole, not simply individual organs, and the massive uptake of this by the pharmaceutical industry is indeed transforming our notions of sex and gender in radical fashion that has been recently analyzed by Paul (Beatriz) Preciado along Foucauldian lines as a neoliberal form of "pharmacopower."[48] While such power may work at the microcapillary level, it is at the level of the whole organism that hormones phenomenologically reveal their powerful effect. Goldstein's work on brain-damaged patients reveals the organism's plasticity, its negotiations with the external world both as potentially catastrophic and as productive of its reality; Catherine Malabou's recent *The Ontology of the Accident* covers strikingly similar ground.[49]

Today, indeed, biology struggles no less with the concept of organism despite its various disciplinary dispersals into ecological, systematic, and molecular frameworks, as indicated by the topic addressed by a recent issue of the journal *Studies in the History and Philosophy of Biological and Biomedical Sciences*: "On Nature and Normativity: Normativity, teleology and mechanism in biological explanation."[50] From a physical perspective, the organization of molecules into arrangements of increasing complexity seems to defy the second law of thermodynamics, which states that things tend toward the lowest possible states of energy: the disorganization and dispersals of entropy. Biologists typically explain this by demonstrating that living cells give off maximally disordered energy in the form of heat, thus offsetting the extra energy it takes for there to be ordered complexity.[51] But this still does not explain why the greater complexity of the cycles of transformation that maintain life might emerge in the first place. Systems chemist Addy Pross has recently argued that, through the concept of "dynamic kinetic stability" a second sort of stability exists in nature that may be mathematically modeled: "Nature's most fundamental drive, dictated by logic itself, is toward greater stability. That drive has a thermodynamic manifestation, as expressed through the ubiquitous Second Law, but it also has a *kinetic* manifestation – the drive toward increasingly persistent replicators."[52] There seems to me to be no great philosophical barrier to thinking of such a drive along Deleuze-Guattarian lines as "desiring production."[53]

And yet, despite political and scientific critiques of the organism, its functional system of parts and wholes, the way that it is both marked as and functions as a primary signifier of totality, hierarchy, substantiality, sovereign power, and all the weight of stultifying metaphysics, the organism still imposes itself upon us as a significant entity. In this phenomenological register it also surely appeared to Aristotle and Theophrastus, during the years when they observed the life-cycles, the manifold structures, and behaviors of the small strange creatures inhabiting a Lesbian lagoon. Might the organism thus carry another kind of valence? One that disrupts and resists what is surely also a neoliberal logic of flexibility, the molecular flow of capitalist logic into every minute of our day and into every pore of our bodies. Such flow is perfectly exemplified by the assaults on sleep through pharmacological and other technical-productive means recently described by Jonathan Crary, insofar as sleep, so necessary at the level of the organism, defies imperatives of accelerating capitalist production and consumption.[54] Mauritzio Esposito, indeed, reads the politics of the organism in a different frame, emphasizing that mechanistic and reductionist approaches in biology support a capitalist ideology of competition, and came to the fore most strongly during the Cold War period "in which group conflict and competition were seen as essential to a pluralistic democratic society." Organismic models, he argues, promote instead a view of society that emphasizes harmony and cooperation.[55] The temporality of the organism, the rhythms it imposes, the zones of privacy upon which it can insist, may yet be a site of resistance to the encroachments of neoliberal capitalism, a slowness that insists upon its needs against capital's ever increasing speeds.

The Aristotelian organism, as I have articulated it, may be both the site of resistance to invasive externalities, and also a site of endless agonism between a logic of hierarchical function on the one hand and the destabilizations of aleatory matter on the other. Aristotle's concern with the non-human organism inevitably opens on to an anthropomorphic concern with the human, that organism whose characteristic functioning is not just a normative conception of health, but also living well as the ζῷον who possesses both λόγος and a political life. The ἐνεργεία of the Aristotelian organism, then, might be understood not simply as a static state of completion, but as a doing, a seeing or a thinking, the human being in its full realization. The *Nicomachean Ethics* offers contemplation as the highest form of human activity, that in which we most resemble the divine νόησις νοήσεως, thought thinking itself, and this seems to confirm the image of the bounded, separate, autarchic, and fully self-sufficient individual. And yet it is also characteristic of humans to engage in the open-ended, indeterminate activities of political life. In this ambivalence of closed and open system, it seems to me that the agonisms and the harmonies indicated at the site of the Aristotelian organism are perhaps inescapable and necessary, in the sense that the Lacanian mirror-stage is a necessary, if truth-compromised, stage through which the infant passes in its ontogenesis. For Lacan, the infant sees itself as a bounded totality in the mirror for the first time, and this vision of unity throws it into an unprecedented state of disorder, the "flutter of jubilant activity."[56] Its recognition of its "unity" is in a profound sense a "misrecognition," not only because the baby does not have the motor skills to act in an orderly way, but also because the organism is constantly in process, constantly realizing indeterminate potentials that are both its own and not its own. But nonetheless, the "false" image that it has formed of itself supports its growing sensation of unification and contributes actively to its integration as ontogenesis proceeds. The imaginary function that "closes off" the organism is certainly supported and "supplemented" by the ready hegemony of substantialist metaphysics and phantasies of sovereignty. And yet a quick glance at the strange proliferations, the beings and becomings found in oceans, lagoons, swamp, and soil may always have the power to carry us away from the narcissistic mirror, and into the lap of the milieu with whose fate our own is always inescapably entangled.

NOTES

[Though recontextualized and lightly edited, some passages in this chapter have previously appeared in Emanuela Bianchi, *The Feminine Symptom*. I thank my editors, Jacob Greenstine and Ryan Johnson, for the kind opportunity to present this work in a new context.]

1. Martin Heidegger, "On the Essence and Concept of *Phusis* in Aristotle's *Physics* B, 1," p. 185.
2. This evocation of the object cannot help resonating with the new status of the object in currently emerging philosophies of object-oriented ontology and speculative realism. While I cannot engage in any substantive way with these movements within the scope of this essay, I do want to emphasize that Aristotle's approach usefully reasserts the ontological primacy of a distinction between technical and natural objects, one that is often minimized in recent discussions of the object qua object.

3. See Charlotte Witt, *Ways of Being*, for an extended discussion of the relationship between *Metaphysics* Books Z, H, and Θ.

4. Aristotle, *Metaphysics* [*Meta.*], H.6, 1045b18–22, translation modified.

5. Since for Aristotle time follows from motion (see Aristotle, *Physics* [*Phys.*], IV.4 212a19 and VII.1 241b28–9), it is anachronistic to designate this as a turn to a temporal frame, but rather one which foregrounds motion and change over stasis.

6. Immanuel Kant, *Critique of Judgement*, pp. 280ff.

7. Elaine P. Miller, "Empedoclean Nature: Nietzsche's Critique of Teleology and the Organism through Goethe and Kant" ["Empedoclean Nature"].

8. Richard Lewontin, "Gene, Organism and Environment," p. 274.

9. See Robin W. Bruce, "A Reflection on Biological Thought: Whatever Happened to the Organism?" p. 356; see also Maurizio Esposito, *Romantic Biology 1890–1945*, especially "Conclusion: Whatever Happened to Organismal Biologies?" pp. 179–88.

10. Gilles Deleuze and Félix Guattari, *A Thousand Plateaus*, especially Ch. 6, "November 28, 1947: How Do You Make Yourself a Body Without Organs?" pp. 149–99.

11. Henri Bergson, *Creative Evolution*, p. 28.

12. Ibid. p. 13.

13. Ibid. p. 17.

14. Ibid. p. 45.

15. Ibid. pp. 43–4.

16. Ibid. p. 94.

17. "Empedoclean Nature," p. 113.

18. See, for example, *Phys.* II.8 198b29–32, which refers to Empedocles rather scornfully thus: "Whenever all the parts came together as if generated for the sake of something, the wholes which were fitfully composed through spontaneity survived, but those which came together not in this manner, like the man-face offspring of oxen mentioned by Empedocles, perished and still do so."

19. Theophrastus, "*On First Principles*," 11a19–10. This empirical claim contradicts Aristotle's insistent refrain that in nature things occur for the sake of what is best "always or for the most part."

20. Gilbert Simondon, *L'Individu et sa Genèse Physico-Biologique*. A summary of this text is available in English as Gilbert Simondon, "The Genesis of the Individual." See also Arne De Boever, Alex Murray, Jon Roffe, and Ashley Woodward (eds.), *Gilbert Simondon: Being and Technology*, and Muriel Combes, *Gilbert Simondon and the Philosophy of the Transindividual*.

21. Carl Zimmer, "Tending the Body's Microbial Garden."

22. According to evolutionary biologist Lynn Margulis, bacteria such as spirochetes (some of which cause syphilis and Lyme disease) may have thus ended up being incorporated into our very physiologies as cilia and sperm tails. See Dorion Sagan, "Metametazoa: Biology and Multiplicity."

23. Ibid. p. 378.

24. Ed Cohen, *A Body Worth Defending: Immunity, Biopolitics, and the Apotheosis of the Modern Body.*
25. Georges Canguilhem, *The Normal and the Pathological*; originally published as *Essai sur quelques problèmes concernant le normal et le pathologique* (1943), and re-published with the title *Le normal et le pathologique, augmenté de Nouvelles réflexions concernant le normal et le pathologique* (1966).
26. What follows is a rather telescopic account of an argument developed more fully in Emanuela Bianchi, *The Feminine Symptom: Aleatory Matter in the Aristotelian Cosmos.*
27. *Meta.* Λ.2 1069b13.
28. *Phys.* I.9 192a24. In fairness to Aristotle he does qualify this by noting that femaleness and ugliness are "accidents" of subjects rather than subjects in themselves, but this does not obviate the force of the analogy.
29. Relevant instances of ῥοπή, often translated as impetus or impulse, occur at Aristotle, *De Caelo*, II.1 297a28, b7, at III.2 310a22, at II.2 305a25, and at IV.1 307b33. A comprehensive analysis of these phenomena may be found in Helen S. Lang's *The Order of Nature in Aristotle's Physics.*
30. Aristotle, *Generation of Animals* [GA], VI.3, 767b3–15.
31. *GA* IV.2 765b28–76a1, 766a9–12.
32. Judith Butler, *Bodies That Matter*, p. 13.
33. Derrida attends to the many aleatory resonances of the notion of the fall – befalling, crashing, letting the chips fall where they may – thus:

> One can fall well or badly, have a lucky or unlucky break – but always by dint of not having foreseen – of not having seen in advance and ahead of oneself. In such a case, when man or the subject falls, the fall affects his upright stance and vertical position by engraving in him the detour of a *clinamen*, whose effects are inescapable.

Jacques Derrida, "My Chances/*Mès Chances*: A Rendezvous with Some Epicurean Stereophonies," p. 5.
34. *GA* VI.1 766a18–22. At 766b15–16 Aristotle says that "if [the male semen] gains the mastery, it brings [the material] over to itself; but if it gets mastered, it changes over either into its opposite or else into extinction." That the continuous scale of temperature should manifest itself "necessarily" in opposites, as manifested by male and female, is difficult to understand. The necessity operating here becomes clearer if we recall Aristotle's insistence that all coming-to-be involves a diremption into active and passive components and thus in the case of sexual reproduction, into male and female.
35. Ibid. IV.2 766a12–14, translation modified.
36. Ibid. IV.3 768b14ff.
37. There is considerable debate as to the status of this claim, but at *GA* I.20 729a32 he writes quite explicitly: "For the nature of the menstrual blood is that of prime matter [κατὰ γὰρ τὴν πρώτην ὕλην ἐστὶν ἡ τῶν καταμηνίων φύσις]." The shift here from the biological to the metaphysical is seamless,

with the menstrual blood clearly standing in here as a perceptible representation of the theoretical substance, of matter as such and in general.

38. *Meta. Z.*9 1034a13.

39. Ibid. 1034a16.

40. Lucretius, *De Rerum Natura*, II.114–28.

41. *Meta. Z.*9 1034b4–7, translation modified.

42. Ibid. 1034a35–1034b4.

43. Ibid. 1034b5–7.

44. Aristotle, *On Coming-to-Be and Passing-Away*, II.9, 335a34.

45. Rebecca Hill, *The Interval: Relation and Becoming in Irigaray, Aristotle, and Bergson*, investigates the topology of proximity and interval in the context of thinking through sexual difference.

46. Margrit Shildrick, *Leaky Bodies and Boundaries: Feminism, Postmodernism and (Bio)Ethics*; Elizabeth Grosz, *Volatile Bodies: Towards a Corporeal Feminism*.

47. See Bruce, "A Reflection on Biological Thought" and Esposito, *Romantic Biology*, for helpful surveys of this movement.

48. W. E. Ritter, *The Unity of the Organism*, vol. 1, especially ch. XIX, "The Significance of the Internal Secretory System," p. 145ff.; Beatriz Preciado, *Testo Junkie*.

49. Kurt Goldstein, *The Organism*; Catherine Malabou, *The Ontology of the Accident: An Essay on Destructive Plasticity*.

50. Relevant articles include Lenny Moss and Daniel J. Nicholson, "On Nature and Normativity: Normativity, Teleology, and Mechanism in Biological Explanation," and Georg Toepfer, "Teleology and Its Constitutive Role for Biology as the Science of Organized Systems in Nature."

51. See, for example, Bruce Alberts et al., *Essential Cell Biology*, pp. 83–4.

52. Addy Pross, "Life's Restlessness."

53. For a helpful examination of this concept see Dorothea Olkowski, "Flows of Desire and the Body-Becoming."

54. See Jonathan Crary, *24/7: Late Capitalism and the End of Sleep*.

55. Esposito, *Romantic Biology*, p. 182.

56. Jacques Lacan, "The Mirror Stage as Formative of the Function of the I as Revealed in Psychoanalytic Experience," p. 5.

BIBLIOGRAPHY

Alberts B., Bray, D., Hopkin, K., Johnson, A. D., Johnson, A., Lewis, J., Raff, M., Roberts, K., and Walter, P., *Essential Cell Biology* (New York: Taylor & Francis, 2010).

Aristotle, *Metaphysics, Books 1–9*, trans. H. Tredennick (Cambridge, MA: Harvard University Press, 1933).

Aristotle, *Metaphysics, Books 10–14; Oeconomica; Magna Moralia*, trans. H. Tredennick and G. C. Armstrong (Cambridge, MA: Harvard University Press, 1935).

Aristotle, *Generation of Animals*, trans. A. L. Peck (Cambridge, MA: Harvard University Press, 1942).

Aristotle, *De Caelo*, trans. W. K. C. Guthrie (Cambridge, MA: Harvard University Press, 1953).

Aristotle, *Physics*, trans. H. G. Apostle (Bloomington: Indiana University Press, 1969).

Aristotle, *On Sophistical Refutations; On Coming-to-Be and Passing-Away; On the Cosmos*, trans. E. S. Forster (Cambridge, MA: Harvard University Press, 1992).

Bergson, H., *Creative Evolution*, trans. A. Mitchell (London: Macmillan, 1954).

Bianchi, E., *The Feminine Symptom: Aleatory Matter in the Aristotelian Cosmos* (New York: Fordham University Press, 2014).

Bruce, R. W., "A Reflection on Biological Thought: Whatever Happened to the Organism?" *Biological Journal of the Linnaean Society*, 112 (2014), pp. 354–65.

Butler, J., *Bodies That Matter* (New York: Routledge, 1993).

Canguilhem, G., *The Normal and the Pathological*, trans. C. R. Fawcett and R. S. Cohen (New York: Zone Books, 1991).

Cohen, E., *A Body Worth Defending: Immunity, Biopolitics, and the Apotheosis of the Modern Body* (Durham, NC: Duke University Press, 2009).

Combes, M., *Gilbert Simondon and the Philosophy of the Transindividual*, trans. T. LaMarre (Cambridge, MA: MIT Press, 2013).

Crary, J., *24/7: Late Capitalism and the End of Sleep* (New York: Verso Books, 2013).

de Boever, A., Murray, A., Roffe, J. and Woodward, A. (eds.), *Gilbert Simondon: Being and Technology* (Edinburgh: Edinburgh University Press, 2012).

Deleuze, G. and Guattari, F., *A Thousand Plateaus: Capitalism and Schizophrenia*, trans. B. Massumi (Minneapolis: University of Minnesota Press, 1987).

Derrida, J., "My Chances/*Mès Chances*: A Rendezvous with Some Epicurean Stereophonies," in J. H. Smith and W. Kerry (eds.), *Taking Chances: Derrida, Psychoanalysis, Literature* (Baltimore: Johns Hopkins University Press, 1984), pp. 1–32.

Esposito, M., *Romantic Biology 1890–1945* (London: Routledge, 2013).

Goldstein, K., *The Organism* (Boston: Beacon Press, 1963).

Grosz, E., *Volatile Bodies: Towards a Corporeal Feminism* (Bloomington: Indiana University Press, 1994).

Heidegger, M., "On the Essence and Concept of *Phusis* in Aristotle's *Physics* B, 1," trans. T. Sheehan, in M. Heidegger, *Pathmarks,* ed. W. McNeill (Cambridge: Cambridge University Press, 1998).

Hill, R., *The Interval: Relation and Becoming in Irigaray, Aristotle, and Bergson* (New York: Fordham University Press, 2012).

Kant, I., *Critique of Judgement*, trans. J. H. Bernard (London: Macmillan, 1914).

Lacan, J., "The Mirror Stage as Formative of the Function of the I as Revealed in Psychoanalytic Experience," in J. Lacan, *Ecrits: A Selection*, trans. A. Sheridan (London: W. W. Norton, 1977), pp. 1–8.

Lang, H. S., *The Order of Nature in Aristotle's Physics* (Cambridge: Cambridge University Press, 1998).

Lewontin, R., "Gene, Organism and Environment," in D. S. Bendall (ed.), *Evolution from Molecules to Men* (Cambridge: Cambridge University Press, 1983), pp. 273–85.

Malabou, C., *The Ontology of the Accident: An Essay on Destructive Plasticity* (Cambridge: Polity Press, 2012).

Miller, E. P., "Empedoclean Nature: Nietzsche's Critique of Teleology and the Organism through Goethe and Kant," *International Studies in Philosophy*, 31.3 (1999), pp. 111–22.

Moss, L. and Nicholson, D. J., "On Nature and Normativity: Normativity, teleology, and mechanism in biological explanation," *Studies in the History and Philosophy of Biological and Biomedical Sciences*, 43.1 (2012), pp. 88–91.

Olkowski, D., "Flows of Desire and the Body-Becoming," in E. A. Grosz (ed.), *Becomings: Explorations in Time, Memory, and Futures* (Ithaca, NY: Cornell University Press, 1999), pp. 98–116.

Preciado, B., *Testo Junkie* (New York: Feminist Press, 2013).

Pross, A., "Life's Restlessness," *Aeon Magazine*, 29 April 2014 (http://aeon.co/magazine/science/stability-how-life-began-and-why-it-cant-rest, accessed 6 August 2015).

Ritter, W. E., *The Unity of the Organism*, vol. 1 (Boston: Gorham Press, 1919).

Sagan, D., "Metametazoa: Biology and Multiplicity," in J. Crary and S. Kwinter (eds.), *Incorporations* (New York: Zone Books, 1992), pp. 362–84.

Shildrick, M., *Leaky Bodies and Boundaries: Feminism, Postmodernism and (Bio)Ethics* (London: Routledge, 1997).

Simondon, G., *L'Individu et sa Genèse Physico-Biologique* (Grenoble: J. Millon, 1995).

Simondon, G., "The Genesis of the Individual," in J. Crary and S. Kwinter (eds.), *Incorporations* (New York: Zone Books, 1992), pp. 297–319.

Theophrastus, *"On First Principles" (Known as his "Metaphysics")*, ed. and trans. D. Gutas (Leiden: Brill, 2010).

Toepfer, "Teleology and Its Constitutive Role for Biology as the Science of Organized Systems in Nature," *Studies in the History and Philosophy of Biological and Biomedical Sciences*, 43.1 (2012), pp. 113–19.

Witt, C., *Ways of Being: Potentiality and Actuality in Aristotle's Metaphysics* (Ithaca, NY: Cornell University Press, 2003).

Zimmer, C., "Tending the Body's Microbial Garden" *New York Times*, 19 June 2012.

CHAPTER 9

Does It Matter? Material Nature and Vital Heat in Aristotle's Biology

Adriel M. Trott

INTRODUCTION

In *Gender: Antiquity and Its Legacy*, Brooke Holmes makes the controversial claim that sexual difference in Aristotle is contingent, belonging to a "realm more fluid and accidental than that of essence and principles – namely, the realm of matter."[1] This position would see the difference between the male and female contributions – semen and menses – as a material one. If it is material, I maintain that it reveals something about how material operates in Aristotle. The effort to distinguish material from form requires affirming either a formal difference between them or a material difference. If the difference between them is formal, as it seems it must be (if form and matter are the contradictories that Aristotle suggests they are), then material is of a different form than form. If the difference is material, as the account of the difference between semen and menses on the basis of degrees of vital heat in Aristotle's biology suggests, then form and matter differ along a continuum, more as contraries that at some degree of heat pass into one another than as contradictories with an excluded middle where the presence of one negates the other. Yet an account of generation that is modeled on artifice, where form is imposed on matter, would seem to require a distinction between the formal and material principles of generation.

In this essay, I frame this question in terms of feminist critiques of the form and material binary, critiques which can be encapsulated in disputes over whether Aristotle's account of generation is a one-sex model or a two-sex model. I turn to Aristotle's account of vital heat to suggest that it is a one-sex model whose difference is on a continuum. I then explain how the difference between contradictories and contraries in Aristotle shows how the difference between material and form, explained through the higher degree of vital heat in semen than in menses, is a difference of contraries and not contradictories and thus a material rather than a formal difference. I conclude that since the two principles are related on a continuum, reproduction should not be conceived through a simple artifice model where form is imposed on matter.

GENDER'S MATTER

The concept of gender as it developed following Beauvoir – "one is not born, but rather becomes, a woman"[2] – allowed feminists to open a space between the biological body and the cultural meaning and expectations of that body. This strategy unsutured gender from sex and liberated women from culturally designated roles otherwise disguised as "natural." Yet the unfortunate consequence of this strategy was to reinscribe the natural at the site of biological sex, making sex what is given and material, the natural element that cannot be altered.

Judith Butler argues that Luce Irigaray falls prey to this problem in her reading of the history of philosophy. Irigaray accuses philosophers from Plato to Heidegger of basing their philosophical systems on a forgotten outside. In her reading of Aristotle, this forgotten outside is matter or nature as givenness. Irigaray accuses Aristotle of resting his conception of the body, the sexed body, on a more primordial forgotten material associated with the mother.[3] As Butler reads her, Irigaray maintains that "the feminine is cast outside the form/matter and universal/particular binarisms" as the "permanent and unchangeable condition of both."[4] Irigaray's strategy is to show the power of mother-matter by showing how the whole project is grounded in some more primordial matter that allows form to appear. Following Irigaray, Emanuela Bianchi argues that Aristotle treats material both as pure δύναμις for form's work and as ἀδυναμία, impotential, having no capacity of its own. These dual roles of material show it to be what Bianchi calls a repressed and aleatory principle that, as repressed and other, returns to trouble the work of form.[5]

Butler worries that Irigaray might be inscribing material and the maternal in this exterior position that makes it the original given, in the same way the gender/sex binary divides culture from nature to challenge what has been construed as natural but ends up more deeply entrenching nature on the other side of the binary. To Butler, Irigaray seems to establish material as the "sign of irreducibility" that bears and supports not only form but cultural construction altogether. Such a view seems to further isolate material and produce a division between what is changeable and cultural from what is natural or a true original ground.[6]

Arguing against the view that constructedness is opposed to materiality, Butler observes that Irigaray's strategy attempts to establish material as a critical ground from which "to verify a set of injuries or violations only to find that *matter itself is founded through a set of violations.*"[7] In this sense, the very natural givenness of material appears constructed.

Irigaray's reading of Aristotle's natural science poses a similar problem to one that arises when political community forms out of the opposition or hier- archization of nature in relation to reason: a fundamental exclusion results from the opposition.[8] For Irigaray, the construction of the feminine outside is due to an opposition and hierarchization of matter in relation to form. Any attempt to recover a robust sense of material in Aristotle thus seems subjected to the problems that Butler finds in Irigaray's reading: either we reinscribe material as this constitutive outside that is other and distinct from form, the "true ground" that is most genuinely given, the real nature, the ur-maternal; or we describe it as always already subjected to form. Or with Bianchi, as both.

Nature is form, actuality, Aristotle insists in *Physics* II.1; yet as an internal principle of movement, an ἀρχὴ κινήσεως, nature must move from within itself to fulfill itself. In sexual reproduction, if material does not have some way of giving rise to the form, then nature is not moving from within itself to fulfill itself, but imposing itself on something other and outside in order to come into being. If nature is form without relation to material, then nature seems to be τέχνη – artifice – where τέχνη is form imposed on matter. However, if, as I argue, nature is not τέχνη, then material cannot be some separate unformed thing that only appears through the imposition of form. Nature as form can- not stand opposed to nature as given material while remaining its own prin- ciple of movement; it then becomes τέχνη – a principle of movement in another form imposed on material, rather than form arising out of material.

When Butler maintains, "if matter never appears without its *schema*" in Aristotle, "that means that it only appears under a certain grammatical form and that the principle of its recognizability, its characteristic gesture or usual dress, is indissoluble from what constitutes matter," she points to how positing separate principles of form and matter, which then conceives of matter as only showing up under the guise of form, is to already stack the deck in favor of form, thereby making it impossible to argue against the stridency of this view of material as stuff that needs form.[9] This account of material's need for form relies on an account of the material principle as already separable and distinct, other, and needing form. But if form comes to be in an intensification of heat in material, an intensification that also occurs in material but to a lesser degree, then there is both a necessary contribution of matter that is other than heat (which is not itself form) and a continuous relation between form and matter. As Holmes writes, "the idea that matter has a (feminine) gender becomes, in Butler's hands, a myth to be exploded."[10] To explode the myth of the feminin- ity of matter without denigrating either femininity or matter is to reconsider anew what material as such is.

Aristotle provides us with both this difficulty and the possible recourse for rethinking it. On the one hand, he defines matter and form as separate prin- ciples. On the other hand, he traces their origin in generation to a process that differentiates along a continuum. So, there is a dual effort in my project: on the one hand, to argue that matter is always already meaningful in Aristotle, and on the other, to show that this meaningfulness does not elide the significance of matter by reducing it to the meaning of form.

ONE-SEX AND TWO-SEX MODELS

Aristotle's account of how semen[11] comes to have the power to bring life into the female menses would seem to be the place to go to consider whether and how the difference between form and matter is material. Thomas Laqueur maintains that sexual difference in Aristotle is not material because semen moves the menses not by material interaction but by intellect.[12] Yet Aristotle's biological account of how semen comes to have the power to concoct suggests that there is something material at the heart of what looks like radical difference in Aristotle. It thus seems then that we need to investigate how semen comes to bring life into the menses to think about how the male contribution differs from the female, which is to say how form differs from material.

I frame this concern within the dispute over whether to read Aristotle's account of sexual difference on a one-sex or a two-sex model. Classical scholarship associates the two-sex model with radical difference and the one-sex model with the failure to think a true contribution of the female, but these distinctions become complicated in any reading of Aristotle.[13] The two-sex model, which seems to portray radical difference and otherness, depicts instead a hierarchy that involves a hidden dependence of the superior principle on the subordinate one, as Irigaray has shown.[14]

The strategic response to the hierarchy traditionally inferred from radical difference has been to challenge how fundamental that difference is by exposing the fluidity of the poles of difference. In Aristotle, the fluidity follows from defining the male as male by a certain activity that is susceptible to fail or be overcome by the female.[15] But affirming the "sliding scale" version of difference moves Aristotle into the one-sex model where the female is a mutilated version of the male.[16] If the two-sex model is supposed to allow for true sexual difference, it does so in Aristotle by making form separable from and superior to matter.[17] If the one-sex model is the solution, it results in a view of difference as simply distance from the norm. The two-sex model posits form and material as contradictories, while the one-sex model makes them contraries. Whatever one might think of Laqueur's historical claims, his analysis of the one-sex and two-sex models is clear: the one-sex model shows that sex was something performed and not essential – male could slide into female – but the consequence of it is that woman is defined as not-man and is devalued.[18] The two-sex model makes women more than just not-men, but then reproduction, and, consequently, matter and woman, are devalued. The one-sex model allows for fluidity without affirmative difference; the two-sex model allows for difference and thereby distinct accounts of the male and female, but introduces a rigid and deconstructive essence of sex, because while it purports to establish distinct essences, the female remains defined in contrast to the male.[19]

While Laqueur seems intent on criticizing the one-sex model, it has several conceptual advantages. As Holmes suggests, the one-sex model is not simply the degradation or distance of woman from the norm, but the recognition of a fundamental unity.[20] If woman is defined in terms of distance from man, a fluidity exists between these positions, where the difference between them is not formal, not a difference of kind, but of degree because a difference in heat. The male has enough heat to concoct or cook the seed to the point where it can bring life into the menses; this concocting can fail or be overridden by the female and the heat that enables it can be found in both male and female bodies.

In what follows, I examine semen's concocting capacity through heat to ask in what terms it divides form and matter. The two-sex model appears to slide into the one-sex model in Aristotle because form is dependent on material, following Irigaray, but the only way for the one-sex model to work in Aristotle (I argue on the basis of this analysis of heat) is if it is rooted in material. Only this account allows us to conclude with Aristotle that heat differentiates the semen from menses. If the feminine principle is the material principle and sexual difference is a material difference, then it would seem that the formal or masculine principle is rooted in and reliant upon the feminine principle. If form is fundamentally other, not on a continuum with the material but entirely differently, effecting change in the menses through the intellect, as Laqueur says, then we have a problem in explaining how the semen comes into contact with the menses so as to form it.[21] Certainly Aristotle elsewhere explains that the form moves the material through the intellect,[22] but that account does not seem to be on display in *Generation of Animals*, where vital heat replaces or serves as the agent of soul in causing life. So the two-sex model makes form dependent on material, making the model itself appear to be a material one and thereby sliding into a one-sex model, which, as I have shown, would need to be material. As Holmes suggests, "if we reconsider the evidence with the idea of a continuum in mind, the binaries that structure sexual reproduction at the level of principle start to soften."[23]

CONTRADICTION AND CONTRARIETY

At *Generation of Animals* I.18, Aristotle maintains that "all the products of semen come into being from contraries [ἐξ ἐναντίων], since coming into being from contraries is also a natural process, for some animals do so, i.e. from male and female."[24] Here male and female are contrary principles that come together to form a third. This is not the coming-to-be of one contrary from its opposite, but it is a becoming that results from the joining of two contraries, as warm comes to be from hot and cold. Three books later, in *Generation of Animals* IV.1, Aristotle writes that the two sexes are opposed – τοῦτον ἀντίκειται – in their ability to "reduce the residual secretion to a pure form."[25] Not only are the sexes opposed, but the force of one sex or its failure can turn the offspring into the same sex or the opposite sex of the principle working on it:

> We must understand besides this that, if it is true that when a thing perishes it becomes the opposite of what it was, it is necessary also that what is not under the sway of that which made it must change into its opposite. After these premises it will perhaps be now clearer for what reason one embryo becomes female and another male. For when the first principle does not bear sway and cannot concoct the nourishment through lack of heat nor bring it into its proper form, but is defeated in this respect, then must the material change into its opposite [τοὐναντίον]. Now the female is opposite [ἐναντίον] to the male, and that in so far as the one is female and the other male.[26]

Here the offspring comes to be out of contraries, and in its coming to be, the material can change from resembling one or the other of the contraries that form it. Note that the embryo itself is called material as a substrate that is coming to be as one sex or the other.

After this passage Aristotle notes that certain parts are principles of the whole body, such that when they change, the whole body does.[27] This leads Aristotle to pose a number of conditions which, if met, would explain when and how the heart and blood are formed:

> The male is a principle and a cause, and the male is such in virtue of a certain capacity and the female is such in virtue of an incapacity, and [. . .] the definition of the capacity and of the incapacity is ability or inability to concoct the nourishment in its ultimate stage [. . .] and [. . .] the cause of this capacity is in the first principle and in the part which contains the principle of natural heat [. . .][28]

If we accept these conditionals, the male and female are contraries or opposites of a kind because of a presence or absence of a capacity to concoct, a capacity that comes about through having sufficient appropriate heat to achieve the right level of concoction.

An opposition is thus set up between the male and the female in reproduction, an opposition of contraries that is based on a capacity or incapacity, which is to say on a form and privation. But we have two accounts of the way that male and female are contraries: one makes male and female opposed as form and privation working on a third substratum – the embryo – and one makes male the form that works on female matter.[29] The latter appears in Aristotle's account of generation as such and the former in Aristotle's account of sexual differentiation. This suggests that the difference that becomes the difference between form and matter is a difference that is located in the body, the material.

Katherine Park and Robert A. Nye explain that both medieval and Renaissance thinkers deny the possibility of a middle between male and female, not just biologically but because the legal landscape has no place for such a middle.[30] But the two kinds of oppositions that Aristotle describes between form and matter show that they are related as both contradictories and contraries. In order for the mapping of form and matter onto male and female to work, they seem to necessarily be contradictories, and yet Aristotle characterizes the distinction more as contraries. In *Categories* 10, Aristotle describes two kinds of contraries: those in which one or the other contrary must belong to that of which they are contraries, as sickness or health must belong to animals' bodies and odd or even must apply to numbers, and those in which neither extreme necessarily belongs to that of which they are contraries, as black and white need not belong to a body and bad or good need not be predicated of men.[31] With the second kind of contrary, the one extreme can change into the other.[32] This kind Aristotle simply calls "contraries." The first maintains an uncrossable distance, and this kind of contrary Aristotle calls "contradictories." In *Metaphysics* Iota, Aristotle writes that "contradiction [ἀντίφασις] admits of no intermediate, while contraries [ἐναντίων] admit of one."[33] Aristotle continues that while contradiction does not allow an intermediate, the change in matter is from contraries. Several chapters later, he writes, "since contraries [ἐναντίως] admit of an intermediate and in some cases have it, the intermediate must be composed of the contraries."[34]

Two chapters later, Aristotle addresses gender and contrariety:

> One might raise the question, why woman does not differ from man in species, female and male being contrary, and their difference being a contrariety [ἐναντώσεως]; and why a female and male belong to it *qua* animal. This question is almost the same as the other, why one contrariety makes things different in species and another does not.[35]

After explaining that contraries that are in formula make a difference in species while contraries in the material do not, he concludes:

> And male and female are indeed modifications peculiar to animal, not however in virtue of its substance but in the matter, i.e. the body. This is why the same seed becomes female or male by being acted on in a certain way. We have stated, then, what it is to be other in species, and why some things differ in species and others do not.[36]

Aristotle begins the next chapter, "Since contraries are other in form [. . .] ." Some kind of difference appears here at the level of material that produces the distinction between male and female, a distinction which is taken to be a difference between what is capable of generating qua form and what only contributes matter to generation, a difference that depends on how the seed is worked on. This view is complicated by the fact that male and female are contraries that necessarily belong to animals, which would seem to make them contraries with an excluded middle, while that which makes them distinct – a degree of heat – would seem to have an intermediate. The female appears to be, or at least to offer, the material that is the underlying thing distinct from the contraries of form and privation, yet she is also the privation of male form in the embryo.

At *Physics* I.7, Aristotle explains generation as something that happens between contraries, "since it is impossible for the contraries to be acted on by each other. But this difficulty also is solved by the fact that what underlies is different from the contraries for it is itself not a contrary [ἐναντίον]."[37] In *Physics* I.9, Aristotle clarifies how the material, as what underlies, differs from privation: "Now we distinguish matter and privation, and hold that one of these, namely the matter, accidentally is not, while the privation in its own nature is not; and that the matter is nearly, in a sense is, substance, while the privation in no sense is."[38] Aristotle continues to refine his definition of matter in this same chapter: "For my definition of matter is just this – the primary substratum of each thing, from which it comes to be, and which persists in the result, not accidentally."[39] In *Metaphysics* Z.8, Aristotle explains that matter is that from which something comes to be and clarifies "let this be taken to be not the privation but the matter."[40]

The shift from male to female occurs between opposites in a way that shows a difference not between form and matter but within the material body, as Aristotle describes the transition that occurs from the offspring being male to the offspring being female in *Generation of Animals* IV.3:

> Now, when anything *departs from type* (ἐξίσταται [note that this is a verbal form of ἔκστασις]), it goes not into any chance thing but into the opposite [ἀντικείμενον], and so too in generation, what isn't mastered necessarily departs from type and comes-to-be the opposite with respect to the *dunamis* with respect to which the generator and mover didn't get mastery. If, then, it's *qua male*, what comes-to-be is female.[41]

Here the change is still at the level of material, as we established earlier, rather than the form as such. Within the material body there are contraries (necessary ones, which would seem to make them contradictories) – male and female – that in fact rise to the level of having the capacity to form the offspring from the generative principles of form and material. These are material contraries that become formal contraries in generation. They become formal contraries, as I will show in the next section, through a material difference: heat.

HEAT IN GENERATION

Aristotle tells us that the male and female both contribute something in generation: residue concocted to various degrees of heat.[42] Aristotle remarks in *GA* II.1 that the semen (σπέρμα) has the principle of motion that brings life into parts, animating them so that they become the parts that they are. In *GA* I.18, Aristotle describes how semen (σπέρμα and σημεῖον) comes to have that principle, beginning, as the feminine contribution does, in nutriment.[43] The nutriment can fail to become semen if the person is too fat because then the residue is being concocted into fat rather than semen (σπέρμα).[44] Thus the process of making semen can fail even in the same body from one time to another.[45] Such failure defines the female as female, "owing to the coldness of her nature."[46] According to this account, if the heat fails to concoct, this failure both signals that the concocting body was female – if what defines the male as male is the ability to concoct – and that what is being worked on will become female. The concoction that forms semen out of residue and that somehow imparts the power to concoct into the semen occurs in the semen through a certain kind of heat, a heat that comes only from other things that share this heat.

Keeping distinct what semen forms and what forms semen, it seems that a certain degree of heat can concoct homogeneous parts – blood, fat, even semen – in a way that thickens them. Still, this heat cannot organize the material into non-homogeneous parts; it cannot bring soul into the material. Aristotle explains that the qualities of these parts may be caused by heat and cold, "yet, when we come to the principle in virtue of which flesh is flesh and bone is bone, that is no longer so; what makes them is the movement set up in the male parent, who is in actuality what that out of which the offspring is made is in potentiality."[47] Semen (τὰ σπέρματα) has the capacity to work the blood up to the point where it has soul, animation, and breath, and to impart such a capacity into the offspring.[48] Soul itself is the animating breath (πνεῦμα), which is heat.[49] Such heat forms the body that will be capable of forming semen by working on the menses to fully concoct it. Successful concoction makes semen out of menses by heating the material to the level where it can generate heat in something else. Failed concoction works at two levels: first, the failure to achieve life; and second, the failure to impart this capacity to achieve life in another to the offspring.[50] A certain degree of heat moves the menses from not having to having breath or soul, which is to say from being material to being form; more heat moves it from not having life to being capable of imparting life. In both cases, this capacity is vital heat.[51]

Before turning to vital heat and its powers, let us review the perplexities that have arisen thus far. Semen is formed by becoming the kind of residue that has sufficient heat, a category of residue that also describes blood, fat, and nutriment. We can deduce that it becomes this kind of residue from another thing that has sufficient heat of the right kind, that is as a result of having been formed from the parent semen. I say deduce because Aristotle offers the account of how the offspring is formed, but the transition into how that offspring is later able to conjure up sufficient heat is not clear, except that it seems initially, by its nature, to have the heat of the father. This process of heat is not a certainty since even the body designated male can fail to produce this semen if it is using that heat to make fat because it has too much nutriment. The same body can both make and fail to make semen if the other nutriments are not in the proper proportion, a proportion that one presumes would follow from having the right kind of heat.

Aristotle writes:

> Now it is true that the faculty of all kinds of soul seems to have a connexion with a matter different from and more divine than the so-called elements; but as one soul differs from another in honour and dishonour, so also the nature of the corresponding matter. All have in their semen that which causes it to be productive; I mean what is called vital heat [θερμόν]. This is not fire nor any such force, but it is the breath [πνεῦμα] included in the semen [σπέρματι] and the foam-like, and the natural principle in the breath [πνεύματι φύσις], being analogous to the element of the stars [τῷ τῶν ἄστρων στοιχείῳ]. Hence, whereas fire generates no animal and we do not find any living thing forming in either solids or liquids under the influence of fire, the heat of the sun [τοῦ ἡλίου θερμότης] and that of animals does generate them. Not only is this true of the heat that works through the semen [διὰ τοῦ σπέρματος], but whatever other residue of the animal nature there may be, this also has still a vital principle [ζωτικὴν ἀρχήν] in it. From such considerations it is clear that the heat [θερμότης] in animals neither is fire nor derives its origin from fire.[52]

Aristotle distinguishes the heat that causes semen to be generative from fire, "which generates no animal." Only "the heat of the sun and that of animals" generates living things. This source is not simply fire, which is elemental and material, but proper (οἰκεῖος) heat, heat from the sun. Fire can form the homogeneous parts (the qualities), but not that which has a function (the ensouled parts). This is the heat proper to bodies that comes from the sun or the earth or the stomach. Aristotle describes this heat as breath, πνεῦμα, and as the heat that is analogous to the heat in the stars, the element of aether. Much later in *Generation of Animals*, Aristotle writes, "animals and plants come into being in earth and in water because there is water in earth, and πνεῦμα in water, and all πνεῦμα is soul-heat [θερμότητα ψυχικήν], so that in a way all things are full of soul."[53] In joining Thales' twin claims that everything is made of water and all things are full of soul, Aristotle associates soul-heat with water and earth in this passage, making it much closer to the elements, against the earlier passage wherein they are distinct. Similarly, in GA II.2, Aristotle defines semen (σπέρμα) itself as water and air after addressing the material properties of water and air in relation to heat.[54]

Friedrich Solmsen ponders the strangeness of the constellation of vital heat, πνεῦμα, and aether in Aristotle: each of these element-like forces are ways that Aristotle tries to think the material site of soul.[55] Aristotle's vacillation between speaking of these as material and at other places as immaterial or divine points to his need to find a material basis for soul while resisting a reduction of soul to material.[56] Solmsen notes that just as Aristotle first defines σπέρμα as πνεῦμα and water where πνεῦμα seems to be merely air, in some places he similarly seems to make fire capable of the kinds of concocting changes attributed to heat. In *Parts of Animals*, Aristotle speaks of fire, breath, and natural heat: fire is the tool the soul uses (such that all animals have an amount of this heat); breath feeds the "internal fire" (where fire or cognates of it are repeated three times in association with the breath); and natural, concocting heat comes from the soul, which is "as it were, set aglow with fire."[57] But Aristotle vociferously rejects their identity in other places (as in the passage above). Solmsen explains the shift from σπέρμα as principle or form in *GA* I to σπέρμα including some material contribution in *GA* II in terms of the shift in focus from the body of the offspring to its soul. It is striking that when the shift is made to the soul, the σπέρμα needs to contribute some material to cause it, that is it needs to be enmattered. So the soul is caused by vital heat, or as Gad Freudenthal argues, vital heat carries the soul, the enforming capacity, and this heat is manifested in πνεῦμα.[58]

Aristotle also says in this passage that vital heat is found in "whatever other residue of the animal nature there may be." One place it is found is in the stomach of both male and female bodies because nutrition requires it. Aristotle explains that nutrition occurs in plants and animals when heat concocts food into blood. In *Parts of Animals*, Aristotle calls the stomach in animals "the internal substitute for the hearth,"[59] since it is where food is concocted into blood, while the earth plays this role for plants.[60] Citing *De Anima* II.4, Paul Studtmann draws a parallel between the heat in digestion and the heat in reproduction, since in both cases, there is a distinction between the kind of heat that causes something to move upward or downward (fire) and the kind of heat that causes matter to emanate it.[61] Different degrees of vital heat seem to produce different degrees of concoction in material, but all things that have nutrition have a vital heat that causes concoction of food into blood. In *Parts of Animals*, Aristotle explains that moist and dry substance is concocted into nourishment "by the force of heat [δία τῆς τοῦ θερμοῦ δυνάμεως]." Since this process is needed for all living things, "it follows that all living things, animals and plants alike, must on this account, if on no other, have a natural source of heat [ἀρχὴν θερμοῦ φυσικήν]; and this, like the working of the food, must belong to many parts."[62] In the next chapter, Aristotle explains that anger produces heat (θερμότητος)[63] and that blood is kept fluid by animal heat (διὰ τὴν θερμότητα τὴν ἐν τοῖς ζῴοις).[64] Thus, Studtmann argues, the semen owes its becoming semen to the same process whereby food is converted into blood,[65] and, we could add, whereby we become angry and our blood remains fluid. Aristotle names fire the source of the heat in the digestive process in *On Youth and Old Age*, where the soul depends upon the digestive processes which depend on natural fire and which can be lost through exhaustion (just as when there is too much heat in a thing burning without extra fuel added).[66]

Vital heat does not seem to be of a different order than of the heat that belongs to all bodies, which turn moist and dry substances into nutriment. Studtmann argues that degrees of vital heat explain the different organizational complexity of nutritive and perceptive organisms, on the basis of his argument that vital heat in the biological works parallels the different types of soul in *De Anima*.[67] The difference between male and female is that less heat is required to maintain certain capacities than is required to generate them.[68] Freudenthal, whom Studtmann appears to be following here, argues that there is thus a difference of degree within vital heat, but a difference of kind between vital heat and elemental heat.[69] Some passages that discuss the difference between male and female seem to designate it as the difference between that which has vital heat and that which has either elemental heat or no heat at all, as when the difference is between what can bring life and what cannot (as when Aristotle says that woman is cold). Other passages, those that draw parallels between the concoction of menses in reproduction and the concoction of food into blood, make vital heat and the power to concoct present in all living things, as when Aristotle writes: "For the earth aids in the concoction by its heat, and the brooding hen does the same, for she infuses the heat that is within her."[70] And again:

> The nourishment again of some is earth and water, of others a combination of these, so that what the heat in animals produces from their nutriment, the heat of the warm season in the environment puts together and combines by concoction out of the sea-water and the earth. And the portion of the vital principle which is either included along with it or separated off in the air makes an embryo and puts motion into it.[71]

Even if a difference of kind between elemental and vital heat is granted, there would remain a strong case that the difference between male and female is a difference in degrees of vital heat. This difference is between the vital heat that can only achieve nutrition and the vital heat that can achieve reproduction, where both are ways of furthering life. If we agree that female bodies do have this nutritive vital heat, then the difference seems to be one of degree. If it is one of degree, then it seems that what is traditionally thought of as a strictly formal principle includes a material aspect, and what is traditionally considered a material principle includes something of what we traditionally attribute to form. On these terms, it seems that the difference between matter and form turns on a temperature – some degree of vital heat after which the soul is present and a degree below which it is not.

ARTIFICE'S NECESSARY CONTRADICTORIES

The account of vital heat presents a model of generation that has the form arising from material. This reading would be challenged in *Generation of Animals* I.22–3, where Aristotle speaks of generation in terms of artifice, where form is imposed on material. Aristotle explains that the carpenter must be connected to the wood and the workmanship. Movement from the carpenter to the material must be connected to the material "as, for instance, architecture is *in* the building it makes."[72] "From these considerations," those of the carpenter and the wood, Aristotle says "we may also gather how it is that the male contributes to generation."[73] He then explains that the carpenter imparts the "shape [μορφὴ] and form [εἶδος]" to the material through motion.[74] As Aristotle writes:

> It is his hands that move his tools, his tools that move the material;
> it is his knowledge of his art, and his soul, in which is the form, that
> move his hands or any other part of him with a motion of some
> definite kind, a motion varying with the varying nature of the object
> made. In like manner, in the male of those animals which emit semen,
> nature uses the semen as a tool and as a possessing motion in actuality,
> just as tools are used in the products of any art, for in them lies in a
> certain sense the motion of the art.[75]

It seems that it is only after the initial moment of generation that nature functions according to an internal principle, but in that initial moment, it remains a model of imposition and mastery. The semen does not become part of the resulting embryo just as no part of the carpenter's art exists in what he makes.[76] The semen is not a part of the offspring, but just a tool of nature to impose form on the καταμήνια. Toward the end of this chapter which concludes *Generation of Animals* I, Aristotle writes, "in all this nature acts like an intelligent workman."[77]

Montgomery Furth argues that the semen itself is not even form, but the tool of the male parent's form. As such, the semen has informational power:

> The *logos* of a pre-determined sequence of physical and chemical
> formative activities ("movements" and "concoctings") which, given
> *catamenia* to work upon, will effectuate a corresponding sequence of
> changes in the catamenial substrate, each change presupposing those
> before it, *via* the postulated physical and chemical mechanisms (as
> "efficient" or "moving causes").[78]

Furth cites *Generation of Animals* II.1, where Aristotle writes: "In a way it is the innate motion that does this [sets up the movement of form in the embryo], as the act of building builds a house."[79] Then in the next paragraph he continues:

> What makes them [the non-homogeneous parts] is the movement set
> up by the male parent, who is in actuality what that out of which
> the offspring is made is in potentiality. This is what we find in the
> products of art; heat and cold may make the iron soft and hard,
> but what makes a sword is the movement of the tools employed,
> this movement containing the principle of the art. For the art is the
> starting-point and form of the product; only it exists in something else,
> whereas the movement of nature exists in the product itself, issuing
> from another nature which has the form in actuality.[80]

Aristotle's account of form as an organizing principle does not seem to allow for a principle of information that is separate from the form as shape. That account seems very much like an account of artifice where the form that generates is an idea in the mind of the artificer, distinct from the form that is the shape. For the account of artifice to work, not only is the information of form distinct from its shape, but also the form has to be a clearly distinct principle from matter. Only if matter is distinct can form be imposed on it. The account of vital heat suggests that the distinction between form and matter arises from out of material and proceeds along a progression from out of material. It proceeds in some material to work it up to the level where it is capable of working up future material, to the point where that future material can work up even further material. Some material must be worked up to a point that is concocted enough to develop nutritive soul, but not worked up sufficiently to be animal soul. This material joins to the other more worked up material to form a living animal offspring. Both kinds of material when they encounter each other have a certain amount of heat from within themselves that brings each to be what it is.

At the outset, it seems that in order for nature to really arise from itself, form in natural generation would need to arise from material. That indeed seems to be the case, though it is true that it arises, that it becomes form, from a vital heat that works the material up to a point where it can do the same to further material. But natural generation is not spontaneous generation; some unifying work is needed between a form that arises from material and a material that becomes form. So when the form comes together, having arisen out of material to join to other material, the form appears to join with its contrary, the contrary from which it has arisen, and in so doing come to some kind of intermediate.

All of this leads to the pressing question that Aristotle's biology raises: is an artifice model of imposition possible, when the imposed form is worked up out of material and imposed on the very material that is also worked up, albeit not as fully worked up? The structure of imposition requires difference and hierarchy. But if the form is worked up from material and imposed and thus joined to material that is less or otherwise worked up, this fusion or joining would seem to collapse the distinction between them. And is not that what natural substance looks like, form that is well-nigh impossible to distinguish from its material?

CONCLUSION

Two points in conclusion. First, we tend to think of "true difference" as formal difference, difference in kind, even as we are pursuing true difference for the sake of elevating the feminine principle, material. We think of difference of degree, difference that is less truly different, as material difference. Where then are we left if the difference between matter and form is itself one of degrees of vital heat, that is a material difference? Where are we left if the difference between the masculine and the feminine is not a formal one? Initially, it seems that this means we are in the one-sex model, the masculine is true sex because it is formal while the feminine aspires toward form. It seems like a less-than-true difference because it is not formal difference. I argue in this essay that the difference between male and female, between form and material, the one based on degrees of vital heat, is a feminine difference, a material one. The feminine principle, material, with its variable degrees of heat, thereby forms the difference between the feminine and the masculine.

Second, the difficult thing about talking about material is that trying to talk about it in any way other than how we have always talked about it requires that we already can talk about it in such an other way. It seems close to impossible to get from here to there without already being there. To challenge the ways by which we think about material in Aristotle requires distinguishing material from, well . . . material, and in this move, we propose that material in Aristotle is not non-form, but rather that it is formal, and therefore better because not as much like material. This is especially a problem for Aristotle, who is generally treated to be the source of the profound distinction between material (stuff, completely unformed, needing something outside of itself to give it shape and meaning) and form (the shape, the source of meaning that makes material show up). If menses is the material, its distinction from semen in terms of degrees of vital heat makes semen form through a material distinction. What this tells us about material is that it is capable of producing a distinction between form and material, which offers us a way to think about material without either elevating material's worth (because it could become *form*) or *devaluing form* (because it is only distinct from material because of some power that is itself material). Such claims would use the language that assumes a great divide and hierarchy between form and material to challenge that divide and hierarchy.

Vital heat does some work for us in thinking through these questions because of its connection to both the elemental and the animate at once. Vital heat is not an on/off switch that makes the residue male or not, but rather a matter of degrees that can fail and be affected by other material. On these terms, material, which in some places Aristotle tries his darnedest to keep from having a crucial explanatory role (in generation specifically and change more generally), comes to have a vital role. In this vital role, material does not look like the material we thought we knew.

NOTES

[I am indebted to the organizers and audience members of the Pennsylvania Circle for Ancient Philosophy meeting in 2014 where I presented this argument for the keynote, especially Rebecca Goldner, Claire Griffin, L. Aryeh Kosman, Christopher P. Long, and Laura McMahon. I am also grateful to the organizers and audience members at the Ancient Philosophy Society meeting in Lexington, KY in 2015 where I presented a version of this essay, especially Emanuela Bianchi and Mitchell Miller. Finally, I would like to thank my summer research student, Jonathan Bojrab, in conversation with whom I was motivated to pursue the distinction between contradictions and contraries to further my case.]

1. Brooke Holmes, *Gender: Antiquity and Its Legacy* [Holmes], p. 43.
2. Simone de Beauvoir, *The Second Sex*, p. 273.
3. Luce Irigaray, "How to Conceive (of) a Girl," in *The Speculum of the Other Woman* [Irigaray], p. 164.
4. Judith Butler, *Bodies That Matter* [Butler], p. 16.
5. Emanuela Bianchi, *The Feminine Symptom: Aleatory Matter in the Aristotelian Cosmos*, esp. Chapter Six, "Sexual Difference in Potentiality and Actuality," pp. 183–222.
6. Butler p. 4.
7. Ibid. p. 5.
8. Adriel Trott, *Aristotle on the Nature of Community*.
9. Butler p. 8.
10. Holmes p. 67.
11. Aristotle uses the term σπέρμα sometimes to refer to seed as such, any contribution to generation, and sometimes to refer to the specific male contribution. Thus some passages where A. Platt (in *The Complete Works of Aristotle*, ed. Jonathan Barnes) translates σπέρμα as semen (such as *Generation of Animals* [*GA*], 725b26ff.) might seem confusing because what is under dispute is not whether the male contribution is much or little, but whether both male and female contributions together are much or little depending on what in the blood is pulled away for nutrition instead of reproduction. (If σπέρμα here means the male contribution, then it does seem to follow that the male contribution is dependent on the availability of material.) Mayhew translates σπέρμα as seed and γόνη as semen. To complicate things, Dean-Jones translates γόνη as both seed and sperm and σπέρμα as semen in the Hippocratic corpus. Dean-Jones, *Women's Bodies in Classical Greek Science* [Dean-Jones], pp. 154, 155n25, 155n26, 165n60, 166n61. James Lennox argues that Aristotle uses σπέρμα somewhat interchangeably with γόνη in *GA* I; in *GA* II and for the rest of *Generation of Animals*, Aristotle seems to use σπέρμα as the generic for seed or contribution and γόνη to refer to the male contribution or semen and καταμηνία to refer to the female contribution or menses.
12. In *Making Sex: Body and Gender from the Greeks to Freud* [Laqueur], pp. 54–5, Thomas Laqueur writes:

> Sperma, for Aristotle makes the man *and* serves as synecdoche for citizen. In a society where physical labor was the sign of inferiority, sperma eschews physical contact with the catemenia and does its work by intellection. The *kurios*, the strength of

the sperma in generating new life, is the microcosmic corporeal aspect of the citizen's deliberative strength of his superior rational power, and of his right to govern. Sperma, in other words, is like the essence of citizen.

Laqueur's account is useful for setting up this distinction between a one-sex and two-sex model, but it is not without serious flaws. As Katherine Park and Robert A. Nye note (in "Destiny is Anatomy"), Laqueur tries to force a distinction between ancient and modern models without sufficient evidence; they help show that it was Aristotelians who were responsible for several views associated with Aristotle, such as the view that the women contribute no seed and that there is a profound incommensurability between the male and female. Helen King dedicates a monograph to responding to and criticizing Laqueur: Helen King, *The One-Sex Body on Trial: The Classical and Early Modern Evidence* [King].

13. As noted by, *inter alia*: Laqueur pp. 28–9; King pp. 40–2; Holmes pp. 39–44.
14. Cf. Irigaray.
15. Holmes pp. 50–4.
16. Helen King and Rebecca Flemming maintain that these are not loaded terms for Aristotle and for Galen as they are for us. King argues that "deformed" and "less perfect" do not carry the judgements for the Greeks that they do for us – though this is somewhat dubious given the centrality of teleology in their work (King p. 41). King quotes Rebecca Flemming who argues that these terms are their way of describing women's "critical inability" to heat their material to the degree where it could impart life-giving breath; see Flemming, *Medicine and the Making of Roman Women*, p. 119.
17. Robert Mayhew's two-sex, two-seed model might complicate this reading of Aristotle. Mayhew attempts to redeem Aristotle by arguing that Aristotle sometimes uses seed in a neutral way to refer to any contribution to generation, that is both semen and menses, so both male and female contribute seed but in different ways (see Mayhew, *The Female in Aristotle's Biology: Reason or Rationalization* [Mayhew], p. 38).
18. Esther Fischer-Homberger, "Herr und Weib," cited by Laqueur p. 8.
19. Laqueur pp. 4–8.
20. Holmes pp. 43–4.
21. This problem is at work in Aristotle's account of how the semen as form works. Lesley Dean-Jones suggests that Aristotle could have allowed that there was material in the semen without detracting from the male superiority he wanted to support, but to do so would make the male hylomorphic, not completely form (in Dean-Jones p. 188).
22. Aristotle, *Metaphysics* [*Meta.*], Z.5.1048a10–14, Z.8.1050a6–10, Z.15–16, Λ.6.1071b30–1, 1072b3–4.
23. Holmes p. 43.

24. *GA* 724b7–10.
25. Ibid. 765b35–766a2.
26. Ibid. 765b35–766a2.
27. Ibid. 766a23–27.
28. Ibid. 766a30–3, 35.
29. This dual conception of material is invoked by Emanuela Bianchi in this volume, "Aristotle's Organism, and Ours." James Bogen argues that Aristotle's use of the term "complete privation" at *Meta.* 1055a33 suggests that there can be partial privation (in "Change and Contrariety in Aristotle," pp. 13–14). See also Mary Louise Gill who argues from *Physics* I.7 and *Generation of Animals* I.18 that material as the ὑποκείμενον in generation has its own proper identity and it remains at work when formed by the form and seed (*Aristotle on Substance: The Paradox of Unity* [Gill], pp. 106–7).
30. Park and Nye, "Destiny is Anatomy," p. 56.
31. Aristotle, *Categories*, 12a1–17.
32. Ibid. 13a19–20.
33. *Meta.* 1055b1–2.
34. Ibid. 1057a18–19.
35. Ibid. 1058a29–36.
36. Ibid. 1058b21–5.
37. Aristotle, *Physics*, 190b32–4.
38. *Physics* 192a4–6. Gill argues that as the substratum material has an identity of its own and it is the subject of generation (not merely of destruction) with reference to *Physics* I.7.
39. *Physics* 192a31–3.
40. *Meta.* 1033a25–6.
41. *GA* 768a2–5. From Montgomery Furth's translation in *Substance, Form and Psyche: An Aristotelian Metaphysics* [Furth], p. 130. Emphasis by translator; brackets are my own.
42. Whether they both contribute something is contested in the literature. Helen King, p. 40, argues that woman does not contribute seed. Mayhew, pp. 34–40, argues that she does.
43. *GA* 725a1–2, 726b2–11, 727a3–4, 727a31–727b5, 728a26–7. Aristotle describes the process of concoction in great detail in *Meteorology* 379b18–35, 381b29–382a5, 382a32–4, 383a1–14, 383b25–6, 384a9–10, 384b4–5. In *Meteorology*, Aristotle describes the work of heat as concoction: "a process in which the natural and proper heat [τοῦ φυσικοῦ καὶ οἰκείου θερμοῦ] of an object perfects the corresponding passive qualities [the dry and moist], which are the proper matter [ἡ οἰκεία ἑκάστῳ ὕλη] of any given object" (*Meteor.* 379b18–20). Aristotle has divided the active work of hot and cold from the passive work of dry and moist and argues that concoction, this heating process, is rooted in the body – "the primary source is the proper heat [θερμότης] of the body" (379b24) – and the end of concoction can be the nature of a thing – "nature, that is, in the sense of the form and essence" (379b26).

Having associated dry and moist with matter and heat and cold with form, Aristotle concludes, "concoction ensues whenever the matter, the moisture, is mastered. For the matter is what is determined by the natural heat in the object, and as long as the ratio between them exists in it a thing maintains its nature" (379b33–5). What is noteworthy in this passage is that form and material are both understood through material processes – heat and cold (both!) are forming processes, and dry and moist (both!) are material that are formed (hot and cold form the passive qualities: *Meteor.* 382a32–4, 383a1–14, 383b25–6, 384a9–10, 384b4–5; dry and moist are both acted on: *Meteor.* 381b29–382a5). Thus the process of formation seems to have worked up from the material level. Because there is considerable dispute regarding whether that account is consistent with the account of *Generation of Animals*, a dispute that would take some space to adjudicate, I have refrained from addressing the *Meteorology* here. Mary Louise Gill argues that either the passive or active element can be at work in elemental change from one element to another: when fire works on earth, its active heat makes it fire, but when fire works on air, the passive dryness makes it fire (in Gill pp. 81–2). Moreover, Gill argues, the elements themselves appear as material that is underlying yet already and always formed, not made up of any simpler ingredients, yet having a distinct character (ibid. p. 82).

44. *GA* 725b31–726a6, see also 727a35–6.

45. Ibid. 726b6–11.

46. Ibid. 728a21. The circularity of this logic is that if the heat fails to concoct this failure both signals that the concocting body is female and that what is being worked on will be female.

47. Ibid. 734b31–5.

48. Ibid. 736b34–737a3, 766a17–20.

49. Ibid. 762a19–20.

50. Here I find myself surprised to side with D. M. Balme over Charlotte Witt, whose work on Aristotle has been influential for me. While I agree with Witt that Balme is wrong to posit a radically individual form in Aristotle, I agree with Balme that the same movement of the semen that generates the offspring differentiates its sex (where I would say that sexual differentiation and the resemblance of the offspring are also of the same order in Aristotle). See D. M. Balme, "Aristotle's Biology is Not Essentialist."

51. The term translated as vital heat is θερμόν. There is no "vital" or "βίος" modifier. Sometimes Aristotle modifies θερμόν with natural or proper (φυσικός or οἰκεῖος). Both Peck and Platt occasionally translate θερμόν itself as "proper heat." Peck translates θερμόν as "hot substance" in the passage below.

52. *GA* 736b29–737a6.

53. Ibid. 762a19–20. My translation, revised from Platt's and Peck's.

54. Ibid. 736a1–2.

55. Friedrich Solmsen, "The Vital Heat, the Inborn Pneuma and the Aether" [Solmsen].

56. Solmsen, p. 122, writes that "all things are full of soul" replaces Thales' "all things are full of gods."

57. Aristotle, *Parts of Animals* [PA] 652b8–16, 473a4–9, and 469b11–17, respectively; cited also by Solmsen at p. 121.

58. Gad Freudenthal argues that the πνεῦμα in Aristotle is a unifying force that keeps a substance together and prevents all the elements from flying in separate directions (Gad Freudenthal, *Aristotle's Theory of Material Substance* [Freudenthal], pp. 137–8). Freudenthal argues that vital heat works on the blood in such a way as to transform it into πνεῦμα which remains in the blood (ibid. p. 125). Freudenthal argues against the view he attributes to Solmsen, that πνεῦμα is the instrument whereby heat is carried through the blood. Freudenthal argues that such an interpretation makes πνεῦμα into a *deus ex machina* since it seems unrelated to any other part of Aristotle's physical theory (ibid. p. 108). Freudenthal's solution is to show that vital heat is not an instrument of the soul that forms; rather vital heat carries the enforming movement, which is to say that it is soul, at once an efficient cause and a formal cause, not merely an efficient cause or tool (ibid. pp. 23–32). Balme argues that πνεῦμα is formed when heat acts on moisture as a result of the body's natural activity, arguing that there is at least a continuum of difference between heat and vital heat, in his commentary of Aristotle's *De Partibus Animalium I and De Generatione Animalium I*, pp. 160–4. Consider also, Aristotle, GA 703a25ff., *De Anima* 416a6–9.

59. PA 650a25.

60. Ibid. 650a2–9, 23–7:

> Now since everything that grows must take nourishment, and
> nutriment in all cases consists of moist and dry substances,
> and since it is by the force of heat that these are concocted and
> changed, it follows that all living things, animals and plants
> alike, must on this account, if on no other, have a natural source
> of heat; and this, like the working of the food, must belong to
> many parts [. . .] But animals, with scarcely an exception, and
> conspicuously all such as are capable of locomotion, are provided
> with a stomachal sac, which is as it were an internal substitute
> for the hearth. They must therefore have some instrument which
> shall correspond to the roots of plans, with which they may
> absorb their food from this sac, so that the proper end of the
> successive stages of concoction may be attained.

61. Paul Studtmann, "Living Capacities and Vital Heat in Aristotle" [Studtmann], pp. 367, 368, 373. Consider *De Anima* II.4, 416b28–9: "All food must be capable of being digested, and what produces digestion is warmth; that is why everything that has soul in it possesses warmth." See also *Meteorology* 379b11, 381b7.

62. *PA* 650a1–5
63. Ibid. 650b36.
64. Ibid. 651a11.
65. Studtmann p. 370.
66. Aristotle, *On Youth and Old Age*, 474a25–474b24.
67. Studtmann p. 372. This view appears traceable to Freudenthal who argues that vital heat produces the *scala naturae* determined in Aristotle by the degrees of complexity of the soul (Freudenthal p. 4).
68. Studtmann p. 373.
69. Freudenthal p. 110.
70. *GA* 753a17–20.
71. Ibid. 762b12–17.
72. Ibid. 730b5–8.
73. Ibid. 730b9–10.
74. Ibid. 730b14–15.
75. Ibid. 730b16–22.
76. Ibid. 730b10–14.
77. Ibid. 731a25.
78. Furth p. 117.
79. *GA* 734b17–19.
80. Ibid. 734b35–735a4.

BIBLIOGRAPHY

Aristotle, *Generation of Animals*, trans. A. L. Peck (Cambridge, MA: Harvard University Press, 1942).

Aristotle, *The Complete Works of Aristotle: The Revised Oxford Translation*, ed. J. Barnes, 2 vols (Princeton: Princeton University Press, 1984).

Aristotle, *De Partibus Animalium I and De Generatione Animalium I (with passages from II. 1–3)*, trans. and commentary by D. M. Balme (Oxford: Clarendon Press, 1992).

Balme, D.M., "Aristotle's Biology is Not Essentialist," in A. Gotthelf and J. Lennox (eds.), *Philosophical Issues in Aristotle's Biology* (Cambridge: Cambridge University Press, 1987), pp. 291–301.

Bianchi, E., *The Feminine Symptom: Aleatory Matter in the Aristotelian Cosmos* (New York: Fordham University Press, 2014).

Bogen, J., "Change and Contrariety in Aristotle," *Phronesis*, 37 (1992), pp. 2–21.

Butler, J., *Bodies That Matter* (New York: Routledge, 1993).

de Beauvoir, S., *The Second Sex* (London: Lowe & Brydone, 1953).

Dean-Jones, L., *Women's Bodies in Classical Greek Science* (Oxford: Oxford University Press, 1996).

Fischer-Homberger, E., "Herr und Weib," *Krankheit Frau and andere Arbeiten zur Medizinsgeschichte der Frau* (Bern: Huber, 1979).

Flemming, R., *Medicine and the Making of Roman Women* (Oxford: Oxford University Press, 2000).

Freudenthal, G., *Aristotle's Theory of Material Substance* (Oxford: Clarendon Press, 1994).

Furth, M., *Substance, Form and Psyche: An Aristotelian Metaphysics* (Cambridge: Cambridge University Press, 1988).

Gill, M. L., *Aristotle on Substance: The Paradox of Unity* (Princeton: Princeton University Press, 1989).

Holmes, B., *Gender: Antiquity and Its Legacy* (Oxford: Oxford University Press, 2012).

Irigaray, L., *Speculum of the Other Woman*, trans. Gillian C. Gill (Ithaca, NY: Cornell University Press, 1985).

King, H., *The One-Sex Body on Trial: The Classical and Early Modern Evidence* (Dorchester: Dorset Press, 2013).

Lacqueur, T., *Making Sex: Body and Gender from the Greeks to Freud* (Cambridge, MA: Harvard University Press, 1990).

Lennox, James, "Aristotle's Biology," *The Stanford Encyclopedia of Philosophy*, Spring 2014 (http://plato.stanford.edu/archives/spr2014/entries/aristotle-biology/).

Mayhew, R., *The Female in Aristotle's Biology* (Chicago: University of Chicago Press, 2004).

Park, K. and R.A. Nye, "Destiny is Anatomy," *New Republic* (18 February 1991), pp. 53–7.

Solmsen, F., "The Vital Heat, the Inborn Pneuma and the Aether," *Journal of Hellenic Studies*, 77 (1957), pp. 119–23.

Studtmann, P. "Living Capacities and Vital Heat in Aristotle," *Ancient Philosophy* (2004), pp. 365–79.

Trott, A., *Aristotle on the Nature of Community* (Cambridge: Cambridge University Press, 2014).

CHAPTER 10

The Modern Aristotle: Michael Polanyi's Search for Truth against Nihilism

David Hoinski and Ronald Polansky

This book tries [. . .] to re-equip men with the faculties which centuries of critical thought have taught them to distrust.[1]

Modern scientism fetters thought as cruelly as ever the churches had done. It offers no scope for our most vital beliefs and it forces us to disguise them in farcically inadequate terms. Ideologies framed in these terms have enlisted man's highest aspirations in the service of soul-destroying tyrannies.[2]

Modern fanaticism is rooted in an extreme scepticism which can only be strengthened, not shaken, by further doses of universal doubt.[3]

It is the height of intellectual perversion to renounce, in the name of scientific objectivity, our position as the highest form of life on earth, and our own advent by a process of evolution as the most important problem of evolution.[4]

Contemporary philosophy of science has been characterized as a debate between realists, idealists, and skeptics about whether science gives us knowledge, and if so what kind.[5] Twentieth-century analytic philosophy featured a debate between logical empiricism, represented by Carnap, Hempel, Reichenbach, and others, and the historicist view of science associated with such philosophers as Hanson, Kuhn, and Feyerabend. The extreme version of this debate, perhaps not held by any of these, would pit a radical objectivism against an equally radical subjectivism. Within continental philosophy, meanwhile, the primacy of consciousness in the natural and social sciences has been emphasized, though it remains a question whether phenomenological and existentialist approaches to science differ significantly from idealism.[6] The phenomenological work of Husserl, toward the end of his life, turned increasingly to the implications of the modern view of science for humanity,[7] and, like Michael Polanyi, saw a correlation between the rise of irrationalism and the straitened outlook imposed on the world by modern natural science. Wilfrid Sellars, from the analytic perspective, provided a comparable critique based on the tension between what he called the manifest image and the scientific image of man.[8] The relationship between science, the theory of knowledge, and the ethical-political implications of both thus came increasingly to the foreground. Contemporary disagreements about the understanding of science and its role tends to bolster the case for skepticism or relativism since, as Plato's Socrates says, intellectual wandering implies absence of knowledge.[9]

The renascence of key Aristotelian lines of thought in the work of Michael Polanyi (1891–1976) offers a critical realism that also does justice to the insights seemingly opposed to it – idealism, phenomenology, and the historicist school – by emphasizing the essential contribution of human beings to knowledge both in and beyond the natural sciences. At the same time, Polanyi's realism combats the skepticism and "dogmatic subjectivity"[10] often associated with these approaches. It does so, however, in a markedly different way from, for example, logical empiricism, which might be seen to exemplify the objectivism Polanyi seeks to overthrow. Polanyi considers objectivism to be problematic for physics and chemistry, and as having an especially pernicious influence in biology, psychology, sociology, and related disciplines. For him the objectivist ideal "falsifies our whole outlook far beyond the domain of science,"[11] perverting our understanding and evaluation of the humanities, ethics, and religion. Objectivism tends to relegate these endeavors to the domain of the merely subjective, hence groundless. Polanyi calls the critical realism he advocates "personal knowledge," which he expects to respond to difficulties in the epistemology of science that he sees playing into contemporary ethical-political problems.

We have three aims: (1) to show how central Aristotelian concerns, such as purpose and structure in nature, and the role of intellect in the human pursuit of knowledge, recur in Polanyi's work; (2) to suggest how Polanyi's rehabilitation of these Aristotelian concerns offers a valuable contribution to contemporary philosophy of science; and (3) to indicate ways that Polanyi's approach to the philosophy of science answers to the ethical-political difficulties that he, like others, sees arising from misconceptions about the nature of science.

Polanyi resembles Aristotle in interesting ways. Trained as a physician and then an active researcher in physical chemistry for many years, Polanyi published numerous scientific papers before turning in the 1940s to philosophical reflection. Thus, like Aristotle, whose philosophy was informed by his biological studies, Polanyi married experience of doing natural science with philosophical reflection. As a philosopher, furthermore, Polanyi like Aristotle worked in many fields, including the natural sciences, psychology, economics, politics, mathematics, metaphysics, religion, fine art, and history. The similarities between the two go even deeper, since for Polanyi all explicit knowledge depends upon tacit knowledge, which entails that we know more than we can say. This shows that human wisdom is never fully formalizable and points to the human involvement in every dimension of theory and practice. Polanyi and Aristotle both emphasize the crucial role played by seeing and intellectual intuition (νοῦς) in science. It follows that science is not something anyone can generate simply by applying a set of rules; rather, it depends at every stage upon an integrating activity of mind, utilizing what has previously been understood. Contrary to the notion that methodical rules can govern scientific investigation impersonally, Polanyi contends that the scientist, or wise person, must learnedly apply what can only be rules of art or maxims, reflecting Aristotle's account of acquired intellectual virtues.

There are, of course, differences between Polanyi's and Aristotle's positions, especially due to their different historical situations. Although both are realists and are optimistic about our ability to make contact with reality through science, Polanyi's view of reality is markedly more cautious and open-ended. Aristotle could see himself as seeking comprehensive understanding in all the most important sciences and, more radically, as bringing philosophy to completion as wisdom. This attitude reflects Aristotle's conviction that the accumulated experience of the cultures of the ancient world had attained as much progressive development as could be achieved.[12] Polanyi, however, confronts a world highly aware of scientific revolutions and progress, illustrated by the examples of Copernicus, Kepler, Newton, Darwin, Planck, and Einstein. Polanyi's commitment to a certain conception of what he calls, after Teilhard de Chardin, the "noosphere" admits that "we may be totally mistaken" about what "we believe to be true and right."[13] Yet he supports our search for truth: he argues that our ability to make statements with universal intent indicates an orientation not merely to what others will accept, or what might prove useful, but toward the way things really are.

Polanyi, admitting that "no man can know more than a tiny fragment of science,"[14] also faces the fact that the sciences have become highly specialized in the modern era. He contends, too, with our modern world that has instruments allowing observations well beyond the unaided senses, major developments in mathematics and natural science, and a complex religious, political, and philosophical heritage foreign, of course, to Aristotle. Can Aristotelian thought retain its purchase on reality in the face of the changes wrought by modern science and, more broadly, the history of over two millennia? Polanyi himself, in light of these developments, characterizes reality as radically open: "In this changing world, our anticipatory powers have always to deal with a somewhat unprecedented situation, and they can do so in general only by undergoing some measure of adaptation."[15]

Because the initial impetus to philosophy came for Polanyi from his political experience, we begin with the political and ethical dimensions of his work.

POLITICS, ETHICS, AND SCIENCE

When Polanyi visited the Soviet Union in 1935, he was profoundly disturbed by a discussion he had with Nikolai Bukharin, at the time a top Bolshevik theorist of Marxism, who insisted that natural science must be subordinated to social needs.[16] On this view, science as a free enterprise for its own sake gives way to a purely instrumental conception of science. What is worse, science is to be brought under state control for economic objectives. Such subordination of science led to the infamous Lysenko case in Soviet biology.[17] Behind Bukharin's argument, Polanyi discerns the irony of a misguided conception of science destroying science itself. Opposition to this outlook (and its appeal at the time to scientists in England) led Polanyi away from active chemical research to philosophical justification of his own view of science emphasizing the essential connection between freedom and truth.

Polanyi traces the historical movement that led to Bukharin from the rise of objectivism in natural science in the early modern period. Objectivism holds that the practice of science can be completely formalized and only what is verified is known. This promotes a materialistic, mechanized worldview, which Polanyi associates, like Husserl, with Galileo, and whose supreme exemplar for Polanyi is the French scientist and philosopher Pierre Simon Laplace (1749–1827). Objectivism's critical emphasis on certainty and impartial verification dares humans to trust in nothing that cannot be empirically verified. Rebelling against a moribund Scholasticism, the early modern philosophers encouraged doubt about any tradition and any reliance on authority. Yet, as Polanyi notes, the corresponding emphasis on knowing for oneself resulted paradoxically over time in the elimination of the personal dimension in the pursuit of truth. Since the critical outlook easily led to extreme empiricism and materialism, it was only a matter of time before Laplace was to envisage a perfectly deterministic and in principle predictable cosmos.[18]

The new scientific outlook contributed to tremendous discoveries and technological advancements; indeed, Polanyi credits scientific rationalism as "a major influence toward intellectual, moral, and social progress."[19] But this critical, skeptical spirit also progressively dissolved traditional ties in all spheres.[20] Scientific rationalism through its rejection of authority led to great misunderstanding of what is requisite for science, which in turn made fertile ground for nihilism or what Polanyi calls "moral inversion." Moral inversion – immorality driven by concealed moral passion – stems from the toxic combination of: (1) the devaluation of ethics, religion, and tradition brought about by the advance of the Laplacean program, coupled with (2) residual Christian moral perfectionism. Polanyi understands the Laplacean program as reducing all reality to matter in motion, hence demolishing much of science, as well as the human good that had hitherto served as the standard for human thought and action. Since the human good and purposes in general are intangible, they have no standing within the domain of objectivist science.

Yet humans still passionately desire the good, but in the absence of any traditional framework to make sense of this desire, humanity increasingly invests
its moral passions in the very objectivism that undermines their true foundation: "The morally inverted person has not merely performed a philosophic
substitution of material purposes for moral aims; he is acting with the whole
force of his homeless moral passions within a purely materialistic framework
of purposes."[21] Paradoxically, with the loss of reliance on Christianity and
the kingdom of God, morally inverted humanity seeks to realize perfection
on earth all the more furiously and unreservedly.

For Polanyi, objectivism and its spirit of universal doubt were embodied
in the nihilism and immoralism of the Soviet and Nazi tyrannies. Focusing
on the Soviet Union, Polanyi assesses why the Stalinist contempt for ordinary
moral standards and disavowal of ideals of justice, equality, and liberty, that
is, its moral inversion, could yet win it intellectual support. Such a contradictory doctrine, he suggests, "enables the modern mind, tortured by moral
self-doubt, to indulge its moral passions in terms which also satisfy its passion
for ruthless objectivity."[22] Soviet Marxism secured loyalty and discredited
opponents by holding that "bourgeois" ideals have immanent in them capitalist material interests, while the proletarian material interests have scientific
and historical objectivity.[23] In this way the regard for justice implicitly propel-
ling Marxism is covered by a supposedly impersonal scientific analysis. Thus
Marxism could deny any force to moral claims while simultaneously relying
on moral passions. Appeal to scientific objectivity apparently exposes hypoc-
risy in others' moral ideals, ignoring that hidden moral motivations drive
this very unmasking.[24] Moral inversion has a double defense: "Any criticism
of its scientific part is rebutted by the moral passions behind it, while any
moral objections to it are coldly brushed aside by invoking the inexorable
verdict of its scientific findings."[25] The combination of scientific objectivity
and disguised moral passion heightens the fanaticism and cynicism characteristic of moral inversion.[26] Even today the worship of "objectivity" in science
promotes skepticism about ethical purposes, and the double-game continues
to be played: questioning the objectivity of claims when they fail to serve
our purposes, and presenting our own purposes as though they were strictly
objective.

The Laplacean conception of science thus has enormous ethical and political consequences. Rejecting this view, Polanyi conceives natural science much
as Aristotle viewed theoretical science, as pursued freely and for its own sake.
Yet Polanyi surprisingly remarks that "[the Greeks] never raised decisively the
issues of intellectual freedom."[27] Plato's cave allegory in *Republic* vii, however, clearly concerns the intellectual liberation resulting from philosophy, and
Aristotle contends that the theoretical life is the most self-sufficient. In fact,
Aristotle and Polanyi both see that self-sufficient life and theoretical research
can only be pursued within a political community. And since politics decides
for the πόλις (or state) what sciences are pursued and how far, in this sense
political philosophy is the architectonic art:

[The human ultimate end] would seem to belong to the most authoritative art and that which is most truly the master art. And politics appears to be of this nature; for it is this that ordains which of the sciences should be studied in a state, and which each class of citizens should learn and up to what point they should learn them; and we see even the most highly esteemed of capacities to fall under this, e.g. strategy, economics, rhetoric; now, since politics uses the rest of the sciences, and since, again, it legislates as to what we are to do and what we are to abstain from, the end of this science must include those of the others, so that this end must be the good for man. (Aristotle *EN* i 2.1094a27–b7)[28]

Politics is the highest field for arranging the community, but Aristotle insists that engagement in theoretical science is and should be the goal of political science.[29] Polanyi concurs that getting the relationship between politics and the sciences right, and seeing truth as the goal of the sciences, is of paramount importance. Since "institutions of higher learning and higher education can be upheld only by public subsidies," the character of public opinion is crucial for the preservation of science as a free enterprise and academic freedom generally.[30] Polanyi speaks of the importance of "indirect appreciation" as crucial to nurturing cultural life including science, because science, philosophy, and other free activities will fare badly with a public that only esteems instrumental value.[31] A major motivation for Polanyi's philosophical reflection is to foster among citizens and scientists a genuine appreciation of the deeper meaning of science, and thus to prepare them for accepting that the standards and values according to which they live are not self-evident. Yet our fallible beliefs can be secured to the extent that we can establish them under the hazardous conditions of personal knowledge.

PERSONAL KNOWLEDGE AND REALISM IN SCIENCE

Polanyi gives a helpful argument for knowledge as personal and against supposing truth a property of declarative sentences:

Any attempt to eliminate this personal coefficient [in statements of fact], by laying down precise rules for making or testing assertions of fact, is condemned to futility from the start. For we can derive rules of observation and verification only from examples of factual statements that we have accepted as true *before* we knew these rules; and *in the end* the application of our rules will necessarily fall back once more on factual observations, the acceptance of which is an act of personal judgment, unguided by any explicit rules. And besides, the application of such rules must rely *all the time* on the guidance of our own personal judgment. This argument formally confirms the participation of the speaker in any sincere statement of fact.[32]

Statements can only be confirmed on the basis of already held beliefs. So "we must accredit our own judgment as the paramount arbiter of all our intellectual performances."[33] Polanyi suggests:

> Objectivism has totally falsified our conception of truth, by exalting what we can know and prove, while covering up with ambiguous utterances all that we know and *cannot* prove, even though the latter knowledge underlies, and must ultimately set its seal to, all that we *can* prove. In trying to restrict our minds to the few things that are demonstrable, and therefore explicitly dubitable, it has overlooked the a-critical choices which determine the whole being of our minds and has rendered us incapable of acknowledging these vital choices.[34]

But this raises the question of how an understanding of science as personal nevertheless remains a conception of science, as distinct from superstitions or subjective whims.

Aristotle shares with Polanyi a realism that emphasizes the human dimension of knowledge. Essential to this realism is the conviction that human powers are adequate to make contact with a multifaceted reality. This requires a suitable connection with tradition and openness to the diversity of what may be known. The modern project of securing justice and improving human life through enhancing human power involved excessive rejection of tradition, which seemed to open the way to endless progress, but took too narrow an approach to knowledge.[35] Humanity thus turned away from a speculative science seeking ultimate causes and principles to the sort of science that could predict how things would happen so that they might be productively utilized.[36] Polanyi displays appreciation of the spirit of ancient philosophizing in coordination with contemporary science.

For Aristotle, in pursuit of science, we move from what is initially intelligible to us to what is more intelligible by nature.[37] This corresponds to Polanyi's basic idea about how objects of focal awareness can become subsidiaries that, in turn, allow us to reorient our focus and gain deeper knowledge. For Aristotle, as for Polanyi, the role of individual human beings in doing science is indispensable for an adequate account of what science is. Aristotle says that science or knowledge aspires to knowledge of causes:

> We think we understand a thing simply (and not in the sophistic fashion accidentally) whenever we think we are aware both that the cause on account of which the object is is its cause, and that it is not possible for this to be otherwise. It is clear, then, that to understand is something of this sort; for both those who do not understand and those who do understand – the former think they are themselves in such a state, and those who do understand actually are.[38]

Knowledge requires the knowing person's awareness of having the peculiar cause or causes. But how do we come to understand causes for Aristotle? It is not ultimately a matter of deduction or syllogism since, as he repeatedly says, demonstrations depend on knowledge of causes, not vice versa. Aristotle rejects that all knowledge is based on demonstration, for this leads to an infinite regress making knowledge impossible, for each premise or proposition of a demonstration would itself be in need of demonstration. It is rather the case that "all teaching and all intellectual learning come about from already existing knowledge."[39] Intellectual processes in conjunction with sense perception lead to the discovery of causes that can then serve as middle terms of demonstrations; hence we move from what is initially intelligible to us to what is intelligible in virtue of itself though grasped by us. Demonstration assumes that we understand the cause and the terms in which the syllogism is set out.[40] Polanyi likewise emphasizes that supporting any new knowledge is a whole background of beliefs and a tacit understanding of the terms in which the knowledge is expressed. His emphasis on personal and tacit knowledge underscores "the contributions made to scientific thought by acts of personal judgment which cannot be replaced by the operation of explicit reasoning."[41]

Polanyi explicates the way knowledge depends on previous knowledge in terms of the relation between tacit and explicit understanding. When we focus on some aspect of reality attempting to know it, we are subsidiarily aware of a wide assortment of factors, ranging from our bodies, to the tools we use, to the theories we employ in order to see reality. In seeking to grasp aspects of reality as wholes, furthermore, we attend subsidiarily to their parts. When we speak we employ words to which only subsidiary attention is paid so that what they mean can receive focused attention. Thus in using speech we have only tacit understanding of our individual phrases and words. Moreover, the motions of our body in producing our speech constitute a yet deeper level of subsidiaries. Polanyi illustrates this tacit dimension ubiquitously in human experience, from using our body in walking or riding bikes, to using our senses in recognizing faces or allowing for perspective, in our thinking in focusing on a logical or mathematical proof while tacitly accepting all the assumptions being made, and so on.

Aristotle's appreciation of how we move our bodies without being aware of all that goes on internally,[42] his awareness that knowledge presupposes knowledge, and his view of speech as employing symbols[43] prefigures Polanyi's treatment of the tacit dimension of personal knowledge. Polanyi and Aristotle would agree "that only a speaker or listener can mean something *by* a word, and a word *in itself* can mean nothing."[44] Names, as Aristotle asserts, are conventional, and only speakers' use of them gives them meaning. This recognition of the "tacit dimension," that is, how our focal understanding is based on what we subsidiarily understand, fits with the Aristotelian approach and makes the strongest counter to the objectivist demand for full clarity, which Polanyi shows unachievable, because all knowledge depends upon further and often tacit knowledge.

Polanyi denies that there is any particular method of scientific research, or set of rules, that will automatically give good results in investigating (here he resembles Feyerabend). He observes:

> Upon examining the grounds on which science is pursued, I found
> that it is determined at every stage by undefinable powers of thought.
> No rules can account for the way a good idea is produced for starting
> an enquiry; and there are no rules either for the verification or the
> refutation of a proposed solution of a problem.[45]

As knowledge depends upon knowledge, and research cannot depend upon strict rules, tradition must have great importance, not only for the transmission of science from one generation to the next, but also as cultivating the scientific sensibility by which knowledge develops. Scientific research, for Polanyi, depends upon the training of scientists in the tradition of science, for only thus do they gain the skilled judgement for assessing current theories and theories under investigation. The role of this training is made evident by the importance of the main centers of science:

> Rarely, if ever, was the final acclimatization of science outside Europe
> achieved, until the government of a country succeeded in inducing
> a few scientists from some traditional centre to settle down in their
> territory and to develop there a new home for scientific life, moulded
> on their own traditional standards.[46]

Polanyi's emphasis on tradition and training corresponds to Aristotle's account of the way that we learn arts and become habituated to moral virtue and develop intellectual virtue. Virtues are appropriate dispositions of the soul. For Aristotle, the well-educated person, that is the person suitably trained, is the one who knows how to appreciate and receive accounts in the different sciences.[47]

Scientific work is the seeing and assessing of some order in nature; those with skill who have received the requisite training and who have the appropriate talent can discern such order and test the reality of this order and its implications. How compelling this perceived order is depends on its improbability of being the case due merely to chance, for "[a chance occurrence] cannot be strictly contradicted by experience."[48] There is always the possibility that the most unlikely apparent order pertains, or that what we take to be a real relation is not one, as humans believed constellations to be real for millennia. New hypotheses may only have apparent or chance confirmation or discomfirmation. As Polanyi emphasizes:

> There is an even wider area of personal judgment in every verification
> of a scientific theory. Contrary to current opinion, it is not the case that
> a proven discrepancy between theoretical predictions and observed
> data suffices in itself to invalidate a theory. Such discrepancies may
> often be classed as anomalies.[49]

Sounding a lot like Kuhn, Polanyi insists that innovations in theory require such a change in outlook that they cannot be viewed as straightforward additions to previous theories:

> Scientific controversies never lie altogether within science. For when a new system of thought concerning a whole class of alleged facts is at issue, the question will be whether it should be accepted or rejected in principle, and those who reject it on such comprehensive grounds will inevitably regard it as altogether incompetent and unsound [. . .] Proponents of a new system can convince their audience only by first winning their intellectual sympathy for a doctrine they have not yet grasped [. . .] Such an acceptance is a heuristic process, a self-modifying act, and to this extent a conversion.[50]

This should be compared to what Aristotle says of gaining new knowledge:

> The acquisition of [knowledge] must in a sense end in something which is the opposite of our original inquiries. For all men begin, as we said, by wondering that the matter is so (as in the case of automatic marionettes or the solstices or the incommensurability of the diagonal of a square with the side; for it seems wonderful to all men who have not yet perceived the explanation that there is a thing which cannot be measured even by the smallest unit). But we must end in the contrary and, according to the proverb, the better state, as is the case in these instances when men learn the cause; for there is nothing which would surprise a geometer so much as if the diagonal turned out to be commensurable.[51]

Learning and defending a new hypothesis require embracing a new framework. Clear but unobvious human desires support this effort.

The innate human love of truth – which recalls Aristotle's insistence that by nature humans desire to know[52] – Polanyi traces back to its prefiguration and origin in our non-human animal ancestors. Polanyi distinguishes three primary sorts of learning that correspond to three principal fields of knowledge. (1) Animals can learn to solve problems, such as finding the way through a maze or figuring out how to use a tool to gain access to food. This is a kind of invention that becomes most fully developed in human technology. (2) Animals can also learn from observing signs, the observational and contemplative approach of which has its complete development in humans' pursuit of natural science. And (3) animals can interpret a situation, as when they understand a maze well enough to use an alternative path upon finding the previously used path is blocked; Polanyi supposes that this full understanding in humans can be seen in mathematical knowledge, in which we have general clarity about the domain.[53] This division rather resembles Aristotle's division of science into practical and theoretical science, with the theoretical sciences including natural science and mathematics.[54] Like Aristotle, Polanyi sees the development of the arts for utility, that is technology, preceding theoretical sciences.[55] Also Aristotle's view of mathematical entities arrived at by abstraction analogously explains why we can have full understanding of such domains.[56] What enables humans to take these sorts of ability beyond that of the animals is our having language:

> The intellectual superiority of man is due predominately to [. . .]
> the representation of experience in terms of manageable symbols
> which he can reorganize, either formally or mentally, for the purpose
> of yielding new information [. . .] To speak is to *contrive* signs, to
> *observe* their fitness, and to *interpret* their alternative relations;
> though the animal possesses each of these three faculties, he cannot
> combine them.[57]

Human use of speech is thus "rooted in the kind of comprehension by which animals make sense of their situation."[58]

Polanyi's reflections on how animals learn, how actual scientific research goes, and his own experience led him to an appreciation of the role of the tacit dimension and the commitment to reality in learning. What a human or an animal seeks to learn, understand, or be able to do poses a problem for the animal or human. This entails the identifying of the problem, the seeking of a resolution to it, and the gaining of this resolution.[59] Polanyi depicts how discovery takes place and has its own standards. Other animals, even worms, can be awakened to the existence of a problem that they need to solve; animals can display unease as they work out a way to deal with the problem; they show excitement as they find a way to resolve the problem; and their self-satisfaction appears as they confidently continue to employ the solution that they have found. Analogously, a person undergoing suitable apprenticeship in science will take on the intellectual passion for contributing to science. Hopefully the emerging scientist envisions a problem needing investigation worthy of his or her intellectual ambition. A worthy problem should be one neither too taxing nor too easy for the investigator and one with intrinsic interest and importance for science, technology, or mathematics.

This problem should engross the person's energies. At nearly all hours, even when the scientist is relaxing or doing other things, the problem occupies some recesses of the mind. It is the intellectual passion of the scientist that demands this occupation with the problem. In relation to the problem and the methods being employed to deal with it, the researcher has some inkling about ways to handle the problem and the outlines of its resolution. Here is where a considerable amount of counterevidence or failure to obtain anticipated confirmation will be rejected or overlooked by the researcher. Polanyi states that the scientist's success will depend ultimately on his capacity for sensing the presence of yet unrevealed logical relations between the conditions of the problem, the theorems known to him, and the unknown solution he is looking for. Unless his casting about is guided by a reliable sense of growing proximity to the solution, he will make no progress towards it. Conjectures made at random, even though following the best rules of heuristics, would be hopelessly inept and totally fruitless.[60]

The researcher's sense of order grasps a reality the proximity to which can be felt by the researcher even before it is well clarified. And the reality of what is sought will only be progressively confirmed by the unanticipated implications of the problem's eventual resolution, if it is resolved. And these unanticipated implications develop in the course of later work by many researchers besides the one or several originally resolving the problem. This shows the reality and significance of what has been sought.[61] Polanyi is convinced that sincere researchers have the personal commitment to pursue a truth that will satisfy universal standards. In human involvement with and resolution of problems in science, technology, and mathematics, the resolution should have universal interest and value, whereas a beast merely seeks a solution peculiarly for itself.

In Polanyi's elucidation of the process of locating problems and their resolution, his realism shines through. If even non-human animals have a heightened sensitivity and growing awareness of their proximity to the resolution of a problem, this clearly also applies to human researchers, and this sense is that of proximity to some reality. If the problem is a technical problem, the solution will show its reality in its successful application. If the problem is one of science, the solution will have the appearance of truth and beauty. Of course the scientist working out the solution will be convinced of its truth and value, and if it wins over others and shows its fertility in having even unanticipated implications, it seems to warrant its acceptance and display its universal relevance.

Comparable to this scenario of research found in Polanyi are the many passages in Aristotle that point to the passions of the researcher driving the pursuit of truth.[62] Moreover, in *Nicomachean Ethics* VI Aristotle speaks of the way the investigator and expert is *in* the truth of the very matters in question.[63] This dwelling in the truth of things well captures the sense of realism for which Polanyi aspires in his account of how the researcher delves into problems, feels the proximity to some reality, and submits to universal standards.

In tracing the continuum of learning from animals to its highest fulfillment in humans, Polanyi conjoins modern evolutionary thinking with an Aristotelian notion of hierarchy in nature and teleology. Aristotle famously thinks that nature works for the sake of something, yet his teleology remains quite sober.[64] Polanyi contrasts "the science of inanimate things, in which no purpose is apparent, and that of living beings which can be understood only in teleological terms."[65] Were there no living things, purposiveness would have no real meaning at all. As Polanyi puts it, "inanimate nature is self-contained, achieving nothing, relying on nothing and, hence, unerring."[66] It is only with living beings that it really makes any difference that nature, the internal principle of motion and rest of natural beings according to Aristotle, works for the sake of something. Plants and animals, the natural beings that manifest purpose, seek to fulfill their natures and have the potential to miss becoming what they were to be: "with [living beings] hazard enters the hitherto unerring universe."[67]

Polanyi challenges the neo-Darwinian belief that higher-level life forms arise by accidental mutations that get favored by their survival ability. Like Aristotle, who looks to emphasize form over matter, Polanyi focuses on the morphological possibility already present to explain the emergence of higher life forms. Polanyi states:

> It is as meaningless to represent life in terms of physics and chemistry as it would be to interpret a grandfather clock or a Shakespeare sonnet in terms of physics and chemistry; and it is likewise meaningless to represent mind in terms of a machine or a neural model. Lower levels do not lack a bearing on higher levels; *they define the conditions of their success and account for their failures, but they cannot account for their success, for they cannot even define it* [. . .] I shall regard living beings as instances of morphological types and of operational principles subordinated to a centre of individuality.[68]

Polanyi summarizes the whole development: "While the first rise of living individuals overcame the meaninglessness of the universe by establishing in it centres of subjective interests, the rise of human thought in its turn overcame these subjective interests by its universal intent."[69] As animals seek the self-satisfaction of solving problems and humans have universal aspirations and standards of greatness, this can be seen at work in the way the emergence of configurations by random processes then become the meaning and controlling factor of the lower parts constituting them;[70] at each level there is "a centre seeking satisfaction in the light of its own standards."[71] This of course corresponds to Aristotle's preference for top-down explanations and the priority of form and actuality over matter and potentiality, for which Aristotle argues in *Metaphysics* Θ.8–9.

Much like Aristotle who, in the *De Anima* and *Parva Naturalia*, has even the functions of plants somewhat centered, and articulates animals as highly centered – that is the senses unite to permit discrimination and self-awareness when awake and general incapacitation in sleep, and animal motion and nutrition derives from the center – Polanyi emphasizes centering in the higher living beings. "But a living individual is altogether different from any of the inanimate things, like tunes, words, poems, theories, cultures, to which we have ascribed meaning before this. Its meaning is different, perhaps richer, and above all, it has a *centre*."[72] This centeredness pertains to the way all life forms, each at its own level, is committed to a purpose.[73] Contrary to the advice of behaviorism, which counsels against observing animals with analogy to ourselves, Polanyi urges that the only way to make sense of animal actions is in "identifying ourselves with the centre of action in the animal and criticizing its performance by standards set up for it by ourselves."[74] As Polanyi insists that we cannot escape evaluating by our own present standards, even if we can appreciate that in the past other standards may have been used, Aristotle assesses his predecessors always in terms of his own standards and the four kinds of causes that he has so carefully elicited.[75] Thus science and life, for Polanyi and Aristotle, have truth and reality as their aim, and personal knowledge pursues these.

TRADITION, FREEDOM, AND THE UNITY OF SCIENCE

Polanyi marshals numerous arguments against "the ideal of scientific detachment," as though science could provide a view from nowhere, from no particular standpoint or set of beliefs. In this, he can be seen to countenance the insights of idealism, phenomenology, and existentialism into the human dimension of all scientific inquiry. And like Aristotle, Polanyi seeks to secure the role of tradition in science while doing justice to the element of freedom necessary for scientific discovery. "Scientific tradition," he remarks, "enforces its teachings in general, for the very purpose of cultivating their subversion in particular."[76] Aristotle typically begins any investigation with a review of the thought of his predecessors.[77] Polanyi, we have seen, emphasizes training in a center of science. Whether research then reinforces and expands and clarifies existing theories or destroys them in whole or in part with a revolutionary new theory, Polanyi has any researcher beginning from existing knowledge. Polanyi thus rejects Cartesian "hyperbolic doubt," for without a beginning in a tradition of beliefs there is no way forward.[78] As he says, "discoveries are made by pursuing possibilities suggested by existing knowledge."[79]

Polanyi stresses the unity of science and at the same time recognizes important distinctions between the different sciences. He conceives unity broadly enough to claim that personal knowledge "bridges the gap between the natural sciences and the study of man,"[80] thus "bringing science and the humanities together."[81] Yet this does not mean that the principles of one science can simply be taken over by another; rather, it indicates that the broad understanding of science as personal knowledge applies to all the different fields of science and to scholarship in the humanities. Aristotle likewise supposes that the same intellectual powers support the various sciences and arts, and the works in the *Organon* are intended for any of the diverse sorts of science, including such fields as rhetoric and poetics. Different sciences do indeed have different principles and purposes. Aristotle frequently rejects the view that there could be one science of everything,[82] and he holds that different sciences must have different principles to account for their different subject matters.[83]

Polanyi indicates that there are three main fields of knowledge where discoveries are made: technology, natural science, and mathematics.[84] Technology is a means through which human beings can make contact with reality, and the same can be said for natural science and scholarship generally. By interiorizing the theories of natural science or the achievements of technology, they become subsidiary parts of our understanding contact with reality. Such tacit knowledge and interiorization is "indwelling."[85]

Natural science may contribute to technological development and technological achievements may aid natural science, but technology and science are not the same thing, and Polanyi sees the attempt to identify them as having deleterious consequences. The sciences, both natural and human, differ from technology in putting us in greater proximity to the reality they seek to encounter, and this is because technology lacks the intellectual element in itself that characterizes the sciences. The difficulty Polanyi sees with technology is that it easily plays into the view that humanity's only real needs are material ones. To suppose that natural science is for utility's sake, for making gadgets that increase our material comfort, is to return to the prescientific outlook when:

> Horoscopes, incantations, oracles, magic, witchcraft [. . .] were all firmly established through the centuries in the eyes of the public by their supposed practical successes. The scientific method was devised precisely for the purpose of elucidating the nature of things under more carefully controlled conditions and by more rigorous criteria than are present in the situations created by practical problems. These conditions and criteria can be discovered only by taking a purely scientific interest in the matter which again can exist only in minds educated in the appreciation of scientific value.[86]

Polanyi sounds much like Aristotle in rejecting the pursuit of natural science for utility rather than for the sake of the knowledge itself. But gaining this appreciation can prove difficult where cultivation has been insufficient and practical interests prevail. Polanyi observes that "in all parts of the world where science is just beginning to be cultivated, it suffers from a lack of response to its true values. Consequently, the authorities grant insufficient time for research; politics play havoc with appointments; businessmen deflect interest from science by subsidizing only practical projects."[87] This of course seems overly optimistic, for similar problems can exist even in the centers of science. Polanyi rightly stresses that valuing science appropriately depends upon sound preparation. Proper education counters some of the dangers of scientism, skepticism, and objectivism, while bolstering rigorous science alive to the personal dimension.

The aim of natural science is truth about its subject matter, which Polanyi and Aristotle unite in seeing as the ultimate goal even of political and economic life. Hence there can be no central control of science, any more than for the economy; rather we must depend upon "spontaneous order."[88] Science requires freedom so that individuals and groups of researchers can pursue the problems that present themselves to them. No one standing beyond the researchers can tell for sure in advance which problems are the really interesting ones.

Even grant programs that are too narrowly designed tend to pervert scientific research instead of supporting it as they are meant to do. Much as Aristotle defends private property and the operation of markets in his *Ethics* and *Politics*, but with advocacy of these as instrumental to the highest culture in theoretical science, Polanyi resists socialism and collective planning, both in science and economic life, as unworkable. Just as no central planner could have all the information reflected in all the areas of scientific research, and cannot foresee the implications of the solutions of problems, so the would-be economic planner cannot have all the information contained in the various prices worked out in the market. Attempts to impose central control of science cripple scientific research, just as similar attempts in the economic domain cripple economic life resulting in oversupply and shortages. Unlike many of his contemporaries in economic thought, however, who also defend markets, Polanyi, much as Aristotle, never loses sight of the hierarchy of pursuits, and hence they both view economic and political life as in service to higher culture.

Polanyi's effort to present a viable "post-critical philosophy" finds him reinvigorating many fundamental Aristotelian approaches.[89] We believe that this reveals the promise of Polanyi's approach while also pointing to the way that various modern developments can be brought into the framework of Aristotelian naturalistic and realistic reflection upon everything that is.

NOTES

1. Michael Polanyi, *Personal Knowledge* [PK], p. 381
2. Ibid. p. 265.
3. Ibid. p. 298.
4. Michael Polanyi, *The Tacit Dimension* [TD], p. 47.
5. David Papineau, *The Philosophy of Science*, pp. 1–20 identifies skepticism, realism, and idealism as the three major generic positions that fight it out over the epistemology of science. Larry Laudan, *Science and Relativism*, presents an imagined dialogue between a positivist, a realist, a relativist, and a pragmatist. Laudan associates relativism with skepticism about the possibility of knowledge in science and further ties this trend to the "unmistakable relativist implications" of the writings of Kuhn and Quine (p. xi). Polanyi attacks objectivism, which he says seems realistic about matter in motion and skeptical about everything else. Objectivism's hallmark is its rejection of the personal dimension in science, which has as its corollary depreciation of the role of tradition and authority in science and generally.
6. See Aron Gurwitsch, *Phenomenology and the Theory of Science*, pp. 10–16 for a forthright acknowledgement of the primacy of consciousness for the phenomenological view of science.
7. See Edmund Husserl, *The Crisis of European Sciences and Transcendental Phenomenology*.

8. Wilfrid Sellars, "Philosophy and the Scientific Image of Man."
9. See Plato, *Alcibiades I*, 111a–12d.
10. *PK* p. 253.
11. Ibid. p. vii.
12. Although this position strikes us as naive, even into the twentieth century philosophers and scientists have in some cases avowed a systematic ambition to complete the philosophical-scientific enterprise.
13. *PK* p. 404.
14. Michael Polanyi, *Knowing and Being* [*KB*], p. 85.
15. *PK* p. 110; see also pp. 124, 196, 208.
16. Polanyi refers to this encounter with Bukharin repeatedly: see Michael Polanyi, *Science, Faith, and Society* [*SFS*], p. 8; *PK* p. 238; *TD* pp. 3–4, 60.
17. For Polanyi's discussion of the Lysenko affair, see Michael Polanyi, *The Logic of Liberty* [*LL*], pp. 72–80. *KB* pp. 24–39 treats the important shift in thought within the Soviet bloc following Stalin's death.
18. For Laplace, the mind knowing all the forces at work in any one moment and the location of all bodies could compute all the past and future. Polanyi comments at *PK* p. 140:

> This ideal of universal knowledge is mistaken, since it substitutes for the subjects in which we are interested a set of data which tell us nothing that we want to know [. . .] That such virtually meaningless information was identified by Laplace with a knowledge of all things past and all things to come, and that the stark absurdity of this claim has not been obvious to succeeding generations since his day, can be accounted for only by a hidden assumption by which this information was tacitly supplemented. It was taken for granted that the Laplacean mind would not stop short at the list of p's and q's at the time t, but proceed by virtue of its unlimited powers of computation to evaluate from this list the events, and indeed all the events, that we might be interested to know.

19. *TD* p. 57.
20. Polanyi observes that the authoritarian dominance of traditional cultural life was broken in the modern period. In previous periods

> society accepted its own structure as permanently established [. . .] during the greater part of recorded history [. . .] a hierarchical social structure was for the most part regarded as essential to the very existence of the body politic. Only after the American and French revolutions did the conviction gradually spread over the world that society could be improved indefinitely by the exercise of political will of the people, and that the people should therefore be sovereign, both in theory and fact. This movement gave rise to modern dynamic societies, of which there are two kinds. When

a society is resolved on a sudden complete renewal of itself, its dynamism is revolutionary; if it aims at a more gradual approach to perfection, its dynamism is reformist. (*PK* p. 213)

See also Friedrich Nietzsche, *The Gay Science*, §346:

Have we not exposed ourselves to the suspicion of an opposition – an opposition between the world in which we were at home up to now with our reverences that perhaps made it possible for us to *endure* life, and another world *that consists of us* – an inexorable, fundamental, and deepest suspicion about ourselves that is more and more gaining worse and worse control of us Europeans and that could easily confront coming generations with a terrifying Either/Or: 'Either abolish your reverences or – *yourselves*!' The latter would be nihilism; but would not the former also be – nihilism? – That is *our* question mark.

21. Michael Polanyi, *Meaning* [M], p. 18.
22. *PK* p. 228.
23. Ibid. p. 229.
24. Polanyi interestingly finds a precursor of this working of moral inversion to discredit what opponents say while employing it itself in a hidden form in Kantian "regulative ideals" about which he asserts:

Knowledge that we hold to be true and also vital to us, is made light of, because we cannot account for its acceptance in terms of a critical philosophy. We then feel entitled to continue using that knowledge, even while flattering our sense of intellectual superiority by disparaging it. And we actually go on, firmly relying on this despised knowledge to guide and lend meaning to our more exact enquiries, while pretending that these alone come up to our standards of scientific stringency. (Ibid. p. 354; see also p. 369)

In the context in which Polanyi offers this, he is arguing that teleology is inevitable in life sciences, though scientists suppose that they must, as scientists, reject final causes.
25. Ibid. p. 230.
26. Polanyi appreciates the richness of the background of moral inversion: "A loathing of bourgeois society, a rebellious immoralism and despair, have been prevailing themes of great fiction, poetry and philosophy on the continent of Europe since the middle of the nineteenth century" (ibid. p. 236). This anti-philistinism led to great art, but prepared the ground for "unscrupulous revolutionary power" (ibid. p. 237).

27. *M* p. 6.

28. Aristotle, *Nicomachean Ethics* [*EN*], I.2, 1094a27–b7; translations of Aristotle are from *The Complete Works of Aristotle*, ed. Jonathan Barnes, with occasional modifications.

29. See ibid. VI 1141a20–22, 1145a6–11, X.7–8.

30. *LL* pp. 50–3.

31. *PK* pp. 220–1.

32. Ibid. p. 254.

33. Ibid. p. 265.

34. Ibid. p. 286.

35. When Descartes in *Discourse on Method*, part 6 speaks of humans becoming "master and possessor of nature" through numerous contrivances that will reduce or eliminate human labor and medical innovations that will secure health, he may envision modern science, conceived as mathematical physics, as returning humans by their own efforts to the Garden of Eden.

36. Consider Hannah Arendt, *The Human Condition*, ch. 6, especially sec. 42. Renewed interest in skeptical texts, such as Sextus Empiricus (see Popkin, *The History of Scepticism from Erasmus to Spinoza*), combined with a Christian view that knowing the essence and purpose of things is reserved for God (see Descartes *Meditations*, AT 55) would contribute to this.

37. Aristotle, *Posterior Analytics* [*Apo*], 71b33–72a5; *Topics.* 141b3–14; *Physics* [*Phys.*], 184a16–26; *Metaphysics* [*Meta.*], 1029b3–12; *EN* 1095b2–4.

38. *APo* I.2 71b9–15.

39. Ibid. 71a1–2.

40. See ibid. I.1 71a11–17.

41. *KB* p. 105.

42. Aristotle, *On the Movement of Animals*, ch. 11.

43. Aristotle, *De Interpretatione* [*DI*], 16a3–4.

44. *PK* p. 252; consider *DI* ch. 4.

45. *PK* p. ix.

46. *PK* p. 182.

47. Aristotle, *Parts of Animals* [*PA*], I.1, 639a1–12; *Meta.* B.3 995a12–14.

48. *PK* p. 37.

49. Ibid. p. 20. Karl Popper, *The Logic of Scientific Discovery*, pp. 75–7 suggests this simple logical analysis for the refutation of hypotheses. Assume hypothesis H, which if true should give the experimental result R, that is, H ⊃ R. But experiment does not yield R, i.e. R is not the case, or ~R. Then by *modus tollens*, H is untrue, i.e. ~H. But Polanyi denies that any earnest scientist gives up so easily as this logic suggests.

50. *PK* pp. 150–1.

51. *Meta.* A.2 983a11–21.

52. Ibid. A.1 980a21.

53. See *PK* ch. 5 and ch. 12 sec. 6.

54. See *Meta.* E.1.

55. Ibid. A.1 981b13–25, A.2 982b11–28.
56. Ibid. M.3.
57. *PK* p. 82.
58. Ibid. p. 250.
59. See *PK* ch.5 sec. 6, 11, and ch. 6 sec. 11.
60. Ibid. p. 128.
61. Polanyi may have a fuller notion of what inspires scientific revolutions than Thomas Kuhn, *The Structure of Scientific Revolution*, since Polanyi does not limit it to handling anomalies: "Some discoveries are prompted by the conviction that something is fundamentally lacking in the existing framework of science, others by the opposite feeling that there is far more implied in it than has yet been realized" (*PK* p. 277).
62. For example, *PA* I.5 645a15–36, and *Meta*. A.1.
63. See *EN* VI 1139a19–31, b14–17, 1140a9–10, b20–1, 1141a17–18.
64. See *Phys*. II.8. In "Is Aristotle's Teleology Anthropocentric?" David Sedley speaks of teleology as anthropocentric. This is a mistaken reading of Aristotle since it misses how it is only in the political rather than the theoretical context that Aristotle suggests any human end of non-human beings. In the theoretical context Aristotle has ensouled beings as definitely purposive, but each natural kind, having its own nature, soberly pursues the natural purpose of its own kind. *Meta*. Λ.10 and *De Anima* II.4, besides the political works, entertains a more unified end of various natural beings.
65. *PK* pp. 175, 394.
66. *TD* p. 44.
67. *TD* p. 91.
68. *PK* pp. 382–3.
69. Ibid. p. 389.
70. Ibid. pp. 384, 396.
71. Ibid. p. 398.
72. Ibid. p. 344.
73. See ibid. p. 363.
74. Ibid. p. 364.
75. See *Phys*. II.1–2, *Meta*. A.3–10.
76. *KB* p. 67.
77. There has been dispute about the role of dialectic and the sifting of ἔνδοξα in Aristotle since G. E. L. Owen, "*Tithenai ta phainomena*," urged its importance (see in favor Martha Nussbaum, "Saving Aristotle's Appearances," and opposed Rob Bolton, "Aristotle's Method in Natural Science: *Physics* I," and Myles Burnyeat, *A Map of Metaphysics Zeta*, p. 79). We think that those opposed only in fact narrow rather than reject the role of dialectic in Aristotle. The dialectic in scientific investigation resembles Socratic ἔλεγχος, from which Aristotle appropriates the approach. For passages in Polanyi that advocate this sort of dialectic, see for example *PK* pp. 267, 269, 294–5.

78. See also Hans-Georg Gadamer, *Truth and Method*, pp. 272–3: "There is one prejudice of the Enlightenment that defines its essence: the fundamental prejudice of the Enlightenment is the prejudice against prejudice itself, which denies tradition its power."
79. *TD* p. 67.
80. *M* p. 44.
81. Ibid. p. 57.
82. See *PA* 641a32–b10, *Meta.* B.2 997a17–25.
83. *APo* I.7.
84. *PK* p. 124.
85. *TD* pp. 17–18.
86. *PK* p. 183.
87. Ibid. p. 182.
88. Mark Mitchell, *Michael Polanyi: The Art of Knowing*, p. 22 relates that Polanyi invented this phrase in his discussions of economics, and it was later taken over by Friedrich Hayek and others who advocate the market system. Hayek acknowledged Polanyi's coining of the term.
89. "Post-Critical" is in the subtitle of Polanyi's major book. In insisting on Polanyi's Aristotelian kinship, we actually go against his own self-understanding. He rather supposes himself more like St. Augustine at the end of antiquity formulating a "post-critical philosophy" and leading the way toward a new world of faith and belief (see *PK* 266–7). But Polanyi, like Aristotle, was himself an active natural scientist concerned with the way to view the various sciences.

BIBLIOGRAPHY

Arendt, H., *The Human Condition* (Chicago: University of Chicago Press, 1958).

Aristotle, *The Complete Works of Aristotle: The Revised Oxford Translation*, ed. J. Barnes, 2 vols (Princeton: Princeton University Press, 1984).

Bolton, R., "Aristotle's Method in Natural Science: *Physics* I," in L. Judson (ed.), *Aristotle's Physics: A Collection of Essays* (Oxford: Clarendon Press, 1991), pp. 1–29.

Burnyeat, M., *A Map of Metaphysics Zeta* (Pittsburgh: Mathesis Publications, 2001).

Descartes, R., *Discourse on Method and Meditations on First Philosophy*, trans. D. A. Cress, 4th edn (Indianapolis: Hackett, 1998).

Feyerabend, P., *Against Method* (London: Verso, 2010).

Gadamer, H.-G., *Truth and Method*, trans. J. Weinsheimer and D. G. Marshall, 2nd rev. edn (London: Continuum, 2004).

Gurwitsch, A., *Phenomenology and the Theory of Science*, ed. L. Embree (Evanston: Northwestern University Press, 1974).

Hanson, N. R., *Patterns of Discovery: An Inquiry into the Conceptual Foundations of Science* (Cambridge: Cambridge University Press, 1958).

Husserl, E., *The Crisis of European Sciences and Transcendental Phenomenology: An Introduction to Phenomenological Philosophy*, trans. D. Carr (Evanston: Northwestern University Press 1970).

Kuhn, T., *The Structure of Scientific Revolutions* (Chicago: University of Chicago Press, 1962).

Laudan, L., *Science and Relativism* (Chicago: University of Chicago Press, 1990).

Mitchell, M. T., *Michael Polanyi: The Art of Knowing* (Wilmington, DE: ISI Books, 2006).

Nietzsche, F., *The Gay Science*, trans. W. Kaufman (New York: Vintage, 1974).

Nussbaum, M. C., "Saving Aristotle's Appearances," in M. Schofield and M. Nussbaum (eds.), *Language and Logos* (Cambridge: Cambridge University Press, 1982), pp. 267–93

Owen, G. E. L., "*Tithenai ta phainomena*," in S. Mansion (ed.), *Aristote et les Problèmes de Méthode* (Louvain: Publications Universitaires de Louvain 1961), pp. 83–103.

Papineau, D., *The Philosophy of Science* (Oxford: Oxford University Press, 1996).

Polanyi, M., *Science, Faith, and Society* (London: Oxford University Press, 1946).

Polanyi, M., *The Logic of Liberty* (Indianapolis: Liberty Fund, 1951).

Polanyi, M., *Personal Knowledge* (Chicago: University of Chicago Press, 1958).

Polanyi, M., *The Study of Man* (Chicago: University of Chicago Press, 1959).

Polanyi, M., *The Tacit Dimension* (Chicago: University of Chicago Press, 1966).

Polanyi, M., *Knowing and Being* (Chicago: University of Chicago Press, 1969).

Polanyi, M., *Meaning* (Chicago: University of Chicago Press, 1975).

Popkin, R. H., *The History of Scepticism from Erasmus to Spinoza* (Berkeley: University of California Press, 1979).

Popper, K., *The Logic of Scientific Discovery* (New York: Basic Books, 1968).

Sedley, D., "Is Aristotle's Teleology Anthropocentric?" *Phronesis*, 36 (1991), pp. 179–96.

Sellars, W., "Philosophy and the Scientific Image of Man," in R. G. Colodny (ed.), *Frontiers of Science and Philosophy* (Pittsburgh: University of Pittsburgh Press, 1962), pp. 35–78.

CHAPTER 11

Diverging Ways: On the Trajectories of Ontology in Parmenides, Aristotle, and Deleuze

Abraham Jacob Greenstine

ONLY ONE ONTOLOGY?

Presently there is a flood of ontologies, an uproar over being. Not only is metaphysics permitted, it has become, perhaps, expected. Not that continental philosophy has returned to some sort of Wolffian systematic science of ontology. Rather, we now find ourselves inundated by a variety of ontological styles: it seems that every philosopher and scholar has their own theory of being. To make our way through this torrent, we might ask: what is ontology? How can we speak of being? Can it be narrated, accounted for, expressed?

In this essay I explore three philosophically and historically decisive answers to these questions: those of Parmenides, Aristotle, and Gilles Deleuze. I examine not only what each thinker says about being, but also how they say it, that is, what the project of ontology is for each. Rather than proposing so many different hypotheses in a single pre-established discourse on being, each of them endeavors to create a new ontology. Parmenides inaugurates ontology, leading us on a journey to the truth through the path of what is. Aristotle, rejecting Parmenides' way of truth, instead proposes a knowledge of being, a science of ontology, which leads in turn to knowledge of the divine as the first causes of things. Deleuze, denying both the truth of Parmenides and the first causes of Aristotle, instead contends that there is only one proposition about being, just a single voice of ontology. Path, knowledge, and proposition: each philosopher institutes his own ontological style. Each defends an ontology apparently unassimilable to the others.

To better motivate this topic, let us begin by considering Deleuze's *Difference and Repetition*, one of the crucial texts of (and behind) contemporary metaphysics. In this work, Deleuze notoriously proposes that "Being is univocal."[1] In contrast to any theory which postulates various categories of things, the univocity of being (that is, the claim that being is univocal) implies that everything is said to be in one and the same way. Deleuze links this univocity with his attempt to think difference in itself, to conceptualize difference without subordinating it to some prior identity. The self-sameness of being is not despite the differences between beings but is, rather, on account of them: "It is being which is Difference, in the sense that it is said of difference."[2] Beyond its role in *Difference and Repetition*, the idea of univocity has shaped much of contemporary metaphysics. Alain Badiou situates his own mathematical ontology against Deleuze's philosophy of difference, arguing that univocity remains a vestige of the transcendent One in Deleuze's project.[3] Moreover, the univocity of being is the source for Manuel DeLanda's popular idea of a flat ontology, which is further employed in the writings of Levi Bryant and Tristan Garcia.[4] Deleuze's proposition is thus a pivotal thesis in today's deluge of ontologies, generating both detractors and defenders.

Yet for Deleuze the univocity proposition is not one ontological hypothesis among many. Instead he defiantly asserts that "there has only ever been one ontological proposition."[5] We should not brush this aside as flippant exaggeration. Ontology, for Deleuze, begins and ends with the univocity of being: "From Parmenides to Heidegger it is the same voice which is taken up, in an echo which itself forms the whole deployment of the universal."[6] Not only is there no project of distinguishing the various senses or categories of being (a project already forbidden by univocity itself), there are no theorems, articulations, or decisions about being beyond univocity. There is no science or path of ontology. All that remains is an "elaboration of the univocity of being."[7] Hence, according to Deleuze, there is no proliferation of ontologies but instead "there has only ever been one ontology, that of Duns Scotus, which gave being a single voice."[8]

While scholars have quarreled over Deleuze's proposition about the univocity of being, the claim about ontology – that there is only one ontological proposition – has been neglected.[9] Yet we must think through this latter contention if we hope to appreciate the novel discourse on being in *Difference and Repetition*. At this point most commentators follow Deleuze's own lead, focusing on the "three principle moments" of univocal ontology, namely the works of Scotus, Spinoza, and Nietzsche. However, in this essay I articulate Deleuze's univocal ontology not as the culmination of some hidden minor tradition, but in contrast to some major ontologies which differ from his own.

One might attempt to find a different sort of culmination, wherein first Aristotle corrects Parmenides and then Deleuze Aristotle. Indeed, these three are so linked, each contending with the one(s) who came before, conceding some points while denying others. While I will address and discuss these critical intertextual references, I am not defending here any image of development from one thinker to the next. Instead, in this chapter I set these various metaphysics against one another, articulating the trajectory of each as it diverges and converges with the others. In what follows we consider each ontological project for its own sake. Let us not be Eleatics, Peripatetics, or (post-)Structuralists. We might characterize our own style as an itinerant, or perhaps zetetic, metaphysics: let us inhabit and explore these doctrines. Let them speak for themselves, whether through myth or by science or in a single echoing voice.

Yet there are other figures, other ontologies, and other discourses: why here privilege these three, about whom we have already heard so much? We could note the nearly suffocating influence on philosophy of the ontologies of Parmenides and Aristotle, and the incipient but growing importance of the writings of Deleuze. More optimistically, we might add that this influence is for good reason – that these philosophers dare to think and speak about being with a creativity and power rarely found and, despite their acknowledged importance, still underappreciated. But broad claims like these hold just as well for a host of other thinkers (insert here whoever you think is of more interest). What remains – some overlap in topics, a gap in the scholarship on Deleuze, a few small but crucial dialogical-intertextual references between these thinkers – may seem like dregs in comparison with the flood of material available to us. However, from these (perhaps contingent) encounters, from the overlaps, gaps, and references, from another reconsideration of Parmenides, of Aristotle, and of Deleuze we can better understand what ontology is and might be, both long ago and still now.

PARMENIDES: "AND STILL ONE TALE OF A WAY REMAINS, THAT IT IS"

Parmenides' *Poem* tells of a three-part journey. In the first, told in the proem, Parmenides is carried along in a chariot guided by the daughters of Helios, and brought "as far as the spirit [θυμός] might reach,"[10] to the audience of an unnamed goddess.[11] Yet rather than finding accomplishment simply in the divine presence, the arrival to the goddess's abode is only a beginning. There, in a divine voice, the goddess informs Parmenides that he must "learn all things,"[12] both the unchanging truth and also the opinions of mortals. These are the second and third parts of the journey, which later readers have called the way of truth and the way of opinion, respectively. These are not ways that Parmenides can travel on foot, nor even by means of a supernatural chariot escorted by maidens; instead he can only accomplish the remainder of the journey by listening and learning from the goddess's tale (μῦθος: "narrative," "story," "myth").[13] This μῦθος performs a dual function: it indicates the way to be taken and guides Parmenides along this path. Narrative can thus grant what heroic labors cannot: access to the "steady heart of well-rounded truth."[14]

More important than access to the goddess herself, or the voyage needed to achieve it, is her lesson and the paths they disclose. Truth is not a matter of a privileged place, or even of a privileged speaker, but instead concerns what is said and how it is said. This divine teaching is transmittable by human words: the goddess orders that Parmenides conveys the μῦθος after he hears it,[15] a command he executes by writing the very *Poem* we read. Hence Parmenides obviates the first part of the journey for future pilgrims: they need not undertake the Orphic expedition to the goddess, but may rather hear the divine μῦθος from Parmenides himself. Anyone with ears to hear or eyes to read – and most importantly, a mind to follow – may hearken to and tell in turn the goddess's tale.[16]

The goddess invokes the first way, "the path of assurance," which "follows the truth,"[17] with the obscure phrase: "that [it] is and that [it] is not not to be" (ἡ μὲν ὅπως ἔστιν τε καὶ ὡς οὐκ ἔστι μὴ εἶναι).[18] This is to be contrasted with the second path, which is "completely impenetrable,"[19] and established with the phrase "that [it] is not and that [it] must not be."[20] The goddess thus riddles her listeners, and the interpretation of these lines is at the crux of contemporary debates about Parmenides' ontology. One problem concerns how to understand ἔστιν, or "is": is it existential, predicative, or perhaps something in between, veridical, or "speculative"?[21] Scholars also disagree about the subject apparently missing from this phrase: some doubt that we are meant to supply one at all, although perhaps the most prevalent view is the one of Jonathan Barnes, who contends that the subject is "*whatever we inquire into*"[22] (implied by the previous line's mention of the "only ways of inquiry").[23] More recently, Palmer argues for a modal interpretation of these passages, contending that the second clauses of each phrase ("is not not to be," "must not be") imply necessity.[24] With all of these hermeneutic possibilities, the goddess's riddle, then, provokes a slew of conflicting interpretations of what the way of truth is.

Yet this is nothing new: Aristotle, while discussing Eleatic philosophy (that of Melissus, Parmenides, and Zeno), asks "since being is said in many ways, how is it said, when they say that all are one?"[25] This proposition, "all are one," is Aristotle's summation of Eleaticism as a whole, and not a direct quotation from Parmenides' *Poem*; regardless, his question indicates a long history of disagreement about Parmenides' doctrines, one which continues in the scholarly debates today. Aristotle, like contemporary commentators, is uncertain of whether Parmenides holds that there is only one being or rather one type of being.[26] We cannot hope here to resolve these difficulties; but since, in this essay, we are more interested in the project of ontology as such than in any particular ontological doctrines, we can concentrate on the explicit features of Parmenides' way of truth.

In Fragments 6 and 8 of the *Poem* the goddess is clear that the way of truth concerns τὸ ἐόν, "being" or "what is." Even G. E. L. Owen, who reinvigorated the hermeneutic disputes over the expression "that [it] is"[27] for the twentieth century, says that "no one will deny that, as the argument goes, τὸ ἐόν is a correct description of the subject [of this passage]."²⁸ The longest surviving section of the *Poem*, Fragment 8, posits and argues for a number of features of τὸ ἐόν, for example that it is undivided, ungenerated, and unified. So even if we do not know whether τὸ ἐόν refers to some single being, a way of being, the totality of beings, or the character of predication, we can still justifiably call this path or way of truth "ontology," using a term anachronistic to classical Greek philosophy.

The goddess distinguishes this ontology, or way of persuasion, both from the impenetrable path of "what is not and must not be,"²⁹ and from the way "along which mortals who understand nothing / amble two-headed,"³⁰ that is, the way which confuses is and is not. (The latter is known as the way of opinion: a path down which the goddess in fact leads Parmenides in latter portions of the *Poem*.) Thus as we travel along the way of truth, inquiring after τὸ ἐόν (being), we cannot mix it with any sort of not-being. It is impossible for not-being to be, or for being not to be.

According to the goddess, ontology is necessary. We are compelled to speak of being, even if the human voice frequently fails to do so. This is clear both at the beginning of the path of truth and along its way. We are constrained to follow this path of "is": "one must say and think that being is; for it is to be, / but nothing it is not."³¹ Meanwhile, the first alternative path, "is not and must not be,"³² turns out to be impossible to follow, since not-being cannot be recognized or indicated.³³ And the second alternative, which confuses being and not-being, which says that not-beings are, "may never be tamed."³⁴ Not only must we pursue ontology, but our other options are either impossible or inconclusive: "and yet a single tale of a way remains, that it is."³⁵ Moreover, necessity guides us along this path of truth. In her tale the goddess shows that being must be "uncreated and indestructible / whole and one-in-kind and steady and perfect."³⁶ Consider, for example, how she demonstrates that being is uncreated:

> But not ever was [being], nor yet will [it] be, since [it] is now
>   together entire,
> One, holding-together; for what birth will you seek of it?
> Where and whence does it grow? Not from not-being will I let
> You say or think: for not said nor thought
> Is it that it is not.³⁷

In these verses the goddess argues from the impossibility of not-being to the claim that being cannot have an origin. A number of passages use the same strategy, arguing from the impossibility of not-being to the necessity of some property of being.

Much of the modal terms in the goddess's tale condition speech and thought, rather than being itself. We are required to speak of being, and cannot utter any word which grants reality to not-being, so long as we follow the truth. Yet, as in the above quotation, these verbal and mental constraints can lead us to conclusions about being. Indeed, at one point in Fragment 8 the goddess affirms that it is the "force of assurance" that does not permit anything beyond being (rather than the existence of any feature or property of being which would inform our assurance).[38] Still, there are a few places in the *Poem* where modal conditions are placed on being itself: for instance, wherever "necessity" proper is named, Ἀνάγκη (in contrast to modal words like χρή, "one must"), the goddess speaks of it as a force (or even as another goddess) that literally shapes being and the world.[39] In general, it seems that any conditions of speech or thought must hold likewise of being, and vice versa: speech, thought, and being are bound by the same demands, "for the same is for thinking and being."[40]

Since necessity guides us to and along the way of truth, we might be surprised that there are any other paths available at all. Although narrative, μῦθος, leads us to ontology, speech also engenders confusion. We saw above that the path of "is not" cannot be indicated, and at one point the goddess says it is "without name."[41] But we might be tempted down the third path, the path of "echoing hearing / and tongue,"[42] the one that confuses being and not-being. This is the great risk of speech: making or using false names while "persuaded that they are true."[43] These are names which cannot refer to any being, like "becoming and destruction" and "not-being."[44] Even as she begins to lead us down this confused way of mortal opinion, the goddess tells Parmenides to hear "the deceptive arrangement of [her] verses."[45] Thus we hear how narrow Parmenides' ontological way is: although the goddess obliges thought and speech to follow the path of truth, "much-experienced habit" easily turns us away from it, to opinion.[46] The necessity of the truth is not guaranteed to mortals, but must be chosen and pursued.[47]

We have, now, the basic trajectory of Parmenides' ontology. Ontology is a way that thought can choose, a path that can be navigated only by hearkening to a μῦθος, which itself can be repeated and transmitted. To journey on this path is to be constrained to think and say being as utterly unconnected to not-being, and hence to find that being is whole, indivisible, and so on. False speech, which mixes being and not-being, puts this journey in danger. Yet if ontology must be chosen, if it is a way to be undertaken, what are we choosing, and to where do we finally journey? The goddess announced this from the start: the "steady heart of well-rounded truth."[48] Truth, ἀλήθεια, is not a feature of this ontological way, not a characteristic of speech or thought, but rather their guide and goal. For this and other reasons Palmer suggests understanding ἀλήθεια in Parmenides' text as "reality."[49] This perhaps goes too far and is too objective: the word ἀλήθεια may refer to being itself, but it also may indicate a change that takes place in those mortals who undertake this journey,[50] and I prefer the more traditional translation of "truth" for preserving this connotation. Whatever way we translate the word, it is surely the case that ἀλήθεια is the real of both the goddess's μῦθος and Parmenides' ontology: we must follow truth in order to think being, and we think being in order to access the truth.

ARISTOTLE: "THERE IS A KNOWLEDGE THAT
CONTEMPLATES BEING AS BEING"

Aristotle, too, is interested in reaching the truth: "it is right also to call philosophy knowledge of the truth."[51] Knowledge, ἐπιστήμη (sometimes translated as "science"), is a state of the soul which discloses truth (ἀληθεύειν).[52] The most choiceworthy kind of knowledge he calls wisdom or first philosophy.[53] Like Parmenides' path, knowledge is bound by necessity: "For we all suppose that what we know does not admit of holding otherwise."[54] Further, as with the goddess's μῦθος, knowledge can be taught and learned.[55] Yet despite their shared pursuit of truth, acceptance of necessity, and commitment to transmission, Aristotle's knowledge of being drastically diverges from Parmenides' path. Knowledge depends on demonstration rather than narrative, and a demonstration is possible only if the terms of one's account are made clear; for this reason, an important component of Aristotle's work is the identification and articulation of different senses of words (or different things which share a name). Moreover, for Aristotle knowledge of something is not just a recognition of its features, but also requires an understanding of its cause.[56] In this section we find that these two tasks (articulating the difference senses of words and inquiring into causes), which are absent from Parmenides' ontological path, are decisive for Aristotle's project of first philosophy, that is, his ontology as wisdom or knowledge of the principles of being.

According to Aristotle, to reach the truth, to gain knowledge, one must rely on λόγοι, accounts (λόγος can be translated in a number of ways, including "speech," "argument," "ratio," "reason"). Knowledge arises from demonstrations, deductions, refutations, premises, conclusions, definitions, and other various kinds of accounts. An account is true or false when it refers or fails to refer to a real state of affairs. But an account might also be ambiguous, indicating more than one state of affairs at the same time. For Parmenides, names are deceptive when they mix together "is" and "is not" (that is, when they fail to indicate anything real), and Aristotle also ensures that his words and accounts refer to something that is, rather than something that only seems to be. With ambiguity, though, we have another type of deception, one where words say too much, rather than not enough. Different things might share one name, and yet have nothing significant in common (for example, a rodent and an electronic device): Aristotle calls these homonyms (or "equivocals").[57] Or there are things which share both a name and some other features, but still do not have a single account (for example, formal and material causes are different sorts of things, but "causes" are not strictly homonymous because they are structurally analogous). It does not matter whether we speak about different senses of a word or different things that share a name; if we do not clarify which thing we mean or which sense we are using, then we cannot achieve knowledge of being or anything else.[58] Aristotle's work is filled with investigations into these things that are neither synonymous (or "univocal," sharing both a name and an account)[59] nor truly homonymous: consider Book Δ of the *Metaphysics*, which distinguishes the various senses of over thirty terms pertinent to first philosophy.

In fact Aristotle criticizes Parmenides precisely for ignoring a major case of polysemy: "false is [Parmenides'] assumption that being is said simply [ἁπλῶς], as it is said in several ways [πολλαχῶς]."[60] Parmenides, not worried about possible homonymy, regards "being" as synonymous, as having just one meaning. Aristotle never attacks this hypothesis as such; the closest he comes is the argument that being is not a class or genus (for a genus cannot be predicated of the differences that divide it into sub-classes, but being is predicated of all things, including these differences).[61] But this argument is effectively an aside, and is made in a passage having apparently nothing to do with Parmenides. Instead, Aristotle typically counters the hypothesis that being is synonymous by articulating the various ways things are said to be. Indeed, he contends that being is simply said in several ways. In the *Metaphysics* Aristotle identifies four primary ways in which things are said to be:

> But since being, said simply [ἁπλῶς], is said in several ways [πολλαχῶς], [1] one of which is according to the accidental, [2] another is as the true, and not-being as the false, and besides these there are [3] the figures of predication [τῆς κατηγορίας] (such as what, of what sort, how much, where, and when something is, and anything else [being] means in this way), and still besides all these [4] [being] potentially and actually.[62]

This is not merely a claim about the word "being," for it also pertains to things themselves (for example: some things are actually so, while others are only capable of being so; some things are accidentally the case, while others are in virtue of what they are). But it is also more than a category theory, wherein everything is one type of being or another (according to the different categories or figures of possible predicates in a judgement), for the figures of predication are only one part of this fourfold distinction. Rather, Aristotle here establishes the different ways beings are. These ways may overlap, for example "is" in "Virgil the cat is striped" accords with the figures of predication, actuality, and also truth. Yet each of these is still an independent and distinct determination, a different way of being, such that one of these determinations might change while the others stay the same.

Although Aristotle does not directly argue against the synonymy hypothesis he ascribes to Parmenides, he does contend that this premise leads to a very un-Parmenidean conclusion, namely that not-being must be.[63] The argument he makes is opaque, and probably not even his own,[64] but it seems to run as follows. Whenever there is predication (or a judgement) the predicate differs from its subject (as being-grey differs from Matilda the cat). And if being is said in only one way, then it must be said either as a predicate or as a subject.

However, either choice implies that not-being must be, despite Parmenides' injunctions against saying not-being. If being is said as a predicate, then it differs from the beings of which it is predicated, which hence must somehow both be and not be.[65] Or if being is the subject (it is *just* what is) then any of its predicates or attributes must both be and not be.[66] Although he admits that some of his predecessors have embraced one or more of these alternatives (perhaps the atomists and Platonists),[67] Aristotle himself can quickly refuse both conclusions as he affirms, against the assumption of this *reductio ad absurdum*, that there are a number of ways in which things are said to be.

Aristotle proposes that "there is a kind of knowledge that contemplates being as being and what belongs to it in virtue of itself,"[68] that is there is an ontological knowledge. Yet there is a tension between the many ways of being and the possibility of this ontology: knowledge investigates the causes of some object, and so we might expect there to be a number of different knowledges for the various ways of being. Of course one could just propose to account for the different senses of being, but this would not be knowledge, for it would not lead to an understanding of the causes of being. To resolve this, Aristotle clarifies that there can be a knowledge of things that are not themselves one, but are "said in relation to one nature, for these too are in a way said as one."[69] For instance, the various kinds of healthy things can be known through medical knowledge insofar as they all relate to health. Being, like health, "is said in several ways, but related to one and to some single nature, rather than homonymously."[70] As everything healthy relates in some way to health, all beings, everything that is, depend on οὐσίαι (sometimes translated "substance," "essence," or "entity"), either by being an οὐσία, or being an attribute of οὐσία, being generative of οὐσία, etc. Οὐσία is the first of the figures of predication, the first category. It can indicate both what something is and that it is. Most importantly, οὐσία is "primary in every way, in accounts, in understanding, and in time."[71] There would be nothing at all if there were not οὐσία. Thus our knowledge of being is a knowledge of οὐσία: "and in fact, what long ago and now and always is sought, and always leads to impasses – what is being? – is just this – what is οὐσία?"[72]

If Aristotle's project of first philosophy were just an investigation into what being is, it would largely be a revision of Parmenides' ontology. Parmenides attempts to establish the features of being, and Aristotle corrects this with an account of οὐσία and its attributes. Yet knowledge of something is more than an account of what it is: knowledge is concerned with why, with the αἰτία, the cause. "Since it is impossible for that of which there is knowledge without qualification to hold otherwise, what is known in virtue of demonstrative knowledge will be necessary,"[73] but most things are not necessary in virtue of themselves, but on account of their causes. So to have knowledge proper we need not only know that something is, and what it is, but also that on account of which it is: "we do not understand the truth without the cause."[74] This is so even for our knowledge of οὐσία: although nothing can exist without οὐσία, we may still wonder why there are οὐσίαι, especially since most οὐσίαι are not simple, but rather a composite of matter and form. Hence Aristotle tells us from the start of his *Metaphysics* that he is investigating causes, that wisdom "must be a contemplation of the first principles and the causes."[75]

Moreover, wisdom, or first philosophy, does not just consider any cause whatsoever, but instead is concerned with the first and highest of principles (ἀρχαί), what is most eminently knowable,[76] what is necessary and simple in itself,[77] what is separate and motionless.[78] If there were no such first causes of things, no οὐσία other than sensible, composite, natural οὐσίαι, then "the study of nature would be the primary kind of knowledge,"[79] that is, wisdom would be nothing but physics. Aristotle, however, contends that there are such separate causes, that in fact they are the divine itself, and he names the study of these causes, knowledge of being as such, theology.[80]

We have, now, the basic trajectory of Aristotle's ontology. Ontology is the highest kind of knowledge, a wisdom that can be achieved only through articulating λόγοι and establishing αἰτίαι. To gain this wisdom is to discover the divine and immutable causes of being as being, and hence to know both what and why being is. There are various ways in which beings can be, and yet being is not homonymous, for every being relates to and depends on οὐσία. First philosophy circulates between ontology, ousiology, archeology, and theology. It would be incorrect to say that the project *Metaphysics* is only one of these; instead, each of these is a different component of a single undertaking.[81] As with Parmenides, Aristotle hopes to reach the truth. Yet while Parmenides' path started with a goddess and from there leads to truth, for Aristotle the highest truth is the divine itself: "The principles of eternal beings are by necessity most true."[82]

DELEUZE: "THERE HAS ONLY EVER BEEN ONE ONTOLOGICAL PROPOSITION"

Deleuze is not interested in discovering – with Aristotle – the divine causes of beings. Nor is he devoted to reaching – with Parmenides – the truth of being as such. He does, in *Difference and Repetition*, establish what we might call a theory of causality, in his examination of the virtual, individuation, and actualization; he also attends to "the most extraordinary play of the true and the false which occurs not at the level of answers and solutions but at the level of problems themselves."[83] Yet no causes and no truths have a privileged relation to being, and ontology is about neither. Moreover, unlike the strenuous μῦθος of Parmenides' ontological path and the various λόγοι of Aristotle's ontological knowledge, Deleuze's philosophy collapses ontology into a single φωνή, or voice: "Being is univocal."[84] Like a narrative or an account, this voice can be transmitted, it echoes; but unlike them it only ever repeats itself, it only ever says the one thing. Deleuze hears this echo in the writings of Parmenides and Aristotle; still, he deliberately and explicitly extricates his project from theirs. In this section we ask why Deleuze's ontology in *Difference and Repetition* diverges so severely, with respect to content and form, from those of his predecessors. In so doing we must consider how the univocity of being relates to the singularity of the ontological proposition, and interrogate the function of an ontology that expresses only one idea.

Difference and Repetition opens with two tasks: to establish a concept of difference ("one which is not reducible to simple conceptual difference but demands its own Idea")[85] and to discover an essence of repetition ("one which is not reducible to difference without concept, and cannot be confused with the apparent character of objects represented by the same concept").[86] Deleuze undertakes the first task by reviewing his predecessors' attempts to account for what difference is. He begins with the philosophy of Aristotle,[87] in which he finds two levels of difference: there are what Deleuze names the "generic differences," the different classes or ways of being that are unassignable to any highest single class, and also the "specific differences," the qualitative differences that divide and subdivide classes into species. These two kinds of differences "are tied together by their complicity in representation,"[88] they reinforce one another and ultimately prop up the genus-species model of representation (the identity of the concept). As noted in the previous section, since specific differences are, since they have being, being cannot be a genus (for a genus cannot coherently be predicated of what differentiates it). If being is not a genus, there must be a number of highest genera, and thus generic differences, that is, a number of different ways of being.

Deleuze is searching for what it is that makes a difference, what differentiates, a concept of difference in itself, absolute. Neither generic difference nor specific difference lead to such a concept, for both are relative to a higher identity. Specific differences are relative to the class, or concept, they subdivide. Generic differences, the highest different ways of being, are relative to and dependent on a primary kind of being, οὐσία (and, in later medieval Aristotelianisms, god), which generates what Deleuze calls an analogy of being (adopting the term from those later Aristotelians). This analogy of being provides us with a "quasi-concept" of being that is neither homonymous/equivocal nor synonymous/univocal. With both specific and generic differences, then, "Difference appears only as a *reflexive concept.*"[89] Specific differences are only discovered by reflection on the identity of quasi-universal concepts; generic differences are only discovered by reflection on the identity of the quasi-concept of οὐσία. Both are subordinate to the generalization-specification representational scheme. For Deleuze, Aristotle only represents the differences of representation itself, "a difference already mediated by representation,"[90] not the differences of particular individuals.

According to Deleuze, this failure to provide an adequate account of difference is not a minor oversight; rather it is an inevitable consequence and "unresolvable difficulty"[91] of Aristotle's ontology. The basis for this failure is the premise that there are different ways of being, or that being is said in many ways. While we might have supposed that these different ways of being furnish us with a concept of difference in itself, they actually institute a schema of representation that prevents us from thinking individuals and their individuating differences. Every being is assigned its way of being, which in turn is further specified and particularized and embodied in some matter. There is no way to talk about the being of the embodied particular as such, only these various classifications. Aristotelian ontology "must essentially relate being to particular existents, but at the same time it cannot say what constitutes their individuality."[92] The issue is less that Aristotle allows for a single quasi-concept of being, a one to which the many senses of being relate analogously, than that he posits more than one way of being at all. These various ways become an obstacle in our effort to account for the being of beings, a net which ensnares our thought while letting pass the object we seek. What is therefore needed is a universal understanding of being, the being of singular beings, indeed of all beings whatsoever: only through this universal can we grasp the individual and conceptualize difference in itself. If we stick with the generic differences of Aristotle, "the genuine universal is missed no less than the true singular: the only common sense of being is distributive, and the only individual difference is general."[93]

Therefore, Deleuze argues, there cannot be multiple senses of being, whether these are understood as analogues or equivocals. There can only be one way of being, it is said in a single voice: being is universal, univocal. Of course there are still differences among beings, but these differences never divvy up being itself; rather we find "a division among those who distribute *themselves* in an open space."[94] To a certain extent Deleuze seems to return to Parmenides' way of truth: being is undivided, unaffected by the comings and goings of beings, it is "the univocity of simple presence."[95] However, Parmenides' truth no more delivers a concept of difference than does Aristotle's first philosophy. If the latter lets difference in itself pass by while thought is ensnared in a net of generalizations, the former excludes all differences whatsoever, relegating them to the second path of mere opinion. For Deleuze being is not said only in and of itself (as in Parmenides' *Poem*), but instead it is said of all beings whatsoever.

This recalls Aristotle's criticism of Parmenides: if being simply is, if it is said in just one way, if it is the single universal predicate, then that of which being is said, beings, are not. Deleuze concedes this point: "Univocal being is indeed common in so far as the (individuating) differences 'are not' and must not be," although he qualifies that this is a peculiar "non-being without negation."[96] Later he recasts this same argument in the terms of the univocity of being: "Univocity signifies that being itself is univocal, while that of which it is said is equivocal."[97] Universal being is what is in common in all beings, but the only thing that all beings share in common is that they differ from one another; the true universal thus is difference itself. In other words, being is indeed, for Deleuze, the self-same; yet what is self-same in beings is only difference. The univocity of being means, simultaneously, the being is said equally of all things, but also that all things are equivocal, unequal.

Every time being is said, it is in one and the same way. Parmenides was right only to permit one way of being, but wrong to make this being coextensive with a singular, most real, true thing. Instead being must be the universal, it must be said equally of all things: it is said of these differences, which somehow are not, it is said of disparate and diverse beings. If being eschews all diversity and forecloses all change, we will fail to grasp both being and difference. For being to be said univocally of all things, it must be "being which is Difference, in the sense that it is said of difference."[98] The philosophy of difference and univocal ontology are mutually implicating: to think difference in itself we must grant the univocity of being, but univocity is only genuine if being is said of differences. We cannot grant that there are different ways of being if we are to establish a concept of difference, for these various generic differences subordinate (true) difference to the identity of the concept and subordinate themselves to the quasi-concept and pseudo-universal of οὐσία. And if we hope to establish the univocity of being, we must grant that being is said of all things, including differences.

Aristotle postulates the many ways of being in part because of his attention to λόγοι: there are many sorts of judgements, many schemas of predication, and these indicate different ways of being. So if being is only said in one way, we might wonder how we can speak of being at all. Deleuze urges us "to replace the model of judgement with that of the proposition,"[99] that is to attend to expression rather than predication. An expression is composed of three independent elements: (1) the designator (that is the word or proposition itself); (2) the referent or designated (that is the thing to which the designator refers); and (3) the sense (that is what is expressed or the attribute of the thing).[100] Two expressions might have the same designator but different senses or referents, as in the case of homonyms. Or two expressions might have the same referent but different senses, indicated by different designators, for example "Virgil and Matilda" and "the author's cats." For being to be expressed univocally, then, it must always have one and the same referent, and it must always have one and the same sense: "Being, this common designated, in so far as it expresses itself, is said in turn *in a single and same sense* of all the numerically distinct designators."[101] Written into the term "univocity" is this idea of a single voice, a φωνή of being.

Because univocal being has always and only one sense and one reference "there has only ever been one ontological proposition."[102] To speak of being is not to attribute a predicate to a subject, but to always express a sole way of being, to designate what is always equal and common in beings. The univocity of being implies that there is only one ontological proposition, that it is singular. Thus follows the unity of ontology: "From Parmenides to Heidegger it is the same voice which is taken up, in an echo which itself forms the whole deployment of the univocal."[103]

Of course, this ontology that says just one thing certainly cannot be Aristotle's project of knowing being as being: even if we disregard the analogy of being, it would still be impossible for univocal ontology to inquire into the cause of beings. Yet we also find Deleuze contrasting the "paths" of Parmenides with the "voice" of ontology. We cannot journey along an ontological way: we cannot (contra Parmenides) establish the features, properties, or attributes of being (even if these are only formally, and not numerically, distinct).[104] That "being" has just one sense implies that being has just one attribute: univocity. To say anything about being – that it is universal, unaffected, undivided, etc. – is always and each time to indicate and intend the exact same thing: "The only realized Ontology – in other words, the univocity of being – is repetition."[105]

If there is only one ontological proposition, what function remains for the echoing voice of ontology? The univocity of being resounds as a demand to be heard. We saw the first demand in the previous paragraph: the ontological proposition acts as a standard for claims about being. Univocity implies that there are no various ways of being, no causes of being, no features or attributes of being (other than univocity itself). This measure is applied even more strictly in Deleuze's examination of the "three principle moments in the history of philosophical elaboration of the univocity of being,"[106] that is, the philosophies of Scotus, Spinoza, and Nietzsche.[107] Deleuze examines not only how each institutes a univocal ontology, but also how the theses of Scotus and Spinoza fail to fully comply with the requirements of univocity. This culminates with a discussion of Nietzsche, wherein we find the fully realized ontology "according to which being is said of becoming, identity of that which is different, the one of the multiple, etc."[108] With this we see the second demand of univocity, also noted above: univocal ontology requires a philosophy of individual difference. The ontological proposition tells us that everything is equal, but "this 'Everything is equal' and this 'Everything returns' can be said only at the point at which the extremity of difference is reached."[109] Although ontology is absolute repetition, what is repeated always differs, as universal being must be of difference itself.

We have, now, the basic trajectory of Deleuze's ontology in *Difference and Repetition*. Ontology is the univocity of being, a single echoing φωνή that says the genuine universality of being. To express this voice is to affirm that being is everywhere equal and the same, and hence to say it strictly of what is everywhere unequal and different. Difference requires the univocity of being, and being in turn calls for difference. This "calling for" or "demand" is the imperative-interrogative aspect of univocity: "The imperatives are those of being, while every question is ontological and distributes 'that which is' among problems. Ontology is the dice throw, the chaosmos from which the cosmos emerges."[110] This ontological demand on beings is pure, that is, necessary and universal: "The gods themselves are subject to the *Anankē* or sky-chance."[111]

KALEIDOSCOPIC ONTOLOGY

So, what is ontology? Unable to confidently propose a single answer, we instead examined three. We considered Parmenides' ontological path, Aristotle's ontological knowledge, and Deleuze's ontological proposition. These thinkers define what ontology can be, for each pursues being to the limits of thought. And while there are certainly other sorts of ontology, both in the history of philosophy and today, these three in particular continue to be decisive, for each presents us with an original and powerful attempt to think through being. Yet what makes these disparate endeavors all ontology? If ontology is said in many ways, do these ways converge? We might be tempted to say that these are three different possible paths, or three ways of speaking of being, or three sciences of being, or perhaps even the echo of a single thought. Yet to affirm any of these is to give priority to one thinker over another. Let us instead consider what is common among them, by noting two of their shared commitments.

All three thinkers agree that it is possible to successfully speak about being, even if they disagree on how to do it. This is the discursive condition for the possibility of ontology. Of course language is not a transparent medium; it indeed poses dangers. These thinkers are attentive to how words distort. Yet linguistic error is neither inevitable nor irreversible: we can work to correct any confusions. Being is not eclipsed by language; it is narrated, accounted for, or expressed therein. Moreover, if ontology can be spoken then it can be repeated, communicated, and transformed. Repeated, in that we can reaffirm and reestablish a discourse of being (even if that discourse is a mere proposition). Communicated, in that this discourse can be heard and learned by others. Transformed, in that those others can modify it as they will, correcting or distorting this discourse about being. The speaking of being hence introduces a historical dimension to ontology.

Further, all three thinkers invoke ἀνάγκη: they link their ontology to the demand of necessity. (In the case of Deleuze we only saw a hint of this, at the end of the fourth section, with the idea of the ontological question and the imperative of being.) The task is not just to say anything whatever about being; rather ontology is constrained to say of what necessarily holds or fails to hold of being. Ontology, the speaking of being, thus occupies the space between being and necessity, between what is and what must be. It articulates the contours of a demand on being itself. While the speaking of being allows for a history of ontology, the restrictions of ἀνάγκη require that ontology hold for all times.

However, we should not presume that ontology is the lowest common denominator of these three projects. The divergences between these thinkers are not so many quirks and idiosyncrasies, but essential to each's very endeavor. They are the media in which ontology happens, and they take it to its extremes. We can quickly review two sets of crucial distinctions.

The first concerns how we speak of being. Parmenides tells us a narrative that leads the reader to an understanding of what features being must have. Aristotle, paying careful attention to the various ways things are said to be, articulates and defends true accounts about being. Deleuze expresses being always and only with a single voice. The first divergence: narrative, accounts, voice – μῦθος, λόγοι, φωνή. Each thinker privileges one of these features of speech in his own attempt to speak about being.

The second concerns the sought for object of ontology. For Parmenides, the goddess promises access to the truth as a result of his journey on the path of being. For Aristotle, wisdom must be of the highest causes of things, and indeed of the divine itself insofar as it is a first principle of beings. For Deleuze, we can only establish a concept of difference in itself by affirming the univocity of being. The second divergence: truth, principle, differences – ἀλήθεια, ἀρχή, διαφορά. Each philosopher establishes his own ontology in pursuit of one of these ideas.

What remains, for us and for the history of ontology writ large, are, again, the gaps, the overlaps, and the dialogical and intertextual references. That is, the question of what each project makes of the others' divergences. Can ontology be successfully uncoupled from truth, as in Deleuze's project, or does ἀλήθεια return with the talk of the genuine universal and difference in itself? What role does the φωνή of the goddess have in Parmenides' μῦθος? What is the relation between λόγοι and narrative? Does Deleuze's model of the proposition successfully supplant Aristotle's thinking of the predication in accounts, or is it merely a supplement? Can Aristotle's hylomorphism account for individual differences? What role does not-being play in the determination of being(s)? If ontology bears a special relationship to ἀνάγκη, then there is a demand to pursue these and other questions. Of course, the answers are beyond the limits of this essay.

NOTES

[I would like to thank Charlie Salem, Ryan Johnson, and Andreea Greenstine for reading through and commenting on drafts of this essay.]

1. Gilles Deleuze, *Difference and Repetition/Différence et Répétition* [DR], p. 35/52.
2. Ibid. p. 39/57.
3. Alain Badiou, *Deleuze: The Clamor of Being*, p. 11.
4. Manuel DeLanda, *Intensive Science & Virtual Philosophy*, p. 41; Levi Bryant, "The Ontic Principle: Outline of an Object-Oriented Ontology," pp. 269–70; Tristan Garcia, *Form and Object*, p. 4.
5. *DR* p. 35/52.
6. Ibid.
7. Ibid. p. 39/57.
8. Ibid. p. 35/52.
9. For some treatments of univocity in the scholarship on Deleuze, consider: Dan Smith, *Essays on Deleuze*, pp. 27–42; Nathan Widder, "The Rights of the Simulacra: Deleuze and the Univocity of Being"; Joe Hughes, *Deleuze's Difference and Repetition*, pp. 52–65; Adrian Parr, *The Deleuze Dictionary*, pp. 196–7, 295–7; Henry Somers-Hall, *Deleuze's Difference and Repetition*, pp. 21–43; Levi Bryant, *Difference and Givenness*. None of these texts

examines the claim that there is only one ontological proposition. In this volume, one should turn to the contribution of John Bova and Paul Livingston, "Univocity, Duality, and Ideal Genesis: Deleuze and Plato," which, by considering the dualism latent in Deleuze's univocity, indeed acknowledges his claim that there is only one ontological proposition.

10. Parmenides, *Fragments* [Parmenides], 1.1; all translations of Parmenides' *Poem* are my own. For Greek texts I used John Palmer, *Parmenides & Presocratic Philosophy* [Palmer], and Hermann Diels and Walther Kranz, *Die Fragmente der Vorsokratiker*. I also consulted Palmer's translation, as well as those of G. S. Kirk, J. E. Raven, and M. Schofield, *The Presocratic Philosophers*, and Richard McKirahan, *Philosophy Before Socrates*.

11. Palmer pp. 51–62, discussing the various possibilities of who this goddess might be, argues that it is Night.

12. Parmenides 1.27.

13. Ibid. 2.1–2.

14. Ibid. 1.29.

15. Ibid. 2.1.

16. Thus the tragedy of losing parts of the text of the *Poem* – we have lost pieces of the divine myth itself through the risk of textual transmission.

17. Ibid. 2.4.

18. Ibid. 2.3.

19. Ibid. 2.6.

20. Ibid. 2.5.

21. For an example of the existential reading, G. E. L. Owen, *Logic, Science and Dialectic* [Owen], pp. 10–16, and Jonathan Barnes, *The Presocratic Philosophers* [Barnes], pp. 160–1; predicative, John Burnet, *Early Greek Philosophy*, p. 178; something in between, Palmer pp. 94–7; veridical, Charles Kahn, "The Thesis of Parmenides"; speculative, Alexander Mourelatos, *The Route of Parmenides*, pp. 47–73.

22. Barnes p. 163.

23. Parmenides 2.2.

24. Palmer pp. 97–100.

25. Aristotle, *Physics* [*Phys.*], I.2, 185a21–2. All translations of Aristotle texts are my own. For the Greek texts I used the Oxford Classical Texts. I also consulted the translations of *The Complete Works of Aristotle: Revised Oxford Translations*, ed. Barnes, and those of Joe Sachs.

26. *Phys.* I.2, 185a23–6.

27. Parmenides 2.3.

28. Owen p. 10.

29. Parmenides 2.5.

30. Ibid. 6.4–5.

31. Ibid. 6.3.

32. Ibid. 2.5

33. Ibid. 2.6–7.

34. Ibid. 7.1.

35. Ibid. 8.1–2.
36. Ibid. 8.3–4.
37. Ibid. 8.5–9.
38. Ibid. 8.12–13.
39. Ibid. 8.16, 8.30, 10.6; similarly with Μοῖρα, fate, at 8.37.
40. Ibid. 3.1. Or "the same is there for thought and that on account which there is thought"; ibid. 8.34.
41. Ibid. 8.17.
42. Ibid. 7.5–6.
43. Ibid. 8.39.
44. Ibid. 8.40.
45. Ibid. 8.52.
46. Ibid. 7.3.
47. Ibid. 8.15–16. It might be noted here that traditionally fragment 7 is seen as contrasting λόγος as something like reason with the echoing hearing and tongue that lead us to error. However, this traditional view has been criticized as misconstruing the text. Consider, for instance, Christopher Kurfess, *Restoring Parmenides' Poem*, pp. 73–83.
48. Parmenides 1.29.
49. Palmer pp. 89–91.
50. For the idea that Parmenides is a type of mystic, consider Peter Kingsley, *In the Dark Places of Wisdom*.
51. Aristotle, *Metaphysics* [*Meta.*], α.2, 993b19–20.
52. Aristotle, *Ethica Nicomachea* [*EN*], VI.3, 1139b15–17.
53. *Meta.* A.2, Γ.4.
54. Ibid. VI.3, 1139b19–21.
55. Ibid. VI.3, 1139b25–35.
56. Aristotle, *Analytica Posteriora* [*APo*], I.2, 70b9–12.
57. Aristotle, *Categoriae* [*Cat.*], 1, 1a1–2.
58. For the argument that homonymy/equivocity is first of all a property of things, not words, consider Joseph Owens, *Doctrine of Being in the Aristotelian Metaphysics*, pp. 107–37.
59. *Cat.* 1, 1a6–7.
60. *Phys.* I.3, 186a24–5.
61. *Meta.* B.3, 998b17–28.
62. *Meta.* E.2, 1026a33–b2.
63. *Phys.* I.3, 186a25–b12.
64. Ibid. 187a1–10.
65. Ibid. 186a25–b4.
66. Ibid. 186a32–b12.
67. Ibid. 187a1–10. There is some scholarly disagreement over who Aristotle refers to in this passage. Most ancient commentators think it is Plato and the Platonist Xenocrates (Alexander of Aphrosias, as recorded in Simplicius, *On Aristotle Physics 1.3–4*, pp. 45, 49; Themistius, *On Aristotle Physics 1–3*, pp. 29–30; Philoponus, *On Aristotle's Physics 1.1–3*, pp. 102–3), while

modern commentators think it is Democritus and Leucippus (W. D. Ross, *Aristotle's Physics*, pp. 480–1; William Charlton, *Aristotle's Physics Books I and II*, p. 63). I see no reason not to suppose that Aristotle meant both the Platonists and atomists. Cf. Aristotle, *De Generatione et Corruptione*, I.8; *Meta.* N.2.

68. *Meta.* Γ.1, 1003a21–2.

69. Ibid. Γ.2, 1003b12–15.

70. Ibid. Γ.2, 1003a33–4.

71. Ibid. Z.1, 1028a31–2.

72. Ibid. Z.1, 1028b2–4.

73. *APo* I.4, 73a21–3.

74. *Meta.* α.1, 993b23–4.

75. Ibid. A.2, 982b9–10.

76. Ibid. A.2, 982a30–b4.

77. Ibid. Δ.5, 1015b11–15.

78. Ibid. E.1, 1026a15–16.

79. Ibid. E.1, 1026a27–9.

80. Ibid. E.1, 1026a18–19.

81. Although perhaps it is appropriate to identify one of them as the overarching task of the *Metaphysics*, to which the others are subordinated. Stephen Menn, *The Aim and Argument of Aristotle's Metaphysics*, argues compellingly and comprehensively that the foremost concern of Aristotle's *Metaphysics* is archeology, the study of the first and highest principles and sources of being. But also consider Pierre Aubenque, *Le Problème de l'Être chez Aristote*, which argues that the project of first philosophy is ultimately, for Aristotle, aporetic; see, in this volume, Pierre Aubenque, "Science Regained," trans. Clayton Shoppa.

82. *Meta.* α.1, 993b28–9.

83. *DR* p. 107/142.

84. Ibid. p. 35/52.

85. Ibid. p. 27/54.

86. Ibid.

87. Ibid. pp. 30–5/45–52.

88. Ibid. p. 34/51.

89. Ibid.

90. Ibid. p. 27/41.

91. Ibid. p. 38/58.

92. Ibid. Of course, here a peripatetic would object: Aristotle does indeed have a theory of matter as the principle of individuation. Consider, in this volume, Emanuela Bianchi, "Aristotle's Organism, and Ours," and Adriel Trott, "Does it Matter? Material Nature and Vital Heat in Aristotle's Biology."

93. Ibid. p. 303/387.

94. Ibid. p. 36/54.

95. Ibid. p. 37/54.

96. Ibid. p. 39/57. A full account of the peculiar non-being of individuating difference is beyond the scope of this essay, although we can mention that individuating differences are non-beings insofar as they are non-actual.
97. Ibid. p. 304/388.
98. Ibid. p. 39/57.
99. Ibid. p. 35/52.
100. In the *The Logic of Sense* Deleuze quickly complicates this distinction with a number of paradoxes; while these certainly develop the idea of univocity in new directions, they are not essential for understanding univocity in *Difference and Repetition* and thus are outside the scope of this essay.
101. *DR* p. 35/53.
102. Ibid. p. 35/52.
103. Ibid.
104. Deleuze seems to waver on whether Spinoza's attributes would also be excluded, that is, whether they express formally distinct senses of being. Consider Gilles Deleuze, *Expressionism in Philosophy: Spinoza*, pp. 104–5; *DR* pp. 35, 303.
105. *DR* p. 303/387.
106. Ibid. p. 39–57.
107. Ibid. pp. 39–42/57–61.
108. Ibid. p. 40/59.
109. Ibid. p. 304/388.
110. Ibid. p. 199/257.
111. Ibid.

BIBLIOGRAPHY

Aristotle, *Aristotelis: Ethica Nicomachea*, ed. J. Bywater (Oxford: Clarendon Press, 1920).

Aristotle, *Aristotelis: Categoriae et Liber de Interpretatione*, ed. L. Minio-Paluello (Oxford: Clarendon Press, 1936).

Aristotle, *Aristotelis: Physica*, ed. W. D. Ross (Oxford: Clarendon Press, 1951).

Aristotle, *Aristotelis: Metaphysica*, ed. W. Jaeger (Oxford: Clarendon Press, 1957).

Aristotle, *Aristotelis: Analytica Priora et Posteriora*, ed. W. D. Ross (Oxford: Clarendon Press, 1964).

Aristotle, *Aristote: De la Génération et de la Corruption*, ed. C. Mugler (Paris: Les Belles Lettres, 1966).

Aristotle, *The Complete Works of Aristotle: The Revised Oxford Translation*, ed. J. Barnes, 2 vols (Princeton: Princeton University Press, 1984).

Aristotle, *Physics*, trans. J. Sachs (New Brunswick, NJ: Rutgers University Press, 1995).

Aristotle, *Metaphysics* trans. J. Sachs (Santa Fe: Green Lion Press, 1999).

Aristotle, *Nicomachean Ethics*, trans. J. Sachs (Newbury, MA: Focus Publishing, 2002).

Aubenque, P., *Le Problème de l'Être chez Aristote: Essai sur la Problématique Aristotélicienne*, 6th edn (Paris: Presses Universitaires de France, [1962] 2013).

Badiou, A., *Deleuze: The Clamor of Being*, trans. L. Burchill (Minneapolis: University of Minnesota Press, 2000).

Barnes, J., *The Presocratic Philosophers*, 2nd edn (London: Routledge & Kegan Paul, 1982).

Bryant, L., *Difference and Givenness: Deleuze's Transcendental Empiricism and the Ontology of Immanence* (Evanston: Northwestern University Press, 2008).

Bryant, L., "The Ontic Principle: Outline of an Object-Oriented Ontology," in L. Bryant, N. Srnicek, and G. Harman (eds.), *The Speculative Turn: Continental Materialism and Realism* (Melbourne: re.press, 2011), pp. 261–78.

Burnet, J., *Early Greek Philosophy*, 4th edn (London: Black, 1930).

Charlton, W., *Aristotle's Physics Books I and II: With Introduction and Commentary* (Oxford: Clarendon Press).

DeLanda, M., *Intensive Science & Virtual Philosophy* (London: Continuum, 2002).

Deleuze, G., *Différence et Répétition* (Paris: Presses Universitaires de France, 1968).

Deleuze, G., *Expressionism in Philosophy: Spinoza*, trans. M. Joughin (New York: Zone Books, 1990).

Deleuze, G., *The Logic of Sense*, trans. M. Lester and C. Stivale, ed. C. V. Boundas (New York: Columbia University Press, 1990).

Deleuze, G., *Difference and Repetition*, trans. P. Patton (New York: Columbia University Press, 1994).

Diels, H. and W. Kranz (eds.), *Die Fragmente der Vorsokratiker*, vol. 1, 6th edn (Berlin: Weidmann, 1951).

Garcia, T., *Form and Object: A Treatise on Things*, trans. M. A. Ohm and J. Cogburn (Edinburgh: Edinburgh University Press, 2014).

Hughes, J., *Deleuze's Difference and Repetition: A Reader's Guide* (London: Continuum, 2009).

Kahn, C., "The Thesis of Parmenides," *Review of Metaphysics*, 22.4 (1969), pp. 700–24.

Kingsley, P., *In the Dark Places of Wisdom* (Inverness, CA: Golden Sufi Center, 1999).

Kirk, G., Raven, J. and Schofield, M., *The Presocratic Philosophers*, 2nd edn (Cambridge: Cambridge University Press).

Kurfess, C., *Restoring Parmenides' Poem: Essays Toward a New Arrangement of the Fragments Based on a Reassessment of the Original Sources* (University of Pittsburgh: http://d-scholarship.pitt.edu/, 2012).

McKirahan, R., *Philosophy Before Socrates: An Introduction with Texts and Commentary*, 2nd edn (Indianapolis: Hackett, 2010).

Menn, S., 'The Aim and Argument of Aristotle's Metaphysics (Draft)' (https:// www.philosophie.hu-berlin.de/institut/lehrbereiche/antike/mitarbeiter/ menn/contents, retrieved January 2015).

Mourelatos, A., *The Route of Parmenides: A Study of Word, Image, and Argument in the Fragments*, revised edn (Las Vegas: Parmenides Publishing, 2008).

Owen, G. E. L., *Logic, Science and Dialectic: Collected Papers in Greek Philosophy*, ed. M. Nussbaum (Ithaca, NY: Cornell University Press, 1986).

Owens, J., *The Doctrine of Being in Aristotelian Metaphysics: A Study in the Greek Background of Mediaeval Thought*, 3rd edn (Toronto: Pontifical Institute of Mediaeval Studies, 1978).

Palmer, J., *Parmenides and Presocratic Philosophy* (Oxford: Oxford University Press, 2009).

Parr, A. (ed.), *The Deleuze Dictionary* (New York: Columbia University Press, 2005).

Philoponus, *On Aristotle's Physics 1.1–3*, trans. C. Osborne (Ithaca, NY: Cornell University Press 2006).

Ross, W. D., *Aristotle's Physics: A Revised Text with Introduction and Commentary* (Oxford: Clarendon Press, 1936).

Simplicius, *On Aristotle Physics 1.3–4*, trans. P. Huby and C. C. W. Taylor (London: Bloomsbury Academic, 2011).

Smith, D., *Essays on Deleuze* (Edinburgh: Edinburgh University Press, 2012).

Somers-Hall, H., *Deleuze's Difference and Repetition: An Edinburgh Philosophical Guide* (Edinburgh: Edinburgh University Press, 2013).

Themistius, *On Aristotle Physics 1–3*, trans. R. Todd (London: Bloomsbury Academic, 2012).

Widder, N., "The Rights of the Simulacra: Deleuze and the Univocity of Being," *Continental Philosophy Review*, 34.4 (2001), pp. 437–53.

CHAPTER 12

Object and Οὐσία: Harman and Aristotle on the Being of Things

Eric Salem

As even a cursory reading of his many books and articles makes clear, Graham Harman means to change the course of contemporary philosophic inquiry in at least two fundamental ways. He wants to revive realism and metaphysics. And he wants to put objects back at the center of metaphysical inquiry.[1] In the case of the first goal, Harman has a number of allies, including his fellow speculative realists; in the case of the second, he is much lonelier. Or at any rate, he has few *contemporary* allies. Harman claims that his object-oriented thinking not only has roots in the "key insights" of Heidegger and Husserl, both of whom have much to say about objects (in spite of Heidegger's aversion to the word); it is even more deeply grounded in Aristotle's thought. As he notes at one point in *The Quadruple Object*, "[my] metaphysics of objects has even deeper roots than [Heidegger and Husserl]. For in a sense, this book seeks only to provide a weirder version of Aristotle's theory of substance."[2]

Harman's attempt to link his own focus on objects to Aristotelian philosophy makes a certain sense. After all it was Aristotle who first put substance, οὐσία, on the philosophic map, in fact made it the central theme of metaphysics: "The thing sought and always causing perplexity as regards what being is, of old and now and always, is just this: what is substance [οὐσία]?"[3] If "substance" and "object" are virtual synonyms, as Harman sometimes suggests, then Aristotle is the first object-oriented philosopher.[4] Moreover, no philosopher has paid more attention to *things* in all their glorious individuality than Aristotle. Consider, for instance, the shelf's worth of books that Aristotle produced on animal life, starting with the *History of Animals* – these texts could only have been produced by someone who spent many years with his eyes wide open, attending to the nearly infinite variety of living things. If Harman wants to ally himself with philosophers who take individual objects seriously in their individuality, neither undermining nor overmining them, Aristotle (along with Leibniz) would certainly be a prime candidate.[5]

Still, it would be a mistake simply to identify Harman's object-oriented thinking with Aristotle's treatment of substance. In the passage already cited, Harman calls his approach to objects "weird," and he is right. What he has to say about objects is decidedly weird, and his approach to objects differs in all sorts of ways from Aristotle's approach, or at least from what is commonly taken to be Aristotle's approach. For Harman, real objects always have a hidden core; they are fundamentally inaccessible to thought and sense. For Aristotle, the opposite seems to be the case: understanding takes work, but the world and things in the world are fundamentally intelligible. For Harman, objects have and do not have their qualities; qualities and the objects they accompany live in constant, polarized tension with one another. Aristotle simply never talks about qualities in this way, and for him some qualities of things function as avenues to the essence of those things. For Harman, objects never really interact; at most they exhibit what Harman calls a vicarious causality. For Aristotle, one might say, the mark of an οὐσία is its ability to bring about change in other things. Above all, and as Harman himself repeatedly emphasizes, the realm of objects is far larger than the realm of substances. Dragons, electrons, and other fictional beings; trees and wooden houses, as well as the carpenters who make them and the termites that devour them; random heaps and random parts – all count equally as objects for Harman. Nature plays no part in the distinguishing of object and non-object. Aristotle's notion of an οὐσία seems to be much more restrictive, and nature does play a central role in the distinguishing of substance and non-substance. Finally, while Aristotle might agree with Harman's own criteria for object-being – autonomy and unity – it seems likely that even here there would be a difference of opinion, in this case about what, exactly, these criteria mean.

Given this multitude of differences, one might think that any attempt at a serious comparison of the two thinkers would be a waste of time: they simply do not share enough common ground. But I plan to take the opposite tack, to take these very differences as an opportunity for further inquiry and an occasion to put each thinker to the test. I start with Harman, sketching out at some length the basic features of his object-oriented ontology, and then bring Aristotle into the picture, as a sort of latter-day commentator. My goal throughout will be to see what light, if any, each thinker might shed on the other and what light, if any, the thinking of each might shed, in spite of their apparent differences, on what they share: an avid and serious interest in what one might call the thinginess of things.

HARMAN

Let us begin where Harman begins in *The Quadruple Object*, with the objects on his desk: pens, eyeglasses, an expired American passport.[6] As he says, all of these and "all such objects must be accounted for by ontology, not merely denounced or reduced to despicable nullities."[7] In other words, if we are to follow Harman's path, we must avoid undermining them – reducing them, as a particle physicist or pre-Socratic philosopher might, to the products or residue of some more fundamental stuff or process – or "overmining" them – treating them, as Hume or a student of Hume might, as needless fictions standing in for bundles of qualities.[8] Instead we must let them be objects. What, then, can we say about them?

Consider Harman's glasses – or some other pair, nearer at hand. Move your head from side to side. Walk around the desk. Leave the room and return after several hours. The contents and configuration of your visual field will change dramatically from moment to moment. Nevertheless, in different moods, in different lights, from different angles, you will always encounter the same object, the same pair of glasses – a one overlaid with a multitude of qualities, a unity accompanied by a series of shifting profiles.[9] But this one – Harman calls it the sensual object – is not a bare unity, identical in all respects to the unity of the pen lying on one side of it or the passport lying on the other. In addition to its sensual qualities, it has real ones, features that set it apart from pens, passports, and everything else. These real qualities might be difficult, even impossible, to list or articulate once and for all; they are not visible or in any other way sensual. But without them the glasses would not be what they are; such qualities make the glasses specific; they are "eidetic."[10]

Now put on the glasses. Use them. As every wearer of glasses knows, the more aware you are of your glasses, the less well you can see with them. They must become invisible to do their work. And the same holds true of the pens we write with, the desks we write on, the air we breathe and, for that matter, our own bodies, including our eyes. We become aware of pens only when they run out of ink, become aware of our eyes only when they become strained by too much reading – when we can no longer use them.[11] This goes to show, someone might suggest, that things like pens and glasses and even eyes are exhaustively defined by their place within a network of human uses: pens not only *have* a purpose, in important respects they *are* that purpose; what it is to be a pen is to perform a function within a larger whole. Harman would disagree. Attending to the way that glasses, pens, and bodies disappear when they are most themselves is of utmost importance, but what we really see here, Harman thinks, is that the reality of objects lies in their withdrawal, their self-concealment, their essential invisibility. Whenever I look at a desk or a pair of glasses – no matter how hard or how carefully I look – I encounter a mere profile, or as Harman likes to say, a caricature or distortion or translation of the object.[12] But the same holds true when I make use of such objects: to use an object is just another way of caricaturing it, of reducing it to its relation to me and other objects I find useful.[13] But real objects are truly auto-nomous: they are independent beings, units governed by their own peculiar laws. Put otherwise: there is more to an object than any encounter – or, for that matter, any series of encounters – with it can yield. Real objects are, as real, isolated from all contact.[14]

We have now reached the threshold of Harman's ontology. We can see, for instance, the beginnings of what he calls the fourfold object, since we now have four items in play, two kinds of objects, real and sensual, and two kinds of qualities, likewise real and sensual.[15] We can also see why something like "vicarious" causation would have to be a feature of Harman's system. Objects are in reality sealed off from one another, and hence incapable of interacting directly with one another. And yet they do interact. Their causal relations and interactions must therefore be indirect, mediated by some third thing.[16]

While these features of the account may be evident enough, some of Harman's most basic claims and assumptions may still seem puzzling or hard for a reader to accept – perhaps especially his claim that every object, however ordinary and insignificant, has a hidden side, an aspect of itself that resists disclosure. But we can perhaps persuade ourselves that Harman is on to something by starting with a more exotic example and working our way down.[17] Take Zamalek, the Cairo neighborhood in which Harman makes his home and which he himself calls an object at the beginning of The Quadruple Object. Neighborhoods can be seen, experienced, and used in a myriad of ways. They can be lived in, strolled through, looked at from above, viewed on maps, related to the cities and nations of which they form part. But neighborhoods also tend to have lives of their own, distinctive ways of being, that even life-long residents (much less sociologists) would be hard pressed to articulate – ways that will endure even as individual residents die or move away but that once lost will be lost forever. This enduring yet fragile hard-to-voice identity is, I would argue, what is real in every neighborhood, in Harman's sense of real. But what holds for the neighborhood surely holds for the street, for the families that live on the street, and for the individuals that make up those families – and if so, then why not for their stuff, too, their pens and eyeglasses and expired American passports? Every object, however ordinary, is like the moon or the force: it has a dark side.

Another feature of Harman's account that the reader may find puzzling involves the relation between the sensual and the real. In The Quadruple Object, in particular, Harman often speaks as if we were dealing with two distinct classes of entities: sensual objects and real objects. But now and then, especially later in the book, he suggests that what he calls the sensual object is simply the manifestation of the real object, its other face as it were.[18] The very expression, "the quadruple object," with its definite article and singular "object," also intimates that the sensual and real are in fact aspects or modes of one being. Why, then, does Harman so often suggest that we are dealing with distinct objects rather than aspects of one? I can think of three reasons. The first is fairly trivial: Harman is making a special effort in The Quadruple Object to be clear and concise about the overall structure of his system, and in the name of clarity and efficiency is willing to allow a certain obscurity to creep into his account. He therefore spends one chapter developing the notion of the sensual object by way of Husserl, another few chapters developing the notion of the real object by way of Heidegger, and does not worry too much about making the connection between them explicit. The second reason is more to the point: were Harman to link the sensual and the real too closely, were he to suggest too emphatically that they are two aspects of one being, we might come away with the impression that every object manifests itself in some fashion or the other. But this is emphatically not Harman's view. Some objects – Harman calls them dormant – are withdrawn, at least temporarily, from all scrutiny. They simply do not appear; they have no sensual "side."[19] In such cases, it makes good sense to speak, not of objects insofar as they are real, but of real objects simply.

The third reason is related to the second, and thinking it through should help us to see that there are also good reasons for speaking of sensual objects, that is, good reasons for attributing a quasi-separate status to the sensual aspect of some objects. In addition, it will give us a sense of just how weird Harman's weird ontology really is. We might admit, on the basis of what's just been said, that some objects are simply invisible. Yet at the same time we might be inclined to think that such objects are exceptions to the rule; most objects, we might suppose, make themselves readily available to the world at large. But this, Harman would say, is a misconstrual of the situation. Invisibility is the default mode of objects. Pens and passports are not there, out in the open, waiting to be seen. To be seen a thing must be encountered *by someone*; the sensual aspect of an object only exists as one side of a relation, at the other end of which is a definite, engaged observer. As a consequence, it makes sense to treat the sensual aspect of the object as a separate being; it lives apart from the real object from which it somehow emerges; at any rate, it belongs to the seer-seen relation at least as much as it belongs to the object. In fact, according to Harman – and here is where things get strange – this sensual object exists as an element or part of a *new* object; it inhabits the "inside" of an object constituted by the relation between observer and observed. To repeat: to be seen or encountered an object must enter into a relation with a second object, and whenever it does, this relation itself counts as a new object.[20]

Two further qualifications need to be introduced here. Thus far I have more or less identified "encountering" with seeing or observing, as if the sensual aspect or object only emerges when human beings, or at least animate beings, meet up with other objects. But Harman will have none of this – it smacks of what he calls the Philosophy of Human Access.[21] Perceiving is one kind of sensual-object-generating relation between real objects – but only one. *Every* genuine encounter between one object and another generates a sensual object, an object derived from the real object encountered, and this sensual object and the encountering object constitute a new object, one that exists independently of the object originally encountered.[22] When I gaze at an apple or grasp it or even eat it, my apple-gazing, apple-grasping, and apple-eating constitute objects in their own right, behind which the real apple lingers, unidentifiable with its visibility or tangibility or edibility. But equally when fire burns cotton (to use a favorite Harmanian example) this fire-burning-cotton constitutes an object in its own right, and what holds in the first case holds in the second: The fire may destroy the cotton but it can no more exhaust the being of the cotton it burns than I can the being of the apple I see or eat; fire encounters the cotton as flammable, but misses its softness and white color.[23] In short, the world is filled with objects that, in their jostling, never really touch, but that, in their never touching, always generate new objects.[24]

The second qualification that needs to be introduced follows directly upon the first. We might be tempted at first to divide objects into two classes: normal objects (like pens and passports) and weird relational objects (like Harman-eyeing-passport or dust-hitting-glasses). But this proves to be another false dichotomy. For just as every genuine relation between objects is itself an object, so every object, however "normal," is itself a system or complex of relations. To return to our earlier example: a neighborhood is a collection of streets, a street is an assemblage of families and shops, a family is a set of individuals, and an individual is a bundle of organs. And what holds for the individual holds for his pens, his glasses and his passport. Everything that is, every entity, leads, as it were, a double life: from one point of view it is an object with its own autonomous life, imperfectly "understood" by all the other objects that see or touch or in any other way impinge on its reality; from another it is nothing but a complex of relations between smaller objects, each caricaturing and being caricatured by one another in turn, and themselves composed of relations between still tinier objects.[25]

We are very far from our starting point. We began, as Harman recommends we begin, in naivety, with simple entities that everyone would call objects: pens, eyeglasses, passports.[26] But now, under his guidance, the world of objects has grown enormously, to include any number of "things" that few of us would earlier have been inclined to call objects. Moreover, even the simple entities with which we began seem far stranger than they did at first, composed as they are of relations upon relations and burdened, as all objects are, with subterranean sides. Confronted by a world of objects that threatens to grow beyond all bounds in both directions, great and small, and where nothing, not even the distinction between object and relation, can be taken for granted, we are bound to have questions. For instance, we might want to ask Harman whether any random collection of entities counts as an object, and if not, if only genuine relations generate or constitute or correspond to objects, as Harman sometimes suggests, what, we might want to know, makes some relations genuine and others not?[27] But I propose that we leave all these and all such questions aside, at least for the time being, and ask instead: what would Aristotle think of Harman's approach? What particular features of his account would Aristotle be likely to agree or disagree with? When Aristotle investigates the being of things is he engaged in the same sort of inquiry as Harman? Does the inquiry into objects have the same character and orientation as the inquiry into οὐσία?

ARISTOTLE AND HARMAN

Let's begin with points of apparent agreement. In the first place, just as Harman puts one sort of entity, objects, at the center of his ontology, so, too, Aristotle puts one sort of entity, οὐσία, at the center of his inquiry into being – recall that Aristotle says, in effect, that the inquiry into being was, is, and always will be an inquiry into οὐσία. In other words, although both authors intend to account for "being as being and what belongs to it in virtue of itself," that is, to account for all beings, both do so by focusing on one type of being and by taking up other beings in relation to it.[28] Second, these central entities, though not, as we shall see, identical with one another, are nevertheless connected to one another, and are connected because Aristotle, like Harman, is committed to beginning with what is "first for us" – with things like pens, glasses, and passports, in Harman's case, and things like human beings, gods, and fire, in Aristotle's.[29] For Aristotle, as for Harman, the task of philosophy is to account for the basic features of our everyday experience, not to explain them away.

Another point of contact or near contact. As we have seen, unity and autonomy are central to Harman's thinking about objects. Every object, real or sensual, is a one with many qualities. And every object, especially every real object, is autonomous – it is essentially unrelated to other objects; indeed its reality lies in this very independence. We find something at least akin to both of these claims in Aristotle. The substantiality of a substance lies, at least in part, in its being a "this something," an individual, that is, something determinate – a one to which all the other features of the thing can be referred.[30] Moreover, the primacy of οὐσία is not only evident in the way we talk – we do not attribute things to qualities but qualities to things and every attempt to define quality or quantity will involve a reference to those things – it is also evident in the most elementary features of our ordinary experience.[31] Οὐσίαι are independent. A substance is separate or separable (χωριστός) from its various features – a man or fire can grow or change color and still remain what it is – while qualities and quantities cannot exist apart from the substances they modify; they are only insofar as there are οὐσίαι.[32] In short, for Aristotle, too, unity and autonomy seem to be characteristic features of the entity that holds his focus.

In fact, a quick glance at some of Aristotle's other inquiries suggests that issues of unity and autonomy are of prime concern to him even outside the domain of "first philosophy" and often shape or even give rise to his most basic insights. The best tragedies (and presumably comedies as well) are well-ordered, unified wholes that represent actions that are themselves whole and complete; bad ones simply string together episodes in a chronological order.[33] The best lives are characterized, not only by excellence of activity, but self-sufficiency, the Aristotelian equivalent of autonomy; too great a dependence on external goods like honor and wealth is a recipe for unhappiness, and the life of contemplation is ultimately judged to be better than a life of action in part because of its greater self-sufficiency.[34] The same standards apply to political life. Self-sufficiency and unity of purpose distinguish the city from other forms of communal life; a city that grows too big (like Babylon) may be powerful, but it will lose the coherence needed for political life, and even a community of the right size that enjoys material self-sufficiency will fail at being a city if it lacks the unity that comes with friendship in a shared understanding of the good life.[35] Finally, who can doubt that Aristotle's apparently limitless fascination with living things has much to do with the way they move through the world as autonomous unities, maintaining relative independence toward the things outside and organic coherence within?

I will have more to say about life and its place within Aristotle's thinking a little later. But for now let us note that up to this point we have seen Harman and Aristotle moving, if not on the same track, then at least on parallel tracks. All that changes, however, just after Aristotle announces that οὐσία must form the center of any serious inquiry into being. For he immediately makes a list of candidate substances that excludes a great deal of what would appear on any list of Harman's: animals, plants and their parts; fire, water, earth and the like; their parts and the things composed of them "such as the heavens and the parts of it, the stars and the moon and the sun."[36] True, Aristotle only says that these things are *thought* to be substances and he seems open, briefly, to considering other possibilities.[37] But the other possibilities he seems most eager to consider are mathematical objects and Platonic forms, and by the end of Book Z of the *Metaphysics* his list of independent things has become even shorter, as if the general view of substance were too generous rather than too stingy.[38] In chapter sixteen he declares that "most of what are thought to be substances are potencies" and proceeds to exclude the parts of animals, as well as earth, fire, and air (as mere parts of the cosmos).[39] Then, in the final lines of Z, Aristotle says that only things (πράγματα) "composed by nature and in accordance with nature" qualify as genuine οὐσίαι.[40] Plants, animals, and the cosmos are the candidates that remain, or at least all that remain among the things that can be perceived. Pens, glasses and passports certainly fail to make the grade, as do, of course, all the more exotic objects described by Harman.

How are we to account for this evident difference between two authors who obviously share a certain amount of common ground? In particular, what leads Aristotle to exclude from the ranks of οὐσίαι things that none of us would presumably have trouble calling objects, for instance all the various products of human artifice? We might be tempted to explain – or explain away – Aristotle's apparent disagreement with Harman as a matter of choice and linguistic history: Harman chooses to give the by now rather empty word "object" the widest possible application, while Aristotle chooses to keep the (in his time) still vibrant word οὐσία confined more or less within the bounds that Plato set for it. In my view, such explanations miss the point. Instead, as I hope to show in what follows, at the bottom of the discrepancy about the range of object-substances lies a dispute between Harman and Aristotle about being and about philosophy – about what beings should form the proper center and starting point of philosophic inquiry and what the proper shape and orientation of philosophy at its most comprehensive should be. But to understand why Aristotle takes the path he does we need to look a bit more at Book Z. Although Aristotle does not argue explicitly against treating products of artifice as genuine οὐσίαι in Z and in fact throughout the book repeatedly uses such products as models for οὐσίαι, nevertheless a little reflection on its arguments can help us to see how such a conclusion would follow.[41]

Let us begin with the two passages cited most recently. In the first, the reason Aristotle gives for calling both the parts of animals and the elements potencies rather than οὐσίαι is that "none of them is one, but they exist like a heap until they are transformed and some one thing is generated out of them."[42] About the parts of animals, in particular, he says "for none of them exists separately, and whenever they are separated, even then, they all exist as material."[43] In the second passage, he says about the οὐσίαι that are formed "according to nature or by nature," that "this nature would appear to be the οὐσία, [a nature] which is not an element but a principle." He then adds, "an element is that which is present as material in a thing and into which it is divided, as is the syllable [ba] into a and b."[44] What can we glean from these passages? To begin with, we can see that, in contrast to what Harman would want to say about objects in general, Aristotle thinks that the parts of substances lack unity, as a group and individually – which means, as he says explicitly at the end of chapter sixteen, that the parts of substances cannot be substances.[45] Moreover, again contra Harman, Aristotle thinks that the parts of substances lack autonomy; they cannot be what they are in separation from the wholes to which they belong; when separated, they devolve into mere material. What makes up for their lack of inherent autonomy and unity – the agreed upon marks of objecthood in Harman and thinghood in Aristotle? An answer is suggested by the second passage and the references in both passages to material. In order for the parts of something to be more than a heap, more than a mass of material, something else has to be present, and this something else cannot have the character of an element or part: the addition of more material, a missing part, will not do the trick. What is needed is form. This is the "nature" that confers unity and autonomy on the thing and its parts and that for this reason can be called the thinghood of an independent thing, the substantiality of a substance, in short the οὐσία of an οὐσία.[46]

What Aristotle is suggesting here surely makes a certain amount of sense. Lungs and livers are fundamentally different kinds of beings than the animals they belong to, for organs have the kind of being they have only in belonging to an organism; they are simply not independent beings. Remove an eye or a foot from an animal; you will not only mutilate the animal; you will also instantly deprive the eye or foot of its being as a potency for sight or a potency for walking. Eye and foot will now be reduced to mere material. The same analysis applies with even greater force to artificial things. Dismantle a house brick by brick, board by board. The bricks and boards that formerly made up the house will literally exist "like a heap"; they will now have the status of materials for house building and will only achieve their former unity if they are given the form of a house once again. Moreover, what holds for the parts of the house will hold for the house as well. I just spoke of the form of a house, but a house has a form only in a manner of speaking – in the same manner as an eye or a roof tile has a form. One can say what it is to be an eye, but what one says will always have reference to the animal it belongs to and that defines its being. Likewise, one can say what it is to be a house, but what one says will have reference to the beings that use it: to be a house is to occupy a certain position within the network of human purposes; it is a potency (a δύναμις rather than an οὐσία) insofar as it is able (δύνασθαι) to serve such a purpose. In the end, a house is no more "substantial," no more an *independent* being, than the bricks from which it made or than the organs of an animal, and the same holds true of every product of human artifice, even, presumably, works of art.

Harman, would, of course, disagree with nearly everything I have just said. Human beings (and other animals) are objects, that is substances. But so are their livers and lungs, their eyes and feet, and all the many things they make, including the houses they live in and the bricks and boards with which they build. Given that "form" applies primarily to living wholes, and given that, as Aristotle uses it, the term marks out one type of "object" over others, does this mean that Harman would reject all talk of forms? The answer, perhaps somewhat surprisingly, is "no." On the contrary, the language of forms is fully incorporated into Harman's system. Form undergoes exactly the same vast expansion as substance: just as every Harmanian object as object is an autonomous unity, so every object as object has a form, or better, is a form or "formal reality," insofar as it is taken as a whole.[47] "Objects encounter their neighbors as unified forms."[48] "Tool-being [another name for "real object"] is a form, a kind of formal cause that acts as substance with respect to its surroundings, but which is born only as a relational composite of its internal elements."[49] In fact, it sometimes looks as if the world is nothing but forms. "What is real in the cosmos is forms wrapped inside forms."[50] "The story of the world is a tale of interacting forms or objects of all possible sizes at all possible levels . . ."[51]

What is absent, then, from Harman's ontology is not the notion of form but only, in his view, an erroneous use of both it and notion of substance, an error based on an "ontic prejudice," that refers "to certain special entities at the expense of others."[52] In other words, "the notion of natural substance makes illicit use of our ontic biases to draw an ontological distinction between substances and non-substances," but thanks, in part, to Heidegger and Whitehead, we have been "liberated" from any "naturalistic view of substance," any tendency to affirm "some pampered set of 'natural kinds' at the expense of other realities."[53] All objects, natural and artificial, share the same formal structure, and in terms of this structure, a clock is as good as a cat: just as a cat is something over and above its parts, so too a clock is something over and above its gears and springs. In both cases the being of object-substances proves to be form.[54]

There is one more term, or really set of terms, in Aristotle's philosophic arsenal that we should reflect on here. Our focus thus far has been on Aristotle's treatment of οὐσία in Book Z. But Books Z–Θ form a unit; they are Aristotle's attempt to think through being as οὐσία by investigating the being of οὐσία. Form and so-called essence (τὸ τί ἦν εἶναι) come to the fore in Z, as the first stage in the attempt to say what οὐσία is. But over the course of Books H and Θ, new terms and combinations of terms come into play. Form is repeatedly identified with activity, ἐνέργεια. (At one point in Book H the coupling "form and activity" or "activity and form" occurs four times in the space of thirteen lines.)[55] The pair form/material are in a certain way replaced by activity/potency. Material itself comes in for renewed treatment: at one point Aristotle says that, "the last stage of material and the form are one and the same thing," at another that "material is in potency because [or in that] it could go toward the form, but whenever it is at work, then it is present in that form."[56] Finally, ἐνέργεια is treated as a near synonym for another new term, ἐντελέχεια, often translated as "actuality."[57]

What are we to make of these claims, shifts, and substitutions, and in particular the emergence of ἐνέργεια? A difficult question, but the beginnings of an answer might go something like this. Form is activity in that activity expresses the manner of being of form, the way in which form unifies the materials of an independent being.[58] The identification of the two tells us that form is not something remote from the thing and its material – instead, it is at work (ἐν-ἔργον) within (ἐν) it, ordering the material, in-forming it, so much so that Aristotle can even say that material at work *is* form. The prime instance of this informing activity is found in living things, but as usual we see something akin to it in the workings of the arts. It is important, as in the case of living things, to think about materials in the right way. A house is not made of trees and dirt. It is made of worked up materials, bricks, boards, and so on, everything that is needed to fashion a house without further ado.[59] But bricks and boards do not a house make. They must be assembled so as to take on the form of a house, and just here the analogy with living things begins to break down. The activity of assembling must occur within the materials of the house, as in the case of a living thing, but the source of the assembling is outside, in the artisan – and so, in a certain sense, is the form. For it is the form in the intellect of the artisan that is the ultimate source of the form of the house, and it is his activity that generates the house.[60] Thus the "form" of the house is a mere arrangement of materials; it is fundamentally inert.[61] Animate form – nature as form – is nothing like this. Not only is the form at work within the animal; it is as sheer being-at-work ultimately responsible for all the activities and motions we associate with animal life: coming into being, metabolizing, growing, moving from place to place, perceiving, and contemplating, everything that has to happen in order for the animal to be and remain complete, to be fully at its end (ἐντελέχεια). Thus Aristotle can say, soon after identifying activity and ἐντελέχεια and right after distinguishing sharply between the activity of the arts and the activities of seeing, contemplating and living, "it is clear that oὐσία and form are being-at-work."[62]

It is perhaps hard to imagine that Harman would find a place within his ontology for this potent sense of form as embedded activity, especially since it is so clearly associated with one type of object, the natural whole. But he does – or at least he seems to. In *The Quadruple Object* Harman says that, "to be an object means to be itself, enacting the reality in the cosmos of which that object alone is capable."[63] In *Guerilla Metaphysics* he speaks of "the very reality of that hammer as it just goes about being itself, unleashed in the world like a wild animal."[64] In *Tool-Being* we get an even more powerful formulation: "Anything, prior to erupting in its explicit form, is real simply by exerting its efforts in the cosmos, by breathing its life into a world that would not have been the same without it."[65] The language of "enacting," "unleashed," "exertion," "breathing," and "life" show that for Harman object-being is anything but inert. Objects in their reality are fully at work. In this, as in his association of objects with form and form-objects with unity and autonomy Harman remains, as it were, a follower of Aristotle.

Still, there is at least one mode of form-as-activity that cannot, in principle, have a place in Harman's thinking about objects. I am thinking of Aristotle's account of knowing in Book III of *De Anima*. Here Aristotle claims, repeatedly, that the intellect is pure potency, capable of becoming all things, and that when we know, we become whatever it is that we know. In such cases, the form that is at work in the object, informing it, now informs us: knowing is the being at work of the thing in the intellect of the knower.[66] There is much that is puzzling here, particularly if we are accustomed to thinking of knowledge as the "product" of our efforts or as the correspondence of thoughts within us to objects outside us. But there is no doubt that the view of cognition that Aristotle lays out here puts him at odds with Harman, since "the eidetic features of any object can never be made present even through the intellect."[67] In Harman's view not even God can enjoy the kind of knowledge that Aristotle characterizes as a human possibility in *De Anima*.[68] For objects are, to use one of Harman's favorite phrases, "dark crystals"; they withdraw from our gaze and indeed from all contact.

We have arrived at a point of sharp disagreement between our authors – or rather, at a second such point. The first had to do with the number of substance-objects, whether they are limited, as Aristotle thinks, to natural wholes, or whether, as Harman thinks, they are virtually infinite. Now we see that, in spite of the striking continuity of Harman's language with Aristotle's, there is at least one matter in which Harman is unwilling to follow Aristotle's lead – his claim that form at work in the thing can become form at work in the intellect of the knower.[69] In what follows I want to assess the significance of these two issues – one concerning the status of nature, the other concerning the possibility of knowledge – within the framework of each author's thinking. But in order to do this we need to take a step back.

COSMOS OR CARNIVAL?

We have been assuming that, whatever their differences, Harman and Aristotle are engaged in substantially the same enterprise. This assumption is in need of some qualification. As Harman makes clear at the outset of *The Quadruple Object* and elsewhere, his goal is to develop an ontology that is as inclusive as possible. This means, in effect, that he is committed to looking for a "formal structure" that will cover anything that might count as an object for us.[70] Of course, since anything that satisfies the structure will then have to count as an object, Harman's approach is liable to generate ever new objects, and this is in fact exactly what we saw happening in part one of this essay. Once Harman finds such a structure – every object contains relations, every relation counts as a new object – it proves to be not only comprehensive but extraordinarily fertile. Yet Harman's approach is not simply positive – it is also in advance committed to the rejection of all ontotheology, that is any attempt in ontology to explain some beings in terms of others or even to single out some beings as more fundamental than others.[71] This commitment is also evident at the beginning of *The Quadruple Object*; it is implicit in Harman's rejection of any over-or-undermining of objects. But this approach to ontology and philosophy so vigorously rejected by Harman is precisely Aristotle's approach. The *Metaphysics* is from the start a search for first causes, for the most fundamental beings, and it culminates in a tracing back of all motion to the divine activity of thought thinking itself.[72] It is, in the end, literally ontotheology. Even Aristotle's investigation of οὐσία at the outset of Book Z is, as it were, ontotheological: he settles on the fundamental being, οὐσία, and then asks what is most fundamental in it; he investigates the οὐσία of οὐσία. And now we come to the main point: Aristotle's claim – which Harman regards as based on an "ontic prejudice" or "ontic bias" – that natural, living wholes (and the cosmos) are substances to a greater degree than organs, elements, and artificial objects is simply another instance of *the same principle* at work: it "privileges" nature over artifice and wholes over parts. In short, Aristotle's disagreement with Harman on this issue is not a random disagreement between two authors who otherwise share much in common. Instead, it is a clear sign of how far apart they are, how different their approaches to philosophy really are.

Can the same be said of the second point of contention? Harman reminds us at critical moments that the focus of his ontology are what Aristotle called "primary substances" – not lion, but this lion, not book, but this copy of this book by this author.[73] But substances in this sense are, as such, unknowable, as Aristotle himself admits in chapter fifteen of Book Z. Now Harman embraces, even relishes and celebrates, this thought, as we've already seen: his real objects are eternally elusive, "dark crystals." But Aristotle clearly has a different approach. He keeps individual things in view, but views them in their intelligibility or as intelligible: all of Aristotle's inquiries approach their objects of investigation under the assumption that those objects are knowable.[74] This is certainly true of the *Metaphysics*: to pursue the question "what is οὐσία?"

is to seek the intelligible cause of οὐσία. In fact, the whole of the *Metaphysics* can be regarded as an elaboration and articulation of the conditions of intelligibility, one that culminates in the claim that the source of order and orderly motion in beings – thought thinking itself – is also the source of their intelligibility. But clearly Aristotle's claims about knowledge in *De Anima* are of a piece with this approach. The thing that Harman would deny outright and that we might find shocking at first – that in knowing we become the thing known – is simply Aristotle's way of expressing that intelligibility in the most direct way he can. (Our way of getting at the same thought is to say, for instance, that someone "lives and breathes" their subject or "knows it inside and out.") Once again, what might seem to be a simple difference of opinion on a particular issue points to a fundamental division. Aristotle and Harman are both thinkers who take their bearings by objects, but the differences in their approaches to beings and the possibility of knowing them put them at opposite ends of the object-oriented philosophy spectrum.

How are we to decide between them? Or must we decide? Each of these approaches makes claims on us that are hard to ignore, and each, I would say, has its advantages. Harman encourages us to cast our net as widely as possible, to remain open to the possibility that even the most ordinary or insignificant of objects, even parts of wholes and man-made objects, might be worthy of our attention. He warns us that new objects can turn up at any moment and that no object can ever be fully understood: there is always "a layer of the world that eludes appearance."[75] Aristotle is no stranger to wonder and to the difficulty of understanding, and he makes a place in his investigations for the artificial and the parts of natural wholes; after all, he wrote the *Parts of Animals*, the *Poetics*, and *On Generation and Corruption*.[76] But he presses us to keep our eyes on the whole and the natural wholes within it. Harman's approach is democratic: all beings and all levels of being matter; equality is primary, and if there is a danger, it is that the very distinction between objects and qualities will simply dissolve and objects will multiply beyond all bounds. Aristotle's approach is aristocratic. The world is finite and nature is a force to be reckoned with; not all beings are created equal, but all find their place and dignity within the whole. If there is a danger, it is that some beings will be too quickly dismissed from consideration and some distinctions too readily assumed to be intelligible.

Put it this way. For Aristotle the world is a cosmos; it falls "naturally" into an ordered array of different domains of inquiry – some higher, some lower – for each of which there is a "natural" mode of investigation.[77] We may be bat-like in our blindness with respect to fundamental matters, but if we remain true to our wonder and willing to follow up our perplexities, genuine progress is possible; there is even the possibility that, now and then, we can share in the very activity that holds the cosmos together.[78] For Harman the world is a much wilder place. That's why he bookends *Guerrilla Metaphysics* with a remarkably vivid (and creepy) description of a carnival: the world is a "carnival of things," full of odd happenings and a constant play of light and shadow, a place where the ordinary can suddenly appear strange and the strange even stranger.[79] Being an ontologist à la Harman means remaining alive to this strangeness and finding ways to do justice to it in speech.[80] By situating ourselves between these two authors, between Harman's carnival and Aristotle's cosmos, and by letting ourselves feel the pressure that each exerts on our thinking about the world, we are better able to ask the question that was asked of old and that must be asked now and always: what is a thing?

NOTES

1. Harman, *Towards Speculative Realism*, pp. 93–121.
2. Harman, *The Quadruple Object* [QO], p. 93.
3. Aristotle, *Metaphysics* [*Meta.*], 1028b1–3. All translations of Aristotle are my own, although I consulted the translations of Apostle and Sachs, as well as the *Revised Oxford Translation*, ed. Barnes (see the bibliography). For the Greek I made use of the Oxford Classical Texts, although I recommend the Loeb series for those starting to look at Aristotle in the Greek.
4. Harman, *Guerilla Metaphysics* [GM], 78.
5. QO pp. 8–13, 17–18.
6. In this section I rely heavily on *The Quadruple Object*; it is the most accessible of Harman's books and the best place for readers new to Harman to start. Readers interested in getting a more complete picture of Harman's thinking should study *Tool-Being* [TB] and then *Guerrilla Metaphysics*.
7. QO p. 5.
8. Ibid. pp. 8–16.
9. Ibid. pp. 24–6.
10. Ibid. pp. 27–30.
11. Ibid. pp. 36–40.
12. Ibid. pp. 44, 75.
13. Ibid. pp. 42–4, 47; GM p. 74. This account of objects in their reality obviously owes much to Heidegger's account of the ready-to-hand in Heidegger's *Being and Time*. But in his claim that use is just another form of distortion, as well as his claim that objects are never simply absorbed into their equipmentality, Harman parts ways with Heidegger (and certainly departs from the standard reading of Heidegger). Harman is happy to concede the point – he claims to be following up a thought that is implicit in Heidegger's approach but that Heidegger himself never quite arrived at.
14. QO p. 47.
15. Ibid. pp. 49–50.
16. Ibid. pp. 73–4.
17. Harman illustrates and argues for this claim at great length in *Tool-Being*. The example I present here is simply meant to illuminate his point for readers unfamiliar with that larger work. I assume that everyone of a certain age knows what it is like to be part of a small, intimate community that then vanishes or dissolves, perhaps overnight.

18. *QO* pp. 75, 111.
19. Ibid. pp. 122–3.
20. Ibid. p. 117; *TB* pp. 260–1.
21. *QO* pp. 60–8.
22. Strictly speaking, every such encounter generates two new objects, since the relations A-to-B and B-to-A are not symmetrical: raindrop-hitting-head is one thing, head-obliterating-raindrop is another: ibid. pp. 75, 117–18.
23. Ibid. pp. 44.
24. *GM* pp. 189–90.
25. *QO* p. 112; *TB* pp. 259–60.
26. *QO* p. 5.
27. Ibid. p. 117; *TB* p. 261. Harman himself worries about this issue. He calls it the "firewall" problem: *GM* pp. 90–1, 95–7.
28. *Meta.* 1003a21–2.
29. Ibid. 1028a17–18, 37.
30. Ibid. 1028a10–16, 25–31; Aristotle, *Categories* [*Cat.*], 3b10–13. The issue of unity, especially substantial unity, turns up repeatedly in the *Metaphysics*. It is also an issue that readers of the *Metaphysics* have long wrestled with. See, for instance, Halper, *One and Many*, pp. xxvi–xxvii, xxix–xxii, xxxv–xxxviii, and Scaltsas, *Substances and Universals*, pp. 107–11, 115, 122–5.
31. *Meta.* 1028a34–6.
32. Ibid. 1028a20–5, 29–31, 33–4, 1029a26–30; *Cat.* 4a10–22.
33. Aristotle, *Poetics*, 1450b24–7, 1451a30–6.
34. Aristotle, *Nicomachean Ethics* [*NE*], 1095b20–6, 1097b6–15, 1177a28–1177b1.
35. Aristotle, *Politics*, 1252b28–1253a2, 1280b30–1281a4, 1326b2–22.
36. *Meta.* 1028b8–13.
37. Ibid. 1028b13–15.
38. Ibid. 1028b16–32.
39. Ibid. 1040b5–8.
40. Ibid. 1041b29–30.
41. I say "genuine" here because in chapter 7 of Z Aristotle seems to allow for the possibility that one might call such objects οὐσίαι in a qualified sense. Consider *Meta.* 1032a20. Aristotle is not being sloppy here; he is allowing his language to reflect an important truth about things. As that chapter shows, houses and chariots share enough common ground with living things to allow for a momentary overlapping of language: both are in some sense organized, generated wholes. And certainly such entities are more οὐσία-like than shapes or colors or even natural, eternally recurring events like eclipses. (Shapes and colors are barely beings, and eclipses, solar and lunar, are not οὐσίαι but relations between οὐσίαι. Of course, as relations they are classic examples of Harmanian objects. See *Meta.* 1028a 13–22, 1044b8–15 and *TB* pp. 277–8.)
42. *Meta.* 1040b8–10.

43. Ibid. 1040b6–8.
44. Ibid. 1041b30–3.
45. Ibid. 1041a2–4
46. Ibid. 1041b4–9.
47. *TB* p. 282.
48. *GM* p. 170.
49. *TB* p. 171.
50. Ibid. p. 293.
51. *GM* p. 170.
52. *TB* p. 275.
53. *GM* p. 76; *TB* pp. 275, 277.
54. *TB* p. 275.
55. *Meta.* 1043a20–33.
56. Ibid. 1045b17–20; 1050a15–17.
57. Ibid. 1044a7–11; 1050a21–3
58. Ibid.1045a20–25. Consider, for instance, Jacob Klein, "Aristotle: An Introduction" [Klein], in *Lectures and Essays*, pp. 180–1, 189.
59. *Meta.*1044a15–23.
60. *Meta.* 1034a9–25; *NE* 1140a10–16.
61. Joe Sachs' footnote on human art in general and houses in particular is helpful on this point. Aristotle, *Metaphysics*, trans. Joe Sachs, p. 159, ftn. 8.
62. *Meta.* 1050a21–1050b2.
63. *QO* p. 74.
64. *GM* p. 74.
65. *TB* pp. 219–20.
66. Aristotle, *De Anima* 429a13–30, 429b6–10, 429b23–430a11, 430a14–16, 19–21. See also Klein pp. 185–7, 190.
67. *QO* p. 28.
68. Ibid. p. 73.
69. If time permitted, this would be the place to take up the issue of causality. Here is a brief sketch of my understanding of the issue. For Harman knowledge must remain incomplete and causality vicarious for the same reason: contact between objects is always indirect. For Aristotle nature as form is not only responsible for the distinctive being of natural wholes and the source of genuine knowledge in beings capable of it; it also makes possible the richest versions of causality: elemental transformations, metabolism, and above all reproduction, the soul's generating of another like itself. As usual we find a weaker analogue in the case of the arts, when the form in the intellect of the artisan, tapping into the powers of a given set of materials, gives rise to the object of a given τέχνη.
70. *TB* p. 275.
71. *GM* pp. 79, 144, 237.
72. *Meta.* 982a28–b10, 983a24–6, 1072a19–b31, 1074b15–34.
73. *QO* pp. 17–19; *TB* p. 247; *Cat.* 2a11–3b33.

74. I do not wish to downplay the tremendous effort required to connect the treatment of οὐσία in the *Metaphysics* with the primary substances of the *Categories*. See, for instance, Michael J. Loux's attempts in *Primary Ousia*, especially pp. 2–5, 8–10, 147–68, 264–74.

75. *GM* p. 10.

76. Consider *Meta.* 982b11–21.

77. Aristotle, *Physics*, 184a17–22.

78. *Meta.* 993a30–b11, 995a24–b2, 1072b14–18, 24–6.

79. *GM* pp. 9–10, 253–4.

80. One might put it this way. For Aristotle nature loves to hide – but she also give us signs, makes herself visible in the very perplexities that bedevil and perhaps discourage us. For Harman, on the other hand, nature not only loves to hide – she does hide; in fact all of being does.

BIBLIOGRAPHY

Aristotle, *Aristotelis: Ethica Nicomachea*, ed. J. Bywater (Oxford: Clarendon Press, 1920).

Aristotle, *Aristotelis: De Arte Poetica Liber*, ed. R. Kassel (Oxford: Clarendon Press, 1922).

Aristotle, *Aristotelis: Categoriae et Liber de Interpretatione*, ed. L. Minio-Paluello (Oxford: Clarendon Press, 1936).

Aristotle, *Aristotelis: Physica*, ed. W. D. Ross (Oxford: Clarendon Press, 1951).

Aristotle, *Aristotelis: De Anima*, ed. W. D. Ross (Oxford: Clarendon Press, 1979).

Aristotle, *Selected Works*, trans. H. G. Apostle, ed. L. P. Gerson (Grinnell, IA: Peripatetic Press, 1982).

Aristotle, *The Complete Works of Aristotle: The Revised Oxford Translation*, ed. J. Barnes, 2 vols (Princeton: Princeton University Press, 1984).

Aristotle, *Aristotelis: Metaphysica*, ed. W. Jaeger (Oxford: Clarendon Press, 1957).

Aristotle, *Physics*, trans. J. Sachs (New Brunswick, NJ: Rutgers University Press, 1995).

Aristotle, *Metaphysics* trans. J. Sachs (Santa Fe: Green Lion Press, 1999).

Aristotle, *On the Soul*, trans. J. Sachs (Santa Fe: Green Lion Press, 2001).

Aristotle, *Nicomachean Ethics*, trans. J. Sachs (Newbury, MA: Focus Publishing, 2002).

Aristotle, *Poetics*, trans. J. Sachs (Newbury, MA: Focus Publishing, 2006).

Aristotle, *Politics*, trans. J. Sachs (Newbury, MA: Focus Publishing, 2012).

Halper, E., *One and Many in Aristotle's Metaphysics: The Central Books*, revised edn (Las Vegas: Parmenides Publishing, 2005).

Harman, G., *Guerilla Metaphysics* (Chicago: Open Court, 2005).

Harman, G., *The Quadruple Object* (Winchester: Zero Books, 2011).

Harman, G., *Tool-Being: Heidegger and the Metaphysics of Objects* (Chicago: Open Court, 2002).

Harman, G., *Towards Speculative Realism: Essays and Lectures* (Winchester: Zero Books, 2010).

Heidegger, M., *Being and Time*, trans. John Macquarrie and Edward Robinson (New York: Harper & Row, 1962).

Klein, J., "Aristotle, an Introduction," in Jacob Klein, *Lectures and Essays*, ed. Robert B. Williamson and Elliott Zuckerman (Annapolis, MD: St John's College Press, 1985), pp. 171–95.

Loux, M. J., *Primary Ousia: An Essay on Aristotle's Metaphysics Z and H* (Ithaca, NY: Cornell University Press, 2008).

Scaltsas, T., *Substances and Universals in Aristotle's Metaphysics* (Ithaca, NY: Cornell University Press, 2010).

PART III

EPICUREANS, STOICS, SKEPTICS, AND NEO-PLATONISTS

CHAPTER 13

Lucretius and Naturalism [1961]

Gilles Deleuze

Translated by Jared C. Bly

Following Epicurus, Lucretius discovered how to determine the speculative and practical object of philosophy as "naturalism." Lucretius' importance in philosophy is linked to this double determination.

The products of nature are not separable from a diversity which is essential to them. But thinking the diverse as diverse is a difficult task upon which, according to Lucretius, all preceding philosophers have shipwrecked.[1] In our world, natural diversity appears in three intersecting aspects: the diversity of species, the diversity of individuals that are members of the same species, and the diversity of parts which compose an individual. Specificity, individuality, and heterogeneity. There is no world which does not manifest itself in the variety of its parts, of its locations, of its coastlines, and of its species that populate it. There is no individual which is absolutely identical to another individual; there is no calf which might be recognized as its mother; no two seashells or grains of wheat which are indiscernible. There is no body composed of homogenous parts; there is no grass or waterway that does not implicate a material diversity or a heterogeneity of elements out of which each species draws the nourishment that is suitable to it. We infer the diversity of worlds themselves from these three points of view: worlds are innumerable, often of different of species, sometimes similar, and always composed of heterogeneous elements.[2]

By what right does one make this inference? Nature must be thought as the principle of the diverse and its production. But the principle of the diverse has sense only if it *does not join* its own elements together into a whole. This exigence should not imply a circle, as if Epicurus and Lucretius simply meant that the principle of the diverse must itself be diverse. The Epicurean thesis is totally other: Nature as the production of the diverse can only be an infinite sum, that is a sum that does not totalize its own elements. There is no combination capable of embracing all the elements of Nature at once, no single world or total universe. *Phusis* is not a determination of the One, of Being, or of the Whole. Nature is not collective, but distributive; the laws of nature (*foedera naturae*, as opposed to the supposed *foedera fati*) distribute non-totalizable parts. Nature is not attributive but conjunctive: it is expressed by the "and" and not by the "is." This and that: alternations and interweavings, resemblances and differences, attractions and distractions, nuances and abruptness. Nature is a Harlequin's cloak made entirely from colored patches and empty spaces, plenitudes *and* void, beings *and* non-being, each one positing itself as unlimited while limiting the other. An addition of indivisible elements, sometimes similar, sometimes different, Nature is indeed a sum, but not a whole. Philosophical pluralism's truly noble deeds commence with Epicurus and Lucretius. We will not see any contradiction between the hymn to Venus-Nature and the essential pluralism of this philosophy of Nature. More precisely, Nature is power [*la puissance*], but this is a power on behalf of which things exist *one by one* without the possibility of being gathered together *all at once*, nor being unified in a combination that would be adequate to Nature or would completely express Nature *at one time*. Lucretius reproached the predecessors of Epicurus for having believed in Being, in the One, and in the Whole. These concepts are fixations of the mind, speculative forms of belief in *fatum*, and theological forms of a false philosophy. The philosophy of Nature is anti-spiritualism, and pluralism is free thought or the thought of freedom.

Epicurus' predecessors identified this principle with the One or the Whole. But what is the one if not a particular perishable and corruptible object that one considers arbitrarily in isolation from all the others? What forms a whole, if not a particular finite combination, full of gaps, that we arbitrarily believe to unify all the elements of the sum? In these two cases, we fail to understand the diverse and its production. One engenders the diverse from out of the one only in presupposing that anything can be born from anything, and thus something from nothing. One engenders the diverse from out of the whole only in presupposing that the elements forming this whole are contraries capable of transforming into one another. This is another way of saying that one thing produces another by changing its nature and that something is born from nothing.[3] Because the anti-naturalist philosophers did not want to account for the void, the void captured everything. Their Being, their One, their Whole are always artificial and not natural, always corruptible, evanescent, porous, crumbly, or brittle. They would prefer to say that "being is nothing" rather than recognize that there are beings *and* there is the void; there are simple beings in the void *and* there is void in composite beings.[4] For the diversity of the diverse, the philosophers substituted the identical or the contradictory, often both at once. It is a question of neither identity nor contradiction, but of resemblances and of differences, of compositions and of decompositions, "of connections, of densities, of shocks, of encounters, and of movements thanks to which everything gains form."[5] Of coordinations *and* of disjunctions, such is the Nature of things.

Naturalism needs a robustly structured principle of causality which can realize the production of the diverse, yet in terms of compositions, of diverse and non-totalizable combinations between elements of Nature.

I – The atom is what must be thought, what can only be thought. The atom is to thought what the sensible object is to the senses: the object which refers essentially to thought, the object which gives way to thought just as the sensible object is that which gives itself to the senses. That the atom is not sensible and cannot be sensible, that it is essentially hidden, this is the effect of its proper nature and not the imperfection of our sensibility. In the first place, the Epicurean method is one of analogy. The sensible object is endowed with sensible parts, yet there is a sensible minimum which represents the smallest part of the object; likewise, the atom is endowed with parts that are of thought; however, there is a minimum of thought that represents the smallest part of the atom. The indivisible atom is composed of thought minima, just as the divisible object is composed of sensible minima, to the extent that one can write:[6]

$$\frac{\text{Sensible Object}}{\text{Sensible Minimum}} = \frac{\text{Atom}}{\text{Thought Minimum}}$$

In the second place, the Epicurean method is one of passage or transition: guided by analogy, we pass from the sensible to thought and from the thought to the sensible through transitions, *paulatim*, at the same time as the sensible composes and decomposes itself.[7] Through this we renounce the ambitions of a false philosophy which at times wishes to think the sensible and other times offers a sensible revelation of thought itself. The sensible object is the absolute object of the senses, the reality of the real as such, just as the atom is the absolute object of thought, the truth of what is thought as such.

2 – The sum of atoms is infinite precisely because they exist as elements that do not create a totality. But this sum would not be infinite if the void were not also infinite. The void and the plenum interweave and are distributed in such a way that the sum of the void and the atoms is itself in turn infinite. This third infinity expresses the fundamental correlation between the atoms and the void. The upper and the lower in the void result from the correlation of the void itself with the atoms; the weight of the atoms (the movement from top to bottom) results from the correlation of atoms with the void.

3 – Atoms encounter one another in the fall, not because of their difference in weight, but because of the *clinamen*. This is because, in the void, all atoms fall at an equal speed: an atom is faster or slower with respect to its weight only in relation to other atoms that impede its fall. In the void, the speed of an atom is equal to its *movement in a unique direction during a minimum of continuous time.*

The minimum of continuous time refers to the apprehension of pure thought. The atom moves "as quick as thought."[8] When we think of the swerve of the atom, it is thus necessary to conceive it as a movement which is made in a time shorter than the minimum of continuous time. The *clinamen* or swerve has nothing to do with an oblique movement which would come to randomly modify a vertical fall.[9] The *clinamen* has always been present: it is not a secondary movement, nor even a secondary determination of the atom's movement which would be produced at any moment in any location. The *clinamen* is the original determination of the direction of the atom's movement, the synthesis of movement and direction. "*Incertus*" does not signify indeterminate but rather unattributable. "*Paulum*," "*incerto tempore*," "*intervallo minimo*" signify: *in a time smaller than the minimum of continuous, thinkable duration*.[10] This is why the *clinamen* does not manifest any contingency or indetermination. It manifests something completely other: the *lex atomi*, that is the irreducible plurality of causes and causal series and the impossibility of joining causes together into a whole. In effect, the *clinamen* is the determination of the encounter between causal series, each causal series being constituted by the movement of an atom and conserving its full independence in the encounter. In the famous discussions that set Epicureans against Stoics, the problem does not pertain to contingency and necessity, but to causality and destiny. The Epicureans, like the Stoics, affirm *causality* (no movement without cause); however, the Stoics desire additionally to affirm *destiny*, that is the unity of causes "between themselves." The Epicureans object to this by asserting that one does not affirm destiny without introducing *necessity*, that is the absolute linkage of effects with one another. It is true that the Stoics retort that they do not introduce necessity at all, but that the Epicureans for their part are unable to refuse the unity of causes without stumbling into contingency and chance.[11] The real problem: is there a unity of causes *between themselves*? Must the thought of nature join the causes together into a whole? The *clinamen* is chance only in one sense: it is the affirmation of the independence and multiplicity of the causal series in themselves.

4 – The atoms have diverse shapes and sizes. However, an atom cannot have just any size whatsoever, since this would attain and exceed the sensible minimum. Moreover, atoms cannot have an infinity of shapes, since all diversity in shape implies either a permutation of the minima of atoms or a multiplication of these minima which would be unable to be pursued to infinity without the atom, once again, becoming itself sensible.[12] The size and shape of the atoms not being infinite in number, there is therefore an infinity of atoms of the same size and shape.

5 – Any atom's encounter with another does not amount to a combination, otherwise the atoms would form an infinite combination. Truthfully, the shock repels as much as it forms combinations. Atoms combine with each other for as long as their shapes allow. Battered by other atoms which shatter their grip, the combinations are disarticulated, losing their elements that create the connection between other compounds. If atoms are said to be "specific germs" or "seeds," it is first and foremost because any given atom does not enter into composition with just any other.

6 – All combinations being finite, there is an infinity of combinations. However, not one combination is formed from a single species of atom. Atoms are specific germs in a second sense: they constitute the heterogeneity of the diverse with itself in the same body. Nevertheless, *in a body*, different atoms tend *in virtue of their weight* to be distributed according to their size: in our world, atoms of the same size group together to form vast composites. Our world distributes its elements in such a way that earth elements occupy the center "expressing" outside of themselves the elements which will form the sea, the air, and the ether (*magnae res*).[13] The philosophy of nature declares the heterogeneity of the diverse with itself *and also* the resemblance of the diverse with itself.

7 – Power [*puissance*] of the diverse and of its production, but also of the power of reproduction of the diverse. It is important to see how this second power ensues from the first. Resemblance ensues from the diverse as such and its diversity. There are neither worlds nor bodies which lose elements at each instant and do not find new ones of the same shape. There are neither worlds nor bodies which do not have for themselves their analogues [*leurs sembla-bles*] in space and in time. It is the case that the production of any composite presupposes that the different elements capable of forming it are themselves infinite in number; they would have no luck encountering one another if each one, in the void, were the only member of its type or limited in number. But, since each one of the elements has an infinity of elements equivalent to it, they do not produce a composite without their equivalents having the same chance of renewing their parts and even of reproducing a similar composite.[14] This argument from probability holds especially for worlds. All the more so, inner-worldly bodies have a principle of reproduction available to them. In effect, they are born in already composed milieus, each one of which groups together a maximum number of elements of the same shape: earth, sea, air, ether, the *magnae res*, the great strata which constitute our world, joining with one another through imperceptible transitions. A determined body has a place in one of these ensembles.[15] This body ceaselessly loses various elements of its compositions, yet the ensemble in which it is immersed procures new ones for it, whether furnishing them directly or transmitting them to it from out of other ensembles with which it communicates. Moreover, a body will itself have related species in other places, in the element that produces it and nourishes it.[16] This is why Lucretius recognizes the last aspect of the principle of causality: a body is not only born from determined elements, which are like *seeds* that produce it, but also takes shape in a determined milieu, which is like a *mother* suitable for reproducing it. The heterogeneity of the diverse forms a kind of vitalism of germs; however, the resemblance of the diverse itself forms a kind of pantheism of mothers.[17]

Physics is Naturalism from a speculative point of view. Yet, in all the preceding theses, the fundamental object of Epicurean physics appeared: *to determine what is really infinite in nature, to distinguish the true infinite from the false.* The first two books of Lucretius are consecrated to this research and, at this level, physics loses all relativity. It is true that this multiplies hypotheses and explications, but only inasmuch as it is a question of a finite phenomenon. The determination of the infinite, on the contrary, is the object of apodictic research. Strangely, it is in this form that physics testifies to its dependence with regard to ethics or to practice.[18] Everything happens as if physics were a means subordinated to practice, but practice would not have found this means all on its own and is incapable [*impuissante*] of achieving its end without it. Practice attains its own end only by denouncing false infinity.

The end or object of practice is pleasure. However, practice, in this sense, only suggests to us all the various means of suppressing or avoiding pain. Yet, our pleasures have more formidable obstacles than pain itself: ghosts, superstitions, terrors, the fear of death, and everything that disturbs the soul.[19] Humanity's portrait is a troubled one, more terrified than in pain. It is the soul's disturbance that multiplies pain, making it invincible, yet its own origin is estranged and more profound. It is composed of two elements: (1) a bodily illusion of an infinite capacity for pleasure which projects into our soul the idea of infinite duration itself; (2) and then the illusion of the infinite duration of the soul, which ceaselessly delivers to us the idea of an infinity of possible pains after death.[20] These two illusions hook together: the fear of infinite punishments naturally sanctions unlimited desires. One must seek out Sisyphus and Tityos on this earth: "It is down here that the sots' life becomes a veritable hell."[21] Epicurus goes as far as to say that, if injustice is an evil, and if licentiousness, ambition, and even debauchery are as well, then it is because we deliver to ourselves the idea of a punishment that could occur at any instant.[22] *To be ceaselessly delivered over to the soul's disturbance* is precisely the human condition, the product of the double illusion: "Today, there is no means, no faculty of resisting at all, since one must fear eternal pains in death."[23] This is why the religious man has two dimensions: avidity and anxiety, a strange complex that generates crimes. The disturbance of the soul is therefore created from the fear of death when we are not yet dead, *but also* from the fear of being not yet dead once we already are.

What is the principle of this disturbance, of this illusion? Lucretius seems to suggest an explanation that relies on *simulacra*, or, more generally, on emanations and emissions. Groups of atoms, which reproduce the exterior form of the composite or transport an intimate quality, ceaselessly detach themselves from the surface or from out of the depths of objects. These emissions are not real objects, although they have a reality. These are the empty, rigid envelopes that only retain a form, empty husks that carry themselves in a straight line, or even shards that only conserve a handful of atoms and disperse in every direction. Moreover, these envelopes, perhaps even the shards, can form spontaneously in the air and in the sky. We are immersed in simulacra; it is through them that we perceive, that we dream, that we desire, and that we act. These phantoms are not real, physical objects, but there is a physical reality to them. They make us perceive what must be perceived, as it must be perceived, and with respect to their condition, to the distance that they must cover, and to the deformations that they undergo. For they transform following obstacles that they encounter in front of them or in accordance with explosions of which they are continually at the center: at the end of a particular trajectory, the visual envelopes no longer strike us with the same vigor, shouts lose their distinctiveness. The error is never therefore in the simulacra themselves, but in our reaction that attributes to the absolute sensible object relative properties that belong to the simulacra. In a similar fashion, the illusion is never in the simulacra themselves, but in the reaction through which we attribute to ourselves spectral desires and fears. In this regard, the simulacra's principal property is the extreme rapidity of their emission and formation. They succeed one another so quickly that one could say that they dance, that, here and there, they form powerful and active beings, infinitely capable of modifying their activity. *Their emission occurs in a time smaller than the minimum of perceived time.*[24] *Such is the source of false infinity*; it is through this that we introduce the image of infinity into our desires and our images of fear and punishment into infinity itself. Lucretius shows that loving desire, incapable of absorbing or possessing its real object, can only enjoy simulacra and knows bitterness and torment in its pleasure that it desires to be infinite.[25] And our belief in gods and the suffering they inflict on us rests on simulacra that before us appear to dance, to speak, to ceaselessly renew themselves, and to represent infinity: all the way down to their voices that seem to promise us eternal pains.[26]

False infinity is the principle of the soul's disturbance. The practical and speculative objects of philosophy as naturalism, science, and pleasure coincide on this point: it is always a question of denouncing the false infinity, the infinity of religion and all the myths in which it is expressed. To whomever asks "what is the purpose of philosophy?" one must respond: who else but philosophy ought to provide the image of a free human, to denounce all the forces which require myth and the soul's disturbance to establish their power? Nature does not oppose custom because there are natural customs. Nature does not oppose convention, since law's dependence on conventions does not exclude the existence of natural right, that is, the existence of a natural function of the law which weighs the illegitimacy of desires with the soul's disturbance that accompanies them. Nature does not oppose invention, since inventions are nothing but the discoveries of nature itself. Yet nature opposes myth. In describing the history of humanity, Lucretius presents us with something like a law of compensation: humanity's unhappiness does not come from its customs, its conventions, its inventions, or its industry, but from the portion of myth that intermingles there and the false infinity that myth introduces into humanity's thoughts and works. Mythical in their principle, royalty, wealth, and property join the origin of language and the discovery of fire and metals; the belief in gods joins the conventions of law and justice; the development of wars joins the implementation of bronze and iron, luxury and frenzy join art and industry.[27] To distinguish in humanity what belongs to myth and what belongs to nature, and in nature to distinguish what is really infinite and what is not: such is the practical and speculative object of naturalism. First philosophy is naturalist; it speaks about nature instead of speaking about gods.[28] Lucretius holds himself responsible for not introducing new myths into philosophy which would remove all positivity from nature. Active gods are the myth of religion just as destiny is the myth of a false physics, and Being, the One, and the Whole are the myths of a false philosophy completely permeated with theology.

Never has one pushed so far the enterprise of "demystification." Myth is always the expression of false infinity and the disturbance of the soul. One of the most profound constants of naturalism is to denounce everything that is sad, everything that is the cause of sadness, everything that requires sadness in order to exercise its power. From Lucretius to Nietzsche, the same goal is pursued and attained. Naturalism makes thought and sensibility into an affirmation. It attacks the prestige of the negative, discharges all power from the negative, and denies the spirit of the negative the right to speak in philosophy. This spirit of the negative that made the sensible into an appearance is again what gathered the intelligible into a one or into a whole.[29] But this whole, this one, was only the nothingness of thought, just as appearance was merely the nothingness of sensation. Naturalism, according to Lucretius, is *the thought of an infinite sum* the elements of which are not composed all at once, but, inversely as well, it is *the sensation of finite composites* which are not added up with each other as such. The multiple is affirmed in these two manners. The multiple as multiple is the object of affirmation just as the diverse is the object of joy. The infinite is the absolute intelligible determination (perfection) of a sum that does not compose its elements together into a whole and the finite itself is the absolute sensible determination (perfection) of everything that is composed. The pure positivity of the finite is the object of the senses; the positivity of true infinity, the object of thought. There is no opposition between these two points of view, but rather correlation. Lucretius established for a long time the implications of naturalism: the positivity of Nature, naturalism as the philosophy of affirmation, pluralism linked to multiple affirmations, sensualism linked to the joy of the diverse, and the practical critique of all mystifications.

NOTES

[This essay was originally published as "Lucrèce et le Naturalisme" in *Les Études Philosophiques*, Nouvelle Série, 16e Année, No. 1 (January–March 1961), pp. 19–29. A second version of this essay can be found in the appendix to *Logique du Sens* (1969). The two versions (1961/1969) have a number of minor and major differences. – eds.]

1. Throughout the critical part of Book I [of *De Rerum Natura*], Lucretius ceaselessly demands a rationale of the diverse.

2. Regarding all these aspects of diversity, see II.342–76, 581–8, 661–81, 1052–6 (see text and translation by Ernout). [Lucretius, *De la Nature*, trans. A. Ernout, 2 vols (Paris: Les Belles Lettres, [1916–20] 2002).]

3. See Book I for the critique of Heraclitus, Empedocles, and Anaxagoras.

4. Regarding the nothingness that eats away at pre-Epicurean concepts, see I.657–69, 753–62.

5. I.633–4.

6. I.749–52 (see also Epicurus, "Letter to Herodotus," 58 [found in Diogenes Laertius, *Lives of Eminent Philosophers*, X.35–83]).

7. III.138–41, 826–33.

8. Epicurus, "Letter to Herodotus," 61–2.

9. II.243–50.

10. "*Intervallo minimo*" is found in Cicero, *De Fato* [*On Fate*], 10.

11. See Cicero, *De Fato*.

12. II.483–99

13. V.449–54

14. II.541–68

15. V.128–31

16. II.1068: "*cum locus est praesto.*"

17. I.168, II.708: "*seminibus certis certa genetrice.*"

18. In effect, while physics deals with a finite phenomenon for which it multiplies explanations, ethics gains little in waiting on it; see Epicurus, "Letter to Herodotus," 79.

19. The beginning of Book II is constructed on this opposition. In order to avoid pain, inasmuch as it is in us, it suffices to have very little . . . *but*, in order to vanquish the disturbance of the soul, a more profound art is necessary.

20. These two aspects are well noted by Lucretius, who insists at times on one and at other times on the other: I.110–19, III.47–73, III.978–1023, VI.12–16. Regarding the body's infinite capacity for pleasure, see Epicurus, *Principal Doctrines*, 20.

21. III.1023.

22. Epicurus, *Principal Doctrines*, 7, 10, 34, 35.

23. I.110–11.

24. IV.768–76, 796.

25. IV.1084–2

26. V.1169–97

27. Book V.

28. Aristotle, *Metaphysics*, 981b.

29. [Deleuze capitalizes these nouns earlier in the essay, but here the capitalization drops out. – trans.]

CHAPTER 14

On Causality and Law in Lucretius and Contemporary Cosmology

David Webb

Written by Lucretius in the first century BCE, *De Rerum Natura* is an elaboration of Epicurean atomism that ranges over the origin of the universe, the formation of worlds, weather systems, the emergence of life and of social order, morality, and much else besides.[1] It can be picked over for interesting anticipations of modern atomism and of evolutionary theory. Yet, as a materialist account of the emergence of order, it depends on an account of causality and law which has some surprises, and it is on these that I want to focus here. The familiar image of atoms moving and combining may lead one to expect that order in the universe depends ultimately on fixed laws governing the movement of atoms. Although there are some grounds for such a reading, they are not compelling, and Lucretius is otherwise quite clear that order consists of regularities that arise locally, varying from time to time and from place to place. That this theory of local regularities has been eclipsed by the assumption that laws are fixed says more about our own views than those of Lucretius. From the standpoint of contemporary approaches to causality, Lucretius' account can be described as a regularity theory, where the regularities in question are a feature of the world (and not just of our perception of it). But it is distinctive in that cause and effect do not always and everywhere proceed according to the same invariable laws. Instead, causality precedes laws, which, as regularities, emerge locally and evolve along with the phenomena they determine. The causal structure of the universe is therefore real, but radically contingent. This idea sets Lucretius' account apart from almost all existing theories of causality and law. Notable exceptions can be found in the work of Charles Sanders Peirce, to some extent in that of Émile Boutroux, and in certain quarters of contemporary cosmology. For example, Peirce writes that "there is room for serious doubt whether the fundamental laws of mechanics hold good for single atoms," and advises that science turn its attention to "a natural history of laws of nature."[2] On his part, Boutroux declares that "it is chance, or destiny, or an ensemble of capricious wills, that presides in the universe."[3] However, in this essay I will focus on the work of Lee Smolin, and in particular on his recent collaboration with Roberto Mangabeira Unger, *The Singular Universe and the Reality of Time*, which presents a comprehensive case for separating causality and law, and recognizing that the laws of nature evolve, an idea he first proposed over twenty years ago in *The Life of the Cosmos*.[4]

Smolin has, for several decades, been at the forefront of research in quantum gravity, which aims to combine the key elements of quantum physics and the theory of general relativity. One of the many challenges this presents is that of bringing together two fundamentally different approaches to space and time. Einstein's general theory of relativity describes space and time as intimately related to events, and as variable according to the perspective or frame of reference one takes up. With no absolute scale of time on which to pin events, a change in perspective may entail a change in the order between events. Ascertaining the causal relations between events is therefore crucial to determining the structure of space and time; or, as Smolin puts it, "almost all of the information needed to construct the geometry of space-time consists of the story of the causal structure."[5] By contrast, quantum physics assumes that space and time are independent of the events that take place in them. So, however strange the behavior of matter at the quantum level may be, there is a certain simplicity to the causal structure. One way to combine these two theories involves introducing into quantum physics the kind of interdependence between events and the structure of space and time that characterizes the theory of general relativity. In this way, the significance of the causal structure of events in the theory of general relativity is carried over to the account of quantum gravity that Smolin and his fellow researchers propose, and thereby to the whole cosmology based on it. However, Unger and Smolin argue that in order for any such account to be successful, cosmology itself must take a further radical step and revise its understanding of the laws of nature and their relation to time.

Unger and Smolin note that physics is still marked by traces of an absolutism that underpinned Newtonian science, most clearly in the assumption that the fundamental equations of science, and by implication the fundamental reality they describe, are timeless. According to this longstanding orthodoxy, the changing universe can be explained by appealing to what does not change, and the aim of science is to discover laws that are universal and eternal. Far from being merely a matter for philosophical speculation that need not trouble science and working scientists, this assumption has, they argue, led contemporary cosmology into dead ends and wild goose chases. Their aim is to root it out, and to show that cosmology can do perfectly well without it.

Although twentieth-century science was marked by at least two decisive breaks with the Newtonian paradigm, in quantum physics and the special and general theories of relativity, the search for a unified law-based account of the universe has remained the norm. In particular, the laws themselves, expressed mathematically, continue to be regarded as timeless, which is to say the laws governing change do not themselves change. Accepting this leaves cosmology facing two fundamental puzzles. First, why are the laws of nature the way they are and not otherwise? Second, why were the initial conditions of the universe as we understand them to have been and not otherwise? The problem is that a scientific account of any given system applies the appropriate laws to the initial conditions without asking where either come from or why they are as they are. There are ways to manage this deficit when dealing with a part of the universe in isolation, but to leave such questions unanswered when dealing with the universe as a whole is to concede that cosmology is radically incomplete. Yet to propose a conclusive "once and for all" answer would invoke a Leibnizian conception of sufficient reason that drags science uncomfortably far from its empirical point of reference. The current orthodoxy leaves cosmology torn between these two unsatisfactory alternatives.

Unger and Smolin's response to this predicament is to challenge the basic assumptions on which it rests, allowing a new possibility to emerge, one in which an adequate cosmological explanation does not have to be "complete" in the Leibnizian sense. Their approach can be encapsulated in what they identify as two cosmological fallacies, a reference both to the fact that they concern cosmology and to the standard objection to the cosmological argument for the existence of God: that it applies to the whole a form of reasoning appropriate only to a part. The first fallacy concerns the Newtonian paradigm according to which to explain how a given system (such as a collection of particles in a box) behaves over time one has to determine the initial conditions (the kind, position, and velocity of all the particles), and then apply the appropriate physical laws. The initial conditions are the starting point for the phenomena that the laws explain, but they are not themselves explained by those laws: "They are assumed rather than explained."[6] This is fine where the task is to explain a well-defined closed system, because there is always an "outside" for the observer and theoretician to occupy, one that is fictitiously timeless. In principle, what is assumed in the account of one part can then be addressed by another, and the universe gradually explained bit by bit. But when the task is to explain the universe as a whole it is impossible to take a position "outside" the system, and there can be no switching of positions to fill out the account. This shows that the assumption of initial conditions becomes problematic when dealing with the universe as a whole. On their part, the laws that are to explain why the initial conditions of the system develop in a given way are regarded as timeless, unaffected by the changes they govern, and having no history of their own. Like the initial conditions of the configuration space, they are assumed by the explanation that follows, and therefore "to ask why they are what they are is to pose a question that lies in principle beyond the limits of a natural science conforming to the Newtonian paradigm."[7] Yet the point of cosmology, Unger and Smolin remind us, is to explain everything, and by adopting a model of explanation that makes this impossible science allows itself to remain shaped by metaphysical forms of thought that it professes to oppose. It is by failing to recognize this, or by ducking the challenge, that Unger and Smolin think science commits the first cosmological fallacy.

Where the first cosmological fallacy concerns a mistake in method, the second, which Unger and Smolin call the "fallacy of universal anachronism,"[8] arises from negligence over what science actually takes to be the case. It is accepted that the universe is cooling down and that the relatively stable structure described by modern science was preceded by a phase in which energy levels were so extreme that the physical laws as we know them could not have applied. In this period, the universe worked in ways we do not recognize and could not derive from observation today. Similarly, it is possible that at some point in the distant future the universe may become quite different to the way it is now, and indeed that there may exist exceptional regions of the universe even now, such as inside black holes, where the laws we see in operation more generally do not hold. The second cosmological fallacy lies in the assumption that the universe we can see now is necessarily a reliable guide to the universe at other times. Unger and Smolin draw a very simple conclusion from all this: that we cannot justify "the immutability of the laws of nature from their overall stability in the observed universe."[9] Having set out these two fallacies, Unger and Smolin go on to elaborate a broad critique of contemporary cosmology, recommending profound revisions to the way science is conceived and practiced that include reversing the priority of structure over history and recognizing that there is a narrative element to scientific explanation. I will say a few words about these ideas later, but first I want to focus here on just two points. The first concerns the relation between laws and the phenomena they are intended to explain, and the second concerns causality and its relation to law.

Science assumes that before a system can be described it must first be partitioned from conditions that are considered to lie outside it. Some of these conditions, such as the precise arrangement of matter a great distance away, can usually be ignored. But other conditions, such as the laws thought to govern the development of the system in question, must be taken into consideration. This works perfectly well when dealing with specific phenomena and small-scale systems, but it becomes problematic when cosmology addresses the universe as a whole. For if, as Unger and Smolin suggest, science should avoid appealing to metaphysical principles, that is, "the explanation for anything in the universe can involve only other things that also exist in the universe,"[10] then the distinction between the initial conditions of the universe and the laws that are to govern its development becomes problematic. In this case, what bears on the development of the universe at any point is no more or less than its total state. The same point can be made by considering the extreme conditions of energy and density in the early universe. At this stage, the distinctions between constituents of nature that are familiar to us today had yet to emerge and there was no "established repertory of natural kinds."[11] Without stable kinds to describe, laws cannot stand apart from the reality they ostensibly govern.

As a consequence, they cannot be universal. In fact, in the most extreme circumstances, the range of law tends towards a point where it coincides with the phenomena it is supposed to govern, because there is no reason to assume that the consistency law requires extends any further.[12] In such conditions, again, the distinction between laws of nature and the phenomena they govern breaks down. As Unger and Smolin are quick to point out, this does not entail the breakdown of order into chaotic confusion, because causal connections continue to be effective even where there is no overarching law to determine how they will occur: "What comes before will always shape what comes later, even if the mechanism of influence may change."[13] Rather than moving from a strongly determined universe to one without meaningful laws, Unger and Smolin argue that laws and the phenomena they govern develop in tandem, their difference being more one of degree than of kind. Although the coeval development of laws and phenomena will be most evident in extreme states of the universe where the degrees of structure and regularity we see today have yet to emerge and the difference between laws and phenomena are consequently slight, the reciprocal effect remains even in regions and periods of stability: it is a matter only of degree and historical perspective.

An obvious objection to raise is that to allow change to be governed by laws that can themselves change is to usher in a crisis in the foundations of science. For if there is no still more fundamental law to determine how laws themselves change, science appears to give up its claim on a final explanation – it can no longer provide the sufficient reason for things being as they are and not otherwise. This is the predicament to which I referred earlier, and which Unger and Smolin call the conundrum of the meta-laws: either there is no law to determine how things change, or there must be a higher-order law that we have yet to find. But the truth is that to phrase the problem this way is to phrase it badly, for science is already unable to provide a sufficient reason for things being the way they are, simply because it cannot account for why the laws and the initial conditions of the universe as a whole are the way they are. Recognizing that there is no need to lament the loss of what science never truly had, Unger and Smolin point out that we are accustomed to think that causality depends on laws, but this is not necessarily the case. Rather, "causality exists without laws, which is a way of saying that causal connections have not acquired, or have lost, the repetitious form, over a differentiated range of nature, that makes it possible to distinguish phenomena from laws."[14] As noted already, this was the condition of the early universe, when the distinction between regularities of nature and states of affairs (or laws and initial conditions) could not be made. In the absence of what we think of as law, "states of affairs may have been excited to higher degrees of freedom and allow for a broader range of adjacent possibles than we usually (but not always) observe in the established universe."[15] Such regularities as there were at this early stage were partial and non-binding, but nonetheless change was not random. As the universe cooled, the structure familiar to us today emerged and regularities became so well established that laws could be separated off from the states of affairs they describe, heuristically at least. They could even be mistaken for laws that are eternally fixed, but this would be to ignore variations in the laws themselves that only become visible over longer periods of time. No one region of the universe or period of its history can be counted on to reveal the most basic truths of nature.[16] Instead, Unger and Smolin argue, "we do better to think of the laws of nature as deriving from causal connections rather than to see the latter as deriving from the former, as we are accustomed to do."[17] This is to say, causal structure comes first and laws follow. It is only when causal structure has reached a settled state that laws can be separated from the phenomena they govern. But this can change. Structure, then, derives from history, and not the other way around. But it also both "constrains and enables later historical development."[18] Accordingly, scientific explanation is itself ultimately historical, tracing events and the way they occur back to what came before without expecting to reach a final point where whole the story began and explanation stops.[19] There is, they suggest, no final answer to the question of why events at a certain point in the history of the universe were as they were, or why the laws that describe their development are what they are. But whereas science that appeals to universal laws has to acknowledge this as an inexplicable limit to its understanding, the model of science that Unger and Smolin propose simply continues to trace conditions and laws back to earlier conditions and laws. In this way, they give up the strictly Leibnizian demand for sufficient reason, while still holding that a reason for why things are as they are and not otherwise can be found, and all this without leaving room for a truth that is in principle beyond the reach of science, and that might be the province of some other, arguably higher, discipline.[20]

I will now tell the story of the precedence of causality to law from the point of view of Lucretius.

Lucretius tells us that his aim in writing *De Rerum Natura* was to release his fellow human beings from the fear inspired by the belief that their lives were subject to capricious and unpredictable gods. To this end, he encouraged the reader to see, following his explanations, that the natural world was governed by stable laws. If this were to mean that the movement and interactions of atoms are everywhere and always the same, one might object that he simply replaced the willful interventions of gods,[21] without considering all the implications of living in a world governed by absolute laws whose origin is unknown and unknowable. Although such laws may be less terrifying, insofar as they may be understood and events made more predictable, they would still be remote and would not themselves belong to the order they governed. Such a view adopts the vantage point of the rebirth of atomism in early modern science and misses much of what is most novel and interesting in Lucretius. In particular, it runs counter to an aspiration running through his work to explain the world from the world itself, and above all on the basis of the principle that only atoms and void exist.[22]

The basic elements of Lucretius' account are simple. The universe is infinite in extent, and has always existed and everything in it is composed of atoms and void. Atoms are infinite in number, but finite in variety and size, and combine to form the ordered world that we see around us. All order emerges as a consequence of chance collisions with no guiding principle or τέλος. Some collisions between atoms lead to combinations that are more stable than others, and some of these recur, and as they do so they form regularities that make subsequent events more or less likely. In this way, pockets of order emerge and persist as atoms combine according to these regularities, but nothing lasts forever and all order is destined eventually to break down, releasing atoms to flow off towards new combinations and new forms of order.[23] The laws that shape events are therefore regularities that emerge from the sequences of events themselves, as they are for Unger and Smolin, and, like them, Lucretius proposes that causality precedes law.[24]

How do atoms actually move, collide, and combine? Imagining something like a beginning, Lucretius sees them raining down uniformly through the void in a laminar flow, driven by their own weight, the heavy and the light moving at the same speed.[25] The fall of atoms in a laminar flow has a mythical quality to it that reminds me of how, it is said, in Romania they used to begin their old tales: "It was a time and it was no time . . ."[26] The account promises both safe harbor and shipwreck. For although the universe has no absolute origin, it has a narrative structure and one can trace events back to an earlier time. Yet in doing so one arrives at a state that contains no information about the initial conditions from which the later universe arose, and next to nothing about the laws that were to give form to that becoming. In this respect the laminar flow plays a role very much like the initial chaos in Hesiod's theogony: lacking all determination, it puts a stop to any narrative driven by the questions "Why this?" and "Where did it come from?"[27] More specifically, the laminar flow does this in the context of a universe that is temporally infinite. Its purpose is to allay any suspicion that further back there may have been a time in which the initial conditions and the law that governed their development were separate. Instead, the separation of initial conditions and laws that is assumed to be fundamental in the scientific account of any given system becomes problematic, as it is for Unger and Smolin when dealing with the universe as a whole. Moreover, Lucretius writes that if the rain of atoms in parallel were not interrupted, then atoms would rain down through the void without colliding, but he does not imply that such an uninterrupted flow actually lasted for any significant period of time: indeed, no period could be significant in a universe that is temporally infinite. The laminar flow has always already been interrupted and, unlike Hesiod's story of the universe, the Lucretian narrative refers back to a state that the universe may not actually have occupied. But whether or not the laminar flow has a place in the chronological series of events, it features in the logical order of the universe. Its primary effect is less to put an artificial stop to the narrative of the universe reaching further and further into the past than to block a particular kind of explanation, that is an explanation that relies on the separation between laws and the conditions to which they apply. The Lucretian story of the rain of atoms tells us not only that the historical narrative has no true beginning, but also that it unfolds without a fundamental separation between laws and initial conditions.

For order to emerge, atoms must collide, and this comes about by virtue of a spontaneous change in direction that Lucretius variously describes using the verbs *depellere*,[28] *declinare*,[29] and *inclinare*,[30] the root of the latter two giving the noun *clinamen*,[31] which is often translated as "swerve," but also sometimes retained without translation.

> While atoms move by their own weight straight down
> Through the empty void, at quite uncertain times
> And uncertain places they swerve [*depellere*] slightly from
>   their course.[32]

The *clinamen* gives the primal equilibrium a needed tilt, and as such serves as a kind of first event, albeit one that is uncaused and which thereby stands as a blank counterpart to the laminar flow it disrupts, each operating as a limit to our understanding. Yet in spite of how it may appear, the *clinamen* is not just an ad hoc device to trigger the processes from which everything will follow in law-like fashion.[33] Such an objection assumes that the *clinamen* should not really happen: it assumes there is a natural motion from which it departs for no good reason. Could the fall of atoms through the void not be such a natural motion, and would such motion not imply the existence of an underlying law? After all, when left to themselves atoms will move this way of their own accord,[34] and this could be described as a kind of natural motion. The truth is it could be so described, but not in the usual sense. According to Newton, a body naturally moves at a constant velocity unless acted on by an external force. When there is a departure from natural motion an explanation is required, and that explanation, which is causal, depends on a law that encompasses both the natural motion and the state to which it is perturbed by the external force: the same laws govern the natural motion of a body, its perturbation, and its motion after the perturbation. But this is not the case in Lucretius. An atom falling through the void by its own weight may be perturbed by a strike from another atom, but the very "first" perturbation is caused by the *clinamen*, which strictly speaking is not an "external force" since the atom is not struck by anything else. Moreover, once atoms begin to collide, the regularities that emerge take over from the basic principles that atoms fall, collide, and combine. Therefore, there is no law that determines both the "natural" system and the perturbed system: each change in the movement of atoms leads directly or indirectly to a change in the regularities that shape the movement of atoms in the future. So while it is true that without the *clinamen* atoms would not collide and therefore could not combine to form the world we see around us, as a spontaneous deviation in the movement of an atom, the *clinamen* does not violate any fundamental physical law, because there are none. The fall of atoms as a laminar flow is not law governed, rather it is simply the condition of equilibrium from which order emerges: both ordered states and the "law" that orders them, which is in fact just a regularity that has reached a settled form.

Smolin makes a similar point from the perspective of contemporary cosmology. There is, he writes, symmetry in a system when it can be changed in a certain respect without disturbing the overall character of that system; for example, a sphere is symmetrical with respect to space, because rotating it does not change its shape. As Smolin notes, the systems in classical and quantum mechanics that have symmetries involve an isolated system moving relative to an external frame of reference.[35] But this cannot be replicated with the whole universe because there is nothing relative to which it can move. Invoking Leibniz's principle of the identity of indiscernibles, Smolin observes that "the universe as a whole has no symmetries."[36] But symmetries are associated with properties that are conserved under transformation, and so "it is then proper to regard the great conservation laws of physics – of energy, momentum, and angular momentum – as emergent and approximate."[37] As a consequence, an account of the universe as a whole can have no global symmetries or conservation laws, which runs directly counter to the received wisdom that the more fundamental the theory the more symmetry it must have. It turns out that this apparently troubling conclusion points cosmology towards a solution for a persistent and difficult problem. For if symmetry were key to a theory of the universe as a whole, one would either have to explain why the symmetry is broken or accept that there is a gap in our knowledge that the theory cannot explain. It is in part to avoid this predicament that Unger and Smolin propose that laws and initial conditions converge when it is a matter of the universe as a whole. They then draw the following conclusion:

> Our universe should not be seen as a vast collection of elementary events, each simple and identical to the others, but the opposite, a vast set of elementary processes, no two of which are alike in all details. At this level fundamental principles may be discerned but there are no general laws in the usual sense.[38]

The basic principles to which Unger and Smolin refer here are higher order regularities that, while not immune from change, change more slowly and help to give form to lower order laws and ultimately to phenomena. They include the principle of least action, and the principle of the conservation of energy.[39] Analogous principles for Lucretius would be those stating that atoms fall by their own weight, and that combinations of atoms are formed as they collide. Such principles provide a general framework within which change occurs but they are not sufficient to determine each interaction. In Unger and Smolin's terms, they do not determine the causal structure of events, which for Unger and Smolin, as for Lucretius, depends on the regularities that form locally in time and space.

Once the rain of atoms down through the void is disrupted by the *clinamen*, a chain reaction of collisions multiplies and spreads. Turbulence ensues, and from this near chaos degrees of order gradually emerge. Lucretius describes the process as follows:

> For sure, not by design or intelligence
> Did primal atoms place themselves in order,
> Nor did they make contracts, you may be certain,
> As to what movements each of them should make.
> But many primal atoms in many ways
> Moving through infinite time up to the present,
> Clashing among themselves and carried by their own weight,
> Have come together in every possible way,
> Tried every combination that could be made;
> And so advancing through vast lengths of time,
> Exploring every union and motion,
> At length those of them came together
> Which by a sudden conjunction interfused
> Often become the beginnings of great things –
> Of earth and sea and sky and living creatures.[40]

The movement of atoms is not coordinated and harmonious, as one would expect if there were fundamental laws. Instead, while the fall of atoms ensures that movement of some kind continues, how atoms combine and the arrangement they assume is a matter of chance. The suggestion that the order of the universe, and more specifically the values of the constants in the fundamental equations of physics, may have arisen purely by chance fell out of favor in modern science as the sheer scale of the odds involved became clear. For there to be order in the universe at all, and certainly on the scale we can see, the constants have to be set to with such precision that chance no longer seems a compelling explanation. It was in part to address this problem that Smolin first proposed the idea that the laws of nature may evolve across the birth and death of many universes, those universes most likely to give rise to order reproducing in such a way that the value of the physical constants settled closer and closer to the values we see in our own universe.[41] Lucretius gets around the problem simply by regarding the universe as temporally and spatially infinite, thereby allowing for all permutations to arise at some point, as different worlds form, grow, decay, and disappear. However, there is a principle of selection at work here, too, insofar as those combinations of atoms which produce order survive and are therefore able to give rise to modifications from which there is then a higher chance of relatively stable states emerging. The essential thing in both cases is that order is not determined in advance by fixed laws working on a determinate set of initial conditions. It is the regularities themselves that draw matter into a settled pattern that repeats and in doing so shapes future events.

When they are sufficiently stable, these regularities constitute laws that are descriptive, in the sense that they pick out the patterns of change and stability that have already emerged. But they are also prescriptive, in the sense that they constrain the movement and combination of atoms, and thereby, within limits, the future. As atoms combine and fall into regular patterns of movement, some events become more likely, and some less, overwhelmingly so in certain cases. As Lucretius writes, we see the seasons pass in regular fashion, animal and plant species reproduce, first beards grow and then with age teeth fall out:

> For since the causes from the first beginning
> Were of this nature, and from the first beginning
> Things happened in this way, in sequence then
> And order fixed they even now recur.[42]

However, the order is never universally binding. It is significant that Lucretius applies the term "fixed [*certo*]" here, to the order of events, and not to a law that might be thought to underpin them. *Certo* means "settled" more than "fixed forever." In particular, it may refer to "what has been agreed" – a fitting sense, given that order emerges from the conjunction of atoms that Lucretius names the *foedera natura* and Michel Serres describes as an alliance or treaty.[43] Such an alliance cannot last forever, because nothing in the Lucretian universe does: "All things are continually in flux,"[44] and even the present arrangement of the earth, the sea, and the sky are expected eventually to break down and give way to other forms of composition.[45] For Lucretius, the question of why certain phenomena occur as they do is not, in the end, a question about laws. It is a historical question. In fact, all fundamental questions are historical, because there is nothing changeless to which the changing world can be referred, or against which it can be measured. Order is local, that is not merely the local manifestation of universal laws and principles, but a singular regularity in which events and the order they exhibit are in continual dialogue. An account of such order will be historical, tracing both the causal series and the causal structure, the sequence of events, and the rule permitting the sequence to continue.

Unger and Smolin embrace this conclusion and argue that cosmology will only be able properly to stake its claim to be "the most comprehensive natural science" when it understands itself as fundamentally a historical science.[46] Cosmology must speak not just of things, events, and the laws by which they are determined, but also of the way the laws evolve, and of the changing causal structure that articulates this evolution. Unger and Smolin (Unger especially) are mindful that a model has already become well established in the social sciences and the life sciences,[47] and acknowledge that their project could be described as bringing such practices to bear on natural science. But it is worth pausing to ask whether the social and life sciences genuinely provide the kind of model actually required by the account Unger and Smolin propose. Evaluating the models of law used in the social and life sciences is too big a task to take on here, but it is possible at least to set out what is at stake.

If "law" is no longer ideal, universal, and fixed, then it needs to be fundamentally rethought, and not just recast in a weakened form. It must not be an essentially changeless law that has had the misfortune to fall into time and then be nudged from one state to another, each time as if fixed for good, until the next change. Such a conception of law would hand down the old assumption that matter is inert and mute, and that it requires an organizing principle of some sort to give it form it and enliven it. Referring to "regularities" is a first step, but the idea that regularity somehow "acts" to sustain a sequence still implies the transcendence of something like a rule to the order of events it governs, which is just what first Lucretius and then Unger and Smolin wish to avoid. The trouble is, the idea of regularity tells us very little about how it sustains itself. The sense of law must properly begin with matter itself and not just be susceptible to change by virtue of matter. On this point, accounts of complexity and emergence offer a way forward, but Michel Serres is particularly helpful.

Thinking of the *clinamen* as the first departure from the laminar flow of atoms raining down through the void, Serres elegantly captures the way that regularities, and thereby laws, emerge when he writes that "the pre-model of the fundamental physics has no laws," but that "as soon as a phenomenon appears, as soon as a body is formed, a law can be expressed."[48] Borrowing from information theory, he likens the emergence of order in the combination of atoms to the emergence of language, as indeed does Lucretius,[49] and observes that "the law repeats the fact itself: as things are composing, the laws express the federated."[50] The code that describes how atoms move and combine arises "as soon as the deviation from equilibrium takes place," and "determination is nothing but the retention of the code."[51] Serres makes no distinction here between code and law, but elsewhere he does, and the difference is significant for the broader account of causality.

Roughly speaking, code and law belong at either end of a process of making sense that begins with matter and ends with science (though science is not the only possible outcome). According to both Lucretius and Serres, everything continually flows, and the only truly basic principle is that everything flows towards equilibrium. Order is the slowing of this return. It is delay. But what causes the delay? And why does a particular order form and not some other? Serres writes that matter's route back to equilibrium is not direct because it flows along paths, which thereby place a constraint on what states can follow from any given configuration. The path is a regularity. But paths are not fixed. They follow the most direct available route back to equilibrium around the obstacles in their way, and these obstacles are simply conjunctions of other paths – other regularities.[52] Matter is simply caught up in a series of games of its own devising. It gets in its own way, diverting itself, giving itself form. There is no law to determine how this must happen, at least no universal law. Sense begins in the form of code as matter first combines. But such code does not necessarily give rise to causal structure. In *L'Incandescent*, Serres writes that things act on one another through the forces they exert, but that they also communicate, exchanging code.[53] Quite distinct from law, code may be the most ephemeral trace of a sequence that does not last, that matter does not remember, long enough to be established as a regularity that we recognize and record. Code is the material analogue of what Leibniz called tiny perceptions (*petites perceptions*), the countless events of sensing that fall below the threshold of consciousness. Causal structure is that code which is sufficiently established in the memory of matter to make the history of a given system or locality calculable, and its future predictable.

Serres concludes that alongside the physics we know, which identifies the causal structure of the physical world, there is a second, which attends to code that has not yet become sufficiently regular to warrant speaking of cause and effect, and that may not ever do so. It takes the form of a historical narrative, tracing the sometimes irregular steps from event to event without the guidance of a fixed law. It is a history of the formation, deformation, and reformation of code. Serres doubts that we have anything like this second science, writing that we still do not have an ear for code that has yet to become cause, for "the clamour of things or the background noise of the world."[54] We still need to learn to remember the world as it remembers, to leave our mark on the world as it marks itself.[55] However, with their inversion of the priority that physics usually accords to structure over history, and their incorporation into cosmology of the precedence of causal structure over law, Unger and Smolin have shown that there are good reasons for science to consider what Serres proposes. In so doing, they have also let us see that Lucretius remains our contemporary.

NOTES

1. The title *De Rerum Natura* [*DRN*] is normally translated either as *On the Nature of the Universe* or *The Nature of Things*, or some close variation. In preparing this essay I have referred to several editions, but have cited the translation by Ronald Melville, published by Oxford University Press.
2. Charles Sanders Peirce, "The Architecture of Theories," p. 164.
3. Émile Boutroux, *De la Contingence des Lois de la Nature* [Boutroux], p. 2.
4. Although Unger and Smolin co-authored *The Singular Universe and the Reality of Time* [*Universe*], the book is divided into two sections, authored individually. Although I will for the most part refer to the section authored by Unger, I will not specify this in my citations, but will note in the text if Unger and Smolin themselves draw the reader's attention to a difference in their views.

5. Lee Smolin, *Three Roads to Quantum Gravity* [*Gravity*], p. 59.

6. *Universe* p. 20.

7. Ibid.

8. *Universe* p. 23.

9. Ibid. p. 267.

10. *Gravity* p. 17.

11. *Universe* p. 269.

12. Ibid. p. 270.

13. Ibid. p. 279.

14. Ibid. p. 270.

15. Ibid. p. 277.

16. Ibid. p. 212.

17. Ibid. p. 281. Boutroux p. 4 proposes a similar idea, when he asks rhetorically: "Do causes merge with laws [*les causes se-confondent avec des lois*], as, in the end, the doctrine that defines laws as an unchanging relation supposes?"

18. *Universe* p. 288.

19. Ibid. p. 372.

20. Unger and Smolin disagree over this point. Unger prefers to dispense with the idea of sufficient reason altogether, whereas Smolin more cautiously proposes to replace it with a "principle of differential sufficient reason" according to which, in choosing between competing theories, one opts for the one that minimizes questions of the form "Why does the universe have property X?" for which there is no rational response – by which he means a scientific response that relies solely on what is within the universe; see *Universe* pp. 367–8, 513–15.

21. *DRN* I.147, II.62.

22. Ibid. I.418–47.

23. These ideas are presented at various points in *DRN*, but in particular at V.107, 245–80, 1341–7.

24. One reason to think that Lucretius regarded the laws of the universe as fixed is that he refers on a number of occasions to the "deep-set boundary stone" marking a limit to what can be and what cannot, and thereby also a limit to the power of religion and its practitioners to intervene (*DRN* I.77, II.1087, V.90, VI.66). Although it may be tempting to see this as an invocation of invariant laws, it is not necessary to go that far. It would be more consistent with the text as a whole to take the expression "deep-set boundary stone" as a reference to the constraints imposed by the basic principles of atomism. For example, everything is born and dies, and this pattern is repeated endlessly across the universe; different stars and planets form and disappear, as do different animals, and the species to which they belong. The principle underlying all of this is that atoms fall, collide, and combine, but this alone does not determine how events in the future will unfold.

25. Ibid. II.230–5.

26. Will Buckingham, *Finding Our Sea Legs: Ethics, Experience and the Ocean of Stories*, p. 90.

27. Hesiod writes: "Chaos was first of all [. . .]" (Hesiod and Theognis, *Theogeny, Works and Days, and Elegies*, p. 27).

28. *DRN* II.219.

29. Ibid. II.221.

30. Ibid. II.243.

31. Ibid. II.293.

32. Ibid. II.217–19.

33. Lucretius appears to endorse the idea that the *clinamen* is necessary to account for the possibility of free will. Although there is textual support for this reading, the argument is far from convincing, and the case for free will seems badly served by spontaneous deviations over which it can have no control. On the other hand, free will depends on not being determined entirely by external stimuli, and the broader account of order in which the *clinamen* plays a vital part involves a conception of order as local that is consistent with the mind having regularities of its own. The will would be the expression of regularities that are neither wholly determined by nature, nor purely spontaneous. Understood in this way, the *clinamen* does make an account of free will possible, but not the one that is most obvious. As Lucretius describes it, free will is an example of more general processes that are marked by greater or lesser degrees of self-regulation, rather than as the exception in a world governed by fixed laws.

34. Ibid. II.202.

35. *Universe*, p. 369.

36. Ibid.

37. Ibid. p. 370.

38. Ibid. p. 371.

39. Unger and Smolin also refer to the principle of the conservation of momentum, the principle of the degradation of energy (Carnot's principle), and the principle of the invariance of the laws of nature for fixed observers or observers in uniform motion; ibid. p. 285.

40. *DRN* V.419–31; Lucretius give a similar description a few pages earlier at ibid. V.187–93.

41. Lee Smolin, *The Life of the Cosmos*. Unger and Smolin put it this way: "Causal continuity between successive universes, or between successive periods in the history of the one real universe, may be stressed but never broken" (*Universe* p. 111).

42. *DRN* V.677–9.

43. Michel Serres, *The Birth of Physics* [*Birth*], p. 113.

44. *DRN* V.280.

45. *DRN* V.91–7.

46. *Universe* p. 42.

47. Ibid. pp. 71–3.

48. *Birth* p. 122.

49. *DRN* II.686–98.
50. *Birth* p. 123; I have modified the translation slightly here. The French runs "La loi répète le fait même: pendant que se composent les choses, les lois disent le fédéré" (Michel Serres, *La Naissance de la Physique dans le Texte de Lucrèce*, p. 152).
51. *Birth* pp. 148–9.
52. Ibid. p. 51.
53. Michel Serres, *L'Incandescent*, p. 60.
54. Michel Serres, *Biogée*, p. 38.
55. *L'Incandescent* p. 60.

BIBLIOGRAPHY

Boutroux, É., *De la Contingence des Lois de la Nature* (Paris: Felix Alcan, 1898).

Buckingham, W., *Finding Our Sea Legs: Ethics, Experience and the Ocean of Stories* (Kingston upon Thames: Kingston University Press, 2009).

Fowler, D., *Lucretius on Atomic Motion* (Oxford: Oxford University Press, 2002).

Hesiod and Theognis, *Theogeny, Works and Days, and Elegies*, trans. D. Wender (London: Penguin, 1973).

Lucretius, *La Natura delle Cose*, trans. L Canali (Milan: Rizzoli, 1990).

Lucretius, *On the Nature of the Universe*, trans. R. Melville (Oxford: Oxford University Press, 1999).

Peirce, C. S., "The Architecture of Theories," *The Monist*, 1.2 (1891), pp. 161–76.

Serres, M., *La Naissance de la Physique dans le Texte de Lucrèce* (Paris: Les Éditions de Minuit, 1977).

Serres, M., *The Birth of Physics*, trans. J. Hawkes, ed. D. Webb (Manchester: Clinamen Press, 2000).

Serres, M., *L'Incandescent* (Paris: Éditions Le Pommier, 2003).

Serres, M., *Biogée* (Paris: Éditions Le Pommier, 2013).

Smolin, L., *The Life of the Cosmos* (London: Phoenix, 1997).

Smolin, L., *Three Roads to Quantum Gravity* (London: Weidenfeld & Nicholson, 2000).

Smolin, L., *Time Reborn: From the Crisis in Physics to the Future of the Universe* (London: Penguin, 2013).

Unger, R. M., *False Necessity: Anti-necessitarian Social Theory in the Service of Radical Democracy* (London: Verso, 2004).

Unger, R. M. and Smolin, L., *The Singular Universe and the Reality of Time* (Cambridge: Cambridge University Press, 2015).

CHAPTER 15

On the Surface: The Deleuze-Stoicism Encounter

Ryan J. Johnson

"THE EVENT OF DEATH"

We begin with two events – two deaths, in fact. The first is the death of the Roman Stoic Seneca.[1] After a complicated history as an imperial adviser to Nero, Seneca was ordered to commit suicide by that infamous Roman emperor. Affirming this fate, Seneca cut an artery on his arm in an attempt to bleed to death. Since he was so old and frail, however, his arteries were weak and barely able to pump blood; death would not be so easy for Seneca. He thus cut arteries on his leg and behind his knees, yet even this did not kill him. Mirroring the famous Socratic manner of death, Seneca then asked for hemlock. Painfully, the hemlock also did not bring the mortal relief. As a last resort, "having been carried into the bath, [. . .] he was asphyxiated by the steam, [and] cremated without any of the solemnity of a funeral."[2] The warm waters finally brought about the event of Seneca's death. The second death is the suicide of Gilles Deleuze. On Saturday, 4 November 1995, after years of pain and suffering, Deleuze leapt from the window of his third-floor apartment, on Avenue Niel in Paris's seventeenth arrondissement. Similar to what he wrote of Beckett, Deleuze had been exhausted by the effects of a lifelong respiratory illness, a tracheotomy, and attacks of suffocation that left him "chained like a dog" to an oxygen machine.[3] In those last few months, he could barely speak or even hold a pen. Defenestration was the evental form of his death.[4] For Seneca and Deleuze, suicide is an event, and as such it is intimately two-sided, simultaneously the most personal and the most impersonal act. Deleuze cites Blanchot in describing "suicide as the wish to bring about the conscience of the two faces of death."[5] The double-sided form of suicide allows us to bring together these two faces of death, two double-sided events, a dual death.

This twofold character, along with the ever-so-thin threshold separating and connecting these two sides, creates a continuous crack in the event. This crack is expressed in the paradoxical Stoic theory of incorporeals and further emphasized in Deleuze's reading of Stoic ontology. In this essay, we explore this strand of the Deleuze-Stoic encounter.

Deleuze explains that the "privileged place assigned to the Stoics is due to their having been the initiators of a new image of the philosopher which broke away from the pre-Socratics, Socratic philosophy, and Platonism."[6] In third-century Rome, a very intriguing double-headed statue expressed these opposed lineages. On one side of the statue is the face of Socrates, on the opposite side is Seneca.[7] Although they share one brain, they engage the world in opposite directions. Each man drank the hemlock, but only one found it deadly. Both are attached along a crack "without thickness," joining and dividing these two faces of philosophy at the backs of their respective heads. Deleuze's encounter with Stoicism begins at this dimensionless border separating Socrates and Seneca. This statue, especially its double-sided structure, expresses the way in which Stoicism initiates a new manner of doing philosophy. This new philosophical manner sparks an alternative philosophical lineage, "a minor tradition," which eventually provokes many of the essential features of Deleuze's own thought.

STOIC ONTOLOGY AND SOMETHING

Keeping with the image of the double-headed statue, let us contrast Platonic and Stoic ontologies. Contra Plato, Seneca writes: "Some Stoics think that the primary genus is 'something' [*quid*]."[8] The Stoics do not contrast nothing and "being" (οὐσία); they contrast nothing and something. Like the Greek Stoics before him, "I [Seneca] divide 'what is' into three species: things are corporeal or incorporeal; there is no third possibility."[9] While it might seem strange that Seneca says there are three species but only lists two, the third species plays more of a polemical role, designating things that do not exist, fictional entities such as Plato's transcendent forms.[10] In fairness, it is not even a third category, but more of a catch-all trash bin for fantastical creatures, or any "bit of Plato's personal baggage."[11]

The real distinction in "something" is modal. Corporeals and incorporeals are both species of something, they are both real, but only corporeals exist. Stoicism is very clear on this point: to be is to be a body. Existence and corporeality are coextensive. Contrary to Platonism, there is no immaterial existence in Stoicism. From beginning to end, Stoicism is a thoroughgoing materialism. The Stoics redeploy the suggestion of Plato's *Sophist* to their own materialist ends. Plato ventriloquizes, "a thing really is if it has any capacity at all [. . .] to do something to something else or to have even the smallest thing done to it."[12] Deleuze (and Spinoza) would agree: to be means to have the capacity act or be acted upon. For the Stoics, only bodies can act and be acted upon.

To exist thus means to be able to engage in causal relations, to bring about effects in and to suffer effects from other bodies. Émile Bréhier, one of the two major influences on Deleuze's encounter with Stoicism, notes that this thesis, another divergence from Platonism, "renders ideal causality completely impossible."[13]

The Stoics postulate another ontological category. While everything is something (every existing thing is a something), something includes that which is beyond body but is not transcendently ideal: incorporeals. Incorporeals are not transcendent forms; immanence characterizes them as much as it characterizes bodies. The difference is that, while incorporeals do not exist, they do subsist (ὑφίστασθαι).[14] Subsistence is neither being nor nothing, but somewhere between both. John Sellars calls them "*non-existent* realities."[15] To differentiate it from Plato's forms, Deleuze sometimes calls this kind of immanent reality "insistence."[16]

Zeno of Citium thought that "it was quite impossible for anything to be acted on by something entirely without body," while Cicero reports, "neither what acts nor what it acts on could be incorporeal."[17] Neither active nor passive, Deleuze calls incorporeals "impassive."[18] While existent bodies have a causal character, incorporeals are not inscribed within the order of causation (which is why Deleuze describes them as effects). Corporeals and incorporeals are both real, insofar as they are both kinds of something, but they are modally different. "The Stoics," Deleuze writes, "are in the process of tracing out and forming a frontier where there had not been one before."[19] Through the construction of this strange ontological frontier, the Stoics "transcend the experiential dimensions of the visible without falling into [transcendent] Ideas."[20] This frontier or surface is the means by which Stoic ontology initiates a new manner of philosophizing.

With this ontological surface, Stoic ontology flattens out the heights of Plato's transcendent metaphysics. No longer is there an ascending movement from depths to height, from particulars to universals, from the darkness of the cave to the bright light of the sun. Instead, the Stoics construct the concept of a flat surface, as paradoxical as it is, that allows continuous passage from corporeals to incorporeals and back again. Distributing the verticality of Platonism onto a single horizontal plane inaugurates a new mode of philosophy, and Deleuze considers this to be an entirely original Stoic achievement, one that further entails an entire ethics.[21] While Deleuze suggests that Plato shows the direction for an overturning of Platonism, "the Stoics," he clearly states, "are the first to reverse Platonism."[22] Recall the two-faced statue: Socrates faces in one direction, perhaps staring up into the height of the transcendent domain, but Seneca looks out in the opposite direction, following the flat surface of something as it stretches out into the distance, perhaps even folding back on itself in the form of a Möbius strip, eternally returning.[23] To give us a concrete image to hold in mind as we progress, we can think of the Stoic surface as the paradoxical middle of the two faces of the Möbius strip.[24]

THE "FOUR" INCORPOREALS

On the traditional reading, the Stoics postulate four types of incorporeals: "[I] sayable [λεκτόν], [II] void, [III] place [τόπον], and [IV] time."²⁵ Part of our argument, though, will be to show how, in the Deleuze-Stoicism encounter, there are not four but three incorporeals: I. Space, II. Λεκτά, III. Time. We begin with void and place.

Space = [I] Void + [II] Place

Sextus clearly explains void and place: "The Stoics say that void is what can be occupied by an existent but is not occupied [. . .] place is what is occupied by an existent [body] and made equal to what occupies it."²⁶ In the extant fragments, the Stoics do not seem concerned that place and void are really only two dimensions of the same concept: space. Place is occupied space; void is empty space. Where bodies are, space subsists; where bodies are not, void subsists. Since place is defined in relation to bodies, it is finite; place subsists as equal in size to the body that occupies it. Void, however, subsists completely independently of bodies, functioning as the empty space outside of all bodies, beyond the totality of "what is," τὸ ὄν, infinitely extending out from the corporeal world in all directions. While place is finite and limited, void is infinite and unlimited.

In order to ensure change in time and space, void and place are necessary. Since they cannot be bodies (for two bodies cannot occupy the same place), void and place are rendered incorporeal, capable neither of acting nor being acted upon. The subsistence of void and place is characterized as "giving way," relenting, unable to offer any kind of resistance. Void yields to bodies and becomes place, and place becomes void when emptied of bodies.

While Deleuze does not write much about void and place, focusing instead on time and λεκτά, we should not pass over this pair of incorporeals too quickly. As we claimed above and will argue below, void and place are two dimensions of the same concept: space. That is, void and place are not two separate types of incorporeals, but are instead two dimensions of one kind of incorporeal. Space is thus the generic name for this first Stoic incorporeal; it is the ever-so-thin cleft separating and connecting void and place. As we will find, this fissure runs throughout the Deleuze-Stoicism encounter.

Λεκτά

A common English translation of λεκτόν is "sayable," and Émile Bréhier translates it with the French word *exprimable* ("expressible"). Λεκτόν is the first term in the Stoic philosophy of language. As this is a materialist account, things begin with bodies, in this case the mouth's production of sounds, which are themselves physical things. Deleuze cites one of Chrysippus' paradoxes: "If you say something, it passes through your lips: now you say wagon, consequently a wagon passes through your lips."²⁷

In order to work through this paradox and discover the Stoic philosophy of language, consider this sentence: "Deleuze has died." The sentence is attributed to a certain state of affairs in the world, although the death subsists only in the writing. In the world, we find only a collection of bodies – an open window, a warm corpse, reddening pavement, confused onlookers, etc. Strangely, there is no death among these bodies. Death does not exist in the world. In the world, there are only bodies intermixing with other bodies, with nouns and adjectives to denote them. Death only subsists in words, such that death is an event expressed by a verb, that is "to die." The sense of the sentence subsists at the thin threshold between the word and the world. Deleuze writes, "physical bodies and sonorous words are separated and articulated at once by an incorporeal frontier. This frontier is sense, representing, on one side, the pure 'expressed' of words, and on the other, the logical attribute of bodies."[28] Bodies are the corporeal finite things, and sense is the infinite expanse playing along the surface of states of affairs.

Now consider the sense expressed in Seneca's "death." In Seneca's last hours, there was a cutting into flesh by a knife. Bréhier mentions cutting in a passage that Deleuze later cites at length:

> So when the scalpel cuts the flesh, the first body produces on the second not a new property but a new attribute, that of being cut. The *attribute*, strictly speaking, does not designate any real *quality* . . ., it is always, to the contrary, expressed by a verb, that is to say it is not a being, but a way of being . . . This way of being finds itself in some way at the limit, at the surface of being, and it is not able to change its nature: it is, in fact, neither active nor passive, because passivity presupposed a corporeal nature which undergoes an action. It is purely and simply a result, or an effect which is not classified among beings.[29]

A cut, like a death, is an incorporeal event. When the knife cuts the skin, we do not say that the knife gave the skin a new quality. Instead, we say that the state of affairs that includes the knife and the skin is not the same as it was. Before, the knife was above the skin; after, the knife is in the divided space of the skin that has acquired the attribute of being a wound. Bréhier explains, "there are no new realities, properties, but only [new] attributes."[30] The skin has the attribute of "having been cut," and the knife has the attribute of "having cut." Nouns denote the various organizations of the states of affairs. The cut, however, expressed by the infinitive verb ("to cut," *couper*) never exists among the corporeal state of affairs, for it is an incorporeal event. It never happens in the world of bodies, but is always what has already happened or is yet to happen. It is neither the active body (knife) nor the passive body (skin), but instead arises as their shared effect. While "wound" and "scar" are qualities of bodies, both nouns, "to cut" is not corporeal, but is rather a verb that contributes an attribute to a body. What it attributes to bodies is an infinitely divisible event that subsists on a frail frontier that leads off in two directions, into the inaccessible past and the unreachable future.

Seneca thus never cuts his arm or leg. It is rather that his skin has already been, or was yet to be, cut. The cut never happens, but subsists as a verb that can be attributed to bodies. Even after several arteries had been severed, he still had to wait for the next event – death. Death, too, never arrives. Seneca never dies, but always "is about to die" or "has died." Death is an impersonal instant that is never present but remains a future that never arrives or a past that has always already passed. "The event is that no one ever dies, but has always just died or is always going to die."[31] For Blanchot, a significant influence on Deleuze's thinking of death, death is impersonal, incorporeal, and infinitive, contained in the verb "to die" (*mourir*).[32] "Death," Deleuze writes, "has an extreme and definite relation to me and my body and is grounded in me, but also has no relation to me at all."[33] Death is immanent but never present in a state of affairs, just as verbs are immanent but never existent in the nouns through which verbs conjugate. Although neither Seneca nor Deleuze ever died, they are now dead. There is no subject in death. Like the infinite verb, death is impersonal and pre-subjective. Deleuze refers to this as the splendor of the fourth person expressed in phrases such as "it rains" (*il pleut*) or "it snows" (*il neige*): "The *they* [*on*] of the pure event wherein *it dies* [*il meurt*] does in the same way that *it* rains [*il pleut*]."[34]

Deleuze pushes the analysis further, prioritizing death to a special evental status. Rather than death being like any other event, "every event," Deleuze writes, "is like death."[35] "To die" is the singular form of the frontier between two domains – life and death – that never relate to each other. Life and death cannot touch.

Let us push Deleuze even further, and consider the eventual status of Seneca and Deleuze's form of death: suicide. Not only is every event like death, but every death and every event is like suicide. While Seneca cuts his arms and legs, he is both active and passive. Suicide brings together activity and passivity in a single body, which is what makes it so personal. Yet the death of suicide, like any death, never happens, which makes suicide so impersonal. Suicide, Deleuze writes, is "impersonal death by means of the most personal act."[36] As such, suicide comes closest to bringing death ("to die," *mourir*) to the present, to now (*maintenant*), although this frontier is never crossed. Bodies and events, like nouns and verbs, are separated by that same surface without thickness that slips through all of Stoic ontology. The second name of this surface is λεκτόν, the second incorporeal.

Deleuze's account of sense emerges out of his encounter with the Stoic concept of λεκτόν. As with λεκτά, Deleuze sees sense as the "*expressed of the proposition.*"[37] For him, sense is neither body nor nothing. It is something. Similar to what Blanchot says about suicide, it is both personal and impersonal; it is what we mean when we speak, but it is also more than that. Since sense exceeds any one person's concept, it is not reducible to a conceptual, sensible, or rational representation, all of which the Stoics consider corporeal. The sense of language subsisted prior to each of us, and it will subsist after death. This is why Deleuze claims that the genetic power of sense "is an impassive and incorporeal entity, without physical or mental existence, neither acting nor being acted upon."[38]

Sextus says it well:

> The Stoics said that three things are linked together, the thing signified and the thing signifying and the thing existing; and of these the thing signifying is the utterance (["Deleuze"][39] for instance); and the thing signified is the actual thing indicated thereby and which we apprehend as subsisting in dependence on our intellect, whereas foreigners although hearing the utterance do not understand it; and the thing existing is the external object, such as [Deleuze] himself. And of these, two are bodies – that is, the utterance and the existing thing – and one is incorporeal, namely the thing signified and sayable [λεκτόν], and this too is true or false.[40]

The λεκτά form a fragile frontier subsisting between pairs of existing bodies; it is what is expressed in, but is not reducible to, an articulated proposition. In between two existing bodies, the signifier and the signified, are the subsistent, incorporeal λεκτά.[41] The key is that λεκτά do not subsist outside of the proposition and its referent. Instead, they inhere or subsist in words. Λεκτά thus have two dimensions, according to the two major kinds of words. Similar to the way in which void and place are two dimensions of space, the verbal and the nominal are two dimensions of λεκτά – verbs express subsistent events and nouns denote existent bodies. As void is unlimited space and place is limited space, verbs are infinitive and unlimited λεκτά and nouns are finite and limited λεκτά. So far, we have seen two primary kinds of incorporeals, and there is one more to cover.

Time

Time is the final incorporeal of Stoic theory. In order to appreciate the full breadth of this ancient-contemporary encounter, we start with Zeno of Citium, the one who founded this ancient philosophical school on that painted porch (ἡ ποικίλη στοά), and map the production of this notion of time through the complicated Stoic account and up to Deleuze himself.

Zeno's definition of time seems to echo Aristotle's definition. In the *Physics*, Aristotle says time is the "number of motion [ἀριθμὸς κινήσεως] with reference to before and after."[42] Similarly, "Zeno said time is the dimension [διάστημα] of all motion without qualification [ἁπλῶς]."[43] Still, while they both define time in relation to motion, there is an important difference: Zeno does not retain the element of calculation or numbering in his definition. Aristotle's account depends more on a counting of what came before and what came after, by how much or how little. Zeno, by contrast, puts time in relation to motion as such, without calculation and without number. Time, for Zeno, is the dimension of motion that is irreducible to quantitative measurement. Unquantified or unqualified movement distributes time not in terms of discrete numbers, but in terms of speed and slowness.[44] Already in Zeno, there is a shift in the ancient thinking of time from quantitative to qualitative measurement, or what Deleuze might call a move from an extensive to an intensive measure of time.

After Zeno, "Chrysippus said time [χρόνον] is [. . .] the dimension [διάστημα] of motion [κινήσεως] accompanying the world's [τοῦ κόσμου] motion."[45] With this definition, Chrysippus develops Zeno's definition in two important ways. First, notice the difference between saying that time is "of" motion, and that it is the dimension "accompanying" motion. When Zeno says that time is the dimension of motion, he implies that movement has a discrete extension, that is it has a determinate beginning and an end, such as five meters, or two kilometers. Although Zeno starts to make the measure of time more intensive, at least compared to Aristotle, for him time is still discontinuous. Chrysippus and all later Stoics, however, complete the transition to the intensive and render time continuous. This is accomplished by means of the second way in which Chrysippus extends Zeno's definition: he connects time to the world's motion, the movement of the κόσμος. The κόσμος, for the Stoics, is infinite in that it endlessly turns in a cycle. Connecting time to the infinite and continuous motion of the cosmic cycles ensures that time is also infinite and continuous. Thus with Chrysippus, time becomes truly continuous.

So far, we have seen that Stoicism, after Zeno, sees time as materially continuous, that is there are no gaps in time. Time is a smooth and unending surface. Stoics also posit time as structurally continuous, that is as infinitely divisible. Against the Epicureans, the Stoics grant no end to the process of cutting time, space, matter, or motion into smaller and smaller parts. "Chrysippus said that bodies are divided to infinity, and likewise things comparable to bodies, such as surface, line, place, void and time."[46] While the materially continuous nature of time entails the infinite stretching of time into the past and future, the structurally continuous nature of time entails some seemingly paradoxical accounts of the present.

If time is infinitely divisible, then the present can be divided endlessly:

> [Chrysippus] says most clearly that no time [χρόνος] is wholly present [ὅλως ἐνίσταται]. For since continuous things are infinitely divisible [τομὴ], on the basis of this division every time too is infinitely divisible. Consequently no time is present exactly, but it is broadly [κατὰ πλάτος] said to be so.[47]

Speaking precisely, time is never present. This is clear for the future and the past. The future and the past cannot, by definition, be present. If they were, they would be the present, and not the future or past. The rub is that this infinite divisibility also applies to the present. Although the present, broadly speaking, seems constituted by part of the past and part of the future, these parts can be divided endlessly. Continuous division implies that the present never is. Hence the paradoxical conclusion: the present is never present, now is never now. This is where Deleuze enters the scene: the present "is subdivided ad infinitum into something that has just happened and something that is going to happen, always flying in both directions at once."[48] Like death, the present never exists, but is instead the nonexistent limit or frontier that endlessly decomposes into the past and the future; it "is" simply the border at which the past and the future meet and separate. We now have some provocative conclusions: since present, past, and future do not exist, time does not exist. Deleuze calls this understanding of time Aion, from αἰών.

Interestingly, the Stoics add a further complication to the paradoxes of time. As soon as they claim that the present is not real, and so never exists, they also say the very opposite of that: "only the present exists [ὑπάρχειν]."[49] The present is real, it seems, but not the past or the future. "The past and the future," they continue, "subsist [ὑφεστάναι], but exist in no way."[50] The present thus has a limited "extension or duration" into which past and future are gathered together or absorbed.[51] In the extended present, "one part of the present time is future and the other past."[52] The extension of the present can both expand and contract. It can expand out to the present day, the present year, even expanding out until it encompasses the time of all bodies, or it can contract down so that it encompasses the time of a single body, however large or small it is. However vast or slim, the present has a finite extension. Deleuze calls this reading of time Chronos, from χρόνος.

Chronos and Aion

While most ancient scholars attempt to explain away the apparent conflict in the Stoic theory of time by stressing one of the two sides of the paradox, at the end of the day they often conclude that the theory is irresolvably fraught. Deleuze, however, does not try to explain away the paradox, but instead sees great power therein. Rather than try to resolve the dynamic tension of the Stoic theory of time, Deleuze greatly appreciates how the Stoic way of formulating problems generates challenging and dynamic concepts: "The genius of a philosophy must first be measured by the new distribution which it imposes on beings and concepts," and this is something that Stoicism accomplishes with their ontology of incorporeals.[53] In Deleuze's eyes, Stoicism is not hopelessly doomed, but instead produces provocative ways of thinking about time, beyond the shadows cast by Socrates, Plato, and Aristotle.

The two parts of the paradox of the Stoic theory of time lead Deleuze to conclude:

> Time must be grasped twice, in two complementary [complémentaires] though mutually exclusive fashions. First, it must be grasped entirely as the living present in bodies that act and are acted upon. Second, it must be grasped entirely as an entity infinitely divisible into past

and future [. . .] Only the present exists in time and gathers together or absorbs the past and future. But only the past and future inhere in time and divide each present infinitely. These are not three successive dimensions, but two simultaneous [*simultanées*] readings of time.[54]

In Deleuze's eyes, the cleavage that acts as the dividing surface between these two seemingly incommensurable accounts of time seems to require two different readings of time. As noted above, Deleuze adapts two classical names for these two readings: Aion and Chronos.

At this point we must be precise in our understanding of the role of time in the Deleuze-Stoicism encounter. We must ask: is Deleuze right in claiming that there are really two different readings of time in Stoicism, Aion and Chronos? Or does it unjustifiably force the Stoics to say something they themselves would not say? Of course we could flippantly refer to Deleuze's famous remark about the buggery of the history of philosophy, it is necessary to remember the most important feature of this reflection on his encounters: "I saw myself as taking an author from behind and giving him a child that would be his own offspring, yet monstrous. *It was really important for me for it to be his own child, because the author had to actually say all I had him saying.*"[55] Let us test whether Deleuze does in fact meet his personal standard of creatively and sensitively engaging with the Stoic theory of time.

Reading the extant passages concerning time attributed to Zeno, Chrysippus, and the other early Stoics, we do not find a single use of the word "αἰών" that has the sense of Deleuze's *Aion*. The only place in which this term appears, in a way, is in Marcus Aurelius' *Mediations*, which was written centuries after the deaths of Zeno and Chrysippus. This is where Victor Goldschmidt, the other major influence on Deleuze's Stoic encounter, and the thinker with the greatest impact on Deleuze's engagement with the Stoic theory of time, turns in order to claim that the Stoics had two distinct accounts of time. Goldschmidt argues that the reason why we do not see two distinct accounts of time in the early Stoics is because Chrysippus had a "negligence with his terminology, [which] we can say was repaired by Marcus Aurelius."[56] Thus Goldschmidt points to a few passages in the *Mediations* that demonstrate how both αἰών and ἄπειρος (the former standardly translated as "eternity" or "age," the latter as "infinite" or "endless"), because they both can refer to eternity and the infinite past and future, are linked.[57] At the same time, John Sellars notes, Goldschmidt overlooks many passages where Marcus Aurelius links ἄπειρος with χρόνος, not αἰών.[58] If Goldschmidt's claim – there are two distinct accounts of time in Stoicism – is based merely on a terminological distinction, then his argument falters due to a lack of textual support.[59]

Yet Deleuze pushes beyond Goldschmidt's influence. Consider what Deleuze says: "The greatness of Stoic thought is to show at once the necessity [*nécessité*] of these two readings and their reciprocal exclusion."[60] While Deleuze follows Goldschmidt in affirming that the Stoics had two readings of time, he further contends that both are equally necessary, complementary, and simultaneous.[61] It is not simply that there are two understandings of time, but also that these two understandings converge in their very divergence.

We can refer to a standard Deleuzian distinction, one that has bubbled below the surface of our entire investigation, in order to make sense of the way in which these two theories of time both converge and diverge. Consider Sellars' clever observation that there is another way to translate the phrase "κατὰ πλάτος" in the already-mentioned Stobaeus passage.[62] Long and Sedley translate this as "broadly." There is, however, another possible translation, one which Goldschmidt himself uses: *l'éntendue*, extension.[63] When we refer to the present as extended through and delimited by the living present of exist-ing bodies, we see time according to extensive measurements: time as χρόνος, Chronos. Given an ongoing state of affairs, we can extensively circumscribe the present as having a finite duration. By contrast, when we consider the pres-ent not as extended but as eternally dislocated, as a continuously displaced and missing center, we consider time according to intensive measurements: time as αἰών, Aion.

What is it to measure time extensively or intensively? An extensive mea-surement of time is something like one minute, two days, three years, and so on. If we divide, for example, one hour in half, we get two half hours. The difference is a mere metric difference, that is there is no real change in kind between one hour, a half-hour, a quarter of an hour, an eighth of an hour, etc. Different extensive measurements are equal and homogenous, that is we can divide into them without changing the nature of what is being divided.[64] An intensive measurement, by contrast, is more like pressure, temperature, or pitch. Such intensities cannot be divided or altered without a change in nature. If we lower the temperature of a gallon of water from 50 to 25 degrees Fahrenheit, we find what was liquid now is ice; if we raise the pitch of a tone by a whole step, we have a new note. Similarly, an intensively considered time is not composed of equal and homogenous parts, but of heterogeneous divi-sions, each of which is infinitely divisible. That is, intensive time is composed of an infinite future and infinite past, separated and connected by a limit, or what Deleuze often calls a singularity. The present does not exist, but instead subsists as "the instant without thickness and without extension," a "pure perverse 'moment,'" an ever-so-thin crack in time.[65]

Chronos is thus the dimension of Stoic time that considers time extensively, while Aion is the dimension that considers time intensively. Chronos is time considered in terms of finite, limited quantities, while Aion is time considered in terms of infinite and unlimited intensities. Part of Deleuze's insight is to demonstrate the simultaneous mutual exclusion and co-necessitation of both Chronos and Aion. Put differently, Deleuze is careful not to sacrifice extensity for intensity, Chronos for Aion, but to demonstrate their immanent relation. The exact nature of this relation is one of Deleuze's greatest contributions to the history of philosophy: the intensive produces the extensive. The reason it is so difficult to see this is because the extensive covers up or hides the inten-sive grounds that produced it. In our case, Chronos hides Aion. It is through

Deleuze's various encounters with figures from the history of philosophy, especially the Stoics, that this intensive-extensive distinction emerges. In the end, Deleuze's encounter with the Stoics forces him to create concepts that show how the intensive and the extensive are two dimensions of the same theory of time. Chronos (extensive time) and Aion (intensive time) are two distinct readings of time, but the key is to see how they are necessary, complementary, and simultaneous understandings of a single incorporeal: time.

THE THREE CRACKED INCORPOREALS

We have now seen how Deleuze engages with some of the most provocative elements of Stoic ontology. Along the way, we have developed a rather unorthodox account of Stoicism, one that does not fully appear in Deleuze's texts but that can be distilled from the contours of his encounter with this ancient Hellenistic school. This less-than-explicit account of the Deleuze-Stoicism encounter is reducible to two claims: there are only three, not four, incorporeals, and each incorporeal has an intensive and extensive dimension.

The reason why commentators usually assert that the Stoics postulated four kinds of incorporeals is reasonably based on the extant ancient texts. Still, we must never forget that none of these are recognized as originating directly from Zeno, Chrysippus, or any of the early Stoics. Our access to the early Stoic ideas thus must pass through various critical and doxographical filters, such as Stobaeus, Sextus Empiricus, Diogenes Laertius, and so on. Since we must rely on the accounts of the critics of the Stoics, we should always recall that these authors often write from partisan, polemical, or even uncharitable perspectives. It is thus likely that there are some, probably significant, differences between what the Stoics themselves thought and what their critics said about them. Remembering this provides sufficient space for the Deleuzian encounter.

It is in this little space that our unorthodox claim appears: there are three incorporeals in Stoicism, and each are split in two. While the extant texts on Stoicism, written by their critics, explicitly give four, not three, incorporeals, this reading of the Deleuze-Stoicism encounter has three distinct advantages. (1) It allays the confusion as to why place and void are considered separate types of incorporeals, when they seem to be rather two ways of understanding space. (2) It helps clarify the clever account of the Stoics' materialist theory of language. (3) It addresses some of the concerns arising from the seemingly paradoxical accounts of time in Stoicism.

As we said, void and place are not simply two distinct concepts, two separate kinds of incorporeals, but instead are two distinct dimensions of a single concept: space. The difference is that place is space considered in terms of the finitude and limits of the bodies that occupy it, and void is space considered independently of bodies, and so as infinite and unlimited. In more Deleuzian language, place is extensive space and void is intensive space. Space is thus one kind of incorporeal, composed of two dimensions – void and place. Space functions as that border without thickness separating void and place. We can twist one of Goldschmidt's diagrams:[66]

Void (infinite/intensive/incorporeal)

SPACE ─────────────|─────────────

Place (limited/extensive/corporeal)

Λεκτά are the second kind of incorporeal. While we have not gone into much detail about the λεκτά in our discussion, much of *Logic of Sense* investigates the ways in which sense relates to linguistic propositions. For our purposes, it is enough to note that there are two dimensions of the λεκτόν: the nominal and verbal.[67] Verbs, especially infinitive and transfinite verbs, are infinite and unlimited λεκτά, and nouns are finite and limited λεκτά. In between is that same ever-so-thin frontier that enters "into the propositions themselves, between nouns and verbs, or, rather, between denotations and expressions."[68] In other words, verbs are intensively considered λεκτά and nouns are extensively considered λεκτά. Although Goldschmidt does not diagram λεκτόν, we can further transplant his diagram thus:

Verb (infinite/intensive/incorporeal)

ΛΕΚΤΟΝ ─────────────|─────────────

Noun (limited/extensive/corporeal)

Time is the third and final type of incorporeal. In the Deleuze-Stoicism encounter, there are two readings of time: Chronos and Aion. Chronos is finite and limited time, wherein only the present exists at a certain duration, while the past and future subsist. Aion, by contrast, is infinite and unlimited time, wherein the none of the present, past, or future exist, but all instead subsist. Put differently, Chronos is corporeal time and Aion is incorporeal time. In Deleuze's terms, Chronos is extensive time and Aion is intensive time. What separates them? That paradoxical surface without thickness that operates throughout Stoic ontology. We can again twist, with yet more changes, Goldschmidt's diagram:[69]

Aion (infinite/intensive/incorporeal)

TIME ─────────────|─────────────

Chronos (limited/extensive/corporeal)

Let us add one more twist to these diagrams. Imagine this: take the ends of the intensive and extensive faces of each incorporeal, twist them and glue them together. We now have three Möbius strips, three paradoxical surfaces, each turning in unison. On each side of the strips are the finite, extended, bodily dimensions – place, noun, Chronos; on the other side are the endless, intensive, separated dimensions – void, verb, Aion. Each side constantly turns into and out of each other.

In conclusion, as place is occupied space and void is unoccupied space, Chronos is filled time and Aion is empty time. As Deleuze says, "Chronos is filled up with states of affairs and the movements of the objects that it measures. But being an empty and unfolded form of time, the Aion subdivides ad infinitum that which haunts it without ever inhabiting it."[70] To this we can add: nouns are filled λεκτά and verbs are empty λεκτά. Nouns are filled by states of affairs (for example, when a denotation corresponds to a state of affairs, it is considered true), while verbs are endlessly empty or displace themselves. Taken together, space, time, and λεκτόν are the three incorporeals in the Deleuze-Stoic encounter. Separating and connecting each of them is that sinuous Stoic surface. Stoic ontology, expressed in its encounter with Deleuze, constructs a dynamic organization composed of intensive and extensive dimensions separated and connected by a single boundary line.

Through it all, paradoxes are not explained away but instead retained for their power to produce a new distribution of thought. The Stoic insistence on retaining the productive promise of paradoxes without recourse to transcendent forms or eternal causes is what, Deleuze argues, makes them innovative initiators of a new image of the philosopher, one that runs counter to Platonism and Aristotelianism. This "new image," Deleuze contends, "is already closely linked to the paradoxical constitution of the theory of sense,"[71] and, we here add, space and time. These three incorporeals are paradoxically structured by the slight Stoic surface separating and connecting their respective extensive and intensive dimensions. It is through this strange account of the incorporeals in Stoic ontology, along with several other paradoxically constituted theories, that the Stoics become the initiators of a new image of philosophy that spawns a lineage of thought leading, eventually, to Deleuze himself.

NOTES

1. Tacitus, *Annals*, 15.62–4.
2. Ibid. 15.64. While Socrates, just prior to his death, asked that a cock be sacrificed to Asclepius, Seneca offered the liquid of the water in which he died as a drink-offering to Jupiter the Liberator; see Plato, *Phaedo*, 118a.
3. Deleuze wrote a delightful essay on the "exhausted" in Samuel Beckett. For an English translation, see Gilles Deleuze, "The Exhausted," in *Essays Critical and Clinical*.

4. The account of Deleuze's death can be found, among other places, in André Pierre Colombat, "November 4, 1995: Deleuze's Death as an Event," which draws a similar line from Stoic deaths to Deleuze's own.

5. Deleuze, *Logic of Sense* [*LS*], p. 156; Deleuze here points to Maurice Blanchot, *L'Espace Littéraire* [Blanchot], pp. 104–5.

6. Deleuze, *LS*, pp. xiii–xiv.

7. *Double Herm of Socrates and Seneca*, Inv. No. Sk 391 (R 106) (Berlin: State Museums, Pergamon Museum, *c.*300–350 AD). In 1813, this double-sided portrait – showing two male heads, back to back – was unearthed in Rome: one was clearly labeled, in Greek, "Socrates," the other, in Latin, "Seneca." See James Romm, *Dying Every Day: Seneca at the Court of Nero*.

8. Seneca, *Selected Philosophical Letters* [*Letters*], "Letter to Lucilius," 58.15. See also the invaluable collection from Anthony Long and David Sedley, *The Hellenistic Philosophers* [*THP*], 27A (for subsequent references to texts from Long and Sedley's collection I will cite the text's location both in *THP* and, parenthetically, in its original source; other places I cite Long and Sedley's commentary through a reference to the page numbers of the pertinent volume).

9. Ibid. 58.14.

10. *THP* 30E (Simplicius, *On Aristotle's Categories*, 105, 8–16). Vanessa de Harven, *The Coherence of Stoic Ontology*, has developed an interesting reading of this third category, which is neither corporeal nor incorporeal, and so expresses a second kind of subsistence.

11. *Letters* 58.18. This move is significant, for it prepares the way for the affirmation of the reality only of individuals or singular things, and the denial of the reality of universals. Spinoza, an early modern Stoic and member of Deleuze's so-called "minor tradition," later makes this move in Book II of his *Ethics*.

12. Plato, *Sophist*, 247e (trans. Nicholas P. White, from Plato, *Complete Works*, ed. John Cooper).

13. Émile Bréhier, *La Théorie des Incorporels dans l'Ancien Stoicism* [Bréhier], p.10. The other major influence on Deleuze's Stoicism is Victor Goldschmidt, whom we address below.

14. *THP* vol. 1, pp. 162–6. The Stoic theory of incorporeals is reminiscent of Meinong's intriguing ontology, which postulates an ontological state between existence and non-existence, which he calls subsistence (*bestehen*); see Alexius Meinong, *Über Möglichkeit und Wahrscheinlichkeit*.

15. John Sellars, *Stoicism*, p. 84; unless otherwise noted, all emphases in quotations are from the original text.

16. Deleuze, *Difference and Repetition* [*DR*], pp. 82, 85, 107.

17. Cicero, *Academica*, 1.39; trans. Charles Brittain, slightly modified. See also *THP* 45A.

18. *LS* p. 20.

19. Ibid. p. 6.

20. Ibid. p. 20; all additions in brackets are my own unless otherwise noted.
21. The entailment of ethics from ontology is a constant theme in the figures with whom Deleuze had his most important encounters. Think of, for example, the continuous movement from metaphysics to ethics or ethics to metaphysics in Spinoza and Nietzsche, two later Stoic sympathizers.
22. *DR* pp. 68, 244; *LS* p. 7.
23. In *The Logic of Sense* Deleuze also uses the Möbius strip imagery to describe both Stoicism and Lewis Caroll (*LS* pp. 11, 20, 123, 337).
24. In fact, a Möbius strip is helpful for thinking about many features of Stoicism, for example their innovations in logic, their productive use of paradoxes, their formulation of an eternal recurrence, and so on.
25. *THP* 27D (Sextus Empiricus, *Against the Professors*, 10.218).
26. *THP* 49B (Sextus Empiricus, *Against the Professors*, 10.3–4).
27. *LS* p. 8; see also Diogenes Laertius, *Lives of Eminent Philosophers*, 7.186. We can understand this process through what Deleuze calls the dynamic genesis of language. Language is made possible by means of "that which separates sounds from bodies and organizes them into propositions, freeing them for the expressive function" (*LS* p. 181). Deleuze articulates three separate stages in this genesis: (1) The primary order of language is sounded out in the depths of bodies, in the guttural cries, cracklings, and burstings of noise erupting out of the sonorous cavities of the body. The clearest examples of this are the noises of an infant. The body of an infant is not a clearly defined and controlled entity, but is rather a disorganized collection of intensities, which emit screams, farts, piss, and various bodily flows. There is no sense to these sounds. They are just noises. It is no coincidence that the infant is the first example of the body-without-organs in *Anti-Oedipus*. (2) Out of the clanging, incoherent noise, the tertiary arrangement emerges. The infant begins to pick up on a repeated sound. The voice of a parent emerges as a "voice from above": "from noises as [. . .] passions of bodies in depth, to the voice as the entity of the heights" (*LS* p. 229). Although the child does not yet have access to the domain of sense lurking within this "familial hum of voices" (ibid.), it does discern a pre-existing and organized system of sounds. The tertiary arrangement of language is the pre-formed system of meaningful words and sentences. (3) The question thus concerns how to move from non-language to language, from noise to meaning. Deleuze's answer is the secondary organization of language, the site of sense (and nonsense). It is called "secondary" not simply to confuse but in order to locate an element of language that lies between the pure noise of the primary order and the meaningful voice of the tertiary arrangement.
28. *LS* p. 91.
29. Bréhier pp. 11–12; as quoted in *LS* p. 5.
30. Bréhier p. 11.
31. *LS* p. 63.
32. Blanchot, p. 160.

33. *LS* p. 151.
34. Ibid. p. 152.
35. Ibid.
36. Ibid. p. 156.
37. Ibid. p. 19.
38. Ibid. p. 20.
39. Sextus uses the name "Dion," but I replaced this with "Deleuze" in keeping with the theme of the essay.
40. Sextus Empiricus, *Against the Professors*, 8.11–12; as quoted in Sellars, *Stoicism*, pp. 61–2. See also *THP* 33B.
41. Stoics make a further distinction between complete and incomplete λεκτά. Incomplete λεκτά are words or phrases that only indicate the potential for sense but do not contain sense, for example, ". . . has died." Bréhier defines incomplete λεκτά as "verbs without subjects," and a complete λεκτόν as a "verb accompanied by its subject" (Bréhier, p. 17). Complete λεκτά convey a sense such that it prevents the need to ask "Who?," Who "has died"? "Deleuze has died."
42. Aristotle, *Physics*, IV.11, 219b1–2.
43. *THP* 51A (Simplicius, *On Aristotle's Categories*, 350, 15–16).
44. Consider *THP* 51B (Stobaeus, 1.106, 5–23).
45. *THP* 51B (Stobaeus, 1.106, 5–23).
46. *THP* 50A (Stobaeus 1.142, 2–6).
47. *THP* 51B (Stobaeus, 1.106, 5–23).
48. *LS* p. 63.
49. *THP* 51B (Stobaeus 1.106, 5–23); I have opted for "exist" to translate ὑπάρχειν, here and in the next quotation, rather than Long and Sedley's choice of "belong."
50. *THP* 51B (Stobaeus 1.106, 5–23).
51. *LS* p. 162.
52. *THP* p. 51C (Plutarch, *On Common Conceptions*, 1081c–1082a).
53. *LS* p. 6.
54. Ibid. 5.
55. Deleuze, *Negotiations*, 5–6; emphasis added.
56. Victor Goldschmidt, *Le Système Stoïcien et l'Idée de Temps* [Goldschmidt], p. 39.
57. John Sellars also points to this, in "*Aiôn* and *Chronos*" ["*AC*"], p. 17. The passage Goldschmidt has in mind is Marcus Aurelius, *Meditations*, 4.3.
58. In both *Meditations* 2.14 and 10.31 Marcus uses the phrase "in infinite time [ἐν τῷ ἀπείρῳ χρόνῳ]."
59. Pierre Hadot offers a similar critique of Goldschmidt (Pierre Hadot, *The Inner Citadel: The Meditations of Marcus Aurelius*, pp. 131–7). Sellars has a helpful list of the various instances of χρόνος and αἰών in the *Meditations* at "*AC*" p. 18.
60. *LS* p. 61.
61. *LS* pp. 5, 61.

62. "Consequently no time is present exactly, but it is broadly [κατὰ πλάτος] said to be so"; *THP* 51B.
63. Sellars records the various ways scholars have translated this phrase, including both Goldschmidt and Hadot ("*AC*" p. 15).
64. *DR* p. 237.
65. *LS* pp. 164, 168.
66. Goldschmidt p. 39.
67. This discussion appears mostly in Series 3–12 of *The Logic of Sense*, but especially in the examination of the four dimensions of the proposition: denotation, manifestation, signification, and sense.
68. *LS* p. 182. For more on Deleuze's account of denotation, as well as the corresponding features of the proposition – manifestation, signification, sense – see the "Third Series of the Proposition," *LS* pp. 12–22.
69. Goldschmidt p. 39.
70. *LS* p. 64.
71. Ibid. p. xiv.

BIBLIOGRAPHY

Aristotle, *Aristotelis: Physica*, ed. W. D. Ross (Oxford: Clarendon Press, 1951).
Blanchot, M., *L'Espace Littéraire* (Paris: Gallimard, 1995).
Bréhier, É., *La Théorie des Incorporels dans l'Ancien Stoicism*, 9th edn (Paris: Vrin, [1928] 1997).
Cicero, M. T., *On Academic Scepticism*, trans. C. Brittain (Indianapolis: Hackett, 2006).
Colombat, A. P., "November 4, 1995: Deleuze's Death as an Event," *Man and World*, 29 (1996), pp. 235–49.
de Harven, V., *The Coherence of Stoic Ontology* (Berkeley: University of California: http://guides.lib.berkeley.edu/dissertations_theses, 2012).
Deleuze, G., *Difference and Repetition*, trans. P. Patton (New York: Columbia University Press, [1968] 1994).
Deleuze, G., *The Logic of Sense*, trans. M. Lester and C. Stivale, ed. C. V. Boundas (New York: Columbia University Press, [1969] 1990).
Deleuze, G., *Negotiations: 1972–1990*, trans. M. Joughin (New York: Columbia University Press, [1990] 1995).
Deleuze, G., "The Exhausted," trans. A. Uhlmann, in G. Deleuze, *Essays Critical and Clinical*, ed. D. W. Smith and M. A. Greco (London: Verso, 1998), pp. 152–74.
Deleuze, G. and Guattari, F., *Anti-Oedipus: Capitalism and Schizophrenia*, trans. R. Hurley, M. Seem, and H. R. Lane (Minneapolis: University of Minnesota Press, [1972] 1983).
Diogenes Laertius, *Lives of Eminent Philosophers*, trans. R. D. Hicks (London: Heinemann, 1925).
Goldschmidt, V., *Le Système Stoïcien et l'Idée de Temps* (Paris: Vrin, 1953).

Hadot, P., *The Inner Citadel: The Meditations of Marcus Aurelius*, trans. M. Chase (Cambridge, MA: Harvard University Press, [1993] 1998).

Long, A. A. and Sedley, D. (eds. and trans.), *The Hellenistic Philosophers*, 2 vols (Cambridge: Cambridge University Press, 1987).

Marcus, A., *Meditations*, ed. and trans. C. R. Haines (Cambridge, MA: Harvard University Press, 1916).

Meinong, A., *Über Möglichkeit und Wahrscheinlichkeit: Beiträge zur Gegenstandstheorie und Erkenntnistheorie* (Leipzig: J. A. Barth, 1913).

Plato, *Complete Works*, ed. J. M. Cooper (Indianapolis: Hackett, 1997).

Romm, J., *Dying Every Day: Seneca at the Court of Nero* (New York: Vintage, 2014).

Sellars, J., *Stoicism* (Berkeley: University of California Press, 2006).

Sellars, J., "*Aiôn* and *Chronos*: Deleuze and the Stoic Theory of Time" (originally in *Collapse*, 3 (2007), pp. 177–205); accessed at http://www.academia.edu/9816442/Ai%C3%B4n_and_Chronos_Deleuze_and_the_Stoic_Theory_of_Time, retrieved 2015, pp. 1–26.

Seneca, *Selected Philosophical Letters*, trans. B. Inwood (Oxford: Clarendon, 2007).

Spinoza, B., *A Spinoza Reader: The Ethics and Other Works*, ed. and trans. E. Curley (Princeton: Princeton University Press, 1994).

Tacitus, *The Annals*, trans. A. J. Woodman (Indianapolis: Hackett, 2004).

CHAPTER 16

Contingency and Skepticism in Agamben's Thought

Gert-Jan van der Heiden

Skepticism is often understood in terms of its epistemological implications alone, namely that we cannot have any certain knowledge. Throughout the history of philosophy, skepticism has been an important partner in conversation for exactly its epistemological position – if only to reject what many consider its unwanted outcomes. In the work of Giorgio Agamben, however, we find another way of retrieving some of the basic terms and concerns of ancient skepticism for ontology. Agamben shows that the skeptic's philosophical vocabulary allows us to articulate an alternative to both the affirmation of being characteristic of ontotheology, as well as the negation of being that characterizes contemporary forms of nihilism.

In this essay, I explore how Agamben retrieves ancient skepticism and how this skepticism informs some of his basic concepts. While Agamben sometimes explicitly refers to the influence of skepticism, at other occasions, his arguments and thoughts are merely marked by several skeptical traces which need to be brought out in a reading of his texts; it is worthwhile to consider both. To examine the skeptical heritage of Agamben's work and its implication for, especially, his accounts of contingency and potentiality which form the heart of his ontological concerns, in this contribution I discuss three different elements: (1) the skeptic formulae, and in particular Agamben's account of ἐποχή and οὐ μᾶλλον; (2) the skeptic passage that may be traced in his usage of the word εὐπορία, which requires some contextualization to understand its meaning and its skeptic kinship; (3) the skeptic overtones in Agamben's reading of the Pauline notion of καταργεῖν, deactivation or suspension.

THE SKEPTIC FORMULA

One of the most important references to skepticism can be found in Agamben's essay "Bartleby, or on Contingency."[1] This complicated essay offers a reading of Herman Melville's story *Bartleby, the Scrivener* in which this story becomes a special kind of experiment, an experiment in ontology. As Agamben explains:

> Not only science, but also poetry and thinking conduct experiments. These experiments do not simply concern the truth or falsity of hypotheses, the occurrence or nonoccurrence of something, as in scientific experiments; rather, they call into question Being itself, before or beyond its determination as true or false. These experiments are without truth, for truth is what is at issue in them.[2]

If we carefully consider this quote, we see immediately how Agamben under-scores the priority of a particular ἐποχή, a suspension of judgement, in relation to the project he undertakes in this essay. Science is focused on judgements concerning the truth or the falsity of certain propositions and hypotheses, or judgements concerning the existence and non-existence of the beings and phenomena it investigates. Science carries out and sets up its experiments so that it can attain this specific goal: to arrive at a judgement. By contrast, the experiments of poetry and philosophy do not have this aim. Rather, the proper domain or place of their experiments can only be reached by a preliminary ἐποχή, namely by the suspension of this quest for truth or falsity. Poetic and philosophical experiments depend on such a suspension not because they are not interested in truth but rather because truth is not presupposed in them as something about which one can judge, as it is in the experiments of science. Or as Agamben puts it: truth is "at issue" in poetic and philosophical experi-ments. Thus poetry and philosophy also examine nature and being, but they do so in different modes than science does. This is the specific role of the sus-pension of judgement that Agamben invokes here: by it, philosophy and poetry aim to enter a domain inaccessible for the sciences, that is for that dimension of human understanding that aims at knowledge. Although skepticism is not mentioned in this particular passage, the skeptical vein of this remark is clear.

According to Agamben, these experiments of thinking and poetry aim at a change of one's mode of existence:

> Whoever submits himself to these experiments jeopardizes not so much the truth of his own statements as the very mode of his existence; he undergoes an anthropological change that is just as decisive in the context of the individual's natural history as the liberation of the hand by the erect position was for the primate or as was, for the reptile, the transformation of limbs that changed it into a bird.[3]

This reference to change shows that what is at stake in these experiments is not the assessment of what is, but rather the possibility of transformation of what we are. This possibility simultaneously brings into play both "what is" and "what is not" in the form of "what can be." One's existence, to put it differ-ently, certainly has some characteristics that can be discovered and examined by the sciences; yet, it is the task of poetry and philosophy to consider our existence not only in light of the characteristics we have, but also in light of the possibility of us lacking these characteristics. The experiments of stories and thoughts thus affect one's dispositions and habits: ἔθος and ἕξις are at stake in poetic and philosophical experiments not as what is already given, ready to be examined, but rather as what is aimed at, as what can be affected and changed. The configuration of human action unfolded by a story may, in a fundamental way, change the actions and behaviors to which the reader is inclined. The configuration of thought unfolded by a philosophy may, likewise, transform the thoughts and convictions to which the reader is inclined. For Agamben, when he speaks about ontology, the questions of disposition and habit are always co-implied.

What type of experiment does ancient skepticism give rise to? To move towards an answer to this question, let me offer another passage, which describes the distinction between the scientific experiment and the poetic experiment, but which also makes a direct reference to ancient skepticism:

> If what is at issue in a scientific experiment can be defined by the question "Under what conditions can something occur or not occur, be true or be false?" what is at issue in Melville's story can instead be formulated in a question of the following form: "Under what conditions can something occur *and* (that is, at the same time) not occur, be true *no more than not be true*?" [. . .] If no one dreams of verifying the scrivener's formula, [that is, "I would prefer not to,"] this is because experiments without truth concern not the actual existence of nonexistence of a thing but exclusively its potentiality. And potentiality, insofar as it can be or not be, is by definition withdrawn from both truth conditions and, prior to the action of "the strongest of all principles," the principle of contradiction.
>
> In first philosophy, a being that can both be and not be is said to be contingent.[4]

Here Agamben makes a number of important connections. First, he shows that the question of whether one should judge or suspend one's judgement need not be conceived as an epistemological question nor as a question concerning the limits and finitude of the human cognitive apparatus. The epistemological approach, which restricts suspension to knowledge and beliefs, assumes that the reality of things and occurrences is fixed and that the only possible complications to this fixity reside in our cognitive access to reality.

Of course, one can approach this question in this way, but Agamben argues here that the skeptical ἐποχή is ultimately, and in its original inclination, concerned not so much with the limits of human cognition but rather with developing a different attitude to exceeding these limits. Thus, despite its epistemological resonance, the question of judgement or suspension of judgement calls for an ontological investigation – at least if we want to understand the underlying ontological issue reflected in this difference between judgement and its suspension. To a certain extent, this need not surprise us: if our capacities to know or to understand make any sense, they should be guided and instructed by the reality that gives itself to be understood; otherwise, Being either becomes merely the product of our cognitive capacities, or it can only be accounted for as pure inaccessibility. In the above quote, Agamben offers a clear account of the distinction between judgement and suspension in ontological terms: whereas the former examines existence in its actuality (a being that either is or is not – a proposition that is either true or false), the latter has access to existence in its potentiality or contingency (a being that can both be and not be – a proposition that can be true no more than not be true).[5]

It is the formula of the "no more than," or οὐ μᾶλλον, that establishes the direct link with ancient skepticism. Οὐ μᾶλλον is used in ancient skepticism to express the indifference between the two alternatives that a judgement offers: true no more than false.[6] According to Agamben, the suspension of judgement with which this formula coincides is not only a form of indifference for the skeptics, but instead the skeptics viewed it "as an experience of possibility or potentiality."[7]

Agamben is here referring to the use of δύναμις by Sextus Empiricus in *Outlines of Pyrrhonism* I.8; yet, his translation significantly differs from the usual one. He translates the first portion of *Outlines* I.8 as a skeptical definition of δύναμις: "The Skeptics understand δύναμις as any opposition between sensibles or appearances and judgments or intelligibles."[8] By contrast, standard translations suggest that δύναμις is nothing but the special capacity or potentiality of skepticism itself: "Skepticism is an ability [δύναμις] to set out oppositions among things which appear and are thought of in any way at all."[9] Whether this difference of translation is important depends, once more, on our conception of the relation between epistemology and ontology. If we understand dimension in epistemological terms alone, then the usual translation, which brackets the ontological register that Agamben includes, is adequate. However, if one understands the epistemological capacity of skepticism as depending on an ontological component, that is that skepticism touches on a genuine feature of reality and leads to an attitude towards the world that captures this basic aspect of the world, then the skeptic's δύναμις to oppose (which leads to the suspension of judgement) aims at δύναμις in the world, one that "shows itself on the threshold between Being and non-Being, between sensible and intelligible, between word and thing."[10] Hence, for Agamben, the skeptic's capacity to affirm neither the sensible nor the intelligible has δύναμις, as what appears on the threshold between sensible and intelligible, as its proper object. Yet, granting that the skeptical δύναμις is the ability to attune ourselves to what happens or "shows itself" on the threshold between sensible and intelligible or between being and non-being, the question remains: is Agamben justified in identifying the object of the skeptical δύναμις with δύναμις itself?

Before answering this question (to which we return in the upcoming sections), let us first analyze how Agamben develops the discovery of δύναμις, as what one finds on the threshold between being and non-being, in a specific conception of ontology of the contingent. Like a few other contemporary authors (we find a similar gesture, for example, in Heidegger and Meillassoux), Agamben shows how this understanding of skepticism and its δύναμις transform Leibniz's famous principle of sufficient reason, which Agamben translates as "there is a reason for which something does rather than does not exist."[11] The term *potius* – "from *potis*, which means 'more powerful,'"[12] and which is translated as "rather" – connects potentiality to reason and subordinates it to Being, Agamben argues. The skeptical formula of οὐ μᾶλλον or "no more than" emancipates Leibniz's "rather" from its subordination to Being.[13] The skeptic formula οὐ μᾶλλον, and more precisely in its form of "Being no more than Non-Being," thus relocates δύναμις. The skeptic interest in ontology neither affirms Being (and the "onto-theo-logical ceremony" that goes hand in hand with it) nor Non-Being (and the "ungrateful guest" of nihilism which accompanies it).[14] The skeptic ἐποχή detaches δύναμις from the primacy of either Being or Non-Being and instead locates it on the threshold of both. This, as Agamben concludes his discussion of skepticism, opens up a new ontology of potentiality and contingency, which he characterizes as follows: "To be capable, in pure potentiality, to bear the 'no more than' beyond Being and Nothing, fully experiencing the impotent possibility that exceeds both."[15]

Yet, what is exactly experienced in this way? Which transformation of existence is at stake in this philosophical experiment of skepticism? In which sense is this an impotent possibility? Why is δύναμις the term to capture this transformation, and why is it the true object of the skeptic capacity to suspend judgement? And how is this related to a specific conception of contingency? Each of these questions requires a deepening of the ontology of potentiality Agamben here announces.

THE SKEPTICAL PASSAGE

At one point in the essay *"Pardes,"* where Agamben reflects on his relation to Derrida's work, he uses the word εὐπορία (transliterated to *euporia*): "The aporias of self-reference thus do not find their solution here; rather, they are dislocated and (according to the Platonic suggestion) transformed into *euporias.*"[16] The idea of the *aporia* (or ἀπορία) is central to Derrida's work and concerns non-passage, a situation in which one cannot pass, in which the road is blocked, obstructed, destroyed, or simply absent. Whereas *aporia* in Derrida's work often is discussed at the point of a dislocating or displacing what one thought was a passage, Agamben suggests in this quote that ἀπορία itself may also be dislocated and, by this, be transformed into an εὐπορία, a good passage, an ease or facility of going through.

To understand the stakes of this transformation of ἀπορία into εὐπορία, a clarification of the philosophical background of these terms may be beneficial. The combination of ἀπορία and εὐπορία – or rather of ἀπορεῖν and εὐπορεῖν – plays a systematic role in Aristotle's conception of the reflection, investigation, or discussion required by first philosophy, as he explains at the beginning of *Metaphysics* B.[17] Here Aristotle argues that a good understanding of a topic requires that one engages with its difficulties or perplexities (ἀπορία) in order to find a way through (εὐπορία) them: only the one who has thus been engaged with the ἀπορίαι of certain problems and found a way out truly understands. One may even understand this conception of the relation between ἀπορία and εὐπορία in terms of Aristotle's understanding of the relation between dialectics and first philosophy: whereas dialectics, as a sort of critical thought, is valuable for its capacity to find the ἀπορίαι of given opinions, it does not attain the true goal of its own enterprise, namely to find a way out of these ἀπορίαι and to enter a state of proper knowledge. In this sense, εὐπορία is nothing but the passageway from dialectics to first philosophy.

If we read Plato as preparing this Aristotelian insight, and we consider "the Platonic suggestion" of which Agamben speaks in "*Pardes*" in light of this understanding of εὐπορία, then Agamben's critique of Derrida would be nothing but a return to the classical metaphysical perspective. Yet, due to its ambiguity, the Platonic dialogues have given rise to more than one descendent: not only to the classical metaphysical point of view of Aristotle, which in a certain sense has become normative in the history of metaphysics, but also to a skeptical heritage. Not only is there a historical link between Plato and skepticism – insofar as Plato's Academy turned skeptical in its middle period under the guidance of Arcesilaus – but there is also a systematic link, as one may perceive a certain skeptical tendency in Socratic dialectic as a quest for ἀπορίαι.

Let us apply these considerations to the terminology of ἀπορία and εὐπορία. In fact, in Plato's dialogues, there are a number of passages in which ἀπορία and εὐπορία come together. In some of them, it seems that an Aristotelian point of view is anticipated. Consider, for example, the following passage: "It is these problems of the one and many, but not those others, Protarchus, that cause all sorts of difficulties [ἀπορίας] if they are not properly settled, but promise progress [εὐπορίας] if they are."[18] A proper treatment of the difficulties promises a way out of the problems – and one might indeed interpret this εὐπορία as leading to the Aristotelian standpoint of a first philosophy. Yet, there are also passages in which it is clear that a more skeptic reversal of the relation between ἀπορία and εὐπορία is brought into play. Consider the following two examples: "For I myself do not have the answer [εὐπορῶν] when I perplex [ἀπορεῖν] others, but I am more perplexed [ἀπορῶν] than anyone when I cause perplexity [ἀπορεῖν] in others."[19] And: "Keep quiet, Hippias. We could well be thinking we're in the clear [εὐπορίᾳ] again, when we've gotten stuck [ἀπορίᾳ] on the same point about the fine as we did a moment ago."[20] The first passage, from the *Meno*, indicates that the difficulties Socrates creates do not stem from some superior knowledge, but rather from his superior being-perplexed. The second example, from the *Greater Hippias*, suggests that, when we think we have found a way out, we might actually find ourselves in an even more problematic position, since we have not recognized the ἀπορία in our supposed εὐπορία. In both cases, the aim of dialectics is not to overcome the ἀπορία but rather to find the ἀπορία since what one takes to be an εὐπορία, a way out, is actually a form of self-deceit. In these two examples, dialectics concerns the dialectician's capacity to find the ἀπορία and to find the opposition that obstructs judgement in the discussion at hand.

If we read Agamben's reference to "the Platonic suggestion" in this way, at first we seem to have a big problem: after all, it seems that we lost the transformation of ἀπορία into a εὐπορία since there is no way out of the ἀπορία. We only have dialectics' way towards the ἀπορία. Indeed, this is our situation, so long as we insist on understanding εὐπορία in the Aristotelian sense of the passage to first philosophy and the way to true knowledge. In light of this interpretation of εὐπορία, to remain on the level of the ἀπορία is to fail to acquire the true end of philosophical inquiry. Yet, if we approach ἀπορία, not from the Aristotelian perspective, but from a more skeptic perspective, another picture arises. The insistence on and persistence of the ἀπορία is not simply a failure, but rather is a εὐπορία in another sense and in another direction: not as the passage to first philosophy, but as a passage to another domain.[21]

Let us consider this in further detail. The skeptical δύναμις, the capacity to find ἀπορίαι and to suspend judgements, opens up a domain in which something unexpected and unforeseeable happens to the skeptic. Sextus offers a beautiful image of this other passageway, which I quote here in full:

> The Sceptic, in fact, had the same experience which is said to have befallen the painter Apelles. Once, they say, when he was painting a horse and wished to represent in the painting the horse's foam, he was so unsuccessful that he gave up the attempt and flung at the picture the sponge on which he used to wipe the paints off his brush, and the mark of the sponge produced the effect of a horse's foam. So, too, the Sceptics were in hopes of gaining quietude by means of a decision regarding the disparity of objects of sense and of thought, and being unable to effect this they suspended judgment; and they found that quietude, as if by chance, followed upon their suspense, even as a shadow follows its substance.[22]

The skeptic's quest thus begins as a quest for a solution to the difficulties it confronts, and sets out on an inquiry that seeks the Aristotelian εὐπορία as its goal. Yet, in its efforts, the skeptic is utterly unsuccessful – at least from the perspective of this goal – and only finds ἀπορίαι. Having at first described skepticism in terms of the ability to oppose, in this passage Sextus describes this the skeptic's capacity as an incapacity, an inability (μὴ δυνηθέντες): the skeptic's power is indeed, as Agamben suggests, an "impotent possibility"[23] since the skeptics are incapable of finding a way out. Yet they embrace this incapacity in their suspension of judgement. To articulate it in Agamben's vocabulary, the characteristic capacity or potentiality (δύναμις as δύνασθαι, as in *Outlines*

I.9) of the skeptics is the capacity or potential not to find a way out of the ἀπορίαι.[24] Yet this incapacity that only finds ἀπορίαι or non-passages turns out to be the skeptical passageway to quietude (ἀταραξία). The opening of this other passage, this other εὐπορία, which is the suspension of judgement, befalls the skeptic by chance and is comparable to a shadow (σκιά) that follows its body (σῶμα). Thus this other, non-Aristotelian εὐπορία is the other side, the shadow of the ἀπορία: it is the ἐποχή of the skeptic. It is the potential not to find a way out (in the Aristotelian sense) that opens up the skeptical way to ἀταραξία.

Reflecting on this discussion, we thus find two different approaches to εὐπορία (both different from the Aristotelian one), and both of them need to be taken into account when we try to understand what Agamben says in his brief but profound comment on Derrida's approach to ἀπορίαι. First, following the skeptic or critical dimension of certain Platonic dialogues, an ἀπορία is a way out of a particular self-deception; while the "pre-aporetic" εὐπορία is marked by self-deceit, an ἀπορία is in a certain sense the true εὐπορία itself since it liberates one from deception.[25] Second, there is the skeptical account of εὐπορία as the shadow of ἀπορία, emphasizing how a seemingly failed enterprise can be caught by the unexpected surprise of another passage; rather than being "pre-" or "post-aporetic," this εὐπορία, as the shadow of ἀπορία, might best be simply called an aporetic (ἄπορος) εὐπορία. This, it seems, is the type of εὐπορία Agamben has in mind in his comment on Derrida: for on the skeptical understanding it is the ἀπορία itself that is the εὐπορία. Moreover, in the skeptical account, the εὐπορία follows the ἀπορία as something unexpected, something that befalls the skeptics in a situation where they experience their incapacity to judge. Hence this experience indeed deserves to be called an experience of potentiality and contingency: the skeptical δύναμις, understood as the power not to judge, stays far from its Aristotelian actualization – from the Aristotelian εὐπορία – but exactly in this way, the skeptic has an experience of δύναμις itself. That is to say, skeptics not only experience ἀταραξία itself, but they also experience the chance of ἀταραξία unexpectedly befalling them. In this way we see how the particular skeptical attitude of thinking – with its δύναμις to reach an ἐποχή, its potential not to pass judgement – is the attitude that is required to experience δύναμις as pure potentiality and contingency. It is this ἔθος of thinking that goes hand in hand with the new ontology of δύναμις that is thus created.[26]

A SKEPTICAL PAUL?

The third and last skeptical moment of Agamben's work can be encountered in what might seem an unlikely place: his engagement with the Letters of Saint Paul. Without going as far as to argue that Paul is really a skeptic, I contend that some of the basic features of Agamben's reading of Paul are akin to what he discerns in the skeptic's discourse and in the skeptical discovery of another passageway out of an ἀπορία. If scholars link Paul's discourse to any Hellenistic school, they usually associate it with Stoicism (and for good reasons); but this reference plays no role in Agamben's discussion of Paul in *The Time that Remains*. Moreover, at important and strategic points, it is also clear that Agamben is not especially interested in the eschatological moments of Paul's letters (which, for Paul, seem to be of fundamental importance). Rather, Agamben focuses on Paul's description and understanding of the time of the "now," a time of crisis – a crisis of the law, of the world, of the people of God, and so on. The question is: how is this crisis not merely nihilistic – the mere destruction of the law, the annihilation of the world, the decay of the people of God, and so on – but how can it offer, in its shadow, a way out?[27] This particular focus allows Agamben to trace features in Paul that are similar to the ones he traces in skepticism.[28]

To make this similarity as clear as possible, let me first offer an Agambian reformulation of the skeptic account of the suspension of judgement. A philosophical dialogue – discussing a topic and its difficulties or ἀπορίαι – aims at a solution of these difficulties. A dialogue works or functions properly if it offers a way out of these ἀπορίαι by means of a solution and towards proper knowledge (that is, the Aristotelian case). By insisting on the ἀπορία and through suspending judgement, the skeptic interrupts this normal and proper functioning; in light of this functioning, the suspension of judgement renders inoperative dialogue as the quest for the proper judgement; it deactivates this dialogical activity. Along with authors such as Jean-Luc Nancy and Maurice Blanchot, Agamben shares an interest in this particular inoperativity that is traced not only in the dialogical inquiries of philosophy, but also in a number of other domains. Yet what is unique in Agamben's thought is how he understands this inoperativity to be something fortunate, as becomes apparent in his account of Paul.[29]

This reformulation of the ἐποχή in terms of inoperativity is helpful when turning to Paul, for the concept of suspension plays a central role in Agamben's interpretastion of Paul. For the purposes of this essay, I limit myself to one (important) example, namely Agamben's attention to the verb καταργεῖν (*katargein*) in Paul's letters. Καταργεῖν is a verb that appears more than twenty times in these letters and, in particular, in the following well-known passage of the *First Letter to the Corinthians*:

> But God chose the foolish things of the world to shame the wise; God chose the weak things of the world to shame the strong. God chose the lowly things of this world and the despised things – and the things that are not – to nullify [καταργήσῃ] the things that are.[30]

One might say that this is indeed one of the more skeptical passages of Paul's, in which the value and the capacity of the wisdom of the world (τὴν σοφίαν τοῦ κόσμου)[31] is doubted, and in which preference is given to what the world deems foolish, base, and despicable. Paul's diatribe against the world and its order leads him, in this passage, to claim that God prefers the lowlifes of this world in order "to nullify the things that are." The verb that is used here, καταργεῖν, to nullify, must be understood correctly. Καταργεῖν does not indicate a simple destruction of the world and its order, since it is not the antonym of ποεῖν. Agamben writes: "As we have seen, this term (which is prudently rendered by Jerome as *evacuari*, 'to empty out') does not mean 'to annihilate, to destroy' [. . .] the positive equivalent of *katargeō* is not *poieō*, but *energeō*, 'I put to work, I activate.'"[32] Καταργεῖν thus expresses something like "to put out of work" or "to deactivate." With this particular sense of the verb in mind, Agamben connects καταργεῖν and κατάργησις to suspension and even translates them as "to suspend" and "suspension" or as "to deactivate" and "deactivation."

Applied to the above quote from Paul, this particular sense of καταργεῖν implies something like the following.[33] The world and its order are marked by distinctions between the strong and the weak, the rich and the poor, those who are something in this order and those who are nothing in this order. In 1 Cor. 1: 27–8, Paul does not simply describe the annihilation of this world and its order but rather the deactivation and suspension of it. This brings into play a particular indecision, which is reminiscent of the skeptic's: rather than destroying the order and either not replacing it or substituting some other well-estab-lished order, the suspension of the order expressed by the verb καταργεῖν puts the given order in another perspective. In particular, through the suspension of oppositions by means of which this order operates, the world is viewed in light of both its contingency and its potentiality. While people tend to comply with this order because they see it as permanent, its suspension does not destroy the world but rather discloses it in its transience. This means two things at once: first, it means that the present order or form of the world has a transitory, con-tingent character – as Paul later insists in 1 Cor. 7: 31 when he writes that the present form of the world, τὸ σχῆμα τοῦ κόσμου, is passing away. However, it also means that what is considered to be nothing is given back its potentiality to be: what is not can yet be otherwise than nothing.

Agamben insists on this reference to potentiality in his account of καταργεῖν, and he contends that Paul's use of the term can be understood as an intervention on the philosophical, Aristotelian thought of the relation between ἐνεργεία and δύναμις, actuality and potentiality.[34] Hence, καταργεῖν is not only the antonym of ἐνεργεῖν, but is, as such, also a concept Paul uses to deconstruct the Aristo-telian scheme of actuality and potentiality. In particular, καταργεῖν as "a taking out of the act" gives rise to another way in which potentiality may realize itself: "Potentiality passes over into actuality and meets up with its *telos*, not in the form of force or *ergon*, but in the form of *astheneia*, weakness."[35] One might be inclined to object: what would an actualization without actuality or work be? In which sense can one think of the τέλος of which Paul speaks without a rela-tion to the Aristotelian δύναμις/ἐνεργεία scheme? Yet, rather than trying to come to terms with such questions, Agamben is solely interested in the strangeness exhibited by Paul's rhetoric, which aims at deactivating the Aristotelian thought of the δύναμις/ἐνεργεία scheme by bringing into play the notion of ἀσθένεια. To understand what this new δύναμις/ἀσθένεια or potentiality/weakness scheme means, one should note that Agamben immediately connects the Pauline notion of weakness to the notion of impotentiality or incapacity (ἀδυναμία). Agamben thinks ἀδυναμία not as simple impossibility but rather as a way to "maintain a kind of potentiality." He explains in "On Potentiality" that "to be potential means: to be one's own lack, *to be in relation to one's own incapacity*. Beings that exist in the mode of potentiality *are capable of their own impotentiality*; and only in this way do they become potential."[36] By connecting impotentiality to weakness, we see the return of a structure similar to the one we found in skepticism. The incapacity of the skeptic to arrive at a judgement is at the same time the skeptic's capacity to not judge and to suspend judgement (and thus to arrive at ἀταραξία as the graceful shadow of ἐποχή). Likewise, in Paul's strange rhetoric, which is not bound by the Aristotelian linking of δύναμις, ἐνεργεία, and τέλος, potentiality is said to find its τέλος in its own incapacity or weakness. This incapacity or weakness is, in fact, Agamben argues, the power, potential, or capacity not to pass into actuality:

> According to Paul, messianic power does not wear itself out in its
> *ergon*; rather, it remains powerful in it in the form of weakness.
> Messianic *dynamis* is, in this sense, constitutively "weak" – but it is
> precisely through its weakness that it may enact its effects – "God
> has chosen weak things of the world to shame the things which are
> mighty" (1 Cor. 1: 27).[37]

The reference here to 1 Cor. 1: 27 (quoted above) indicates two things. First, impotentiality or weakness is in fact a potentiality, namely as the potential not to affirm or be integrated into the order of the world. Second, weakness, as potentiality, truly deactivates this order. It is exactly for this reason that God chooses the weak things and the things that are not (τὰ μὴ ὄντα). The weak and the things that are worth nothing cannot actualize their potential in the order of the world; thus they are exemplary of a weakness that, in light of the καταργεῖν (the suspension or deactivation of the existing order), turns out to be a potentiality, namely the potential not to affirm this order.

These final remarks also make clear that the suspension of the order of the world should not be understood as an effort on the part of Paul to simply inverse the existing order, giving riches to the poor and power to the weak. Rather, the transitory nature of the world, which is disclosed by the suspension of its order, is otherwise denied in and by this order; this ordered world claims permanence for itself and, therefore, it does not discern the crisis it is in. Paul's καταργεῖν aims at tearing down this form of (self-)deception of the order of the world, and thus at showing that, in a certain sense, all things are in the same situation as the lowlifes, the poor and the weak. In this Pauline logic that connects δύναμις to ἀσθένεια, it is exactly to the weak that potentiality is returned by the suspension of the order of the world.[38]

THE ONTOLOGY OF POTENTIALITY

Skepticism, as I noted at the beginning of this essay, is usually discussed in terms of its epistemological impact and, more precisely, the claim that we cannot attain certain knowledge. Agamben, however, notes that the philosophical vocabulary of ancient skepticism is not developed solely for an epistemological position, but, perhaps more significantly, concerns a specific ontology of δύναμις. This ontology, as his account of philosophical and poetic experiments indicates, goes hand in hand with a particular conception of δύναμις according to one's ἔθος and habits. If we consider the particulars of this ontology of δύναμις or potentiality, it is clear that it is indeed developed through skeptical means. I have discussed how Agamben's approach to ἐποχή, the suspension of judgement, and the concept of inoperativity all belong to a particular skeptical heritage. The skeptics, as Sextus already indicates, are the ones that "keep on searching."[39] This quest continues because the skeptic cannot find proper and stable answers, but only problems and difficulties; hence the skeptic school is also called aporetic (ἀπορητική).[40] This failure to arrive at proper knowledge deactivates and suspends a particular conception of philosophical thinking. However, as Agamben argues, this process, which is a failure from the Aristotelian point of view, is not so when considered from the skeptic's perspective: this process depends on and discloses a particular conception of δύναμις. The incapacity to reach a conclusion is the potential not to participate in the order of an Aristotelian first philosophy – much like the way in which Paul describes the incapacity of the powerless as the potential not to participate in the order the world prescribes. This is the δύναμις of the skeptic in a double sense. As *genitivus subjectivus*, it is the disposition of the skeptic expressed in the Agambian formula of "the potential not to . . .," as in the potential not to affirm or deny. At the same time, however, the insistence on this potential not to . . ., its becoming a *habitus* or ἔθος of skeptical thinking itself, leads neither to nothing nor to mere failure. By accident and chance, it discloses another ontological conception of δύναμις. As *genitivus objectivus*, the δύναμις of the skeptic offers a conception of potentiality that is no longer subordinated to actuality. Rather, as Agamben reads in Paul, it leads to a conception in which weakness or impotentiality is power. Thus it is in the form of this particular weakness in which δύναμις is given back to what is (as well as what is not).

It is important to note that in both the skeptical and the Pauline case, this emphasis on the importance and power of weakness or failure is not simply a counter-model either to the Aristotelian conception of an εὐπορία out of the encountered ἀπορίαι or to the concept of ἐνεργεία as the goal of δύναμις. A counter-model suggests that one might choose. Rather, the skeptic's account of philosophical inquiry, as well as the Pauline account of the present order of the world, both depart from an experience of crisis and ἀπορία. The order of the world cannot maintain its permanence, and the ἀπορίαι presented to thought do not allow an Aristotelian way out. It is in response to this experience of a crisis of thought and world that a new reappraisal of weakness is to be found:

by making this weakness or incapacity one's habit, and by insisting on the potential not to be integrated into a particular mode of thinking or a particular order of the world, another power is generated. One may call this a power of resistance to the normal sense of εὐπορία – finding solutions to given problems, or negotiating with the given order of the world – and at the same time it is a power of chance or contingency which is granted another εὐπορία.

NOTES

1. Giorgio Agamben, "Bartleby, or On Contingency" ["Bartleby"].
2. Ibid. p. 260. Here I only develop Agamben's description of the experimental role of stories and philosophy in line with the philosophical experiment of skepticism. For a more extensive consideration of how Agamben uses Bartleby, see Gert-Jan van der Heiden, "Reading Bartleby, Reading Ion: On a Difference between Agamben and Nancy."
3. "Bartleby" p. 260.
4. Ibid. pp. 260–1; unless otherwise noted words in brackets are my own.
5. An interesting discussion may arise at this point between the attention to contingency both in Agamben's work and in Quentin Meillassoux, *After Finitude*, and their differing accounts of the principle of contradiction with respect to the contingent.
6. See Sextus Empiricus, *Outlines of Pyrrhonism* [*Outlines*], trans. R. G. Bury, I.188–90. In his essay, Agamben connects this skeptical formula of οὐ μᾶλλον to Bartleby's formula "I would prefer not to" (see "Bartleby" p. 253–9).
7. Agamben, "Bartleby, or On Contingency," p. 257. He derives this from a quotation from Sextus Empiricus which he translates as follows:

> The Skeptics understand potentiality-possibility [*dynamis*] as any opposition between sensibles and intelligibles. By virtue of the equivalence found in the opposition between words and things, we thus reach the *epokhē*, the suspension, which is a condition in which we can neither posit nor negate, accept nor refuse. (Ibid.; bracketed insertion included by Agamben)

In the Loeb edition, the same quotation is translated as follows:

> Scepticism is an ability, or mental attitude, which opposes appearances to judgments in any way whatsoever, with the result that, owing to the equipollence of the objects and reasons thus opposed, we are brought firstly to a state of mental suspense and next to a state of "unperturbedness" or quietude. (*Outlines* I.8)

Sextus continues: "Now we call it an 'ability' [δύναμιν] not in any subtle sense, but simply in respect of its 'being able' [δύνασθαι]" (ibid. I.9).

8. Modified from "Bartleby" p. 257; translation of *Outlines* I.8.

9. Sextus Empiricus, *Outlines of Scepticism*, trans. Julia Annas and Jonathan Barnes, I.8.

10. Agamben, "Bartleby, or On Contingency," p. 257.

11. "Bartleby" p. 258.

12. Ibid.

13. "The formula emancipates potentiality [. . .] from both its connection to a 'reason' (*ratio*) and its subordination to Being" (ibid.).

14. Ibid. p. 259.

15. Ibid.

16. Giorgio Agamben, "*Pardes*: The Writing of Potentiality," p. 217. There are a few other occurrences of this term in Agamben's *oeuvre*: see Leland de la Durantaye, *Giorgio Agamben*, p. 134.

17. Aristotle, *Metaphysics*, 995a24–b4 (see *The Complete Works*, ed. J. Barnes). According to Heidegger, this form of reflection is διαλέγεσθαι; see Martin Heidegger, *Grundbegriffe der Aristotelischen Philosophie*, pp. 158–61.

18. Plato, *Philebus*, 15b–c; all translations of Plato are from *Complete Works*, ed. John Cooper.

19. Plato, *Meno*, 80c–d.

20. Plato, *Greater Hippias*, 298c.

21. Elsewhere, I have discussed the role of this εὐπορία in relation to the ἀπορία of dialogue in terms of Plato's *Parmenides* in order to articulate Agamben's perspective on the problem of plurality (in relation to both Badiou and Nancy); see Gert-Jan van der Heiden, *Ontology after Ontotheology: Plurality, Event, and Contingency in Contemporary Philosophy*, pp. 117–26, and Gert-Jan van der Heiden, "Deciding on Plurality? Plato's Parmenides between Badiou and Agamben," pp. 204–6.

22. *Outlines* I.28–9.

23. "Bartleby" p. 259.

24. Note that indeed, in *Outlines* I.9, where Sextus glosses δύναμις with the verb "to be able" (δύνασθαι), he uses the same verb (δύναμαι) as the one he uses in I.29 to say what the skeptics cannot do (μὴ δυνηθέντες). It is thus indeed a capacity that is at first experienced as an incapacity – and therefore indeed deserves to be called, in an Agambian vein, a potential not to . . . (find a way out).

25. For the difference between pre-aporetic and post-aporetic εὐπορία in Plato, consider Frisbee C. C. Sheffield, *Plato's Symposium: The Ethics of Desire*, p. 70ff. The post-aporetic εὐπορία, as it is called here, indicates that ἀπορία, as a way out of self-deception, is itself a form of progress – and in this sense it compels us to "be optimistic about inquiry" (p. 71).

26. See "Bartleby" p. 259.

27. One striking passage can be found in Giorgio Agamben, *The Time that Remains* [*Time*], 55–7.

28. A more elaborate account of these suspensions can be found in my forthcoming article, "Suspending the World: Paul's Proclamation of Contingency."

29. One of the most important discussions in which this inoperativity plays a role is the discussion on community, and I agree with De la Durantaye that, whereas Agamben is not unique in his understanding of the aporias of community, the *euporia* he finds there is unique, cf. De la Durantaye, *Giorgio Agamben*, 161.

30. 1 Cor. 1: 27–8; translation from the *New International Version* (*NIV*).

31. 1 Cor. 1: 20.

32. *Time* p. 96. Here, of course, we also see the intrinsic connection between κατάργησις and the French term *désoeuvrement*, translated as inoperativity: ἐνεργεία or being at work (*oeuvre*) has as its antonym being out of work (or action).

33. Note that Agamben himself chooses in this context a different passage from Paul related to the suspension of the law (*Time* p. 96), although he also refers to 1 Cor. 1: 27–8 in this section (p. 97) and also mentions it elsewhere (p. 10).

34. He notes that Paul was familiar with this opposition and uses it (at least twice) in his letters, see *Time* p. 90.

35. Ibid. pp. 96–7.

36. Giorgio Agamben, "On Potentiality," p. 182. At this point, Agamben refers to Aristotle, *Metaphysics*, 1046a32. He makes this reference again at *Time* p. 97.

37. *Time* p. 97.

38. The type of potentiality that arises is discussed in another, famous passage of the *First Letter to the Corinthians*, namely 1 Cor. 7: 28–31. Here, the passing away of the order of the world is connected to a particular ἔθος that relates to the world in attunement with its passing away. The ἔθος is not simply one of impossibility or incapacity in the everyday sense, but one of ὡς μή, of "as not," as Agamben translates this Pauline phrase: the weak and powerless are not only weak, but they do the things in the world in light of their potential not to . . .

39. *Outlines* I.3–4.

40. Ibid. I.7.

BIBLIOGRAPHY

Agamben, G., "Bartleby, or On Contingency," in G. Agamben, *Potentialities: Collected Essays in Philosophy*, trans. D. Heller-Roazen (Stanford: Stanford University Press, 1999), pp. 243–71.

Agamben, G., "On Potentiality," in G. Agamben, *Potentialities: Collected Essays in Philosophy*, trans. D. Heller-Roazen (Stanford: Stanford University Press, 1999), pp. 177–84.

Agamben, G., "*Pardes*: The Writing of Potentiality," in G. Agamben, *Potentialities: Collected Essays in Philosophy*, trans. D. Heller-Roazen (Stanford: Stanford University Press, 1999), pp. 205–19.

Aristotle, *The Complete Works of Aristotle: The Revised Oxford Translation*, ed. J. Barnes, 2 vols (Princeton: Princeton University Press, 1984).

Barker, K. L., Burdick, D. and Burdick, D. W. (eds.), *The NIV Study Bible: New International Version* (Grand Rapids: Zondervan Bible Publishers, 1995).

De la Durantaye, L., *Giorgio Agamben: A Critical Introduction* (Stanford: Stanford University Press, 2009).

Heidegger, M., *Grundbegriffe der Aristotelischen Philosophie*, Gesamtausgabe Band 18 (Frankfurt am Main: Vittorio Klostermann, 2002).

Meillassoux, Q., *After Finitude: An Essay on the Necessity of Contingency*, trans. R. Brassier (New York: Continuum, 2008).

Plato, *Complete Works*, ed. J. M. Cooper (Indianapolis: Hackett, 1997).

Sextus Empiricus, *Outlines of Pyrrhonism*, trans. R. G. Bury (Cambridge, MA: Harvard University Press, 1933).

Sextus Empiricus, *Outlines of Scepticism*, trans. J. Annas and J. Barnes (Cambridge: Cambridge University Press, 2000).

Sheffield, F. C. C., *Plato's Symposium: The Ethics of Desire* (Oxford: Oxford University Press, 2009).

van der Heiden, G.-J., "Reading Bartleby, Reading Ion: On a Difference between Agamben and Nancy," *International Yearbook for Hermeneutics*, 12 (2013), pp. 92–108.

van der Heiden, G.-J., *Ontology after Ontotheology: Plurality, Event, and Contingency in Contemporary Philosophy* (Pittsburgh: Duquesne University Press, 2014).

van der Heiden, G.-J., "Deciding on Plurality? Plato's Parmenides between Badiou and Agamben," in G.-J. van der Heiden (ed.), *Phenomenological Perspectives on Plurality* (Leiden/Boston: Brill, 2015), pp. 195–209.

CHAPTER 17

Plotinus' "Reverse" Platonism: A Deleuzian Response to the Problem of Emanation Imagery

Gina Zavota

The concept of emanation is central to Plotinus' ontology, appearing throughout the *Enneads*. It has, however, been historically difficult for modern interpreters to grasp, due to the often vague, metaphorical language with which Plotinus discusses it. As far back as 1937, A. H. Armstrong sums up the state of research by stating that "the difficulty is not so much to discover what Plotinus meant by 'emanation' [. . .] The difficulty is to see what the precise philosophical meaning of this conception is."[1] Most scholars, he claims, acknowledge this difficulty but do not attempt any serious resolution of it. In the intervening decades, there have been surprisingly few attempts to address this problem directly. Lloyd Gerson has argued that Plotinus' metaphysics is not truly emanationist at all, but is more accurately labeled "instrumental creationism," the qualification "instrumental" being necessary to maintain the simplicity of the One – the ultimate source of all things – in Gerson's analysis. But even Gerson acknowledges that this description is only acceptable "if it is allowed that instrumental creationism is a legitimate species of creationism." If not, "then Plotinus' metaphysics is not accurately called creationist. But it is not emanationist either. I do not have a convenient label to offer for this alternative."[2] As we will see momentarily, there is good reason to doubt whether Plotinus' metaphysics is emanationist in the usual sense of the word. Rather than attempting to stretch the notion of creationism or of emanationism far enough to accommodate the system presented in the *Enneads*, I would like to suggest a new context within which to understand it, namely the ontology of Gilles Deleuze. While this may at first seem like an arbitrary combination of two incompatible philosophers, I hope to show that there are certain aspects of Deleuze's ontology, such as its emphasis on difference, decentralization, and generativity, that make it effective as a tool for rethinking Plotinus' system. While Deleuze's rejection of Platonism is clear from even the most cursory reading of his work, I believe his thought can nonetheless be fruitfully applied to those aspects of Plotinus' system, such as emanation, which deviate from the thought of Plato.

The doctrine of emanation can be seen as a response to the central ontological question, posed by Plotinus in *On the Three Primary Hypostases*, of "how from the One [. . .] anything else, whether a multiplicity or a dyad or a number, came into existence, and why it did not on the contrary remain by itself, but such a great multiplicity flowed [ἐξερρύη] from it as that which is seen to exist in beings."[3] This "flowing" gives rise to the lower hypostases, Intellect and Soul, as well as the realm of Nature and the individual objects within it. As Armstrong points out, there is no single Greek word or phrase which is translated as "emanation," but rather a collection of diverse metaphorical descriptions meant to illustrate the process. The language of "flowing" and "overflowing" is often used to describe emanation, as in *On the Origin and Order of the Beings Which Come After the First*: "This, we might say, is the first act of generation: the One, perfect because it seeks nothing, has nothing, and needs nothing, overflows [ὑπερερρύη], as it were, and its superabundance makes something other than itself."[4] Along with this, Plotinus often uses the language of radiation, and the familiar images of the circle and the sun, to describe the relation of the lower hypostases to the One. In *On the Primal Good*, for example, while describing the manner in which all things are directed toward the One or Good, he states that the Good

> must stay still, and all things turn back to it, as a circle does to the
> centre from which all the radii come. The sun, too, is an example,
> since it is like a centre in relation to the light which comes from it and
> depends on it; for the light is everywhere with it and is not cut off
> from it.[5]

On one level, these metaphors are not difficult to understand: emanation is an outpouring of some sort, from a single, central source to a multiplicity of individual objects. However, if we pause for a moment to consider what Plotinus says about the nature of the One, the descriptions above become less satisfying, for it becomes difficult to see how anything could ever flow, radiate, or grow out of it. To begin with, the One is not an intellect, as one might expect of the source of all things. Plotinus states that "the Good must be simple and without need, it will not need thinking [νοεῖν]; but what it has no need of will not be present with it."[6] Furthermore, the One or Good is not to be identified with any thing of this world, or with the totality of things in the world. While these things are, in a sense, "in" Intellect – the realm of Being – they are not in the One. As Plotinus states in *On the Three Primary Hypostases*:

God is not one of all things; for this is how all things come from him, because he is not confined by any shape . . . One is one alone: if he was all things, he would be numbered among beings. For this reason that one is none of the things in Intellect, but all things come from him.[7]

In addition, as mentioned above, the One is absolutely simple, "for if it is not to be simple, outside all coincidence and composition, it could not be a first principle."[8] Plotinus also frequently stresses that the One "stays still," that it "must not be the Good by activity or thought, but by reason of its very abiding. For because it is 'beyond being,' it transcends activity and transcends mind and thought."[9] We thus have the paradox of a first principle which is prior to thought, motion, differentiation, and multiplicity of any sort, which is perfect and complete in itself, but from which multiplicity nonetheless flows or emanates. In what is perhaps an attempt to address this issue, Plotinus states that "nothing can come from [the One] except that which is next greatest after it,"[10] and also next in simplicity, stillness, etc.: namely, Intellect. All subsequent created things, in which ever greater degrees of complexity and motion are manifested, thus flow only indirectly from the One. Nonetheless, the question of how anything at all issues from it remains unanswered.

Plotinus seems to be aware of this paradox, for at certain points he indicates that his emanationist metaphors are not entirely accurate. Most significantly, through much of *On the Presence of Being, One and the Same, Everywhere as a Whole*,[11] a two-part treatise comprising texts VI.4 and VI.5 in the *Enneads*, he seems to reject emanationism outright. At one point, for instance, while attempting to explain the unity of the intelligible, he asks us to imagine a small, luminous body placed inside a larger transparent sphere. He goes on to argue that

since the light does not come from the small bodily bulk [. . .] suppose that someone took away the bulk of the body but kept the power of the light, would you still say the light was somewhere, or would it be equally present over the whole outer sphere? You will no longer rest in your thought on the place where it was before [. . .] but you will be puzzled and put in amazement when, fixing your gaze now here and now there in the spherical body, you yourself perceive the light.[12]

This striking passage leads Armstrong to claim that "we have no longer emanation but immanent omnipresence" and that "there seems to be a struggle between a doctrine of emanation and one of immanent omnipresence, which finally issues in an outspoken pantheism."[13] While I believe that the claim of pantheism is somewhat of an overstatement, I agree that this passage seems to indicate a rejection of emanationism. When the source is removed, it no longer makes sense to speak of light emanating from somewhere to somewhere else, spreading out or splitting into parts, or indeed to speak of any sort of motion or process at all – the light just *is*, its existence known simply through the luminosity of the outer sphere.

This unusual language in VI.4–5 has been the subject of much scholarly attention. While most of the literature on this treatise concerns the lower hypostases, as opposed to the One, it provides an illuminating glimpse of how contemporary scholars have attempted to reconcile passages like the one quoted above with Plotinus' more general ontology. Dominic O'Meara, responding to an article by J. S. Lee, asserts that, inasmuch as the intelligible is immaterial and unextended, it is meaningless to speak of it being divided into parts, or of something participating in only a part of it.[14] Eyjólfur Emilsson extends this analysis to the realm of Soul, which he takes to be the main topic of VI.4–5, stating that "the whole of soul must presumably be present to whatever any soul is present to. In other words, the doctrine of the unity of soul is just a special case of the divisibility of being."[15] However, while these analyses are extremely helpful in clarifying the way in which Intellect or Soul can be present in their entirety to individuals, the authors take Plotinus' rejection of emanation imagery in these treatises as problematic primarily when we attempt to reconcile VI.4–5 with the rest of the *Enneads*. For example, Emilsson states that

> relating our treatises to other Plotinian works poses difficult questions. This is so because here Plotinus goes very far in rejecting the language of emanation and even that of reflection as mere metaphors liable to mislead us. As he depends on this sort of language elsewhere [. . .] our treatises may leave us somewhat baffled as to what to make of those other passages.[16]

While I agree that the language of VI.4–5 causes a special problem in developing a systematic understanding of Plotinus' ontology, I believe that it is possible to reconcile this apparent rejection of emanationism with Plotinus' somewhat reluctant acceptance of it elsewhere, while also providing at least a feasible answer to the question of how anything came from the One in the first place. While the One is admittedly not the subject of *On the Presence of Being Everywhere*, the question of how something indivisible, unmoving, and simple can give rise to anything applies with even greater force to the One than it does to the lower hypostases. Rather than relegating this treatise to special consideration apart from the rest of the *Enneads*, then, I instead take Plotinus' indication here that the One is a source by some means other than straightforward emanation as a starting point from which to rethink this key aspect of his ontology.

I now turn to the work of Gilles Deleuze, in particular his own rather distinctive ontology. Before I begin, a few caveats are in order. First, it barely needs to be said that the differences between the metaphysical commitments of Plotinus, a third-century Platonist, and Deleuze, a twentieth-century poststructuralist and empiricist, are vast. Nonetheless, I believe that some of Deleuze's central ontological insights are applicable even within the extremely different context of Plotinus' work, for reasons that will hopefully become apparent shortly. In addition, it is impossible to do justice to Deleuze's ontology in a paper of this length, and thus my discussion of it will of necessity be limited to a brief overview of a few central concepts. While this will force me to pass over many important nuances in Deleuze's thought, I am hopeful that even this cursory examination will be sufficient to demonstrate that this line of inquiry holds promise. With that said, I will now turn to my overview of some of the most relevant Deleuzian notions.

For the purposes of this project, one of the key texts for consideration is *Difference and Repetition*, an important work from 1968 in which Deleuze presents a critique of what he considers to be an ontology of identity and representation, as seen in Plato, Hegel, and most of the other central thinkers in the Western philosophical tradition. In its place, he proposes an ontology of difference, comprised of three registers: the virtual, the intensive, and the actual. He emphasizes throughout that his distinguishing of the virtual from the actual does not imply that the virtual is a realm of mere possibility and is therefore less real than the actual. On the contrary, "The virtual is opposed not to the real but to the actual. *The virtual is fully real in so far as it is virtual.*"[17] Elsewhere, he adds that "the only danger in all this is that the virtual could be confused with the possible. The possible is opposed to the real [. . .] The process [the virtual] undergoes is that of actualisation."[18] Furthermore, this actualization should not be thought of in the sense in which an acorn can be said to actualize its potential when it becomes an oak tree. Rather – using the language and theoretical framework of differential calculus – Deleuze characterizes actualization in terms of "differential elements" of a "virtual Idea" (or sometimes "virtual multiplicity"), which are actualized as they enter into "differential relations" determined by "singular points." To give an example that will hopefully help clarify this barrage of terminology, Deleuze describes the virtual Idea of language as "a virtual system of reciprocal connections between 'phonemes' which is incarnated in the actual terms and relations of diverse languages."[19] In other words, from the full continuum of possible human vocalizations, the "differential elements" – the phonemes – of a particular language are actualized through their mutually determinative "differential" relations within that language. This implies that an individual sound has no linguistic significance outside of a particular language in which it is actually used, and outside of the ways in which it is combined with other sounds into meaningful units of that language. The "singularities," or "pertinent peculiarities,"[20] of a given language are those points that define the structure and development of the language; for example, the changes in how a given set of vowel sounds is pronounced in a certain area can mark the birth and evolution of a new regional dialect of the language. Thus, while the capacity for the development of any and all languages is inherent within the virtual network of differentially connected phonemes, the process of actualization takes place only when actual speakers begin to communicate with each other through meaningful combinations of these elements.

Units such as groups of speakers who share a dialect – which are intermediate in size and complexity between individual speakers and the set of all speakers of the language – are a good example of Deleuze's third ontological register, the intensive. The intensive is, in essence, the means by which the virtual is actualized.[21] It possesses certain quantifiable attributes, such as, in the case of a linguistic group, the geographical distribution of speakers, their socioeconomic conditions and average level of education, who they generally converse with, and so on, which determine how any given individual will speak. In summary, then, the virtual Idea of "language," while fully real, is only actualized in the individuals who speak a particular language, each uttering combinations of phonemes in a way that is determined by what Deleuze refers to as the "intensive" properties of his or her local linguistic community. He is borrowing a term from the sciences, where an intensive property is a property such as temperature, which is not divided when the substance that has the property is divided. Thus, if a gallon of 100-degree water is divided in half, the two resulting half-gallons are not each at 50 degrees. However, each half-gallon of water will weigh half as much as the gallon did; weight, in contrast to the intensiveness of temperature, is an extensive property. For Deleuze, intensiveness indicates an inherence of the property in the thing that is not present with extensive properties, which seem to be instilled in objects through some external mechanism. Put differently, having a certain weight is not a property of the water per se, but of the contingent fact that the water happens to be in a particular size container; when it is poured into two smaller containers, we think of the same overall volume of water as being comprised of units that weigh less than the previous one did. In an important sense, then, the water's weight is a property of the container, not the water itself.

It is worth taking a step back from our analysis here in order to better understand how Deleuze conceives of intensive connections among elements, which he sometimes refers to as "assemblages." They are, as he puts it, "rhizomatic." In botany, the term "rhizome" refers to "a horizontal, usually underground stem that often sends out roots and shoots from its nodes,"[22] as is the case with many common plants, such as ginger, bamboo, and several types of fern. Deleuze discusses the notion most thoroughly in the introductory chapter of *A Thousand Plateaus*, coauthored with Félix Guattari. There they contrast the rhizome with two other types of organic structure: (1) that of a typical tree, which has roots, a trunk, and branches. Deleuze and Guattari consider this "arborescent" organization to be an inadequate representation of the ontological structures they are exploring, because of its centralized and hierarchical nature. They also contrast the rhizome with (2) the radicle-system, where "radicle" refers to the first shoot that emerges from a seed and grows downward, providing an anchor for the developing roots. When a main root is severed or its growth is otherwise aborted, "an immediate, indefinite multiplicity of secondary roots grafts onto it and undergoes a flourishing development."[23]

While this radicle-system might seem like a less hierarchical alternative to the traditional, arborescent model, Deleuze and Guattari counter that "the root's unity subsists, as past or yet to come, as possible."[24] Thus the goal of the radicle, like that of the arborescent structure, is the establishment of a centralized root system, whenever that may become possible. In other words, the destruction of a control center does not result in a decentralized system, but rather in a system seeking to re-establish a central locus of power.

A rhizomatic structure is, by contrast, distributed and decentralized from the start and not in any way driven toward centralization. Deleuze and Guattari use the term to draw attention to several of the central characteristics around which they construct their decentralized, non-hierarchical ontology. In the opening pages of A Thousand Plateaus, they enumerate six "approximate characteristics of the rhizome"[25] that help to clarify their use of the term. The first two, considered together, are "principles of connection and heterogeneity," or the fact that "any point of a rhizome can be connected to anything other, and must be. This is very different from the tree or root, which plots a point, fixes an order."[26] Unlike the arborescent root structure, in which a path from one root tip to the next inevitably involves doubling back toward the center, the parts of the rhizome are connected laterally in a nonhierarchical network; there is no central point toward which every route must lead and each area in the rhizomatic structure has multiple connections with many others.

In addition, the rhizome is inherently multiple, unlike the radicle structure, in which multiple shoots sprout up from a destroyed or aborted central root with the "memory" of that root and the "intention" of establishing another centralized system. The figure of unity thus overshadows the arboreal and radicular systems in a way it does not in a rhizomatic arrangement, due to the latter's "principle of multiplicity." Put another way, there is no level or "plane" above that on which the connections of the rhizome exist, no external power directing those connections. They state that a rhizome "never has available a supplementary dimension over and above its number of lines" or connections, referring to this network of connections as a "plane of consistency of multiplicities" in which the multiplicities are defined based on the connections made and the trajectories or "lines of flight" through which those connections are established.[27] There is no internal organizing principle or essential structure to the rhizome, nothing that would inevitably point to another plane, or to a form, ideal, model, or central locus of control in which the pattern of connection is formed.

Fourth, the "principle of asignifying rupture" states that "a rhizome may be broken, shattered at a given spot, but it will start up again on one of its old lines, or on new lines."[28] Unlike in the case of the radicle structure, in which a destroyed central root leads inevitably only to the appearance of radicles which mimic that now absent central root, when a rhizome is severed, new lateral connections appear on the plane of consistency, or old ones are reactivated and strengthened, in an unpredictable fashion. Again, there is no controlling principle or model external to the plane of consistency itself, so there is nothing to impose the same response after each rupture. In other words, the rupture does not in any way point to a dimension supplementary to the plane of consistency, as the damaged radicle-system always points to the possibility of a central root. Finally, Deleuze and Guattari describe what they call "principles of cartography and decalcomania."[29] Decalcomania is the decorative technique of transferring patterns to pottery or to other materials. It is thus a mapping from one medium onto another, with results that can constitute quite a transformation from the original image, unlike a simple tracing, in which the result is meant to resemble the original as closely as possible. With respect to the rhizome, this means that there are multiple points of entry into the system, as in an animal's burrow; in addition, each time the animal enters the burrow, it has multiple possible paths from which it can choose. As opposed to the repetitive tracing of the same route, with the same goal, as in a daily commute to work or school, a journey from one point to another within a rhizomatic structure is open-ended and variable.

From this overview of the nature of rhizomatic connections, it should be clear that one of the primary features of Deleuze's ontology is its decentralized nature. Replacing an ontology of identity with one of difference entails, first and foremost, dispensing with the notion that individual members of a "species" – whether a biological species or something like a linguistic community – are united through a shared essence that exists on or points to a dimension external to the plane of consistency. Rather, the real, historical processes accounted for by Deleuze's intensive register allow for the actualization of the virtual in ways that differ from individual to individual. In place of a single, unifying essence, there are numerous distinct individuals, each related to others by the material conditions of their existence. Deleuze expresses this succinctly in *The Logic of Sense*, where he states that "To reverse Platonism is first and foremost to remove essences and to substitute events in their place."[30]

How could this "reversal" of Platonism possibly help us shed light on the ontology of such a thoroughly Platonic thinker as Plotinus? First and foremost, in the notion of actualization through increasing particularization and activity, it gives us a new way to conceive of how anything could arise from the One. Deleuze is very clear that "actualization comes about through differentiation, through divergent lines, and creates so many differences in kind by virtue of its own movement."[31] While Deleuze's virtual register does not possess the simplicity of Plotinus' One, Deleuze also does not characterize it in terms of difference in the same way as he does the intensive, which "includes the unequal in itself"[32] and "affirms difference,"[33] or the actual, in which heterogeneity is even more pronounced. Instead, the virtual is a field of differential connections among elements such as phonemes (in the case of the Idea of language), none of which are inherently preferred over any others. Manuel DeLanda explains this succinctly when he describes the virtual as "a *continuum* which yields, through progressive differentiation, all the discontinuous individuals that populate the actual world."[34] One of main points upon which Deleuze insists across his ontological works is that the existence of these individuals is not the result of a process of creation or causality, at least not in the sense in which this requires a creator or cause outside the individual itself. Rather, he borrows the mathematical notion of a function or operator, such as addition, which is defined by the effect it has on operands, not by a particular result. As Deleuze puts it, "the quasi-cause does not create, it operates."[35] This focus on activity and differentiation is reminiscent of the language that Plotinus uses to speak of Soul's presence in individual bodies, explaining that Soul "leapt out, we might say, from the whole to a part, and actualises itself as a part in [the world]."[36] This particularization and separation takes place "not spatially, but [the soul] becomes each particular thing in its activity."[37]

Returning to the question of what to make of Plotinus' emanation imagery and his apparent abandonment of it in VI.4–5, the same principles of activity, differentiation, and decentralization apply. Plotinus conceives of Intellect's generation from the One in terms of action, but not in terms of causality in our typical understanding of the word. Rather, the intellect is generated through its own turning back or returning to contemplate the One: "How then does [the Good] generate Intellect? Because by its return to it it sees: and this seeing is Intellect."[38] This return to the Good is inherently generative; indeed, it is the motion by which Intellect constitutes itself by distinguishing itself from that from which it came. The initial moment of Plotinian ontology is thus defined by difference, by Intellect's divergence from the One even as it turns back toward the One in contemplation. From Intellect proceeds Soul, a "restlessly active nature" which is "always moving on to the 'next' and the 'after,' and what is not the same"[39] and which is actualized in individuals by means of yet further differentiation. Further differentiation leads to further generation, and while a simple, unmoving first principle is the ultimate source of all things, the process of generation is described throughout in terms of actualization and differentiation from it – the sort of continuum of "progressive differentiation" to which DeLanda refers. As Deleuze asserts, "actualization is creation."[40]

This should prompt us to think of generation not as a flowing outward from a source, but rather as a process of relational self-determination – a series of "differential relations" through which all created things are constituted, as with the process by which the virtual is actualized by means of the intensive. From here, we can answer the question of how the One gives rise to anything when it is simple, complete, and unmoving by asserting that it is not a motion or process initiated by the One that causes everything to "emanate" from it, but rather its difference from everything created. Beginning with Intellect, all generation is a turning toward the One and a self-constitution through differentiation from it. The One initiates no action, it simply "abides." As Plotinus frequently reminds us, "The One did not in some sort of way want Intellect to come into being [. . .] for if this was so, the One would be incomplete."[41] While it is immeasurably greater than, and, in this sense, on a "plane" external to that of Intellect, it does not provide an ordering principle for Intellect, being prior to all conceptions of ordering or rules, which by definition imply a multitude of factors to order or regulate.

Recalling Deleuze's conception of the virtual as a field of differential dispersion, through which the rhizomatic connections of the intensive register emerge, we can gain new insight into statements such as "if anything comes into being after [the One], we must think that it necessarily does so while the One remains continually turned toward itself,"[42] and that this occurs "without the One moving at all, without any inclination or act of will or any sort of activity on its part."[43] The One does not move, will, or actively cause Intellect to come into being any more than the virtual imposes an order upon the intensive plane of consistency; rather the intensive is defined by the rhizomatic structure of self-organizing connections among elements, without reference to any external ordering principle. The virtual is thus not the source of these emergent structures in the way in which emanationist images would portray the One as the source of Intellect, that is as the sun is a source of light or a spring is the source of flowing water – another possible reason to rethink the import of such images. While Plotinus employs this imagery in an attempt to explain how Intellect, which he describes as "all movement filling all substance [. . .] always one thing after another,"[44] can come from the One without the latter moving or changing in any way, it is ultimately inadequate, as he himself acknowledges. This is the case primarily because it depicts the One as a source in far too active of a sense – as imbued with some sort of excess which overflows it – hence Plotinus' removal of the central source entirely in the controversial passage from *On the Presence of Being Everywhere* under discussion here.

Deleuzian ontology thus gives us a way to understand how Intellect can, in a sense, generate itself as it turns back to contemplate the One. This idea is in keeping with the way in which Plotinus describes contemplative activity throughout *On Nature and Contemplation and the One*, his most significant treatise on the topic. Speaking in the voice of Nature, he indicates the inherently generative character of contemplation: "My act of contemplation makes what it contemplates [. . .] as I contemplate, the lines which bound bodies come to be as if they fell from my contemplation."[45] Later in the treatise, he explains how Intellect's contemplation, while stronger and less "active" than that of Nature, nonetheless generates Intellect itself. Unlike with Nature or Soul, for Intellect, contemplation and its object are one. However, this unity is not the same as that of the One, for contemplation is inherently multiple. Thus, "when [Intellect] contemplates the One, it does not contemplate it as one: otherwise it would not become intellect."[46] As described earlier in this essay, it is through this contemplative activity, through this turning to regard the One, that Intellect emerges as a self-organizing principle. Thus the One, in its "everlastingness and generosity," is the "productive power of all things"[47] not by actively creating, overflowing, or radiating in the manner implied by emanationist metaphors, but rather by being what Intellect joins with in contemplation, in an act through which Intellect is constituted. The ability of the

Deleuzian framework to conceptualize such a means of "creation" is another significant feature that I believe makes it a superior means of conceiving of Plotinus' ontology as compared to the emanationist imagery with which he himself is dissatisfied.

Before concluding, I would like to articulate one final advantage that I believe this account has over the traditional explanatory frameworks used to address the question of how things proceed from the One, namely the facility with which Deleuze's ontology handles interactions between incommensurables. As DeLanda points out, "an assembly process may be said to be characterized by intensive properties when it articulates *heterogeneous* elements as such," giving as an example "the assemblage formed by a walking animal, a piece of ground and a gravitational field."[48] Even this most basic configuration illustrates the way in which an assemblage can be made up of vastly different elements from different orders of existence: in this case, an organic, living being; an inorganic compound; and one of the fundamental forces governing the natural world. Clearly none of these components is permanently altered in a significant fashion through this interaction, yet the connections giving rise to this transitory configuration of animal, ground, and gravity are no less significant because of this. Deleuze himself, when speaking of such intensive assemblages, writes that:

> It is no longer a question of imposing a form upon a matter but of elaborating an increasingly rich and consistent material, the better to tap increasingly intense forces. What makes a material increasingly rich is the same as what holds heterogeneities together without their ceasing to be heterogeneous.[49]

Admittedly, Deleuze is referring to elements that exist on the same "plane of consistency," whereas Plotinus' hypostases are not only on different planes, but actually *are* those different planes. But far from making the application of Deleuzian thought to Plotinian ontology inappropriate, this further speaks to its applicability. The incommensurability, the utter difference between the hypostases, is a constant theme in the *Enneads*, in statements such as "there must be something simple before all things, and this must be other than all the things which come after it, existing by itself, not mixed with the things which derive from it."[50] In his ontology of difference, Deleuze starts from the assumption that unlike elements, as well as more similar ones, can combine to form assemblages. There is no priority of the homogenous over the heterogeneous – if anything, the reverse is true. Likewise, Neoplatonic ontology begins with the assumption of radically different ontological realms between which there is necessarily some kind of commerce, mirroring Deleuze's starting point. Emanationist explanations still remain within the paradigm of sameness that characterizes the ontology of identity against which Deleuze is reacting.

Our tacit assumption that only like entities can interact leads to all sorts of difficulties in interpreting Plotinian texts, not least of which is the trouble caused by Plotinus' abandonment of emanation imagery in *On the Presence of Being Everywhere*. O'Meara characterizes the root of such problems as "difficulties we have in reconciling the omnipresence of soul in the corporeal world with the non-corporeal, size-less (ἀμεγέθης) nature of soul and with the indivisibility of soul implied by its sensory unity (ὁμοπαθής)."[51] According to O'Meara, Plotinus is quick to diagnose the problem, inasmuch as he "finds at the root of our difficulties with intelligible omnipresence a tendency to treat the intelligible as if it were material."[52] Plotinus himself takes great care to avoid this tendency, and admonishes us to do so as well throughout the treatise, most notably in the following passage:

> When one was speaking about those things [of the lower world] one
> would reason logically from that nature and from what is held to
> be true about it [. . .] But when, on the other hand, one engages in
> reasonings about the intelligibles, the right way would be to take the
> nature of substance about which one is concerned and so establish
> the principles of one's reasonings, without passing over, as if one had
> forgotten, to the other nature.[53]

Here, Plotinus reminds us to reason about intelligibles in an appropriate fashion, namely by employing "intelligible principles of intelligibles and those which belong to true substance."[54] In other words, we should refrain from attributing properties such as spatial location, divisibility, and temporality to intelligibles. Likewise, we must remember that we can only have probable knowledge about the things of this world, not the kind of certainty that could come from reasoning about intelligibles. In short, we must develop a facility for conceiving of two distinct orders of being, each with its own set of principles and properties, as part of a union (in this case, ensouled human beings) in which neither component becomes like the other. Plotinus has already alluded to the necessity of reorienting our thinking in this way in the first part of the double treatise, where he states that "nothing prevents different things from being all together, like soul and intellect and all bodies of knowledge, major and subordinate."[55] This fundamentally heterogeneous sort of assemblage is precisely what Deleuzian ontology excels at conceptualizing.

I hope to have provided a compelling argument in support of approaching certain aspects of Plotinus' ontology from a Deleuzian perspective. In the end, however, the question could be raised as to whether this account might not simply be another metaphor to describe a process that is essentially indescribable. After all, the Plotinian One is ontologically prior to Intellect, thought, and language, and thus prior to any attempt to rationally understand its workings. Could it be that metaphor is the best we can hope for when we discuss it? And if this is the case, what makes a Deleuzian explanation any better than the metaphors of flowing or radiating that Plotinus clearly finds inadequate? As to the contention that this may be merely one metaphor among many, I concede that this may, in fact, be the case. In one sense, talk about first principles as far removed from normal human experience and comprehension as Plotinus' One is bound to be somewhat metaphorical, and it is impossible to know the extent to which Plotinus himself felt that he could ever hope to give more than a metaphorical description of the process by which anything proceeds from it. That having been said, there is value in a metaphor that more fully and accurately illustrates something, and thus in arguing for the superiority of one account over another, even if neither is a literal description of Plotinus' conceptions. With this essay, I hope to have presented at least a few compelling reasons to adopt a Deleuzian framework for the interpretation of key elements of Plotinus' ontology, rather than accepting the traditional emanationist explanation. Inasmuch as the former gives us fruitful new insight into how constantly moving, differentiated Intellect proceeds from something as radically different from it as the motionless, perfectly unified One, I believe that it is, if nothing else, a closer approximation to the perhaps ineffable truths that Plotinus so frequently tried to articulate.

NOTES

1. A. H. Armstrong, "'Emanation' in Plotinus" [Armstrong], p. 61.
2. Lloyd P. Gerson, "Plotinus's Metaphysics: Emanation or Creation?" pp. 574.
3. Plotinus, *Enneads*, trans. A. H. Armstrong, V.1.6.5–7.
4. Ibid. V.2.1.5–10.
5. Ibid. I.7.1.24–8.
6. Ibid. V.6.4.1–3 (*On the Fact that That Which Is Beyond Being Does Not Think*).
7. Ibid. V.1.7.19–23.
8. Ibid. V.4.1.11–13 (*How That Which Is After the First Comes from the First, and On the One*).
9. Ibid. I.7.1.17–21. "Beyond being" is a reference to *Republic* VI. 509b9, where Plato states that the Good is "ἐπέκεινα οὐσίας."
10. *Enneads* V.1.6.40–1.
11. Ibid. VI.4–5.
12. Ibid. VI.4.7.28–40.
13. Armstrong p. 62.
14. Dominic O'Meara, "The Problem of Omnipresence in Plotinus' Ennead VI, 4–5: A Reply" [O'Meara], *pp.* 70ff. See also Jonathan Scott Lee, "The Doctrine of Reception According to the Capacity of the Recipient in 'Ennead' VI 4–5," to which O'Meara was replying, and Michael F. Wagner, "Plotinus' Idealism and the Problem of Matter in 'Enneads' VI 4 and 5."
15. Eyjólfur Emilsson, "Plotinus' Ontology in Ennead VI.4 and 5," p. 97.
16. Ibid. p. 87.
17. Gilles Deleuze, *Difference and Repetition* [DR], p. 208.

18. Ibid. p. 211.
19. Ibid. p. 193.
20. Ibid. p. 203.
21. To take another example, Manuel DeLanda, in his *Intensive Science and Virtual Philosophy* [DeLanda], explains the intensive by borrowing from evolutionary biology the notion of a "deme," or a local population of members of a particular species that interbreed and thus share a gene pool (pp. 53–5).
22. http://www.yourdictionary.com/rhizome
23. Gilles Deleuze and Félix Guattari, *A Thousand Plateaus* [ATP], p. 5.
24. Ibid.
25. Ibid. p. 7.
26. Ibid.
27. Ibid. pp. 8–9.
28. Ibid. p. 9.
29. Ibid. p. 12.
30. Gilles Deleuze, *The Logic of Sense* [LS], p. 53.
31. Gilles Deleuze, *Bergsonism*, p. 43.
32. *DR* p. 232.
33. Ibid. p. 234.
34. DeLanda p. 72.
35. *LS* p. 147.
36. *Enneads* VI.4.16.28–30.
37. Ibid. VI.4.16.34–5
38. Ibid. V.1.7. 5–6.
39. Ibid. III.7.11.14–18 (*On Eternity and Time*).
40. *Bergsonism* p. 98.
41. *Enneads* V.3.12.28–31 (*On the Knowing Hypostasis and That Which Is Beyond*).
42. Ibid. V.1.6.17–19.
43. Ibid. V.1.6.25–8.
44. Ibid. VI.7.13.41–3 (*How the Multitude of Forms Came into Being, and on the Good*).
45. Ibid. III.8.4.8–11.
46. Ibid. III.8.8.31–2.
47. Ibid. V.4.1.34–6.
48. DeLanda, p. 67.
49. *ATP* p. 329.
50. *Enneads* V.4.1.5–8 (*How That Which Is After the First Comes from the First, and on the One*).
51. O'Meara p. 63.
52. Ibid. p. 65.
53. *Ennead* VI.5.2.16–21; also quoted by O'Meara.
54. Ibid. VI.5.2.8–9.
55. Ibid. VI.4.11.11–13.

BIBLIOGRAPHY

Armstrong, A. H., "'Emanation' in Plotinus," *Mind*, 46.181 (1937), pp. 61–6.

DeLanda, M., *Intensive Science & Virtual Philosophy* (London: Continuum, 2002).

Deleuze, G., *The Logic of Sense*, trans. M. Lester and C. Stivale, ed. C. V. Boundas (New York: Columbia University Press, 1990).

Deleuze, G., *Bergsonism*, trans. H. Tomlinson and B. Habberjam (New York: Zone Books, 1991).

Deleuze, G., *Difference and Repetition*, trans. P. Patton (New York: Columbia University Press, 1994).

Deleuze, G. and Guattari, F., *A Thousand Plateaus: Capitalism and Schizophrenia*, trans. B. Massumi (Minneapolis: University of Minnesota Press, 1987).

Emilsson, E., "Plotinus' Ontology in Ennead VI.4 and 5," *Hermathena*, 157 (1994), pp. 87–101.

Gerson, L. P., "Plotinus's Metaphysics: Emanation or Creation?" *Review of Metaphysics*, 46.3 (1993), pp. 559–74.

Lee, J. S., "The Doctrine of Reception According to the Capacity of the Recipient in 'Ennead' VI 4–5," *Dionysius*, 3 (1979), pp. 79–97.

O'Meara, D., "The Problem of Omnipresence in Plotinus' Ennead VI, 4–5: A Reply," *Dionysius*, 4 (1980), pp. 61–74.

Plotinus, *Enneads*, trans. A. H. Armstrong, 7 vols (Cambridge, MA: Harvard University Press, 1966–88).

Strange, S. K., "Plotinus' Account of Participation in *Ennead* VI.4–5," *Journal of the History of Philosophy*, 30.4 (1992), pp. 479–96.

Wagner, Michael F. "Plotinus' Idealism and the Problem of Matter in 'Enneads' VI 4 and 5," *Dionysius*, 10 (1986), pp. 57–83.

PART IV

POSTSCRIPT

CHAPTER 18

From Metaphysics to Ethics (with Bernard Stiegler, Heraclitus, and Aristotle)

Kurt Lampe

"From metaphysics to ethics": what kind of transition is signaled by this title? Certainly it is not a matter of progressing from an axiomatic foundation to its corollaries, or shifting attention from one discrete domain to another. Just as this volume has not explored unidirectional "influences" (Latin *influo*, "flow into") from ancients to moderns, but rather cultivated their ongoing interactions, similarly we do not want to think metaphysics as a reservoir from which ethics are "derived" (Latin *deriuo*, "channel away"). Contemporary continental philosophies, like most Greek and Roman philosophies, tend to develop as complex *Gestalten*: metaphysical, ethical, and many other practico-theoretical facets co-emerge out of inchoate impulses, guided by various reflective practices. This could be illustrated from many preceding chapters. For example, to return to the middle of this book, and the beginning of Greek philosophy, Bartlett shows how the Parmenidean constellation of thinking, being, and not-being is reinvigorated in Badiou's "event." Badiou's evental politics and erotics are not additions to this foundation, but other facets of the same emerging Gestalt. Similarly, on the daring but erudite reconstruction of Peter Kingsley, Parmenides' ontology, like his poetic imagery, belongs to an entire program of initiatory rebirth.[1] Thinking metaphysics and ethics together acknowledges the organic composition of so-called "first philosophy" with self-cultivation and self-conversion.

Rather than revisiting moments from the preceding chapters, in this postscript I would like to illustrate this point with a contemporary philosopher who has so far remained in this book's footnotes: Bernard Stiegler. Stiegler is best known for his philosophy of technics, which seeks to overturn "metaphysics," that is transcendent and originary regimes of being and truth, on at least two fronts: first (1) he posits a "default of origin," which all organismic systems endlessly supplement, thus transforming themselves toward a completion they never achieve; second (2) he emphasizes the ways in which human systems distribute themselves – their drives, desires, cognition, and so on – across technical objects. The upshot of (1) is that humans and the reality we disclose are always becoming, never fixed in being; the upshot of (2) is not only to entrench and complicate (1), since human self-supplementing is distributed across both social and technical organs, but also to implode most existing metaphysical schemes, since they exclude technology. For Stiegler, this overcoming of "metaphysics" has deep ethico-political motivations: unless we can effectively critique how our psychosocial, economic, and ecological reality comes to be, we will be unable to solve geopolitical problems or make our lives worth living.[2]

Stiegler frames his anti-metaphysical technics with an extremely uncharitable reading of Plato's *Phaedrus* and *Protagoras*, which builds on Derrida's well-known chapter, "Plato's Pharmacy."[3] But despite his belief that ancient philosophers neglected technology and his hostility to "metaphysics," Stiegler draws opportunistically on Greek and Roman philosophemes that we would usually classify as metaphysical – in other words, doctrines or images that concern being, change, causation, time, and so on. In the process he not only enriches his own theorizing, but also allows us to invest ancient texts with new significance. Here I will briefly visit just two examples.

HERACLITUS

I begin with a typically elliptical fragment of Heraclitus, which Stiegler creatively decompresses. "*Human minds*," Stiegler writes,

> are never satisfied in the state of domestication [. . .] On the contrary,
> they always need to create fantasies that *escape* from that control,
> and lie hidden in the shadowy place of mysteries at the heart of those
> *crypts* to which, as Heraclitus says, *physis* ('being' for the mystagogue
> Heidegger) loves (*philein*) to withdraw (*kruptestai*), where there
> is light, or fire, or at least *warmth* – the very crypt before which
> Heraclitus wants to place his Laws.[4]

Here Stiegler's principal reference is obviously fragment DK B123: φύσις κρύπτεσθαι φιλεῖ. Mainstream anglophone scholars translate "nature loves to hide" or "the real constitution is accustomed to hide itself."[5] For them, φύσις is the referent for what Heraclitus calls "the shared λόγος" or simply "the λόγος."[6] Thus the fragment alludes to the subject's difficulty in perceiving, cognizing, and expressing (λόγος) the paradoxical harmonies of objects-out-there (φύσις). By contrast, Pierre Hadot translates the fragment as "what unveils is also what veils," or "what is born wants to die."[7] Here we are on rather different philosophical terrain. The "mere metaphor" of what nature "loves" to do, its regularities, has become a deep mystery about impersonal organic drives, which blur the subject-object dichotomy. Stiegler hints at a similar reading, beginning with his gloss of φύσις as "'being' for the mystagogue Heidegger." For Heidegger, Heraclitean φύσις designates the transcendental clearing in which beings are disclosed by and for humans.[8] As he translates the fragment, "Being [emerging appearance] intrinsically inclines toward self-concealment."[9] In other words, disclosure always forecloses other configurations of reality. Beyond the finite dwelling of Dasein lie "mysteries,"[10] as Stiegler signals by speaking of "the shadowy place of mysteries" and calling Heidegger a "mystagogue."

So Stiegler appropriates Heraclitean φύσις as a principle of beings' emerging appearance, unveiling, or birth, while redeploying the infinitive κρύπτεσθαι to allude to beings' correlative disappearance, veiling, and death: a mystery. This reading is obviously metaphysical, but what does it mean?

It is precisely by adding ethical and political nuances that Stiegler sheds light on this question. First, in a manner appropriate to Heraclitus' polysemous Greek, Stiegler elaborates κρύπτεσθαι into two French forms: he speaks of "those *crypts* to which, as Heraclitus says, *physis* loves to withdraw." While "to withdraw" (*se retirer*) is an uncontroversial translation for the present middle/passive infinitive κρύπτεσθαι, "crypts" (*cryptes*) is not philologically motivated. By supplementing "to retire" with "crypts," underground chambers of burial and worship, Stiegler hints that the mystery of concealing and dying requires cultivation. One of the key messages of *Taking Care of Youth and the Generations* is that intergenerational care (parenting, education, and the institutions and technology that support them) sustains the "organs" and "circuits" of desire and belief. Desire and belief involve selecting from the manifold of experience in order to configure a past and aspirations for the future. They are the sublimated and socialized products of each person's or community's impetus toward supplementing their originary lack. Since Stiegler often names this care *philia*,[11] from φιλία, the verb φιλεῖ ("loves") in φύσις κρύπτεσθαι φιλεῖ reads as an allusion to the inseparability of worlding from interpersonal caring. Love, friendship, worship, and cultivation: taken together with the technologies across which they are distributed, these are the psychosocial "organs" that support shared cognitive and affective orientations, through which beings emerge from φύσις.

But this psychosocial sharing must not exclude the mystery of Being. When Stiegler says that Heraclitus "wants to place his laws" before this crypt, he presumably has in mind the report that Heraclitus deposited his book in the temple of Artemis at Ephesus.[12] Artemis is a goddess of borders and transitions, which often involve the explosion and reconstitution of regimes of meaning.[13] Like her brother Apollo, sometimes considered the patron deity of philosophy, she has both civilizing and enigmatic, terrifying aspects.[14] Her temple is thus a thought-provoking symbol for the "infinite" or "incalculable" spaces of concealment required by the unveiling of φύσις. Stiegler writes that "*human minds* [. . .] are never satisfied in the state of domestication [. . .] On the contrary, they always need to create fantasies that *escape* from that control."[15] In other words, because of our originary default and complex distribution of energies across technologies, human psyches and societies cannot stand still; we must continuously evolve toward our individuation-to-come. We can only do this if we refrain from freezing and mortifying our hopes and beliefs. That is why it is not only nature that loves to hide, but human fantasy that "lies hidden" in the crypt, "where there is light, or fire, or at least *warmth*." "Escaping" (*échapper à*) and "lying hidden" (*gésir*) are additional Stieglerian supplements for the meaning potential in κρύπτεσθαι. It is not only shared psychosocial organs that must be nourished, but also the infinite beyond in which these organs "grow" (φύσις < φύω, "grow"). The sharing of norms must be complemented by critical management of this un-domesticable facet of human individuation. In this way Heraclitean fire will continue to provide its world-disclosing "light" and life-supporting "warmth," sustaining the world and the people and societies in it.

ARISTOTLE

We can further illuminate the interplay of metaphysics and ethics in Stiegler's philosophy by turning to his appropriation of Aristotelian theology. Though Aristotle's works are intact and prosaic, unlike Heraclitus' ambiguous fragments, his esoteric style and theoretical complexity make his god as puzzling as Heraclitus' nature. On Stephen Menn's reading, which cogently situates Aristotle in the context of his predecessors, the key features of Aristotle's deity are absolute goodness and continuously active thinking.[16] This would be clear enough, but it becomes challenging when we add that, in order to be absolutely good and continuous, god's thinking must not have any independent content: god must be self-sufficient "thinking of thinking [νόησις νοήσεως]."[17] Furthermore, Aristotle wants this "thinking of thinking" to be the principle of all activity in the universe, and to hold this position by virtue of its lovability: in some sense, everything must be oriented toward love of god.[18] Finally, he notoriously concludes his *Nicomachean Ethics* with the assertion that the best life for humans lies in godlike thinking, even though such contemplation is only intermittently possible.[19] This is hard to understand, not only because it threatens to render superfluous the previous nine books on moral virtues, but also because god's thinking is neither readily intelligible nor, to many modern readers, particularly attractive. What form of thinking is this? How does it organize the universe? How and why does that universe love it? Why should humans emulate it?

A good entry point into Stiegler's creative solution to this puzzle is his warning about "the destruction . . . of *theos*, of that which according to Aristotle animates each soul, as absolute singularity."[20] Let us focus on the claim that Aristotle's god is an "absolute singularity." What does this mean?

For Stiegler, there are basically two types of singularities. First are the infinite and incalculable objects projected by interpersonal caring and its technologies, which give that caring and technology their orientation. Examples include art, justice, virtue, beauty, the triangle, the bee, or the French language.[21] The infinite object of justice, for instance, (ideally) gives orientation to education, legislation, legal proceedings, and their techno-material apparatuses. In Stiegler's terminology, such objects do not "exist," but "consist": "justice certainly does not exist on earth, and will never exist. Who, however, would dare to suggest that this idea does not consist, and does not merit being *maintained*, and even *cultivated* in young souls [. . .] ?"[22] Here we see the second domain of Stieglerian "singularities." Parental and educational "cultivation" of "young souls" not only "maintains" the consistence of justice, it also singularizes those souls. In other words, infinite objective singularities like Justice facilitate the infinite (inter) subjective process of self-singularization. They provide an organizing space for people's and groups' self-projection toward their futures. This is why Stiegler says that god, as a singularity, "animates each soul": if objective singularities admitted interpretive closure, this space would close up, threatening our sense of being alive. At the same time, the "existence" of worldly things would fade into mere "subsistence": there would be an "*interruption* of making-world – of the psychic and collective individuation that a world is."[23] In other words, if the psychosocial and technical organs of worlding sickened, things would lose their haecceity, their existence: in Heraclitean terms, φύσις would be entombed in the mortifying concealment of its own crypt.

Why does Stiegler call god an absolute singularity? Because it is the very plane on which objective singularities consist, and toward which subjective singularities are oriented.[24] On this basis, we can formulate Stiegler's implicit solutions to the conundrums with which we began. What form of thinking is god? How does it organize the universe? For Stiegler, god is the principle of those singularities which are the condition of the possibility of the thinking that makes both individuals and the world exist. In other words, god's consistence gathers and guarantees the consistence of justice, the bee, the French language, and so on. And those consistences permit the existence (emergence into being) of acts of justice, individual bees in all their specific and conspecific variations, and French grammar, vocabulary, and its dialects. How and why does the universe love god? Because, as the gathering of singularities, god is the object of the ceaseless self-supplementing projection of all individuals, groups, and technical apparatuses. (In this regard, god's place in atheistic culture is taken by the Freudo-Lacanian Thing.)[25] In other words, god represents a remedy for our originary lack, inasmuch as the process of remediation makes us and our world exist.

Why, finally, should humans emulate god? On the one hand, it is perhaps not even intelligible for humans to emulate god as horizon of singularities. But if, following Aristotle, we choose to represent this horizon as the continuous actualization of singularities,[26] then we can follow Stiegler in speaking of the need to "elevate" our psychosocial and technical organs toward this actualization:[27] we must sublimate our individual and collective neediness, since otherwise we either succumb to repressive norms, whose singularities have died, or act out addictively or destructively. Unlike many readings of Aristotle, this by no means implies abandoning moral virtues for theoretical contemplation. The challenge to "elevate" ourselves toward god comes up in every psychosocial and techno-material domain.

CONCLUSION

It will be evident that Stiegler does not aspire to rigorous scholarly readings; rather, he creatively supplements and redeploys texts with a view to his own ends. For him, texts are elements of interpersonal distributed systems, whose vitality lies in ongoing individuation.[28] In this postscript I have focused on illuminating how ancient metaphysical ideas help him to express ethico-political problems. At the same time, and in a similar spirit of supplementation, I have oriented my commentary on Stiegler toward classic interpretive challenges at the interface between metaphysics and ethics in Heraclitus and Aristotle.

Could ancient metaphysics, in turn, nourish further developments in Stieglerian ethics and politics? Stiegler identifies the apparatuses of hyperindustrial consumerism and mobile digital media as the greatest modern challenges to the existence of individuals and their worlds. The solution is to "elevate" these systems toward the horizon of singularities, which Stiegler constantly presents in cultic, mystagogic, and spiritual terms. At the same time, he insists that the god of traditional religions is dead.[29] Could the "soft," pantheistic polytheisms of ancient philosophy help us to develop the spiritual organs we need – especially those of us insufficiently "inspired" by the Pauline spirituality of Gianni Vattimo, Julia Kristeva, or John Caputo? Ancient metaphysics, with its polymorphous relations to "the gods," undoubtedly has much still to offer to contemporary continental ethics.

NOTES

1. Peter Kingsley, *In the Dark Places of Wisdom and Reality*.
2. Stiegler repeats and varies these core positions across his publications. He explicitly engages with the field of "distributed cognition" in "Relational Ecology and the Digital *Pharmakon*." See also the bibliography for the main texts under discussion. Further, I made use of the collection of resources at arsindustrialis.org/les-pages-de-bernard-stiegler.
3. Bernard Stiegler, *Technics and Time 1: The Fault of Epimetheus* [*Epimetheus*], especially pp. 95–100, 185–203; Jacques Derrida, *Dissemination*, pp. 67–186.
4. Bernard Stiegler, *Taking Care of Youth and the Generations* [*Youth*], p. 38 (translation modified).
5. G. S. Kirk, J. E. Raven, and M. Schofield, *The Presocratic Philosophers*, p. 182; Charles Kahn, *The Art and Thought of Heraclitus*, p. 109.
6. For example, at DK B1, 2, 50, 80, 89, 113–14.
7. Pierre Hadot, *The Veil of Isis: An Inquiry into the History of the Idea of Nature*, p. 11.
8. Martin Heidegger, *Introduction to Metaphysics* [*Introduction*], [87]; *Early Greek Thinking*, pp. 112–13.
9. Brackets in original (*Introduction* [87]).
10. See Thomas Sheehan, "A Paradigm Shift in Heidegger Research," pp. 198–9.

11. For example, Bernard Stiegler, *The Decadence of Industrial Democracies* [*Decadence*], pp. 15, 17, 87, 129; *Youth* pp. 3, 13, 27, 169, 185; Stiegler, *What Makes Life Worth Living: On Pharmacology* [*Worth Living*], pp. 35, 65, 72.

12. Diogenes Laertius, *Lives of Eminent Philosophers*, 9.6.

13. Jean-Peirre Vernant, *Mortals and Immortals: Collected Essays*, pp. 195–243; Hugh Lloyd-Jones, "Artemis and Iphigeneia," pp. 87–102.

14. See especially Marcel Détienne, *Apollon le Couteau à la Main: Une Approche Expérimentale du Polythéisme Grec.*

15. *Youth* p. 38.

16. Stephen Menn, "Aristotle and Plato on God as Nous and as the Good."

17. Aristotle, *Metaphysica* [*Meta.*], Λ.9 1074b34–6. On the pertinence of *De Anima* III.5 to Aristotelian god, see Victor Caston, "Aristotle's Two Intellects: A Modest Proposal."

18. *Meta.* Λ.6–7; see also Aristotle, *Physica*, VIII.1–6. The precise relation of these two texts is debated. Contrast J. L. Ackrill, *Aristotle the Philosopher*, pp. 128–34 with Jonathan Lear, *Aristotle: The Desire to Understand* [*Lear*], pp. 293–309.

19. Aristotle, *Ethica Nicomachea*, 10.7–8, especially 1177b26–1178a8, 1178a7–24; *Meta.* Λ.7 1072b15–27.

20. *Decadence* pp. 85–6.

21. On "singularities" and "consistences," to which Stiegler frequently alludes, see especially *Decadence* pp. 89–93, 116–19, 124–7; *Worth Living* pp. 32–4, 43–8; *Youth* pp. 41–6, 68–71, 100–6; Bernard Stiegler, *Acting Out*, pp. 5–7.

22. *Decadence* p. 90.

23. *Decadence* p. 105; see also *Worth Living* pp. 64–5.

24. *Worth Living* pp. 61–2; *Youth* pp. 108–9; *Decadence* pp. 87–90, 124–7, 136–7, 149–51.

25. *Worth Living* p. 62.

26. Consider Lear pp. 293–306.

27. *Decadence* pp. 132–61.

28. *Decadence* p. 137; *Epimetheus* p. 235; *Youth* pp. 81–2.

29. See especially Bernard Stiegler, "Constitution and Individuation," note 6.

BIBLIOGRAPHY

Ackrill, J. L. *Aristotle the Philosopher* (Oxford: Clarendon Press, 1981).

Aristotle, *Aristotelis: Ethica Nicomachea*, ed. J. Bywater (Oxford: Clarendon Press, 1920).

Aristotle, *Aristotelis: Physica*, ed. W. D. Ross (Oxford: Clarendon Press, 1951).

Aristotle, *Aristotelis: Metaphysica*, ed. W. Jaeger (Oxford: Clarendon Press, 1957).

Aristotle, *Aristotelis: De Anima*, ed. W. D. Ross (Oxford: Clarendon Press, 1979).

Caston, V., "Aristotle's Two Intellects: A Modest Proposal," *Phronesis*, 44.3 (1999), pp. 199–227.

Derrida, *Dissemination*, trans. B. Johnson (London: Bloomsbury, 2004).

Détienne, M., *Apollon le Couteau à la Main: Une Approche Expérimentale du Polythéisme Grec* (Paris: Gallimard, 1989).

Diels, H. and Kranz, W., *Die Fragmente der Vorsokratiker*, vol. 1, 6th edn (Berlin: Weidmann, 1951).

Diogenes Laertius, *Lives of Eminent Philosophers*, trans. R. D. Hicks (London: Heinemann, 1925).

Hadot, P., *The Veil of Isis: An Inquiry into the History of the Idea of Nature*, trans. M. Chase (Cambridge, MA: Harvard University Press, 2006).

Heidegger, M., *Early Greek Thinking*, trans. D. F. Krell and F. A. Capuzzi (New York: Harper & Row, 1975).

Heidegger, M., *Introduction to Metaphysics*, trans. G. Fried and R. Polt (New Haven, CT: Yale University Press, 2000).

Kahn, C. H., *The Art and Thought of Heraclitus* (Cambridge: Cambridge University Press, 1979).

Kingsley, P., *In the Dark Places of Wisdom* (Inverness, CA: Golden Sufi Center, 1999).

Kingsley, P., *Reality* (Inverness, CA: Golden Sufi Center, 2003).

Kirk, G. S., Raven, J. E., and Schofield, M., *The Presocratic Philosophers*, 2nd edn (Cambridge: Cambridge University Press, 1983).

Lear, J., *Aristotle: The Desire to Understand* (Cambridge: Cambridge University Press, 1988).

Lloyd-Jones, H., "Artemis and Iphigeneia," *Journal of Hellenic Studies*, 103 (1983), pp. 87–102.

Menn, S., "Aristotle and Plato on God as Nous and as the Good," *Review of Metaphysics*, 45.3 (1992), pp. 543–73.

Sheehan, T., "A Paradigm Shift in Heidegger Research," *Continental Philosophy Review*, 34 (2001), pp. 183–202.

Stiegler, B., *Technics and Time 1: The Fault of Epimetheus*, trans. R. Beardsworth and G. Collins (Stanford: Stanford University Press, 1998).

Stiegler, B., *Acting Out*, trans. D. Barison, D. Ross, and P. Crogan (Stanford: Stanford University Press, 2009).

Stiegler, B., *Taking Care of Youth and the Generations*, trans. S. Barker (Stanford: Stanford University Press, 2010).

Stiegler, B., *The Decadence of Industrial Democracies*, trans. D. Ross and S. Arnold (Cambridge: Polity Press, 2011).

Stiegler, B., "Relational Ecology and the Digital *Pharmakon*," trans. P. Crogan, *Culture Machine*, 13 (2012), pp. 1–19.

Stiegler, B., *What Makes Life Worth Living: On Pharmacology*, trans. D. Ross (Cambridge: Polity Press, 2013).

Stiegler, B., "Constitution and Individuation" (http://arsindustrialis.org/node/2927, accessed 12 July 2015).

Vernant, J.-P., *Mortals and Immortals: Collected Essays*, ed. F. I. Zeitlin (Princeton: Princeton University Press, 1991).

Index